IT MATTERS

ENGLISCH FÜR IT-BERUFE

von
Brad Courtney
Robert Kleinschroth
Isobel Williams

unter Mitarbeit der Verlagsredaktion

Cornelsen

IT MATTERS

Verfasser/in:	Brad Courtney, Melbourne
	Isobel Williams, Berlin
Verfasser KMK-Seiten:	Robert Kleinschroth, Heidelberg
Berater/innen:	Antje Baehr, Essen; Annette Fauth, Freiburg; Jan Richter, Freiberg
Projektleitung:	Simone Conrad
Außenredaktion:	James Abram
Redaktionelle Mitarbeit:	Thomas Adam, Christine House, Oliver Busch (Wörterverzeichnisse)
Bildredaktion:	Gertha Maly, Christina Scheuerer
Layoutkonzept:	finedesign, Berlin
Gesamtgestaltung und technische Umsetzung:	vitaledesign, Berlin
Umschlaggestaltung:	vitaledesign, Berlin
Coverfoto:	Fotolia/.shock
Illustrationen:	Oxford Designers & Illustrators

Erhältlich sind auch:
Handreichungen für den Unterricht mit MP3-CD und Online-Zusatzmaterialien
ISBN 978-3-06-451524-6

Soweit in diesem Lehrwerk Personen fotografisch abgebildet sind und ihnen von der Redaktion fiktive Namen, Berufe, Dialoge und Ähnliches zugeordnet oder diese Personen in bestimmte Kontexte gesetzt werden, dienen diese Zuordnungen und Darstellungen ausschließlich der Veranschaulichung und dem besseren Verständnis des Inhalts.

www.cornelsen.de

Die Webseiten Dritter, deren Internetadressen in diesem Lehrwerk angegeben sind, wurden teilweise von Cornelsen mit fiktiven Inhalten zur Veranschaulichung und/oder Illustration von Aufgabenstellungen und Inhalten erstellt. Alle anderen Webseiten wurden vor Drucklegung sorgfältig geprüft. Der Verlag übernimmt keine Gewähr für die Aktualität und den Inhalt dieser Seiten oder solcher, die mit ihnen verlinkt sind.

1. Auflage, 3. Druck 2020

Alle Drucke dieser Auflage sind inhaltlich unverändert und können im Unterricht nebeneinander verwendet werden.

© 2018 Cornelsen Verlag GmbH, Berlin

Druck und Bindung: Livonia Print, Riga

ISBN 978-3-06-451522-2
ISBN 978-3-06-451523-9 (E-Book)

PEFC zertifiziert
Dieses Produkt stammt aus nachhaltig bewirtschafteten Wäldern und kontrollierten Quellen.
www.pefc.de

PEFC/12-31-006

Vorwort

IT Matters 3rd edition ist die vollständige Neubearbeitung des bewährten Englisch-Lehrwerks für IT-Berufe an Berufsschulen sowie für die innerbetriebliche Aus- und Weiterbildung.

Das Lehrwerk setzt Englischkenntnisse voraus, die dem Niveau B1 des Europäischen Referenzrahmens *(Common European Framework of Reference)* entsprechen. Es deckt die Themen der aktuellen Lehrpläne der Bundesländer für Englisch in der Berufsschule konsequent ab.

IT Matters 3rd edition besteht aus zwölf Units, die flexibel einsetzbar sind. Jede Unit umfasst vier abgeschlossene Lernsituationen, die jeweils in einer Doppelstunde bearbeitet werden können. Eine Unit ist wie folgt aufgebaut:

Foundation: Diese Doppelseite bietet Ihnen mit technischem Grundwissen und elementarem Themenvokabular einen Einstieg in das Thema der Unit.

Part A/B: Diese stark technisch ausgerichteten Module können je nach Umfang der Inputmaterialien jeweils zwei oder drei Seiten umfassen. Hier werden fachspezifische Schwerpunkte der Unit mithilfe authentischer und aktueller Materialien behandelt.

Communication: Berufliche Kommunikation steht im Fokus des abschließenden *Communication*-Teils. Ein „Das kann ich"-Kästchen – eine Checkliste zur Selbstevaluation – rundet die Unit ab und ermöglicht es den Lernenden, über ihren persönlichen Lernerfolg zu reflektieren.

Alle Lernsituationen sind so konzipiert, dass sie ausgelassen oder zu einem anderen Zeitpunkt behandelt werden können. Somit berücksichtigt die Modulstruktur einer jeden Unit die organisatorische Vielfalt des Englischunterrichts und schafft größtmögliche Flexibilität im Unterricht.

Besonderer Wert wird in diesem Lehrwerk auf **Handlungsorientierung** und direkten Berufsbezug gelegt: Jedes Modul beginnt mit einer branchenspezifischen *Situation* und führt über handlungs- und kompetenzorientierte Lernschritte zu einem Handlungsprodukt. Dieses Lernziel ist jeweils zu Beginn des Moduls mit einem Pfeil gekennzeichnet und ermöglicht so eine schnelle Orientierung.

Unterschiedliche Aktions- und Sozialformen ermöglichen zudem den Einsatz von kooperativen Lernformen und fördern **eigenverantwortliches Lernen**.

Um der Heterogenität der Auszubildenden gerecht zu werden, finden sich zahlreiche Aufgaben zur **Binnendifferenzierung** in den Units. Diese sind mit einem Strich unter der Aufgabenziffer gekennzeichnet und verweisen auf editierbare Kopiervorlagen in den Handreichungen, die alternative Bearbeitungsmöglichkeiten für die jeweilige Aufgabe zur Verfügung stellen.

Zur Vorbereitung auf die **KMK-Prüfung** für Niveau B1 und B2 werden anhand von sechs Unterrichtseinheiten und einer kompletten Musterprüfung prüfungsrelevante Materialien und Aufgaben angeboten und so eine systematische Prüfungsvorbereitung ermöglicht.

Grundlegende grammatikalische Strukturen werden durchweg im **situativen Kontext** vermittelt, ergänzt durch eine systematische Grammatikübersicht im Anhang. Zur Erweiterung des berufsrelevanten Wortschatzes wird schwieriges **Fachvokabular**, das zum Verständnis der Materialien notwendig ist, in jedem Modul in einer *Toolbox* gesondert hervorgehoben. Eine umfangreiche *Unit word list* mit allen neuen Wörtern in chronologischer Reihenfolge wie auch eine *A–Z word list* mit allen neuen Wörtern in alphabetischer Reihenfolge befinden sich im Anhang, ebenso wie berufsbezogene *Useful phrases,* die eine effektive berufliche Kommunikation erleichtern.

Sämtliche Audiomaterialien finden Sie in den Handreichungen für den Unterricht. Typische Sprachhandlungssituationen im Berufsalltag werden multimedial mit visueller Unterstützung trainiert: Diese visualisierten Hörtexte sind mit ▶ gekennzeichnet und schulen effektiv das Hör- und Sehverstehen. Ein Webcode, mit dem Sie die visualisierten Hörtexte aufrufen können, befindet sich ebenfalls in den Handreichungen.

Die Verlagsredaktion sowie das Berater- und Autorenteam wünschen Ihnen viel Erfolg und Freude mit *IT Matters 3rd edition.*

Table of contents

1 My company

FOUNDATION: A company profile

Situation: You are an apprentice IT administrator with a German company that also has lots of trainees from abroad.
→ **You write a short profile of your company in English for the apprentice file.**

1 Reading a company website

Before you write the profile, you read another company's English profile online.

ANC Adler Network Components – a global player

A Adler Network Components is a German producer of device connection technology. Its head office is in Duisburg in North Rhine-Westphalia. The company was founded in July 1948 by Hans-Joachim Adler and his wife, Luise. Today, Adler Network Components is still a family business. It is run by Wolfgang and Suzanne Adler and their two children, René Adler and Mareike Adler-Schmidt.

B The structure of the company looks like this:
Wolfgang Adler – Chairman of the Board, General Partner
Mareike Adler-Schmidt – General Partner, Senior Vice President Finance and Purchasing
René Adler – General Partner, Senior Vice President New Technologies
Suzanne Adler – Partner, Senior Vice President Sales and Marketing

C Although it is a family business, Adler is also a global player. There are 11 factories, located in Germany, the Netherlands, France, Great Britain, Romania, the USA and China. Forty-seven sales companies look after Adler's customers worldwide. The company employs around 4,000 people, including over 500 engineers and IT specialists.

D Adler Network Components develops, manufactures and sells electrical and electronic cables and connectors. Our products are used in mechanical engineering, factory automation, data processing and networks, industrial electronics and telecommunication.

E Vocational training and apprenticeships for young people play a central role in the company.

A Match the headlines 1–6 to the paragraphs A–E. There is one headline more than you need.

1 Company structure	**3** About Adler	**5** Introduction to Duisburg
2 Interesting information for trainees	**4** Adler's customers	**6** Adler worldwide

 **TOOLBOX**

apprentice – *Lehrling, Auszubildende/r*	IT administrator – *IT-Kaufmann/-frau*
apprenticeship – *Lehre, Ausbildung*	vocational training – *Berufsausbildung*

B Say if the following statements are true or false according to the text. Correct the false statements.

1 Adler Network Components is a multinational company.
   False: Adler Network Components is a family business and is well known abroad, but it is not a multinational.
2 Adler's head office is in Germany.
3 The company was founded over 70 years ago.
4 No one from the original family works for the company any longer.
5 All production is done in Germany.
6 Adler has an international sales team.
7 The company sells to customers in many different sectors.
8 There are no training possibilities at Adler.

2 Introducing a company

Some young people are introducing themselves and the companies they work for.

2))) Copy the grid below into your exercise book. Then listen and complete the grid.

Name of company	Sector	Head office	Size
BCC Electronics	■1	■2	medium-sized
International Solutions	■3	■4	start-up
Nilsson Construction	building	■5	■6
Han Gao	■7	■8	■9
Jahn Services	■10	■11	■12
Aikon	■13	■14	■15

3 Making notes about your company

A Make notes that you can use to give a short description of your company. Cover the points below:

– name of the company
– sector
– location
– number of employees
– what the company does
– target group/customers
– some competitors

> **→ Asking for information**
>
> **Who** do you work for?
> **What** is the name of your company?
> **Where** is the company located?
> **How many** employees does your company have?
>
> › *Grammar: Questions and short answers, page 162*

B 👥 Talk with a partner. Your partner will ask you questions about your company. Use the notes above. **You have three minutes to answer.**   › *Useful phrases: Describing companies, page 150*

4 Writing the company profile

Now it is time to write the company profile for the apprentice file.

👥 On your own, or with your partner, write a short profile of your company. Structure your information under the headings you used for exercise 3A above. Present your company to the class and be prepared to answer questions from the audience.   › *Useful phrases: Describing companies, page 150*

 TOOLBOX

head office – *Zentrale, Hauptsitz*
medium-sized company – *mittelständischer Betrieb*

multinational company – *multinationaler Konzern*
start-up – *Start-up(-Unternehmen)*

PART A: The layout of a company

> **Situation:** You have just started a job at Accensys GmbH, a subsidiary of a large multinational IT services company. You are attending the company's induction week in Atlanta in the United States.
> → **You show a visitor around your training company's premises.**

1 Looking at a company layout

You are shown to a desk and start the electronic introductory course that explains the Accensys company structure, activities and the layout of the Atlanta head office.

A Look at the company layout shown in the introductory course. Find the departments on the map that match the German words (1–8).

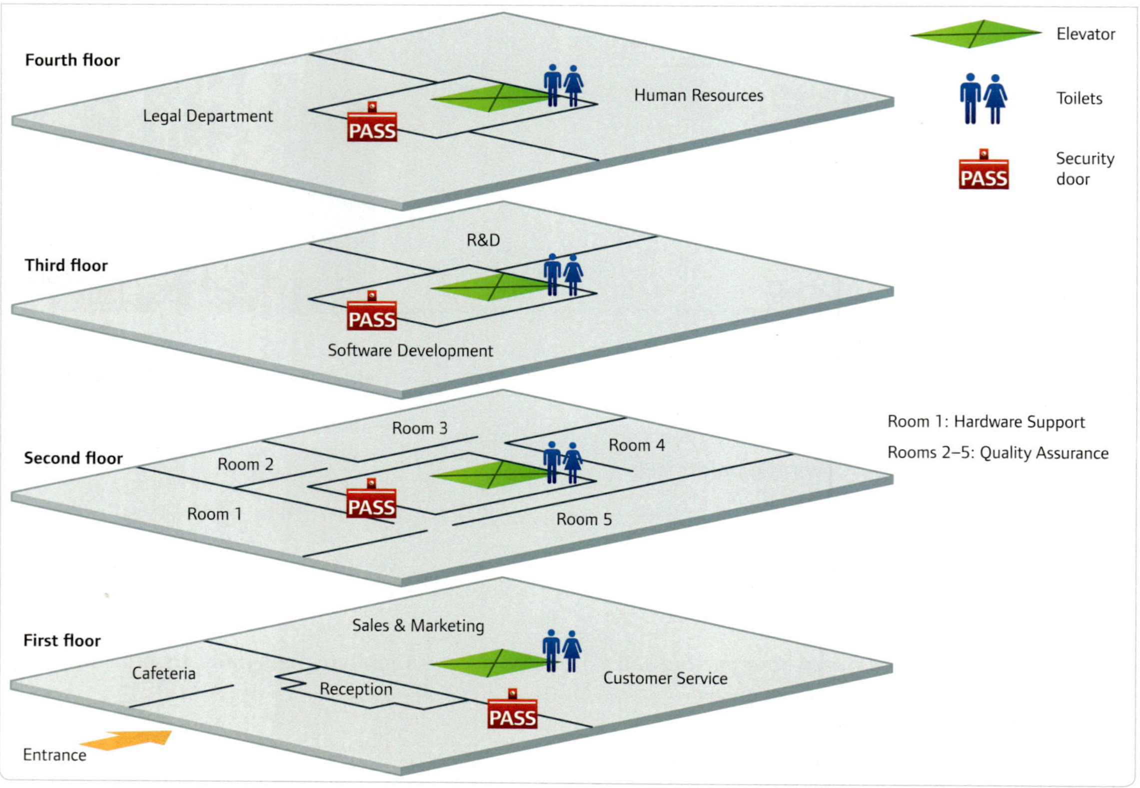

Fourth floor
- Legal Department
- PASS
- Human Resources

Third floor
- R&D
- PASS
- Software Development

Second floor
- Room 3
- Room 2
- Room 1
- PASS
- Room 4
- Room 5

Room 1: Hardware Support
Rooms 2–5: Quality Assurance

First floor
- Sales & Marketing
- Cafeteria
- Reception
- PASS
- Customer Service
- Entrance

Legend:
- Elevator
- Toilets
- Security door (PASS)

1	Personalabteilung	5	Qualitätssicherung
2	Vertrieb	6	Rechtsabteilung
3	Hardware-Support	7	Kundendienst
4	Forschung und Entwicklung	8	Softwareentwicklung

Infobox

BE: lift	AE: elevator	Aufzug
second floor	third floor	2. OG
first floor	second floor	1. OG
ground floor	first floor	Erdgeschoss

 TOOLBOX

department – *Abteilung*
induction – *Einführung*

layout – *Raumaufteilung, Plan*
subsidiary – *Tochterfirma*

B Which department names from exercise 1A match these descriptions?

1 Promotes the business to customers to increase sales of its products and services.
2 Makes sure that the software meets the technical standards.
3 Recruits and interviews new employees and handles staff relations, benefits and training.
4 Handles internal and external legal issues for a company.
5 Maintains and repairs the employees' computers and company-owned servers.
6 Creates, documents and debugs software used by customers and/or employees.
7 Creates innovative new products and/or improves existing products and production methods.
8 Provides information about products and services, replies to customer complaints and questions.

2 Listening to a guided tour

Edwina Chan, who is part of the IT Services team, takes the new employees on a tour of the Atlanta office.

A 3))) ▶ Listen and match the sentence beginnings (1–11) with the endings (a–k).

1	We'll start our tour …	a	the third floor is an open-plan office.
2	There are two teams …	b	we'll take the elevator to the first floor.
3	The door just in front of us …	c	me up the stairs to the third floor.
4	You can find them by …	d	ahead along the walkway, we'll be able to see …
5	The elevators are located …	e	leads to the Quality Assurance team.
6	Now, I'd like you to follow …	f	here on the second floor.
7	As you can see, …	g	could I ask you to please keep quiet.
8	Before we go on, …	h	over there in the corner.
9	If we walk straight …	i	in the middle of each floor.
10	They are located …	j	going along this corridor and through the door at the end.
11	After that, …	k	located on this floor.

B 3))) ▶ Listen again and put the items/places (a–h) in the order they are mentioned in the tour.

4 a elevators   1 c second floor   2 e Quality Assurance   7 g Software Development
3 b Hardware Support   6 d third floor   8 f R&D   5 h stairs

3 Giving directions

You and another new employee are standing at the reception desk on the ground floor (BE)/first floor (AE).

👥 Work with a partner and use the Accensys layout on page 8.

Partner A: Choose three departments and ask your partner how to get to them.
Partner B: Tell your partner how to get to the department that he/she asks about.

Swap roles when you have finished.

➡ Giving directions

Go down the corridor to the last door on the right.
Take the elevator up/down to the third floor.

› Grammar: Imperatives, page 162

› Useful phrases: Showing visitors around the company, page 150

4 Showing a visitor around your company

Now it is time to give visitors a guided tour of your training company.

👥 Work with a group of students that work at the same company as you. Draw a floor plan of the building that you work in and then take the class on a guided tour.

› Useful phrases: Showing visitors around the company, page 150

PART B: The structure of a company

> **Situation:** You have just started a job at Accensys GmbH, a subsidiary of a large multi-national IT services company. You are attending the company's induction week in Atlanta in the United States.
> → **You describe the structure and key roles of your training company.**

1 Understanding a company organization structure

You and the other new employees are attending a presentation by Ben Webster from the Human Resources (HR) department. He's explaining the company organigram.

A ◀)) Listen to Ben's presentation and complete the missing information in the Accensys organigram with words from the list.

Chief Digital Officer (CDO) · Chief Executive Officer (CEO) ·
Chief Technology Officer (CTO) · Head of IT Operations ·
Head of Software Engineering · Project Managers · Quality Assurance Managers

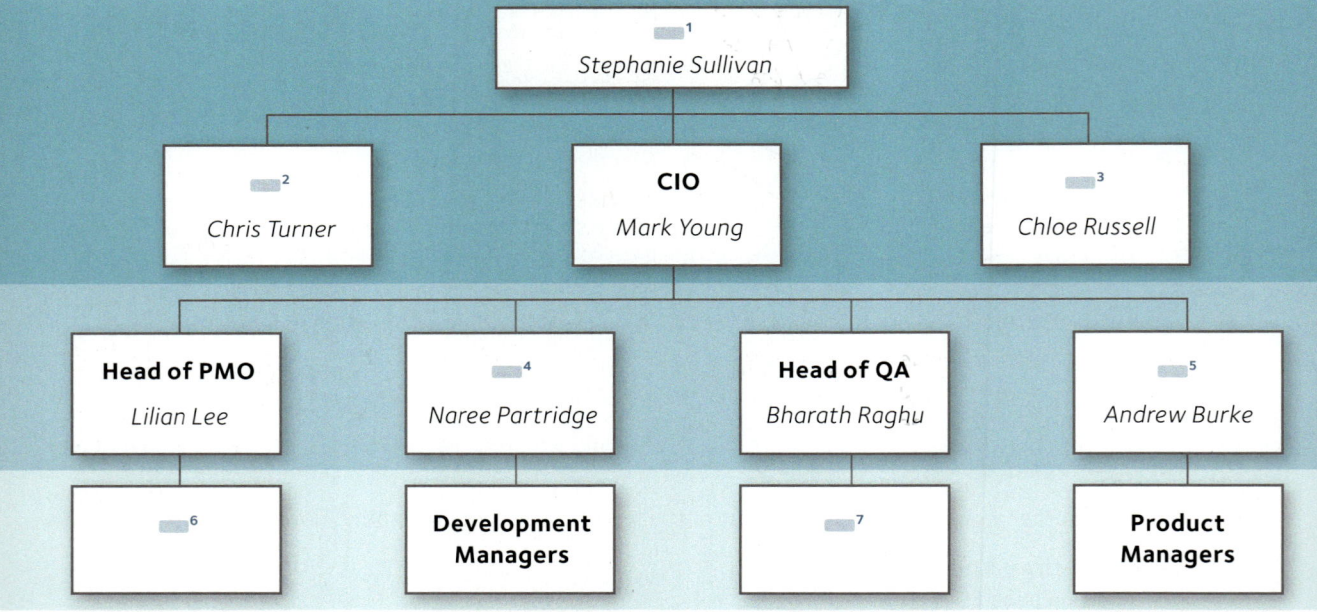

B ◀)) Listen again and complete the gaps with the missing words.

Stephanie Sullivan	It's my ▬▬¹ to set the overall company ▬▬² and strategies, and to manage the company.
Chris Turner	I report directly to the CEO. I deal with ▬▬³ architecture, platforms, ▬▬⁴ processing, system analysis, and so on.
Mark Young	I am responsible for deciding how we use ▬▬⁵ in Accensys to maximize benefit to the company and ▬▬⁶. I also report to the CEO.
Lilian Lee	I supervise a large team of project managers. I liaise with all of the ▬▬⁷ teams to make sure that we deliver our ▬▬⁸ on time.
Bharath Raghu	I manage the ▬▬⁹ teams. I make sure that we release high-quality software ▬▬¹⁰ to our clients.
Andrew Burke	I keep our ▬▬¹¹ and software ▬▬¹² running so that both we, and our clients, can perform our daily tasks.

2   Joining a project

You receive a welcome email from the project manager that you will be reporting to later.

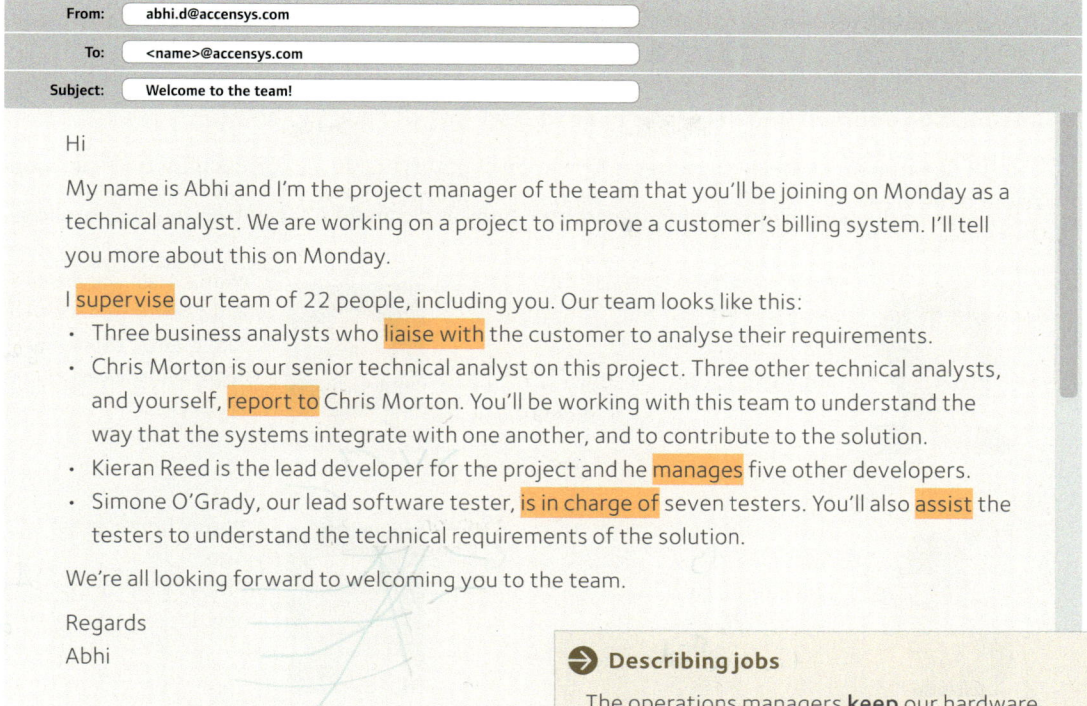

From:	abhi.d@accensys.com
To:	<name>@accensys.com
Subject:	Welcome to the team!

Hi

My name is Abhi and I'm the project manager of the team that you'll be joining on Monday as a technical analyst. We are working on a project to improve a customer's billing system. I'll tell you more about this on Monday.

I supervise our team of 22 people, including you. Our team looks like this:
- Three business analysts who liaise with the customer to analyse their requirements.
- Chris Morton is our senior technical analyst on this project. Three other technical analysts, and yourself, report to Chris Morton. You'll be working with this team to understand the way that the systems integrate with one another, and to contribute to the solution.
- Kieran Reed is the lead developer for the project and he manages five other developers.
- Simone O'Grady, our lead software tester, is in charge of seven testers. You'll also assist the testers to understand the technical requirements of the solution.

We're all looking forward to welcoming you to the team.

Regards
Abhi

> **➔ Describing jobs**
>
> The operations managers **keep** our hardware platforms running.
> The development managers **make sure** our software products get to our clients.
> Mark Young **is** responsible for deciding how we use technology. He **reports** directly to the CEO.
>
> › *Grammar: Simple present, page 162*

Read the email and then describe the following relationships in the team, using the highlighted verbs. The first one has been done for you.

1	The project manager	supervises	a team of 22 people.
2	You		the senior technical analyst.
3	The lead developer		five developers.
4	The business analysts		the customer.
5	The lead software tester		seven testers.
6	The technical analysts		Chris Morton.
7	You		the testers.

3   Describing the structure of your training company

Now it is time to describe your training company to your classmates.

A   Work in groups of students from the same training company. Decide together what information you want to include on an organization chart, then draw it. Make sure you include the main departments and the names and job titles of people in important positions.

B   Tell students from another group about the structure of your training company. Use your organization chart and describe the team that you work for. Explain the team structure and the relationship between the members of the team.

> › *Useful phrases: Describing jobs and responsibilities, page 151*

COMMUNICATION: Introductions and small talk

Situation: You work in the IT department at Mech-On, a Nuremberg-based engineering company.
→ **You look after a visitor from England until your supervisor, Ms Müller, is ready to meet him.**

1 Introducing yourself and others to colleagues

The HR department at Mech-On stores information about its employees on computerized personnel files.

A 5))) **Listen to the people introducing themselves. Copy and complete the entries in your notebook.**

Name: Martyna Nowak
Age: ■¹ 42
Place of birth: Poland
Job description: ■² *product manager*

Name: Halil Özdemir
Age: ■³ 29
Place of birth: ■⁴ *germany*
Job description: training supervisor

Name: Deema Mansour
Age: ■⁵ 19
Place of birth: Syria
Job description: ■⁶ *trainee IT administrator*

Name: Robert Klein
Age: 21
Place of birth: ■⁷ *Austria*
Job description: ■⁸ *qa tester*

Name: Canan Tolon
Age: ■⁹ 25
Place of birth: Turkey
Job description: ■¹⁰ *business analyst*

Name: Alexei Melnyk
Age: 39
Place of birth: ■¹¹ *Ukraine*
Job description: ■¹² *software developer*

B You have three minutes to introduce yourself to the other people in the class.

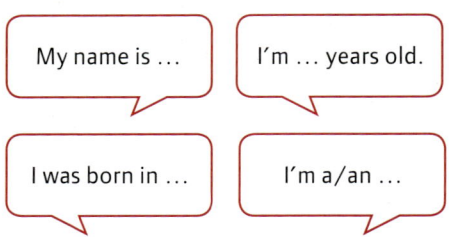

My name is …

I'm … years old.

I was born in …

I'm a/an …

> → **Asking about jobs**
>
> What **do you do**? – I'm **a** trainee. / I'm **an** IT administrator.
> What **is** your job? – I'm **a** software developer. / I'm **an** analyst. (NOT: ~~My job is …~~)

C Introduce one of the people you met to the rest of the class.

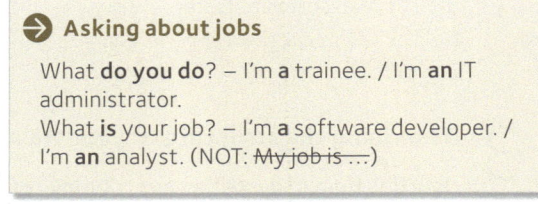

This is …

He's/She's … years old.

He/She was born in …

He's/She's a/an …

› *Useful phrases: Making introductions, page 150*

2 Making formal introductions

A 👥 Work with a partner. Introduce yourself in a formal way to your partner (a visitor).

B 👥 Now formally introduce your partner to another pair.   › *Useful phrases: Making introductions, page 150*

3 Making small talk

A 👥 In groups, choose suitable topics for small talk in business. Say which topics you should avoid.

holidays   your city/town   religion   the journey to the meeting place

illnesses   sport   politics   the weather   pay   where someone works

B Match the questions (1–5) to the possible responses (a–e).

1 Is this your first time in Berlin?
2 How is your hotel?
3 It's lovely weather, isn't it?
4 How was your journey?
5 Where are you based?

a Yes. It's fantastic. We've been very lucky this year.
b Very nice. I travelled by train this time.
c Yes. I've heard that it's a very interesting city.
d Fine. I have a good view from the window in my room.
e In Scotland. In Edinburgh, in fact.

4 Meeting and greeting the visitor

Now it is time to meet the visitor. You know that the person Ms Müller is expecting is called Mr Brown.

A 👥 Work in groups of three. Complete the dialogue. Then close your books and practise the dialogue.

You	*Excuse*[1] me. *Are you*[2] Mr Brown?
Visitor	Yes, I am.
You	I'm (own name). ▬▬[3] do you do? ▬▬[4] to Mech-On.
Visitor	Thank you. It's ▬▬[5].
You	I'm afraid Ms Müller has been held up, but she'll be here in a few minutes. ▬▬[6] your coat?
Visitor	Yes, thank you. Here you are.
You	▬▬[7] you like something to drink?
Visitor	Yes, please. I'd like a cup of coffee with milk and sugar.
You	Here you are. Is this your ▬▬[8] in Germany?
Visitor	No. I've been here before, but only on holiday.
You	Oh. Here's Ms Müller now. Mr Brown, ▬▬[9] Ms Müller.
Ms Müller	▬▬[10] morning, Mr Brown. Sorry to keep you waiting.
Visitor	No problem. Your assistant has been looking after me very well.

➡ **Offering help/refreshments**

Can I take your coat?
Would you like something to drink?
Would you like some tea or coffee?

› *Useful phrases: Showing visitors around the company, page 150*

B 👥 Write your own dialogue and practise it in your group.

DAS KANN ICH (Unit 1)

– Ein kurzes Firmenprofil meines Ausbildungsbetriebs auf Englisch erstellen. (Foundation)
– Meinen Arbeitsplatz im Ausbildungsbetrieb auf Englisch beschreiben. (Part A)
– Die Organisationsstruktur meines Ausbildungsbetriebs auf Englisch beschreiben. (Part B)
– Englischsprachige Besucher/innen empfangen und jemandem vorstellen. (Communication)

2 My workplace

FOUNDATION: Internal communication

Situation: Your firm is carrying out measures to improve internal communication among teams.
→ **You do a survey to find out which means of communication your colleagues use and what improvements they would like.**

1 Talking about communication at work

   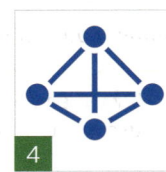  

A   What method(s) of communication do you use most at work? Make a list.

B   👥 Work with a partner. Talk together about the advantages/disadvantages of the means of communication on your lists.

C   👥 Work with another pair. Rank the types of communication according to how useful they are when you are at work.

2 Getting the message across

Three employees are discussing their company's decision to improve internal communication. (The discussion is in three sections.)

David	Marta	Janek
Software tester	Business analyst	Software developer

 **TOOLBOX**

to access information – *auf Informationen zugreifen*
face-to-face meeting – *persönliches Treffen/Gespräch*

to share information – *Informationen teilen*
to synchronize files – *Dateien abgleichen/synchronisieren*

A   6))) ▶ Listen and say who expresses the following opinions.

1   A face-to-face meeting is good when you want to make a quick decision.
2   When you want a quick decision in writing, it's better to send a text message.
3   It doesn't take long to write an email.
4   You need to be at work to access the intranet.
5   You can access cloud storage from anywhere.
6   Slides should only be used for graphic images and shouldn't have a lot of text.

B   6))) ▶ Listen again and complete the notes on the advantages and disadvantages of the different types of communication systems below.

1   If the other person isn't around, you can't have a ▭ . *f-f meeting*
2   Good options for making a ▭ are using the telephone for a phone call or a text message.
3   One of the things people really dislike about emails is that ▭ .
4   An intranet is ▭ *structured* so it's easy to find the information you're looking for.
5   The advantage of using the cloud is that the company can ▭ with clients.
6   When they're full of text, slides are ▭ . *boring* *fail waste of time* *share data*

3 Carrying out a survey

You do a survey among your colleagues to find out their ideas about internal communication.

A   In class, brainstorm ideas for questions for your survey.

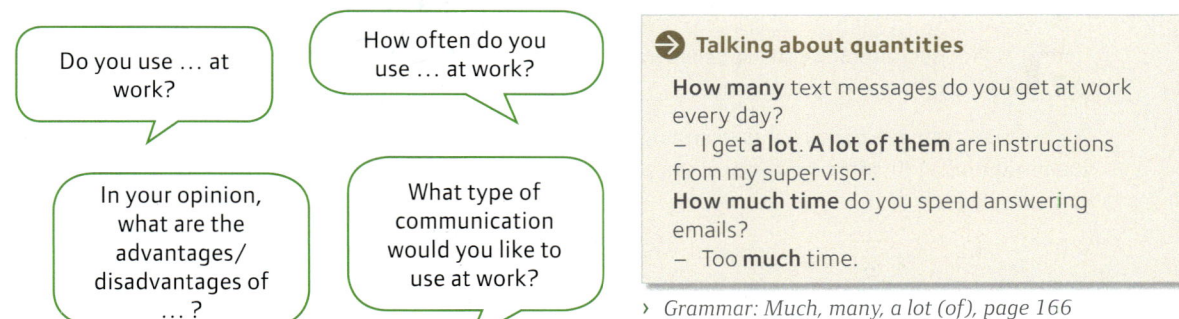

Do you use … at work?

How often do you use … at work?

In your opinion, what are the advantages/ disadvantages of … ?

What type of communication would you like to use at work?

→ **Talking about quantities**

How many text messages do you get at work every day?
– I get **a lot**. **A lot of them** are instructions from my supervisor.
How much time do you spend answering emails?
– Too **much** time.

› *Grammar: Much, many, a lot (of), page 166*

B   Make two charts to record the results of your survey.

1 Communication we use at work			
type of communication	How many people use this?	advantages	disadvantages
email	H̶H̶T̶ I I	you can send attachments	too many emails every day

2 Communication we would like to use at work	
type of communication	advantages

C   Use the results of your survey to make suggestions on how to improve internal communication in your firm.

15

PART A: IT job profiles

Situation: It's your first day as a software developer at Hillier Recruiting, a large recruitment company with its headquarters in Sydney, Australia. You learn about the working conditions and some of the jobs in the company.
→ **You write a profile of yourself for your company's intranet.**

1 Understanding working conditions

Sandra Grima from Human Resources explains some of the working conditions at Hillier Recruiting to a group of new employees.

A   7))) **Listen and note the numbers Sandra gives for each of these aspects of the working conditions.**

1   annual leave days *1   20 days*
2   paid sick days per year *2   10 days*
3   unpaid leave allowed per year *3   2 weeks*
4   leave allowed to be saved *4   6 weeks*
5   hours that employees must be working *5   10 am to 3 pm*
6   latest time to be in office without permission *6   8 pm*

B   7))) **Listen again and complete the sentences with the missing words.**

Here at Hillier Recruiting, we're big believers in providing a work-life balance that suits each employee, so we try to offer flexible working conditions.

For example, you get 20 days of paid annual leave and ____¹ take up to 10 days of paid sick leave. We also ____² you to take an additional two weeks of unpaid leave each year and save up to six weeks of leave if you like longer holidays.

You ____³ work remotely if you choose to, which means that you ____⁴ be in the office every day but you ____⁵ co-ordinate the days that you work from home with your boss.

Although we offer flexible start and finish times, you ____⁶ start and finish at any time of day and ____⁷ be working between 10 a.m. and 3 p.m. In addition, you ____⁸ be in the office after 8 p.m. without permission. You ____⁹ take up to one hour for lunch.

In the office you ____¹⁰ wear formal clothing but your clothes ____¹¹ be neat. You ____¹² wear jeans and a clean T-shirt, if you like – the IT department is quite casual – but you ____¹³ wear shorts.

C   **Summarize the things you are allowed to do and the things you are not allowed to do at Hillier Recruiting.**

Things you are allowed to do	Things you are not allowed to do
wear jeans and a T-shirt ____	____
Things you must / have to do	**Things you don't have to do**
____	____

> → **Expressing permission and obligation**
>
> You **may** take up to an hour for lunch.
> You **must not** wear shorts.
> You **may not** be in the office after 8 p.m.
> You **have to** wear neat clothing.
> You **don't have to** be in the office every day.

› *Grammar: Modals and their substitutes, page 167*

2 Talking about working conditions

During a break, you talk to some of the other new employees.

A Work with a partner. Discuss your answers from exercise 1C and put them into order, starting with the things that you think are most important. Add any other things you can think of.

B Compare your results with another pair.

3 Working with a team

You have joined an IT project that is delivering new functionality to the job applicant system at Hillier Recruiting. You look up the profiles of the other team members on the company intranet.

Software tester: Akio Ishikawa

Hi everyone – my name is Akio Ishikawa and I'm a graduate software tester on this project. I work very closely with the business analysts to under-stand what the software has to do. I create scenarios and test data which I use to test our software against the requirements. I don't like finding bugs and defects in the software, but it is better for me to find them than the users!

I like to keep work casual – I feel more creative in jeans and a T-shirt! I prefer late starts and late finishes and love to work from home as I have a long commute to work. I like to get to know my colleagues, too, so I like to have long lunches with a group. My family is in Japan, so I usually take longer holidays to spend time with them.

Project manager: Patricia Ganley

Hi, my name is Patricia and I'm excited to be the project manager in this team! Overall, I'm responsible for delivering the project on time and at the cost expected.

I provide the project sponsors with updates on our projects and raise problems with them. Together, the sponsors and I try to remove any roadblocks that are slowing down the project team. I also work with other project managers to understand how our projects affect one another.

I start early and leave the office late and often take work home with me – there's so much to do as a project manager! I take a few short holidays a year but usually have to be forced to take leave. I often eat lunch at my desk but I like to organize team lunches once a month. My friends think I'm a workaholic … and they're probably right!

Software developer: Saurabh Chawla

Hi team – my name is Saurabh Chawla and I'm happy to be part of the project as a software developer.

I write the code that delivers the functionality that our customers want, so I have a close relationship with the business analysts who help me understand the requirements. I like easily understandable code, so I make sure that my code is explained with detailed comments. I like to start early and leave early as I have two daughters that I love to spend time with. I enjoy a full and productive work day, but I like to separate work and family life, so I don't work from home at all. You'll normally find my holidays are at the same time as school holidays.

 TOOLBOX

---

bug – *Bug, Fehler*	to raise a problem – *auf ein Problem aufmerksam machen*
to deliver – *liefern, in die Tat umsetzen*	scenario – *Szenario*
functionality – *Funktionen*	test data – *Prüfdaten*
to provide – *zur Verfügung stellen*	to write (software) code – *(Software-)Code schreiben*

A   Write the following phrases as responsibilities and say which of the three roles they belong to. Use the information from the profiles on page 17 and the language box to help you.

project manager · software developer · software tester

1 debug own software code
A software developer is responsible for debugging his/her own software code.
ST **2** ensure that software meets requirements
PM **3** remove obstacles for project team
ST **4** create scenarios and test data
SD **5** explain code with detailed comments
PM **6** co-ordinate all teams in project
SD **7** fix defects raised by testers
PM **8** deliver project on time and at cost expected

> **Describing responsibilities**
>
> **It's** the software developer's **responsibility to** write …
> The project manager **makes sure that** the project …
> I **am responsible for** debugging …
> **My role/job is to** deliver …
> **It's up to me to** maintain/update …

› *Useful phrases: Describing jobs and responsibilities, page 151*

B 👥 Work with a partner. The following are standard documents that are part of a software project. Which job profile do you think they belong to? Explain your answers.

1 project timeline PM
2 test scenarios ST
3 code comments SP
4 defect reports ST
5 project costs PM
6 interface specification SD
7 project plan PM
8 test plan ST

> *The project manager probably writes the … because he/she is responsible for …*

4 Writing a profile for the company intranet

Now it is time to write your own profile for your training company's intranet.

A   Write a profile of yourself in English. Include the following information:

- your name and role
- your responsibilities
- the documents you write
- who you work with
- your preferred ways of working

>

> **Talking about likes and dislikes**
>
> I enjoy/dislike **working** in a team.
> I want **to write** software code.
> I like **to start / starting** early in the morning.
> I'd prefer **to work** from home more.

› *Grammar: Verb + to-infinitive or -ing form, page 165*

B   When you have finished, pin your profile on the wall and do a gallery walk.

› *Useful phrases: Describing jobs and responsibilities, page 151*

 TOOLBOX

defect – *Defekt, Fehler, Mangel*
document – *Datei, Dokument*

interface – *Schnittstelle, Interface*
responsibility – *Verantwortung, Zuständigkeit*

PART B: Ways of working in a team

> **Situation:** You are working on a project that is moving into the development phase.
> → **You give feedback to your project manager on how you prefer to work in different situations.**

1 **Reading about different ways of working**

Your project manager sends you an email about teamwork during the development phase.

Subject: Teamwork

Hi team

I've talked to several team members about the best way to work as a team now that we are moving into the development phase of the project. I'd like to share the results of those conversations and propose some guidelines for effective team output.

At the request of the development team, we're going to have daily 15-minute stand-up meetings every morning to provide updates and set our goals for the day. Even though I prefer more formal meetings with agendas, I understand that the software development team would rather not have them. I'll keep formal meetings to a minimum.

I've arranged for us all to sit together on Level 2. Sitting together allows us to have spontaneous discussions about issues and brainstorm solutions more quickly, which I really like. The software developers agree with this, however they ask that we don't include them in spontaneous discussions as they need time to concentrate on building software. If you have questions, they'd prefer you to add them to the Wiki pages rather than asking them directly.

If you do feel the need for a quiet space for a period of time, feel free to move to a hot desk. But please don't spend all your time sitting alone – you are all critical members of the team!

Finally, the executives have asked us to be paperless. As you know, I favour printed documents, but the software development team's preference is also electronic documentation. We have invested in the tools, such as Confluence and Jira, so I'd like us all to support this.

If you have any questions or concerns, please let me know.

Justin

A **Say whether the following statements are true or false. Correct the false statements.**

1 The project manager spoke to company executives about the best ways to work.
2 Formal meetings will not be used for this project at all.
3 The team will all sit together on Level 2.
4 The software development team want questions emailed to them.
5 Hot desks are available for people that need some quiet working time.
6 The software development team have asked for the project to be paperless.

TOOLBOX

---

agenda – *Tagesordnung*
development phase – *Entwicklungsphase*

to propose – *vorschlagen*
spontaneous – *spontan*

B Fill in the table with the preferences of the development team and the project manager for different ways of working.

Project manager	Software developers
formal meetings	▬▬
▬▬	▬▬
▬▬	▬▬

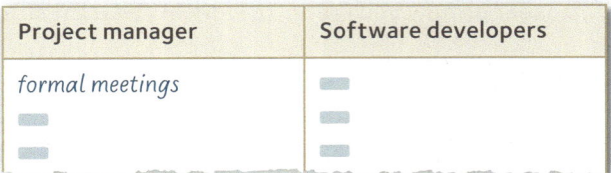

➜ **Talking about preferences**

I **prefer** formal meetings to stand-up ones.
The team **would rather** not have formal meetings.
Their **preference** is for electronic documentation.
I **favour** printed documents over electronic documentation.

2 Comparing ways of working

The development team chat about ways of working after the meeting.

jarred: Hi everyone. Following on from the PM's email, I wanted to share this well-known article about ways of working. (http://paulgraham.com/makersschedule.html) 9:34 AM

david: Thanks – this is great! My opinion is just the same as the author's. It's better to acknowledge everyone's preferences rather than pretend we all work in the same way. 9:35 AM

kevin: I'm glad the PM shared our point of view earlier today. I find answering spontaneous questions more difficult and less useful than setting aside 30 mins every morning to answer questions. 9:35 AM

jessica: I agree. I think many people expect instant answers nowadays, because of the internet, IM, etc. and I think that has made our productivity worse than before. 9:35 AM

david: I'll also add that most questions do not need to be answered instantly. Most questions are not as important as people think they are. 9:36 AM

kevin: Agreed, but I find myself wanting instant answers too. I guess I'm no better than anyone else. :-/ 9:36 AM

jarred: I think choosing a starting point to work together and then adjusting it as we go along is the best way to work together over the lifetime of the project. 9:37 AM

david: Jarred, your opinion is similar to mine. Saying that it is final is the worst thing for the team. It's definitely smarter for us to change when we need to. 9:37 AM

jessica: I think that we can all agree that not changing when we need to is the least effective option. 9:38 AM

➜ **Comparing things**

Meetings are **not as important as** people think they are.
It's **smarter** for us to change when we need to.
Answering spontaneous questions is **more difficult than** setting aside time every day.
It's **better** to acknowledge preferences **than** pretend we're all the same.
Adapting as we go along is **the worst** way of working together.

› *Grammar: Comparatives and superlatives, page 166*

A   Complete these sentences using phrases from the IM chat.

1   David's opinion is *the same as* the author's.
2   David thinks that it ▭ to acknowledge everyone's preferences rather than pretend that we're all the same.
3   In Kevin's opinion, answering spontaneous questions ▭ and ▭ setting aside 30 minutes every morning.
4   Jessica thinks that the expectation of instant answers has made their productivity ▭ before.
5   David says that most questions ▭ people think they are.
6   Jarred thinks that adjusting as they go along ▭ to work together.
7   David's opinion is ▭ Jarred's and he thinks that it's definitely ▭ for them to change when they need to.
8   Jessica believes that not changing when they need to ▭ option.

B   👥 With a partner, compare the ways you prefer to work individually and as a team.

3 Thinking about location

The development team meet to brainstorm changes to the way they work together.

A   8))) Listen to the discussion and note down the answers to the following questions.

1   How is the project progressing compared to the schedule?
2   How often is Jessica interrupted by questions or noise?
3   Which team get loud when they are busy?
4   What is a real downside to open-plan floors?
5   What does Dave do when he works at home?
6   What two suggestions are made to improve the situation?

B   8))) Listen again and complete the sentences with the missing words and phrases.

1   I'd like to discuss the ▭ of the locations of the team members.
2   We still feel that we are being interrupted too often, which is a ▭ for all of us.
3   That would also remove the ▭ of distraction from the other teams on the floor.
4   The major ▭ in working from home is that there are no distractions.
5   But ▭ , we can't come and ask you a question.
6   That may be a ▭ for you, but for me it's a huge ▭ .
7   It's definitely an ▭ if there are no distractions.

4 Explaining how you prefer to work

Your supervisor asks you to give feedback on the right balance between distractions and teamwork.

A   👥 Work with a partner. Think about the pros and cons of each of the following ways of working:

- remote working / working from home
- working in an open-plan office
- having to answer questions instantly
- using electronic communication
- communicating face-to-face

B   👥 Work in small groups. Make a list of the ways that you work and communicate to do the following:

- find or clarify information
- solve a complex problem
- argue the advantages and disadvantages of a solution
- get help or ask for advice

C   Use your notes from exercises 4A and 4B to give a short presentation to the class. Explain the advantages and disadvantages of each way of working and state which way you prefer, giving reasons.

› *Useful phrases: Giving presentations, page 151*

COMMUNICATION: Telephoning

Situation: You are working in the UK subsidiary of Fischer Digitaltechnik GmbH.
→ **You call a client and leave a voicemail message. Later, you take a message.**

1 Making a telephone call

Your supervisor has left you a note asking you to call a customer, Mr Dalton.

First, check the phrases for making a call. Put them in the order you will use them when you call.

a Could you ask … (*name*) to call me back?
b Good morning/afternoon.
c I'd like to speak to / leave a message for … (*name*).
d I'm calling on behalf of … (*name*).
e It's about the …
f My number is …
g Thank you. Goodbye.
h The details are as follows: …
i This is … (*name*) from Fischer Digital Ltd.

> · *Phone Esher Engineering to confirm the update for their components database.*
> · *Say that you're calling on my behalf.*
> · *Ask to speak to Roger Dalton. He's the factory manager.*
> · *Tell him that two IT service technicians will be at the factory at 8.30 on Tuesday, 7 June.*
> · *The update should be completed by 12.30 at the latest.*
> · *If you only get voicemail, ask for Mr Dalton to call you back to confirm the date and time.*
> · *Give him your mobile number.*
> *Thanks.*

2 Leaving a voicemail message

When you call Esher Engineering, you only get voicemail, so you have to leave a message for Mr Dalton.

👥 Work with a partner. Use the phrases in exercise 1 and the note above to complete the voicemail message.

"Good morning. This is ▬▬[1] from Fischer Digital Ltd. I'm calling ▬▬[2] my supervisor, John Hall.
I'd like to ▬▬[3] Mr Dalton, the ▬▬[4]. It's ▬▬[5] update for your components database.
The ▬▬[6]: We'll be sending ▬▬[7] to your factory at 8.30 on Tuesday, 7 June. The update should be completed by 12.30 ▬▬[8].
▬▬[9] Mr Dalton ▬▬[10] to confirm the details? My ▬▬[11] 0177 58412503. ▬▬[12]. Goodbye."

3 Preparing to take a call in English

Match the English sentences (1–10) to the German equivalents (a–j) on page 23.

1 I'm sorry, I didn't understand. Could you repeat that, please?
2 I'm afraid the line is engaged.
3 I'm sorry, … (*name*) is unavailable at the moment.
4 Please hold the line.
5 Who's calling, please?

6 Would you like to speak to someone else?
7 Would you like to leave a message?
8 I'm trying to connect you.
9 I'll put you through.
10 Could you spell your name, please?

 **TOOLBOX**

to be unavailable – *nicht zu sprechen sein*
to connect sb – *jdn verbinden*

engaged – *besetzt*
extension – *Durchwahl*

a   Bleiben Sie bitte dran.
b   Der Anschluss ist besetzt.
c   Ich stelle Sie durch.
d   Ich habe nicht verstanden. Bitte wiederholen Sie.
e   Buchstabieren Sie bitte Ihren Namen.

f   Möchten Sie mit jemand anderem sprechen?
g   Ich versuche, Sie zu verbinden.
h   Möchten Sie eine Nachricht hinterlassen?
i   Die Person, mit der Sie sprechen möchten, ist im Moment nicht da.
j   Wie ist Ihr Name bitte?

4 Taking a message

Your colleague, Julie Matthews, takes a call from a supplier.

9))) Before you listen to the call, complete the dialogue using phrases from exercise 3. Then listen and check.

Julie   Fischer Digital Ltd. Julie Matthews speaking.
Liam   Can I speak to Martin Brown in Hardware Support, please?
Julie   *Who's calling please* [1]?
Liam   This is Liam Donnelly.
Julie   I'm sorry, ▬ [2]?
Liam   It's L I A M D O double-N E double-L Y. I'm calling from Adler Network Components in Manchester. It's about the cables Mr Brown ordered.
Julie   Thank you, Mr Donnelly. I'll try Mr Brown for you. Please ▬ [3].
Liam   Thank you.
…
Julie   Mr Donnelly. I'm sorry, Mr Brown is ▬ [4] at the moment. Would you like to ▬ [5]?
Liam   Yes. All right. Anyone in Hardware Support will do.
Julie   Thank you. I'll ▬ [6].
…
Julie   I'm sorry, Mr Donnelly. I'm afraid the line ▬ [7]. Would you like to ▬ [8] for Mr Brown?
Liam   Yes, please. Would you tell Mr Brown that the cables he ordered aren't available and ask him to call me to discuss an alternative. My telephone number is 161 839 5005 and the extension is 822.
Julie   ▬ [9]. I didn't ▬ [10]. Could you ▬ [11], please?
Liam   Sure. It's 161 839 5005, extension 822.
Julie   Thank you, Mr Donnelly. I'll make sure that Mr Brown gets the message.

> **→ Giving telephone numbers**
>
> Say each digit separately, except for double digits, e.g.
> 01233455 = "oh (*AE*: zero) one two double-three four double-five".

5 Role-play: A telephone call

 Work with a partner. **Partner A** and **Partner B**: Look at File 1 on page 134.

› *Useful phrases: Telephoning, page 152; Taking telephone calls, page 152*

DAS KANN ICH (Unit 2)

– Eine Umfrage über Kommunikationsmittel im Betrieb durchführen. (Foundation)
– Mich und meine Arbeit in einem Tätigkeitsprofil auf Englisch beschreiben. (Part A)
– Meine bevorzugten Arbeitsbedingungen auf Englisch beschreiben und begründen. (Part B)
– Eine Nachricht auf einer Mailbox hinterlassen; eine Nachricht weiterleiten. (Communication)

 TOOLBOX

mobile phone (*AE*: cell phone) – *Handy*
to put sb through – *jdn durchstellen*

voicemail – *Mailbox*

1 Interaktion: B1

Sie befinden sich auf der CEBIT in Hannover.

 Erstellen Sie in Partnerarbeit einen Dialog auf Englisch anhand folgender Rollenkarten.

Partner A:
Ihre Firma entwickelt intelligente Computerspiele. Sie übernehmen gerade den Standdienst.

– Sie stellen sich interessierten Besuchern/ Besucherinnen vor, beantworten Fragen u. a. zu:
  • der *gaming software* Ihrer Firma
  • den Hardware-Voraussetzungen
  • dem Standort ihrer Firma usw.
– Sie fragen den/die Besucher/in nach
  • seiner/ihrer Firma
  • dem zurzeit meistverkauften Computerspiel
– Sie geben dem/der Besucher/in auf Verlangen:
  • Verkaufsliteratur
  • eine Demo
  • Ihre Visitenkarte

Sie verabschieden sich nach kurzem Smalltalk über Erfahrungen mit Computerspielen usw.

Partner B:
Sie sind bei MacGaming im Einkauf tätig, einer internationalen Kette, die Computerspiele vertreibt. Sie finden einen Messestand für *gaming software*.

– Sie stellen sich dem/der Firmenvertreter/in vor und stellen Fragen u. a. zu:
  • dem Angebot der Firma
  • den Hardware-Voraussetzungen
  • den Preisen
  • der Gewährleistung usw.
– Sie beantworten Fragen zu:
  • Ihrer Firma
  • dem von MacGaming meistverkauften Computerspiel (*Battlefield 1*)
– Sie bitten um Kataloge und Demos

Sie geben dem/der Firmenvertreter/in Ihre Visitenkarte.
Sie verabschieden sich nach kurzem Smalltalk über Erfahrungen mit Computerspielen usw.

2 Produktion: B1

Für den neuen Internetauftritt Ihrer Firma T&P soll die Rubrik „About us" aktualisiert werden.

Verfassen Sie anhand der untenstehenden Tabelle eine kurze Firmengeschichte auf Englisch.

1992	Start-up-Gründung T&P in Garage in Dublin durch die ehemaligen IBM-Angestellten Tom Clark und Paul Kuhn – Erstellung von Software für Dubliner Buchladen
1993	erstes Produkt: T&P-93, Software für Kleinbetriebe – vier Kunden – großer Erfolg
1995	Umzug nach Bonn – neues Produkt: T&P-95 für Gehaltsabrechnung (*payroll accounting*) – Vermietung an mittelständische Firmen
1997	Einstellung von vier Software-Ingenieuren – steigende Kundenzahl – 30 % Umsatzsteigerung
1999	bestes Jahr – sechs Angestellte – neues Produkt: T&P-FA für Buchhaltung (*accounting*)
2002	schlechtes Jahr – Feuer im ersten Stock – Geräte defekt – Verlust wichtiger Kunden – Lieferschwierigkeiten
2005	T&P gewinnt Copyrightprozess – erhält 120.000 € Schadenersatz
2007	Erweiterung des Teams auf 18 Mitarbeiter – Unfalltod des Firmengründers Tom Clark
2010	neuer Partner: Fritz Keil – Kauf von AP-GamingSoftware – Umsatzzunahme um 25 %
2016	Kooperation mit französischer Firma – Entwicklung von cloud-basierten Dienstleistungen
2017	Pläne für Investition in Internet der Dinge (*IoT*) und AR (*augmented reality*) – Suche nach Partnern

3 Mediation: B1

Sie sind Praktikant/in in einem deutschen Unternehmen, das Software für Computerspiele entwickelt.

Ihr Chef gibt Ihnen den folgenden Text und bittet Sie, ihm die wichtigsten Informationen stichpunktartig auf Deutsch per E-Mail zu schicken, weil er sie als Handout für einen Vortrag nutzen will.

Ihre E-Mail sollte folgende Aspekte berücksichtigen:

- Vorteile vertikaler Hierarchien
- Vorteile flacher Hierarchien
- Mitverantwortung der Mitarbeiter
- Feedback durch Kunden

Welcome to Steamboat Software!
Welcome to the world of 'flat'!

The military and many traditional business corporations rely heavily on hierarchy as a way of maintaining predictability and reliability – two important elements for businesses with customers who desire predictable and reliable products. A traditional hierarchy simplifies planning and makes it easier to control a large group of people from the top down.

However, we don't think that this is the right model for an entertainment company such as Steamboat Software. We recruit intelligent and innovative people – like yourself – and we agree 100% with Steve Jobs, who once said: "It doesn't make sense to hire smart people and tell them what to do. We hire them to tell us what to do!"

Hiring creative, innovative people and telling them to sit at a desk and do as they're told wastes 99 per cent of their talent. We want innovators to innovate and creators to create, and that means maintaining a working environment where you'll be able to do exactly that.

That's why Steamboat Software doesn't have a hierarchy. We're flat, which is our way of saying that we don't have any management and nobody "reports to" anybody else. We do have a founder, but even he isn't your manager. Now that you are part of the team, you have the chance to create opportunities and take risks. You can start your own projects and see them through to the end product.

Our flat structure removes the barriers between your work and the customers who enjoy the results of your work. Almost all companies claim that "the customer is boss", but here that statement is at the heart of what we do. There's nothing stopping you from finding out for yourself what our customers want, and then giving it to them.

"Wow, that sounds like a lot of responsibility," you might be thinking to yourself – and you're right. We've chosen you to work here because we know that you're talented; but we also believe that you are capable of running this company, because, in many ways, that's what we want you to do!

3 Computer hardware

FOUNDATION: Hardware components

Situation: You are getting work experience as an IT salesperson at a large electronics store in the UK.
→ **You help customers choose the right computer and understand the choices they are making.**

1 Identifying hardware components

Before you start work, you check that you know the English names of the most important pieces of computer hardware.

Match the names in the list to the photos (1–8).

central processing unit (CPU) · graphics card · hard disk · keyboard · monitor · motherboard · mouse · random access memory (RAM)

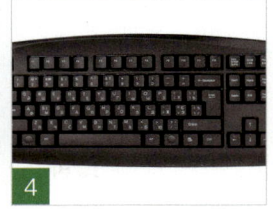

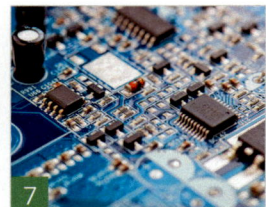
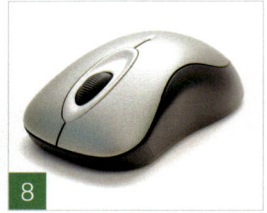

2 Explaining the functions of hardware components

A customer is interested in buying a gaming computer for his children but is worried about the price of some of the components.

Match the correct answers (a–g) on page 27 to the customer's questions (1–7) below.

1 Why do I need such a powerful graphics card?
2 Can I spend less on the CPU?
3 And the motherboard?
4 Do I need much RAM?
5 OK, what type of monitor do you recommend?
6 I suppose I'll need a big hard disk, too, right?
7 Can I at least get a cheap keyboard and mouse?

a   Although it houses all of the components, such as the graphics card and CPU, you don't have to spend a lot to get a good one.

b   It is important as it stores information that the CPU needs to use really quickly, for example things displayed on the screen. However, you can start with a mid-range amount and upgrade it easily later on.

c   It's a key part of a good gaming system. It turns the information from the CPU into the pictures that you see on the monitor. It needs to be very fast for gaming so the game runs smoothly.

d   Not necessarily. This is where your data gets saved, but online games don't take up much space because they aren't saved on your computer.

e   Well, this is the part that lets you see what's happening in the game. It doesn't need to be bigger than 24" but it is important to have a fast refresh rate, otherwise the game will look unclear.

f   You could, but because it processes every single instruction, I wouldn't recommend it. It's like the brain of the computer.

g   You could, yes. These are your input devices and are how you interact with the game. Gaming versions may have extra keys and buttons, but they don't make a big difference.

3   Discussing peripherals and connectivity

A customer is talking to a colleague. She has just started doing freelance graphic design work from home. She wants to set up a home office and asks for advice on peripherals.

A   10))) ▶️ **Listen to their conversation and match the peripherals (1–6) to the connection methods (a–f) your colleague recommends. Some of them have two possibilities.**

1	headset	a	3.5 mm jack
2	speakers	b	Bluetooth
3	monitor	c	Ethernet cable
4	external hard drive	d	HDMI
5	printer	e	USB-C
6	modem	f	Wi-Fi

B   10))) ▶️ **Listen again and complete the statements.**

1   Get a Bluetooth version and ▬ your computer – it's very easy and convenient.

2   You should ▬ the normal 3.5 mm jack because the audio quality is better.

3   I want something that I can easily ▬ and work with two screens.

4   You only need one USB-C cable to ▬ the monitor to your computer.

5   It also comes with an adapter in case someone else needs to ▬ your monitor.

6   You can even ▬ into this monitor so you don't have to plug and unplug it.

7   You can ▬ your Wi-Fi network and print.

4   Analysing your own computer hardware

To make sure that you know all the English names, you decide to make a list of the peripherals you sell and the ways that they can be connected to a computer or smartphone.

A   👥 **Work with a partner and make a list of the ways that you connect hardware to your computer, smartphone and/or tablet. How do you connect and why?**

B   👥 **Present your list to the class and discuss any differences in how you choose to connect peripherals.**

> *Useful phrases: Giving presentations, page 151*

 TOOLBOX

connectivity – *Anschlüsse*   peripheral – *Peripheriegerät*

PART A: Hardware installation

Situation: You work as a computer technician at Dream AR, a software development company that is expanding into augmented and virtual reality.
→ **You explain to a colleague how to install a hardware component.**

1 Reading an instruction manual

The laptops of some developers need to be upgraded for augmented reality (AR). You look up the instructions for replacing some of the key hardware.

Replacing internal hardware components

Preparation
Warning: Turn off your laptop. Wait ten minutes after shutting down the computer to let the internal components cool before continuing.

- Disconnect the power adapter, Ethernet cable, USB cables, security lock, and any other cables connected to the laptop to prevent damage to connections.
- Turn the laptop over and remove the ten screws that secure the bottom case using a Phillips screwdriver.
- Take the bottom off the laptop case. It should come off fairly easily, but you may need to lightly force it.

Replacing a hard drive
- The hard drive is held in place by a little piece of plastic. Unscrew the screws holding the plastic piece in place.
- Gently lift the hard drive out of the chassis and disconnect the mSATA ribbon.
- Unscrew the four small posts on each side of the hard drive with a Torx screwdriver. Then, screw the posts into the new hard drive.
- Connect the mSATA ribbon to the new hard drive and place it back in the laptop. Re-attach the plastic piece holding the drive in place.

Replacing or adding RAM modules
- Push the levers on the sides of the RAM module in an outward direction to release the module from the memory card slot.
- When the module pops up, find the half-circle notches on the module. Hold each RAM module by its notches and slide it out from the slot.
- Align the notch on the gold edge of the RAM replacement module with the notch in the lower memory slot.
- Tilt the card and push the memory into the slot.
- Use two fingers with firm, even pressure to push down on the memory module. You should hear a click when you insert the memory correctly.

 **TOOLBOX**

---

case – *Gehäuse*
chassis – *Montagerahmen*
lever – *Hebel*
notch – *Einkerbung*

ribbon (cable) – *Flachbandkabel*
screw – *Schraube*
slot – *Steckplatz*

👥 Work with a partner. Take it in turns to ask and answer the following questions about the text on page 28. Use suitable verbs from the list in your answers.

align · disconnect · find · hear · hold · push · remove · slide out · tilt · turn over · unscrew

1 What do you do to prevent damage to connections?
Disconnect the power adapter and any other cables connected to the laptop.
2 How do you remove the bottom case?
3 What do you do before you take the hard drive out?
4 What do you do with the mSATA ribbon when replacing a hard drive?
5 How do you release the module from the memory slot?
6 What do you do after the RAM module pops up?
7 How do you remove the RAM module?
8 What do you do with the replacement RAM module?

> 🔘 **Giving instructions**
>
> **Turn off** your laptop.
> **Disconnect** the power adapter.
> **Take** the bottom off the laptop case.

› *Grammar: Imperatives, page 162*

2 Reading about augmented reality peripherals

Development and testing an AR application requires a lot of new hardware. You've just received the first delivery of new hardware and read some information about the equipment and how to use it.

Headset

A full 360 degrees of head motion can be tracked by the headset using multiple embedded sensors. The display has a 90 Hz refresh rate with 2160 × 1200 pixel resolution for a truly realistic experience.

There are two options for connecting the headset to the computer.
1) Headset cable – the cable plugs into the thunderbolt port on the headset. The cable powers the headset, which allows unlimited playing time and offers the lowest latency.
2) Headset wireless adapter – the wireless adapter also attaches to a thunderbolt port on the strap of the headset and lasts about three hours. The latency is slightly higher than with a cable. A wireless unit must be installed in your computer as the headset communicates with the PC via a proprietary wireless protocol.

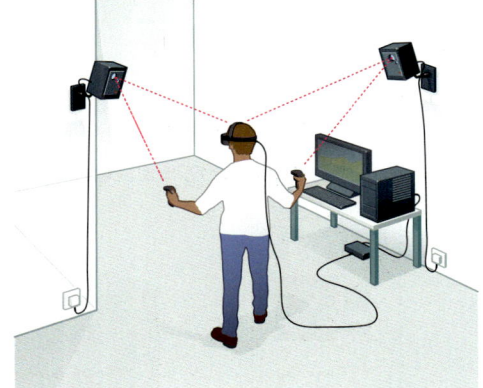

Handsets

The handsets are used to map the movement of each hand via 64 sensors in each handset. They are battery powered and a full charge provides four hours of use. They can be charged using the supplied micro-USB cables. They are connected to the headset via Bluetooth.

 TOOLBOX

charge – *Ladung*
latency – *Verzögerung, Latenzzeit*

to map – *erfassen*
proprietary – *firmeneigen, urheberrechtlich geschützt*

Base stations

The physical location of the user is monitored by the base stations using an infrared connection with the headset. They must be installed above the head height of the user (mounting kits are included). They must be positioned to have a clear view of the user and must be connected to a power source via the power cable. You require at least two base stations and can use up to four.

Peripheral tracker

Real objects (e.g. tennis rackets, plastic weapons) are turned into input devices by the peripheral tracker. It can be attached to any object using tape or a strap and communicates with the headset via Bluetooth. Up to eight can be used simultaneously and a charged battery gives six hours of use.

A   **What do the following numbers refer to?**

a   360 degrees   **b**   2160 × 1200 pixels   **c**   three hours   **d**   64   **e**   at least two   **f**   up to eight

B   **Summarize each piece of hardware mentioned in the following table.**

Hardware	Headset	Handsets	Base stations	Peripheral tracker
Function of hardware?				
How is it powered?				
What is it connected to? How?				

> ### ➔ Describing capability
>
> The handsets **are connected** to the headset via Bluetooth.
> A full 360 degrees of head motion **can be tracked** by the headset.

> › *Grammar: Passive forms, page 164*

3   Replacing a graphics card

A colleague asks you how she can upgrade the graphics card on her home computer.

Describe the steps to replace the graphics card using these pictures as a guide.

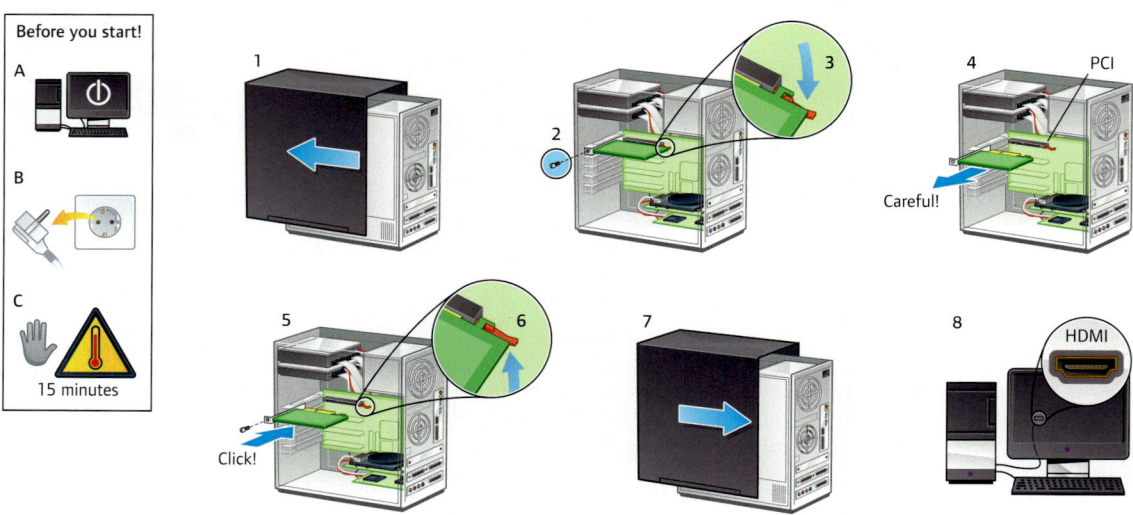

> › *Useful phrases: Giving instructions, page 152*

PART B: Computer configuration

Situation: You work as a computer technician at DIY Hardware, a large hardware store chain that operates throughout Canada.
→ **You match a computer to a colleague's needs.**

1 Assessing someone's computer requirements

Your colleagues often come to tell you about their computer hardware requirements.

I'm in Marketing and Branding. I need a computer with high performance graphics and a lot of RAM as I produce videos and other marketing material that are used by the sales team, appear on our website or are printed. I need to use a high-resolution monitor with accurate colour reproduction.

I'm in the Human Resources department so I usually speak to people instead of working on the computer. I only use mine to write emails, put information on the company intranet or input data into our HR system.

I work in Customer Support and help customers with questions about billing, warranties, returns as well as other questions about the products we sell. I don't really mind what type of computer I have as I mainly use it to look up information – I don't think I need anything high-powered and I don't know much about computers.

I'm an account manager and I travel a lot to meet clients. I need something that is light-weight and looks good, so I take a hybrid device. It has a solid-state drive that lets me load videos and documents quickly. It's easy to carry and I can use it as a tablet if I want to. It also connects to many monitors so that I can connect to a large monitor without worrying about an adaptor.

I'm a software developer and I need a computer with a fast CPU so that I can compile my software code and load all my applications quickly. I have two monitors so that I can see requirements on one screen and the software code on the other. I also need a lot of RAM.

I'm a financial analyst so I spend a lot of time working on spreadsheets. It's important that I have a fast machine because I perform a lot of complex calculations and I'm always in a rush to give my boss something. I need a large monitor, too, so that I can see as much of the spreadsheet as possible

Which of the highlighted jobs or departments needs each of these hardware features? Sometimes more than one answer is possible.

1 fast graphic performance
2 easy to carry / lightweight
3 lots of processing power
4 special monitor
5 fast load times
6 nothing special

2 Listening to someone's computer requirements

Your team provides computers to the employees of DIY Hardware. Your colleague, Geoff Wiley, tells you about Sean Santoro, a new sales representative who has just started with the company.

A   11)))   ▶   **Listen and note down which of the following Geoff thinks are Sean's computing needs and why.**

- fast processor
- lots of storage space on the hard drive
- ✗ – good looking computer
- ✗ – portability
- ✗ – lots of connection options

- ✗ – large high-resolution monitor
- ✗ – fast document loading times
- powerful graphics card
- ✗ – wireless connectivity
- ✗ – long-lasting battery

B   11)))   ▶   **Listen again and complete Geoff's assessment of the best computer for Sean.**

1 A desktop is *not fit-for-purpose* and a laptop is the  ~~computer~~ for him. *most appropriate / suitable*
2 Something with a lot of connection options is ___.
3 Light-weight and a long lasting battery are ___ for his needs. *spot on*
4 A 128 GB hard drive is ___. *more than enough*
5 An overly fast processor isn't ___ due to cost.
6 A solid-state drive is ___. *advisable / appropriate*
7 I told him that it would be ___ given his needs. *inappropriate*
8 All things considered, configuration 1 is ___ for him. *the best fit*

3 Talking about customized computers

You and your colleagues often talk about your own PCs and how you like to customize them to your needs.

👥 **Discuss any experience you've had with customized computers with a partner. Think about the aspects below and report your experiences to the class.**

- Why did you need to customize the computer?
- What components did you add to your computer?
- Did the customized computer meet your requirements?

4 Matching a computer configuration to a user's needs

You have received an email from Human Resources requesting new computers for three new employees.

👥 **Working with a partner, choose one employee to match a computer to and give reasons for your choice of computer. Use the computer configurations 1–3 in the table on page 33.**

> ➡ **Saying whether something is suitable**
>
> A laptop is the **most appropriate** computer for him.
> A desktop is **not advisable** due the cost.

 **TOOLBOX**

configuration – *Konfiguration*	portability – *Transportierbarkeit*
high resolution – *hohe Auflösung*	solid-state-drive – *Solid-State-Laufwerk*
light-weight – *leicht*	wireless – *drahtlos*

From:	michael.y@diyhardware.ca
To:	hardwaresupport@diyhardware.ca
Subject:	Computers for new employees

Good morning

Could you provide new computers for these three employees? They are all starting on Monday.

Thanks, Michael

Kate McMillan: graphic designer
– Manipulates large image files
– Creates website graphics
– Creates posters for marketing

Glen O'Brien: software developer
– Writing, compiling and debugging software
– Tracks defects on intranet ticketing system
– Needs to view multiple documents at same time

Amanda Sandilands: financial analyst
– Attends meetings
– Reads and edits spreadsheet reports
– Email, web browsing

	Configuration 1	Configuration 2	Configuration 3
Model	Microsoft Surface Pro laptop/tablet hybrid	Acer laptop + external monitor	Apple iMac
Operating system	Microsoft Windows	Microsoft Windows	Apple Mac OSX
CPU	Dual-core processor	Dual-core processor	Quad-core processor
RAM	4 GB	8 GB	16 GB
Hard disk	128 GB SSD	512 GB HDD	256 GB SSD, 1 TB HDD
Monitor	12.3 inch	laptop: 13.3 inch external: 22 inch	27 inch
Resolution (pixels)	1440 × 900	laptop: 1440 × 900 external: 1920 × 1080	5120 × 2880
GPU	Integrated graphics	Integrated graphics	Dual graphics cards
Connectivity	USB-A × 2, SD Card slot, Wi-Fi, Bluetooth	Wi-Fi, Bluetooth, VGA, DVI, USB ×4, Ethernet	USB-C × 4, headphone
Battery life	9 hours	6 hours	–
Weight	0.78 kg	2.19 kg	9.5 kg

COMMUNICATION: Emails

Situation: You are getting work experience at HardWareHouse Ltd, an IT hardware wholesaler. Your supervisor asks you to take care of a customer enquiry.
→ **You write an email to a customer.**

1 Giving email addresses over the phone

You check the English for some of the symbols that appear in email addresses.

A Match the symbols (1–6) to the words (a–f).

1	+	**4**	-	**a**	at	**d**	plus
2	_	**5**	.	**b**	dot	**e**	number
3	@	**6**	3	**c**	hyphen	**f**	underscore

B **12))) Listen to your supervisor and a customer on the phone. Which email addresses are correct?**

1
a tm.martin@hard_warehouse.co.uk
b tmmartin@hardware-house.co.uk
c tm.martin@hardware_house.co.uk

2
a maryannbrown@5+5_services.net
b mary-anne-brown@5+5services.net
c maryann-brown@5+5services.net

C 👥 **Work with a partner. You are going to dictate email addresses to each other.**

Partner A: Look at File 2 on page 134.
Partner B: Look at File 5 on page 136.

> Can you spell that, please?

> Could you repeat that, please?

2 Writing a subject line

The first indication of what is in an email is the subject line. This must state clearly what the email is about.

A 👥 **Work with a partner. Study the subject lines (1–6) below and find an email which …**

1	is a request for information.	**a**	Subject:	Need your help with English
2	gives information about a meeting.	**b**	Subject:	New venue for event on Saturday
3	asks for assistance.	**c**	Subject:	Flyer (attached)
4	contains new information.	**d**	Subject:	Meeting 25.03. Starting time?
5	announces a change of plan.	**e**	Subject:	Update on project
6	is a covering letter for a brochure	**f**	Subject:	Agenda

B 👥 **With your partner, write suitable subject lines for the following emails (1–6).**

1 Sorry, I would like to change the date of the meeting to Friday 12 July.
2 Could you send me information about the presentation, please?
3 I am on holiday from 21.03 till 04.04 inclusive and will answer emails when I return.
4 I am writing to confirm your application for a stand at the Technical Trades Fair. The stand number is C208.
5 As promised, here is the link to the website www.tipsformails.com.
6 This is just to let you know that I am interviewing a new technician at 12.30.

TOOLBOX

hyphen – *Bindestrich, Minus*   underscore – *Unterstrich*

3 Writing a reply to an email enquiry

Your supervisor gives you the enquiry below and asks you to reply by email.

Dear Sir or Madam

We have studied your catalogue on the internet and are interested in your ergonomic mouse devices
(catalogue number SP 492876) and your keyboards (catalogue number SS 8592201).
We would like to order 100 of each item.
We would also like to order 200 8 GB USB sticks and 200 16 GB USB sticks.
Please let us know if you have these items in stock.

Yours faithfully
Robert Johnson
CompuStore Ltd

Use a suitable greeting and subject line and reply to Mr Johnson. Include the following points:

- Thank him for his enquiry.
- Say that the mouse devices, keyboards and USB sticks are in stock.
- Say you will dispatch them next week.
- Say that you look forward to doing business with him in the future.
- Use the correct complimentary close.

› *Useful phrases: Writing emails, page 153*

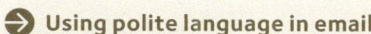 **Using polite language in emails**

Could and *would like* are more polite than phrases with *can*, *need* or *want*.
~~Can~~ you let me know by Monday? → **Could** you let …
I ~~need~~ the information today. → I **would like** the …
We ~~want~~ to have a meeting. → We **would like** to …

› *Grammar: Modals and their substitutes, page 167*

 Salutation and complimentary close in emails

If you do not know the name of the person you are writing to, begin your email with *Dear Sir or Madam*.
If you do not know your business partner well, use a formal salutation and complimentary close.

	Salutation	Complimentary close	
Formal (to unknown person)	Dear Sir or Madam	Yours faithfully	
Formal (to person whose name you know)	Dear Mr/Ms Smith	Regards Best regards	Best wishes Yours sincerely
Less formal	Dear Paul / Hi Paula Good morning, Paul	Regards Best regards	Best wishes All the best

---

DAS KANN ICH (Unit 3)

- Eine Liste der englischen Bezeichnungen für IT-Anschlüsse zusammenstellen. (Foundation)
- Einem Kollegen / Einer Kollegin erklären, wie man eine neue Grafikkarte installiert. (Part A)
- Computerhardware an die Bedürfnisse von Kollegen und Kolleginnen anpassen. (Part B)
- Die E-Mail eines Kunden / einer Kundin auf Englisch beantworten. (Communication)

 TOOLBOX

complimentary close – *Grußformel (am Briefende)*
salutation – *Anrede*
subject line – *Betreff*

Best regards / Regards – *Viele Grüße/Mit freundlichen Grüßen*
Yours faithfully – *Mit freundlichen Grüßen*
Yours sincerely – *Mit freundlichen Grüßen*

4 Computer software

FOUNDATION: Graphical user interfaces (GUIs)

Situation: You work in the IT Support department of a financial services company in Sydney, Australia.
→ **You help a colleague navigate a computer interface.**

1 Navigating a desktop or laptop graphical user interface (GUI)

A new employee asks you about the Apple OSX GUI. She has only used Windows computers in the past.

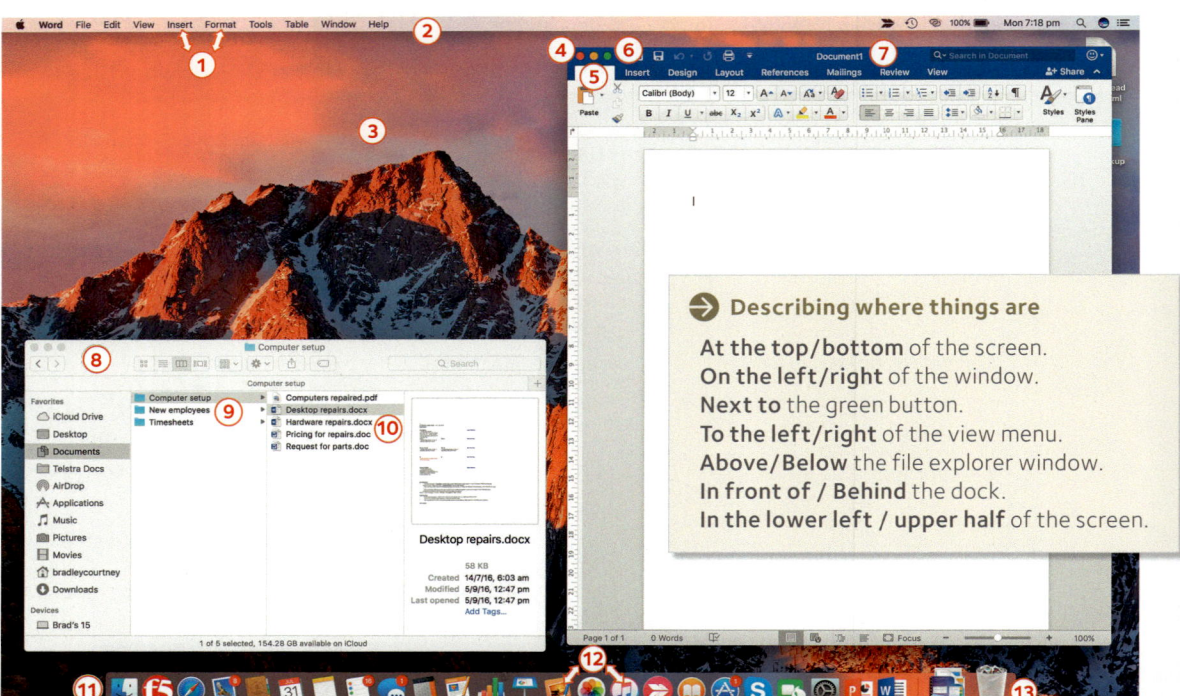

Describing where things are

At the **top/bottom** of the screen.
On the **left/right** of the window.
Next to the green button.
To the **left/right** of the view menu.
Above/Below the file explorer window.
In front of / Behind the dock.
In the **lower left / upper half** of the screen.

A Match the GUI components from the list to the numbers (1–13) on the screenshot.

application icon · application window · close button · desktop · dock · file · file explorer · folder · maximize button · menu bar · menus · minimize button · wastepaper basket

B Describe where each of the GUI components is located on the screen above to help your colleague find them.

2 Navigating a smartphone GUI

Your team maintain a 'Tips and Tricks' page to help the sales team use the FindYourWay maps app.

FindYourWay – Tips and Tricks

Maps

You can use maps in either portrait or landscape mode by rotating your phone.

Choose a destination and get directions
- **Press and hold** on the place on the map you want to mark as your destination. A pin will drop onto the map and an address and car symbol will appear.
- **Tap once** on the car symbol and you will be shown a route from your current location to the destination.

Zoom-in
- Place two fingers close together on the screen and then **spread** them to control zoom-in precisely.
- **Double tap** the place you want to zoom into on the screen to zoom in in steps.

Zoom-out
- Place two fingers on the screen and then **pinch** to control zoom precisely.
- Do a **two-finger tap** on the screen to zoom out in steps.

Scroll
- To scroll slowly through a map, touch the screen and **drag** your finger in any direction on the screen.
- To scroll quickly through a map, **swipe up, down, left or right** through the map.

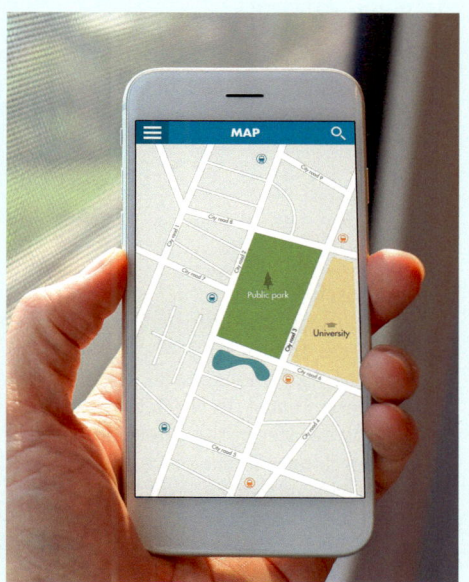

A You want to add some icons to the FAQ page to make it easier for some of the non-native employees to understand gestures. Match gestures to each of these icons using phrases from the text.

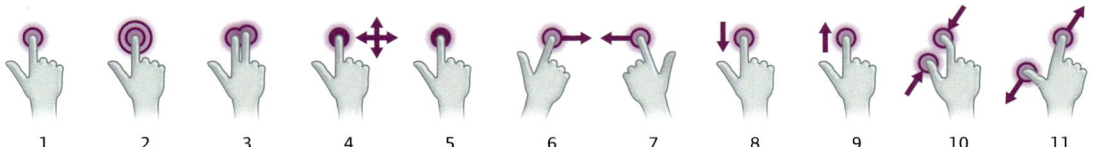

B Work with a partner. Write a set of English instructions to answer these FAQs using a smartphone that you have. When you have finished, compare your answers with another pair.

1 How do I delete an app?
2 How do I find a document on my phone?
3 How do I turn on the flashlight?
4 How can I see the widgets?
5 How do I zoom in to a PDF?

› *Useful phrases: Navigating GUIs, page 153*

3 Explaining smartphone functions

A colleague asks you to explain how some of the functions on his new smartphone work.

Work with a partner. Each choose one or two smartphone functions. Write some instructions on how to use the function. Read the instructions to your partner and see whether he/she can perform the function.

PART A: Software installation

Situation: You work in the Release Management team at Allotel, a British telecommunications company located in London. The team co-ordinate the large number of software releases that take place across the entire company.

→ **You report back to your supervisor on the progress of a software installation.**

1 Installing software

The team use a cloud-based release management solution and they have recently purchased a licence for an extension package. You read the installation instructions.

Pre-installation steps
- Make sure you have sufficient privilege to perform the installation. (You must have 'Administrative' level access or higher.)
- Under the 'Extensions' menu, choose 'Add new extension'. Enter the URL provided in your licence confirmation email. To check that the URL is valid, look for a green tick that will appear next to the URL. The transfer of the extension package will begin automatically after validation.
- The unpacking will take place on your cloud environment, so you need to ensure that you have enough available space to allow for transfer and installation of the temporary installation files. To do so, check the 'Available space' option in the environment settings and make sure you have at least 600 MB available to allow for the uncompressed files.

Installation steps
- Click 'View components'. You'll see a list of components in the package as well as a list of connected apps.
- To check that the components and any connected apps shown are acceptable, ensure that no other component and apps appear in the 'Acceptable' list. Then select 'Continue'.
- A dialog box appears showing all the websites that the package communicates with. (We recommend using SSL for transmitting data.)

Post-installation steps
*Note that these are general steps. You should take additional steps to verify your specific settings.
- To confirm that the package installed successfully, check that it is visible in the 'Active extensions' menu.
- To confirm access is correct, verify that a user that you expect to use the additional features can see the extended menu options.
- Confirm the installation files have been deleted. They should have been automatically removed as part of the installation.

 **TOOLBOX**

administrative level – *Administratorenebene*	privilege – *Berechtigung*
cloud-based – *cloud-basiert*	uncompressed – *unkomprimiert*
extension package – *Erweiterungspaket*	to verify – *überprüfen*
free/available space – *verfügbarer Speicherplatz*	visible – *sichtbar*

A   **Read the additional instructions below and decide which heading from the installation instructions on page 38 each one belongs to.**

1   To check that your environment meets the minimum requirements, verify the environment information in the environment settings.   → *Pre-installation steps*
2   Select 'Yes' to grant access to these third-party websites and click 'Continue', or click 'Cancel' to stop the installation of the package.
3   To verify that the selected third-party websites have access, confirm that 'Verified' appears next to each website (they have been pinged in the background).
4   To make sure that the download was successful, check that 'Download complete' appears next to the extension name. Then click 'Install'. You'll see a message that describes the progress and a confirmation message after the installation is complete.
5   Ensure that users not required to use the extension cannot see the extended menu options.
6   Confirm that all users are logged out of the environment by ensuring that no users are listed in the 'Logged in users' panel on the bottom-right of the screen.

B   **Now explain how to carry out the following tasks using information from the text and exercise 1A.**

How do I ...
1   make sure that the URL for the extension package is valid?
2   check that the environment has sufficient space?
3   ensure that the components and any connected apps shown are acceptable?
4   verify that the environment meets the minimum requirements?
5   verify that a user expected to use the additional features can do so?
6   check that the package has been installed successfully?
7   confirm that the selected third-party websites have access?
8   ensure that all users are logged out of the environment?   › *Useful phrases:*
9   check that the download has been completed successfully?   *Installing software, page 153*

2   Understanding failure and error messages

You need to give an update to your boss on the progress of critical releases and you use the most recent automated report from the release management system.

Overnight patch deployment report – 19th October

MS Visio patch – Deployed 11.38 p.m.

Deployed to 213 users
Deployed successfully to 127 users
Failed to install for 86 users
Main reasons for failure
- 56 did not start because users delayed the installation
- 16 did not complete as a result of users not having latest version of MS Office
- 10 did not start as users have not logged in since the patch was released
- 4 failed as a result of insufficient privileges

Critical security flaw update 5.1.23.2 – Deployed at 2.54 a.m.

Deployed to 15435 users
Failed to install on 3456 users
Main reasons for failure
- 2309 installations did not start because users delayed the installation
- 332 did not start due to users having not logged on since the patch was released
- 243 did not complete because users do not have dependent programs installed
- 188 did not download as a result of connectivity interruptions

---

Answer your boss's questions on the report on page 39.

1 What was the failure rate of the MS Visio patch?
2 What was the success rate of the critical security flaw update?
3 How many installations were delayed by users?
4 How many failures were caused by software issues?
5 What was the main reason for failure of both patches?
6 What two software issues caused failures?
7 What were the other reasons for failure?

➜ Talking about cause

56 did not start **because** users delayed the installation.
10 did not start **as** users have not logged on since the patch was released.
188 failed **as a result of** download interruptions.
332 did not start **due to** users having not logged on since the patch was released.

3 Reporting on results

You are attending a meeting with your manager to provide updates on the software patches that are in progress. The meeting starts in one hour, so you call your colleague to talk about the progress of your respective areas of responsibility.

👥 Work with a partner. Partner A: Look here. Partner B: Look at File 3 on page 135.

A Answer your partner's questions about the patch releases using the report below.

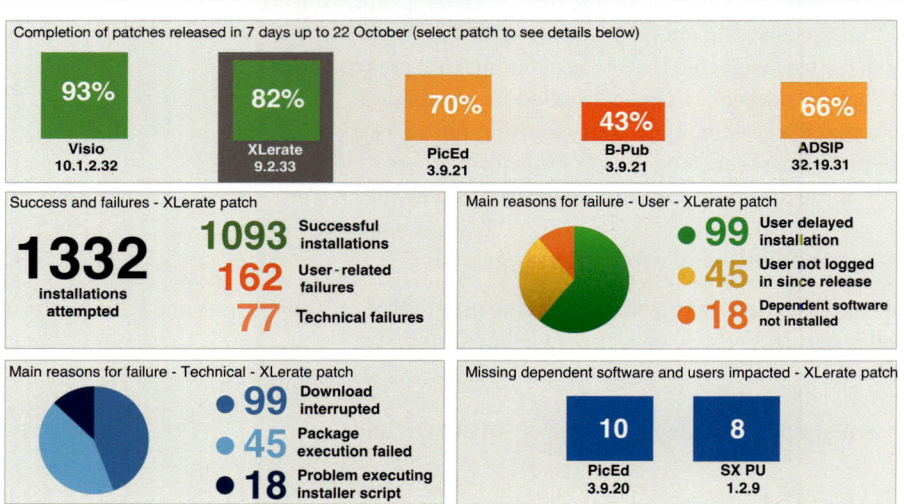

B Ask your partner questions to find out the following information:

– the progress of the patches released in the week up to 11 April
– the success rate of the TDS patch
– the main reasons for failure for the TDS patch
– if there is dependent software that is causing problems

› Grammar: Questions and short answers, page 162

TOOLBOX

to delay sth – *etw verschieben*	to release – *freigeben, veröffentlichen*
to deploy – *bereitstellen*	security flaw – *Sicherheitslücke*
failure – *Fehler*	success rate – *Erfolgsquote*

PART B: Software configuration

Situation: You work in the Release Management team at Allotel, a British telecommunications company located in London. You are looking at ways to improve the success of the enterprise software releases.
→ **You advise a colleague on configuring software installations.**

1 Configuring software releases

You look at the current configuration options for your software updates.

Software release configuration

Set your preferences to deploy applications, software updates and maintenance scripts to your users and make selections on the level of control you give them.

The default options are set to give users no control.

You can edit your selections at any time.

Force install
Choose whether to force install for
- ● all software
- ○ critical software only
- ○ no software

Select how to force install software
- ☑ Force install by a specified date and time (date/time must be set for every release at release time)

- ☐ Force install after a given duration after release
  Choose the duration after which force install occurs.   Every [2]   period [▼]

User controlled configuration
Decide which configuration options you want to give your users

- ☑ Allows users to delay software installation?

- ○ Force install after [   ] delays   ○ Never force installs

- ☑ Make software available for users to install when requested

- ● All software   ○ Non-critical software only

Select which configuration options a user can have

- ☐ Set software to automatically install outside working hours
- ☑ Set working hours?   Start time. [9:00 AM]   end time [   ]   [Save] [Cancel]

A   **Copy and complete the table for each GUI element named in the screen above.**

Component	Number on screen	Number checked	Number unchecked	Number populated	Number unpopulated
Radio buttons	7 (3 sets)	▭	▭		
Check boxes	▭	▭	▭		
Text fields	▭			▭	▭
Drop-down fields	▭			▭	▭
Buttons	▭				

B Match the descriptions to the GUI elements.

1	Radio buttons	a	are used when you want to perform an important action.
2	Check boxes	b	allow you to select one or more values from a hidden list.
3	Text fields	c	allow you to select one value from a set of values on screen.
4	Drop-down fields	d	are used to enter values like names, addresses and notes.
5	Buttons	e	only allow two values – true and false – for a given field.

C Complete the notes on how to configure the following using the words from the list. Some words can be used more than once.

choose · control · decide · enter · give · options · preferences · select · set

- The administrator ▦¹ the ▦² using the configuration options.
- To allow users freedom, ▦³ them as much ▦⁴ as possible.
- To ▦⁵ to force install software for critical software only, you have to ▦⁶ the first radio button selection.
- The user controlled configuration section allows you to ▦⁷ which configuration ▦⁸ to ▦⁹ to users.
- To ▦¹⁰ the duration after which force install occurs, you have to ▦¹¹ a number into the duration text field and ▦¹² a value from the drop-down box.

D 👥 Discuss with a partner the options you would choose if you wanted to a) give users as little choice as possible, or b) give users as much choice as possible. Compare your ideas with another pair.

2 Taking action to achieve desired outcomes

You listen to your boss and a colleague, Gavin, discussing how best to configure the software installation for the company's employees.

A 13))) Listen to their conversation and give the reasons why your boss thinks the following suggestions won't work.

- forced updates
- telling how many times they can delay an install
- emailing users
- installing on startup

B 13))) Listen again and complete the sentences, using the prompts in brackets.

1 If we minimize the options that users have, … (secure software environment)
   we will have a clean, secure software environment.
2 If we allow them to control when their updates are installed, … (fewer complaints)
3 (restrict / control) … if we want to do our job properly.
4 If we want a good balance, … (allow / delay / installation)
5 If we want them to have control, … (tell / how many times / delay)
6 If we send them an email to explain how important installs are, … (less likely / delay)
7 (call / complain / slow startup) … if their battery goes flat in the middle of the day.

> ➔ **Talking about consequences**
>
> **If** we **minimize** their options, we **will have** secure software.
> We **should minimize** their options **if** we **want** secure software.

› *Grammar: Conditional sentences, page 164*

3 Writing instructions to configure software

You've received an email from a colleague asking for advice on the best balance of configuration options.

A   **Read the email and note down the following:**

– the outcomes you would expect for the options mentioned
– some pros and/or cons of each option

B   **Compare your notes with a partner and come to an agreement on the recommendations you would give your colleague.**

C   **Write an email reply to your colleague with your recommendations and the reasons behind them.**

From:	bernd.schwang@allotel.co.uk
To:	intern@allotel.co.uk
Subject:	Using the force?

Hi,

I'm trying to configure how much control users receive over software installation and am having trouble finding the right balance. I know you've done this before, so I want to ask you for some advice (pros/cons). Here are some of the options I'm considering:

– Install on startup
– Install on shutdown
– Install on inactivity
– Install in the background if upgrade does require the computer to be restarted. If so, force restart outside of office hours.
– Install between 12 a.m. and 5 a.m.
– Download installation files when connected to network and install even if not connected to network
– Communicate with users to tell them why installs are so important
– Communicate to users that find their computers have been restarted overnight and confirm that all of their files will be saved

Any help would be appreciated.

Cheers,
Bernd

PS – hope you like the Star Wars reference!

› *Grammar: Conditional sentences, page 164; Modals and their substitutes, page 167*

 **TOOLBOX**

default option – *standardmäßige Option*	preferences – *Einstellungen*
to force (an) install – *eine Installation erzwingen*	shutdown – *Abschalten, Herunterfahren*
inactivity – *Inaktivität*	software script – *Software-Skript*
outcome – *Ergebnis, Resultat*	

COMMUNICATION: A short presentation

Situation: Some trainees from the UK are soon going to start work at your company.
→ **You give a short presentation to the new trainees about your work.**

1 Thinking about the contents of a presentation

Your supervisor gives you a list of points you should include in your talk.

what the company does · your department · what you do

A Work with a partner. Read the list and decide together what you would like to add to your supervisor's list above. Make notes.

B Compare your notes with another pair and decide on the final points you will cover. Make a mind map.

C Agree on the order you will present the contents. Make a numbered list. Write the name and date of your talk at the top of the list.

Presentation to new trainees: 08.07.20..
1 Introduction (self/the company)
2 ▬
3 ▬

2 Writing the presentation

A Use your mind map and the list from exercise 1 to write your text. Follow this structure.

Introduction	– Say in a few words what you are going to talk about.
Main part	– Use one paragraph for each topic.
	– Use signposts to move from one subject to the next.
Conclusion	– Summarize the main ideas.
	– Invite questions from the audience.

B Check the text together for clarity and correctness as follows.

- Is the information in the text correct? If not, correct it.
- Is the spelling and grammar correct? Use your dictionary and the list of phrases on page 45.

3 Making a prompt card

A presentation comes across best when the presenter looks at the audience and speaks naturally. As it is difficult to do either of these things when you read from a text, you should make yourself a prompt card.

A Follow the steps below.

- Highlight important words and phrases in your text.
- Copy the words and phrases onto an index card.
- Include signposts to structure the ideas.

> – *manufacturing company*
> – *workshop*
> – *apprentice ...*

B Practise your presentation in your group, using only your prompt card.

➡️ **Structuring a presentation**

Introduction
My name is … and this is my colleague, …
We are … apprentices at … (*name of company*) in Germany.
This morning/afternoon, I'm / we're going to give a short talk/presentation on …
I/We will be happy to answer any questions at the end of the talk.

Main part
I've/We've divided the talk/presentation into … parts.
First/Firstly, … / Second/Secondly, … / After that … / Finally, …

Signposts
To begin with … / Next …
Now … / I would also like to mention …

Conclusion
To conclude, … / To sum up, …
I'd/We'd be happy to take questions now. / Does anyone have any questions?
Thank you for listening.

4 Giving your presentation

It is time to give your presentation and to give each other feedback.

A Decide who is going to speak first in your group. When it is your turn, stand up, look directly at the audience and smile. Then speak freely and clearly using your prompt card. Ask for questions at the end.

B Give each other feedback using this feedback sheet. Give points from 1 to 3.
(1 point = needs improvement,
2 points = good,
3 points = very good)

› *Useful phrases: Giving presentations, page 154*

Presentations feedback		Points
Content	you covered all the necessary points	▭
	you used examples to support your points	▭
Structure	your talk was easy to follow	▭
	you used useful phrases to structure your talk	▭
	you summarized the main ideas in your conclusion	▭
Presentation	you smiled and looked friendly	▭
	you spoke clearly and freely	▭
	you looked at the audience when you spoke	▭
Dealing with questions	you dealt with questions in a friendly manner	▭
	you answered all the questions clearly	▭
Overall score for the presentation		▭ /30

DAS KANN ICH (Unit 4)

– Einem Kollegen / Einer Kollegin die Bedienung einer Benutzeroberfläche erklären. (Foundation)
– Einen Bericht über die Fortschritte bei einer Softwareinstallation geben. (Part A)
– Einen Kollegen / Eine Kollegin beraten, wie man eine Softwareinstallation konfiguriert. (Part B)
– Eine kurze Präsentation über meine Arbeit für neue Auszubildende halten. (Communication)

1 Hörverstehen: B1/B2

Sie absolvieren derzeit ein Praktikum in New York. Ihre Kollegin möchte sich in einem Apple Store Apple Watches anschauen. Ein Verkäufer wird auf sie aufmerksam.

14))) Hören Sie das Gespräch und machen Sie sich Notizen zu den folgenden Fragen. Beantworten Sie anschließend die Fragen in ganzen Sätzen auf Deutsch.

1 Mit welchen Funktionen der Uhr ist Susan bereits vertraut?
2 Wie ruft man das Dock auf?
3 Was für ein Applemodell trägt Kevin?
4 Welche zwei Möglichkeiten gibt es, um einen Überblick über die Apps zu erhalten?
5 Welche Funktion haben die *Activity Rings*?
6 Wie motiviert die Uhr den/die Träger/in, sich mehr Bewegung zu verschaffen?
7 Welche Körperfunktionen misst die Uhr? Welche nicht?
8 Welche technischen Daten erwähnt Kevin?

2 Produktion: B1

Sie sind Praktikant/in bei T&P in Luton, UK, einem Unternehmen mit Schwerpunkt Business Software für mittelständische Unternehmen. Ihr Vorgesetzter bittet Sie, neue Laptops bei der Firma DIY Hardware zu bestellen. Sie sollen aber vorher einen Kostenvoranschlag (*quotation*) für einen Laptop einholen, den Sie für die Softwareentwicklung für geeignet halten.

Verfassen Sie eine E-Mail an DIY Hardware in englischer Sprache unter Berücksichtigung folgender Punkte:

– förmliche Anrede
– Informationen über Ihre Firma
– Angebot über einen Laptop Ihrer Wahl
– Konfiguration – geeignet für Software-Entwickler
– Frage nach Rabatt bei Bestellung von fünf Geräten
– Frage nach der Lieferzeit und Verfügbarkeit
– Grußformel

3 Produktion: B2

Sie sind Praktikant/in bei T&P. Sie beantworten per E-Mail die Fragen Ihres englischen Freundes, der Probleme mit seinem langsamen Computer hat.

Schreiben Sie ihm eine E-Mail in englischer Sprache unter Berücksichtigung folgender Punkte:

– Bezug auf die E-Mail Ihres Freundes
– Entfernung von Datenmüll
– Gewinnung von Speicherplatz
– Endgültiges Löschen von Dateien (Shreddern oder Deinstallieren?)
– Programme zur Beschleunigung des PC
– Datensicherheit bei häufigem Surfen im Internet
– freundschaftlicher Abschluss

Mediation: A2 / B1

Die Tochter Ihres Bekannten wünscht sich eine Tattoo-App für ihr Smartphone. Bevor Ihr Bekannter den Wunsch seiner Tochter erfüllt, bittet er Sie, ihm das Wichtigste des folgenden englischsprachigen Texts per E-Mail auf Deutsch mitzuteilen.

Fassen Sie die wichtigsten Fakten des Textes auf Deutsch zusammen. Berücksichtigen Sie dabei folgende Fragestellungen:

– Für wen ist InkHunter geeignet?
– Wie lädt man die App herunter?
– Wie projiziert man ein Tattoo auf die Haut?
– Entstehen Kosten?

InkHunter

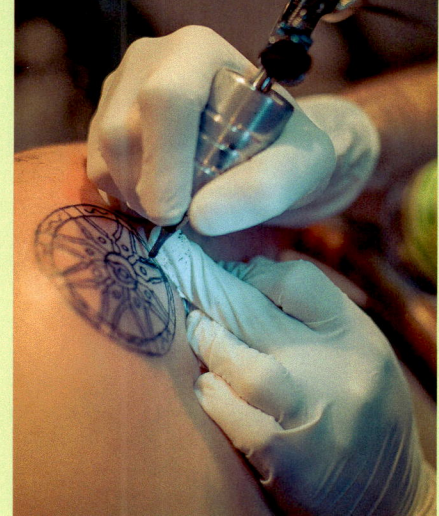

Think before you ink. See what you get before you make a decision for life you might repent one day. For people who for years have been toying with the idea of getting a heart tattooed on their right shoulder, but lacked the courage to enter a tattoo shop, InkHunter is exactly the right app. It is an app for Android and iOS devices using augmented reality that allows you to try on virtual tattoos to get a better idea of what the design will look like before it is inked forever.

Before you can actually start the app, you are required to log in with an email or via your Facebook account. Then you draw a marker, a square of three lines, on your body in the place where you want the design to appear in 3D mode. You will be asked for permission to use the camera of your smartphone. Then it will project in real time any tattoo design of your choice on any part of your body. You can choose the tattoos from the gallery of the available designs, create your own sketches or even use photos from your own collection. Now you can play around with colour and size and look at it from different angles. If you want to be absolutely sure before you go under the needle, save a photo of it and share it with friends to get second opinions.

InkHunter was created by a team of software engineers based in Ukraine. It is free to download and use, but encourages users to buy tattoo artists' designs if they try one.

5 IT security

FOUNDATION: Unauthorized access

Situation: You work in the IT department at Hoffman Auditing, a tax consultancy in Auckland, New Zealand. The company has discovered that several customer accounts have recently been hacked.
→ **You write an email to your customers with advice on how to avoid cybercrime.**

1 Identifying types of attack

Your department head gives a presentation to the company's senior managers about the hacks.

A 15))) ▶ **Listen to her presentation and match the hacking methods (1–6) with the PowerPoint slides (A–F).**

1 phishing
2 worms
3 backdoors
4 man-in-the-middle
5 injection attacks
6 social engineering

A
- exploits flaws in database
- hides in files that seem normal
- installs software with hidden commands

B
- listens to communication between a user and the network
- monitors and records communication
- infects many users that work in cafés and on public Wi-Fi networks

C
- pretends to be from a trustworthy organization
- asks the recipient to click on a link
- links to websites that are infected with malware

D
- exploits weaknesses in people, not software
- hacker pretends to be a real customer
- persuades users to open an email they've been sent containing malware

E
- provides access to a network by bypassing normal authentication
- hides in inactive state and is very difficult to detect
- often starts via a trojan

F
- copies itself and spreads to other computers on a network
- sends sensitive documents back to the hackers
- uses network bandwidth to send information

 TOOLBOX

authentication – *Authentifizierung*	to infect – *infizieren*	recipient – *Empfänger/in*
to bypass – *umgehen*	malware – *Schadprogramm(e)*	trojan – *Trojaner*

B 15)) ▶ **Listen again and complete the statements of caution that your manager uses. The first one has been done for you.**

1 The findings show that our employees don't seem to *pay attention to* our warnings about cybercrime.
2 We send an information email to our employees each month. I can only repeat what we say there: ▬ phishing.
3 Our network monitoring team continues to ▬ for worms.
4 We continually ▬ for communications that are going to unidentified locations.
5 Many of our staff work in cafés, even though they have been told to ▬ they use secure networks.
6 These are hard to detect, so we ask employees to ▬ anything that just doesn't look right.
7 Our employee training contains lessons on how to ▬ social engineering.

> **Exercising caution**
>
> Beware of …
> Guard against …
> Keep an eye out for …
> Pick up on …

› *Grammar: Imperatives, page 162*

2 Warning employees about cybercrime

The IT department at Hoffman Auditing has created a cybersecurity FAQ page for its employees.

Match the situations (A–G) to the explanations (1–7) on the FAQ page.

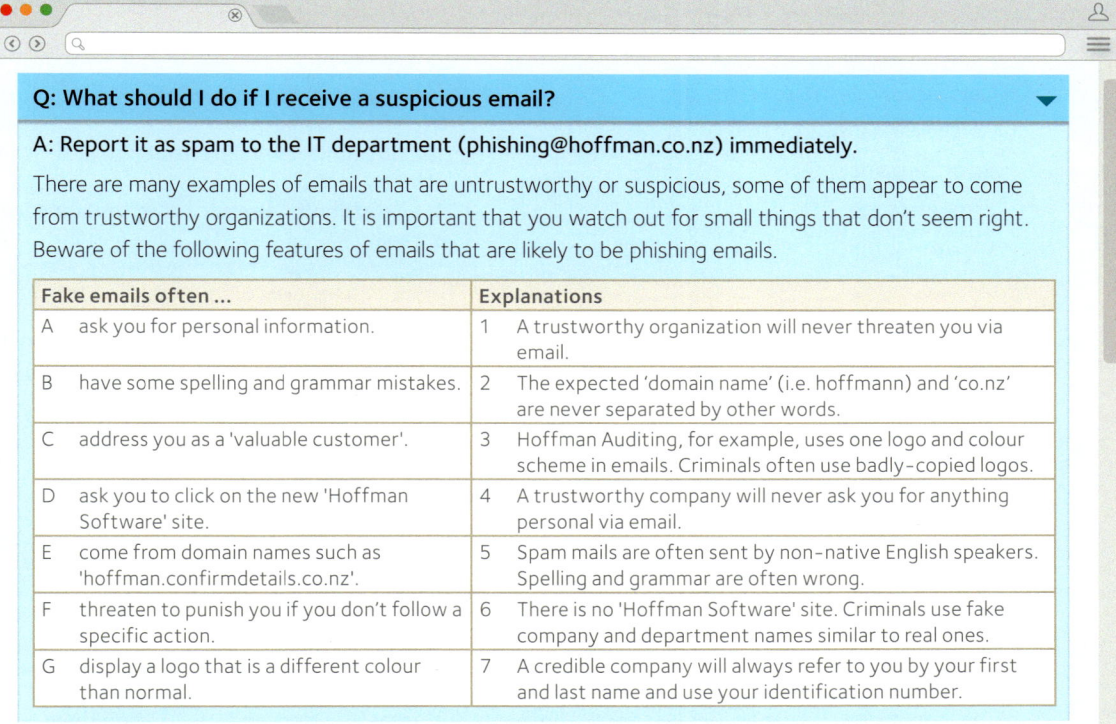

Q: What should I do if I receive a suspicious email?

A: Report it as spam to the IT department (phishing@hoffman.co.nz) immediately.

There are many examples of emails that are untrustworthy or suspicious, some of them appear to come from trustworthy organizations. It is important that you watch out for small things that don't seem right. Beware of the following features of emails that are likely to be phishing emails.

Fake emails often …		Explanations	
A	ask you for personal information.	1	A trustworthy organization will never threaten you via email.
B	have some spelling and grammar mistakes.	2	The expected 'domain name' (i.e. hoffmann) and 'co.nz' are never separated by other words.
C	address you as a 'valuable customer'.	3	Hoffman Auditing, for example, uses one logo and colour scheme in emails. Criminals often use badly-copied logos.
D	ask you to click on the new 'Hoffman Software' site.	4	A trustworthy company will never ask you for anything personal via email.
E	come from domain names such as 'hoffman.confirmdetails.co.nz'.	5	Spam mails are often sent by non-native English speakers. Spelling and grammar are often wrong.
F	threaten to punish you if you don't follow a specific action.	6	There is no 'Hoffman Software' site. Criminals use fake company and department names similar to real ones.
G	display a logo that is a different colour than normal.	7	A credible company will always refer to you by your first and last name and use your identification number.

3 Warning customers about cybercrime

Your manager asks you to write to Hoffman's customers with tips on how to guard against phishing emails.

Write an email to Hoffman's customers. Make sure you tell them what to do if they receive a suspicious email. Explain some of the things that Hoffman does to minimize the risk to customers.

Use the FAQ page and the language of exercising caution to help you. Make sure you tell them:
– to watch out for cybercrime but not panic
– how to identify a real email from Hoffman
– what to do if they receive a suspicious email that claims to be from Hoffman

PART A: Internal access and acceptable use

Situation: You work in the IT department at Hoffman Auditing, a tax consultancy in Auckland, New Zealand. One of your jobs is to provide technical support to employees.
→ **You summarize the terms of acceptable use and internal access at your training company.**

1 Understanding access privileges

A colleague receives a call from Esther Smith, a Hoffman tax consultant, about a problem she is having with an application.

A 16))) **Listen and complete the following form about Esther's request.**

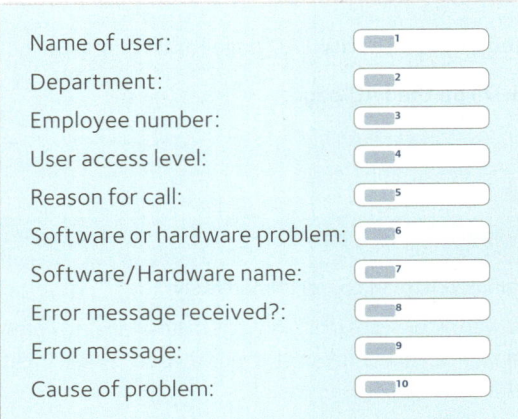

Name of user: [____]¹
Department: [____]²
Employee number: [____]³
User access level: [____]⁴
Reason for call: [____]⁵
Software or hardware problem: [____]⁶
Software/Hardware name: [____]⁷
Error message received?: [____]⁸
Error message: [____]⁹
Cause of problem: [____]¹⁰

> **⊘ Expressing permission and restrictions**
>
> I **am (not) allowed/permitted** to install software from the internet.
> You **do/don't have permission** to download videos.
> They **do/don't have access** to the company intranet.

› *Useful phrases: Explaining access requirements, page 154*

B 16))) **Listen again and complete the email to Esther Smith containing the audio management software links and a summary of the call and her access level. Use phrases from the telephone conversation to help you.**

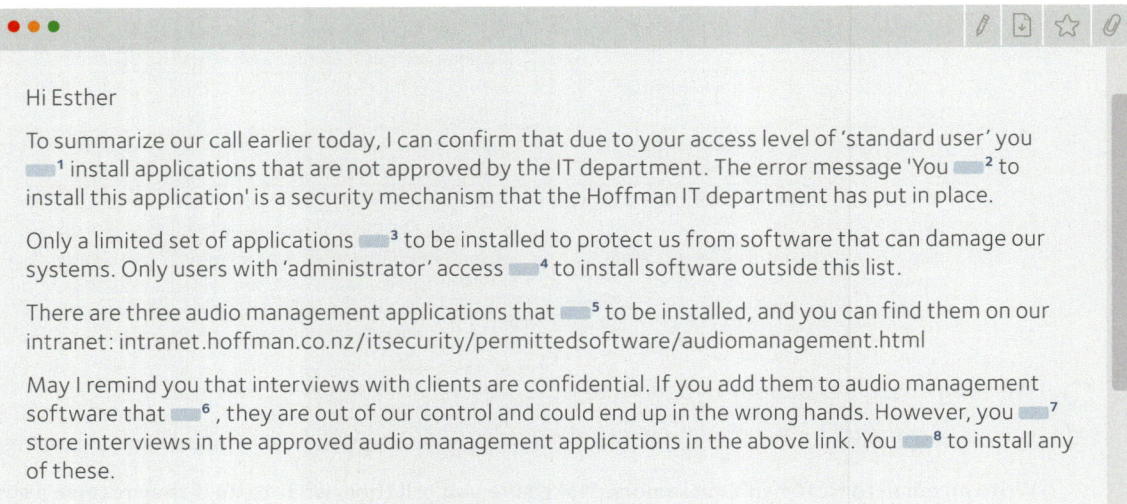

Hi Esther

To summarize our call earlier today, I can confirm that due to your access level of 'standard user' you [____]¹ install applications that are not approved by the IT department. The error message 'You [____]² to install this application' is a security mechanism that the Hoffman IT department has put in place.

Only a limited set of applications [____]³ to be installed to protect us from software that can damage our systems. Only users with 'administrator' access [____]⁴ to install software outside this list.

There are three audio management applications that [____]⁵ to be installed, and you can find them on our intranet: intranet.hoffman.co.nz/itsecurity/permittedsoftware/audiomanagement.html

May I remind you that interviews with clients are confidential. If you add them to audio management software that [____]⁶, they are out of our control and could end up in the wrong hands. However, you [____]⁷ store interviews in the approved audio management applications in the above link. You [____]⁸ to install any of these.

 **TOOLBOX**

acceptable use – *zulässige Nutzung*   confidential – *vertraulich*

2 Defining acceptable use

Hoffman has recently changed their acceptable use policy, which means employees have to complete online training to demonstrate that they understand the new policy.

A   Match the following words and phrases to their German equivalents.

1	circumstance	a	Ausnahme
2	to contravene sth	b	gegen etw verstoßen
3	controversial	c	Ruf, Ansehen
4	defamation	d	schaden
5	exception	e	umstritten
6	to harm	f	verbieten
7	to prohibit	g	Verleumdung
8	reputation	h	Umstand

B   Read the activities (1–9) below. Think about what might be in the new acceptable use policy. For each activity, discuss with a partner whether you think it is (probably) allowed or not allowed.

1   reading an online newspaper for a few minutes per day
2   emailing customer lists to a personal computer
3   sharing individual employees pay details
4   storing personal videos
5   storing images that show discrimination based on race or religion
6   playing networked games
7   watching a press release video from Hoffman's competitors
8   sending personal emails from a work computer
9   using social media (Facebook, Twitter) from a Hoffman computer

C   Now read the acceptable use policy and confirm your answers to exercise 2B.

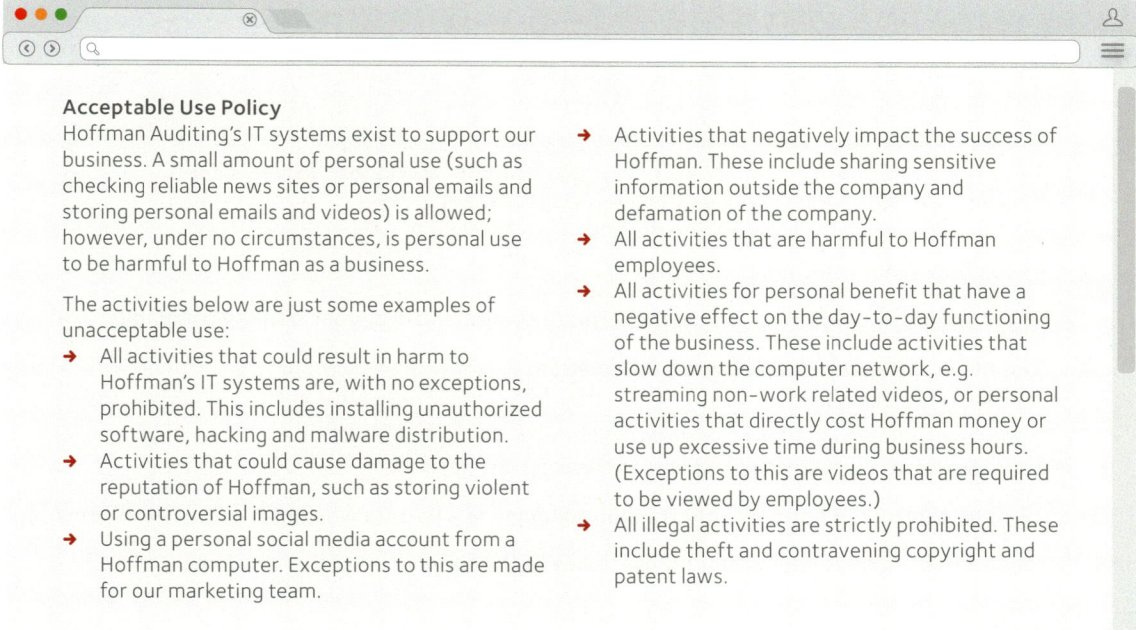

Acceptable Use Policy

Hoffman Auditing's IT systems exist to support our business. A small amount of personal use (such as checking reliable news sites or personal emails and storing personal emails and videos) is allowed; however, under no circumstances, is personal use to be harmful to Hoffman as a business.

The activities below are just some examples of unacceptable use:

➔ All activities that could result in harm to Hoffman's IT systems are, with no exceptions, prohibited. This includes installing unauthorized software, hacking and malware distribution.

➔ Activities that could cause damage to the reputation of Hoffman, such as storing violent or controversial images.

➔ Using a personal social media account from a Hoffman computer. Exceptions to this are made for our marketing team.

➔ Activities that negatively impact the success of Hoffman. These include sharing sensitive information outside the company and defamation of the company.

➔ All activities that are harmful to Hoffman employees.

➔ All activities for personal benefit that have a negative effect on the day-to-day functioning of the business. These include activities that slow down the computer network, e.g. streaming non-work related videos, or personal activities that directly cost Hoffman money or use up excessive time during business hours. (Exceptions to this are videos that are required to be viewed by employees.)

➔ All illegal activities are strictly prohibited. These include theft and contravening copyright and patent laws.

D   With your partner, compare this policy with your own company's policy and discuss the differences.

3 Reading about remote network access

Hoffman Auditing has introduced some new options for accessing the company network.

> The NextGen remote network access (RNA) allows access to the company network when you are at home or on the road. It allows access from your company-owned or personal computer via a virtual private network (VPN) connection.
>
> The table below lists the options available for authentication:

Authentication option	Requires app	Other restrictions
SMS	No	Requires mobile cellular coverage.
Call	No	Requires a desk phone or call forwarding to your mobile.
Email	No	Needs access to email via smartphone, tablet or computer.
Soft token	Yes	Requires a smartphone or tablet with app installed; does not require network access.
Hard token	No	Needs a registered and working hardware token.
Push notification	Yes	Requires a smartphone or tablet with app installed and network access via cellular or Wi-Fi.

A Match the four images to the correct authentication option in the table above.

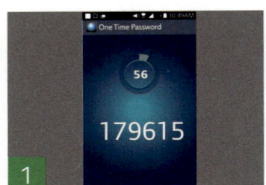  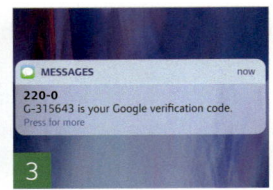 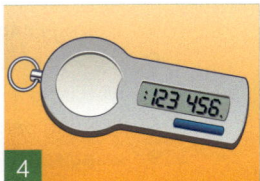

B 👥 Discuss all the possible authentication options in each of the following situations with a partner.

You are …
1 at a meeting room in your company building with your laptop only (no desk or mobile phone).
2 at home with your personal computer and smartphone with the app installed.
3 somewhere where mobile phone reception is weak, but you have your smartphone with the app installed.
4 at a café and only have a mobile phone with no internet access (not a smartphone).
5 in an hotel with a hard token and a laptop with Wi-Fi connection.

4 Accessing your company systems

Now it is time for you to summarize the terms of computer use at your training company.

A First of all, write down the following information:
– where you can log in from
– what you are (not) permitted to do with your company computer
– what options you have to gain access to the company network

B 👥 Then explain the policy at your training company to a partner who notes down the information.

C Your partner explains your computer use policy to the class.

> › *Useful phrases: Explaining access requirements, page 154*

 TOOLBOX

token – *Marke, Token*   notification – *Benachrichtigung*

PART B: External access

> **Situation:** Hoffman Auditing maintains a cloud-based data store of information that is accessible by clients. Securing the cloud is important as the clients' financial information is highly confidential.
> → **You explain security procedures to a company client.**

1 Reading about client portal access

You have created a flow chart to explain the steps that the company two-factor authentication (2FA) takes to determine whether access will be granted.

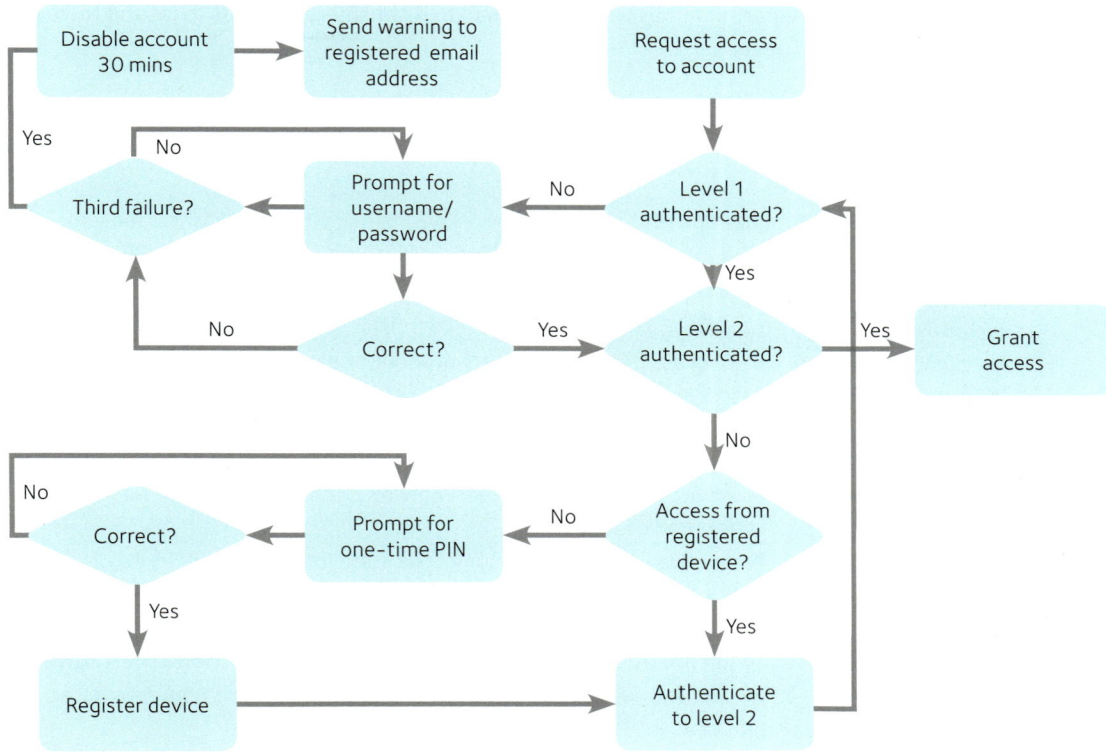

A According to the diagram, under what conditions do the following events happen?

1 an account is disabled   *An account is disabled when a user fails login three times.*
2 a user is granted access to the site
3 a user is prompted for their one-time PIN
4 a user is prompted for username and password
5 a warning is sent to the registered email address
6 a device is registered

 **TOOLBOX**

---

to disable – *sperren*
to grant access – *Zugang gewähren*
one-time PIN – *einmaliger PIN-Code*

prompt – *Eingabeaufforderung*
to request access – *Zugang anfordern*
two-factor authentication – *Zwei-Faktoren-Authentifizierung*

B 👥 **Think about your own smartphone. Ask and answer the following questions with a partner.**

1 What happens when you fail login?
   I am prompted to ...
2 What happens when you purchase an app?
3 What happens when you reset your password?
4 What happens when you remove your SIM card?
5 What happens when you decide to not use a passcode/fingerprint?

> ➡️ **Describing decision points**
>
> Your account **is disabled** when you fail login three times.
> You **are prompted** for a username when the system authenticates the request.

› *Grammar: Passive forms, page 164*

2 Staying up to date

Hoffman Auditing's IT department has written an email to its business partners to inform them of some new improvements to IT security.

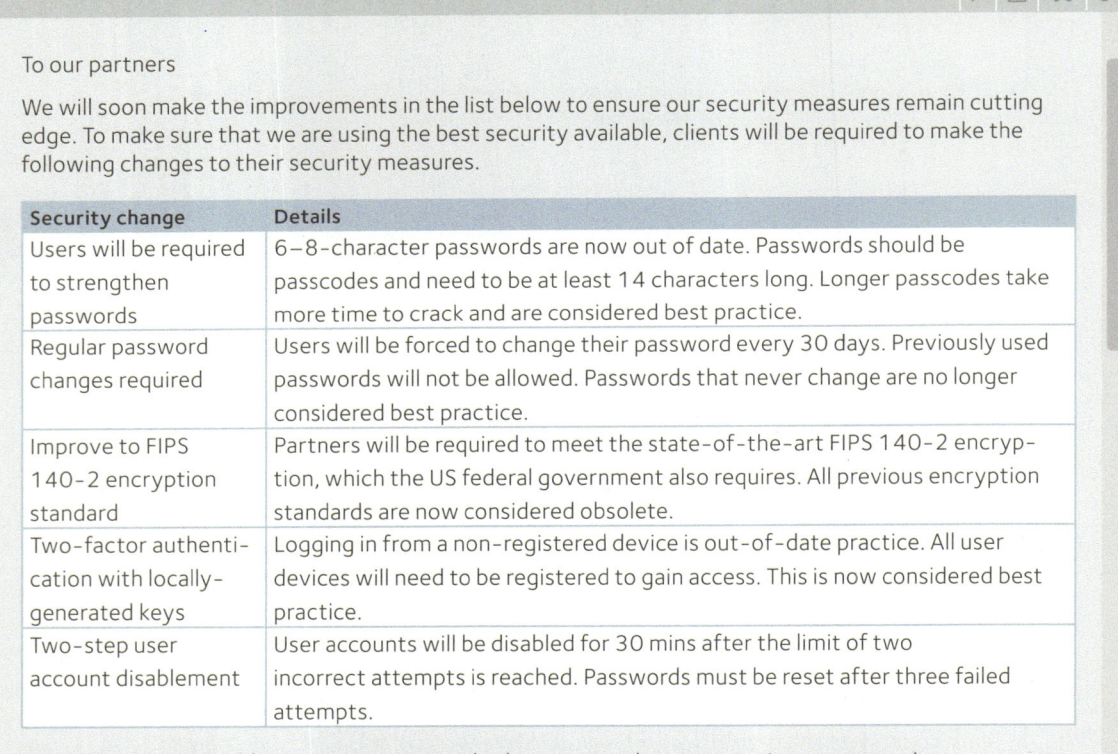

To our partners

We will soon make the improvements in the list below to ensure our security measures remain cutting edge. To make sure that we are using the best security available, clients will be required to make the following changes to their security measures.

Security change	Details
Users will be required to strengthen passwords	6–8-character passwords are now out of date. Passwords should be passcodes and need to be at least 14 characters long. Longer passcodes take more time to crack and are considered best practice.
Regular password changes required	Users will be forced to change their password every 30 days. Previously used passwords will not be allowed. Passwords that never change are no longer considered best practice.
Improve to FIPS 140-2 encryption standard	Partners will be required to meet the state-of-the-art FIPS 140-2 encryption, which the US federal government also requires. All previous encryption standards are now considered obsolete.
Two-factor authentication with locally-generated keys	Logging in from a non-registered device is out-of-date practice. All user devices will need to be registered to gain access. This is now considered best practice.
Two-step user account disablement	User accounts will be disabled for 30 mins after the limit of two incorrect attempts is reached. Passwords must be reset after three failed attempts.

We will continue to update our security standards to ensure that our practices are up to date.
FAQs on the topic can be found at: www.hoffman.co.nz/itsecurityfaqs.html

---

 **TOOLBOX**

---

best practice – *optimale Vorgehensweise*
cutting edge – *hochmodern, auf dem neuesten Stand der Technik*
encryption – *Verschlüsselung*

obsolete – *veraltet, überholt*
out of date – *veraltet, überholt*
state of the art – *auf dem neuesten Stand der Technik*

A   Say what the article on page 54 considers the following to be.

1   6–8-character passwords *are considered out of date.*
2   14-character passcodes …
3   Frequent password updates …
4   Passwords that never change …

5   FIPS 140-2 encryption …
6   Other encryption standards …
7   Unregistered devices …
8   Registered devices …

B   Create the FAQ page by writing short answers to the following questions that explain what Hofmann Auditing's business partners will be required to do. Use the words provided to help you.

> **➜ Talking about requirements**
>
> Access **will be granted** to authorized users only.
> Weak passwords **will not be accepted**.

› *Grammar: Passive forms, page 164*

1   What are the minimum password requirements? (users/forced)
    Users will be forced to use a minimum of 14 characters.
2   How often do I need to update my password? (you/require)
3   How many login attempts do I have before my account is disabled? (login attempts/limit)
4   How long is my account disabled? (your account/disable)
5   What encryptions standards do I have to meet? (you/require)
6   Can I access Hoffman via my unregistered device? (access/restrict)
7   Can I use passwords that I've previously used? (previous passwords/accept)

3 Presenting a new security measure to clients

Hoffman has developed a way for their clients to log in to their website without the need to enter a password each time. The new system uses a single sign-on (SSO).

Prepare a presentation of the single sign-on for your clients using the diagram and list below. Include the following points in your presentation:
– the security standards that clients will be required to meet
– a description of how your security mechanism works, including the key decision points

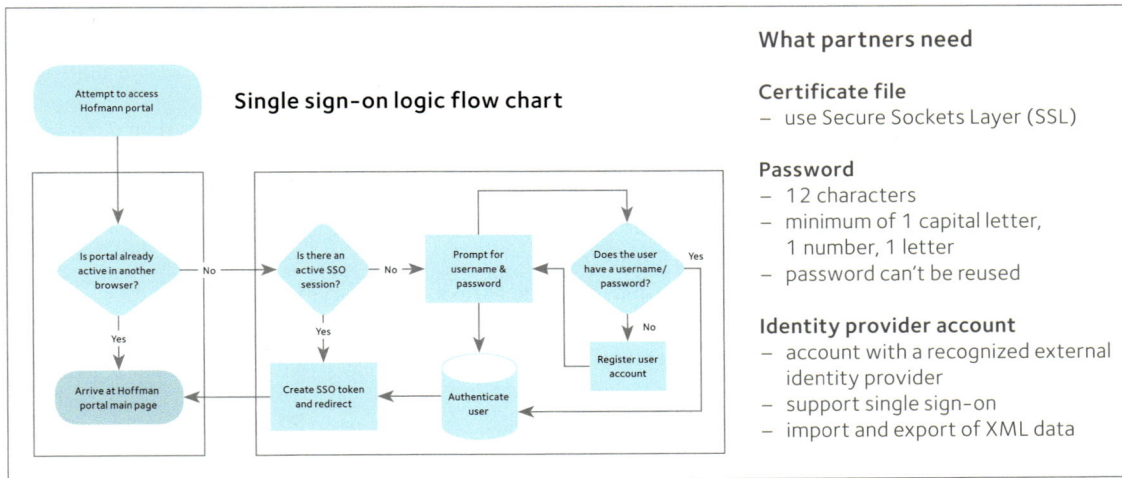

Single sign-on logic flow chart

What partners need

Certificate file
– use Secure Sockets Layer (SSL)

Password
– 12 characters
– minimum of 1 capital letter, 1 number, 1 letter
– password can't be reused

Identity provider account
– account with a recognized external identity provider
– support single sign-on
– import and export of XML data

› *Useful phrases: Giving presentations, page 151*

 **TOOLBOX**

SSL (Secure Sockets Layer) – *Methode zum verschlüsselten Senden von Daten via Internet*
XML (Extensible Markup Language) – *erweiterbare Auszeichnungssprache*

COMMUNICATION: Graphs and charts

Situation: You are part of the IT Security team at AGM Bank in London. Like many banks, AGM Bank is under constant attack from cybercriminals.

→ **You give a presentation about the trends and cost of cybercrime.**

1 Listening to trends in cybercrime

You attend a presentation by the Head of IT Security about cybercrime at AGM Bank during the previous year.

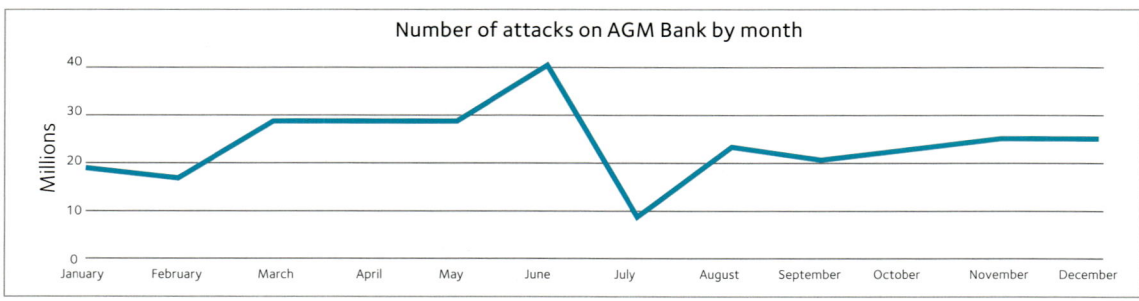

A 17))) **Look at the graph and decide which months the following numbers refer to. Then listen to the presentation to check your answers.**

1   39.75m   2   22.3m   3   25.2m   4   19.08m   5   9.76m   6   28.13m

B 17))) **Listen again and match words from the two boxes to complete the description of the trends given by the Head of IT Security.**

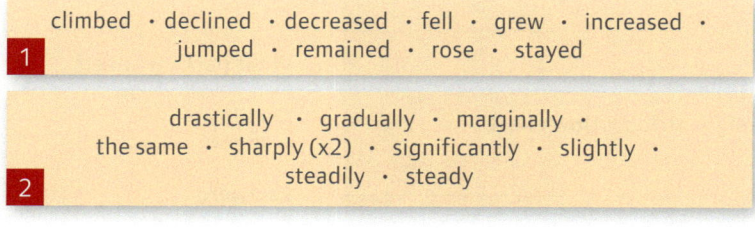

> **→ Talking about change**
>
> The number of attacks **decreased slightly** last month.
> Then they **jumped sharply** in October.

> *Grammar: Simple past, page 163; Adjectives and adverbs, page 166*

1   In general, the number of detected attacks ▬▬ last year, with some peaks and troughs midway through the year.
2   The number ▬▬ in February, as they have tended to do in previous years.
3   After it ▬▬ in March, it levelled off and ▬▬ until May.
4   In June, attacks ▬▬ again and that was the peak for the year.
5   Strangely, they ▬▬ the next month to only 9.76 million.
6   Following that trough in July, the number of attacks ▬▬ in August to 22.3m and then ▬▬ in September.
7   The number of attacks then ▬▬ over the last quarter of the year, then ▬▬ from November to December.

2 Describing cyberattack figures

You and your colleagues are discussing the figures for cyberattacks over the last two days at a regular team meeting.

👥 **Work with a partner. Partner A: Look at File 4 on page 135. Partner B: Look at File 6 on page 136.**

3 Analysing the cost of cybercrime

You attend a presentation about the cost of cybercrime at AGM Bank bank last year.

Complete the following using the phrases from the list and the information in the pie chart.

a bit less than a third · about a tenth ·
approximately a quarter · around twice ·
in the region of two-thirds · just over half ·
just under a fifth · roughly three times

1 Phishing and social engineering accounted for ▭ of costs.
2 Malicious code cost us ▭ as much as malware.
3 ▭ of cost came from web-based attacks.
4 ▭ is caused by viruses and worms.
5 Malicious insiders, web-based attacks and malicious code made up ▭ of the costs incurred.
6 ▭ of costs came from malicious insiders, web-based attacks, malicious code and phishing and social engineering.
7 Web-based attacks, malicious code make up ▭ of costs incurred.
8 Web-based attacks cost us ▭ as much as phishing & social engineering.

Cost breakdown per attack type

- virus & worm
- malicious insider
- web-based attack
- malicious code
- phishing & social engineering
- botnet
- malware

24.69% · 18.85% · 18.17% · 14.55% · 9.78% · 9.61% · 4.34%

4 Giving a presentation on cybercrime

Now it is time for you to give a presentation about the trends and costs of cybercrime.

First, prepare notes and then give your presentation to the class. Your presentation should include the following information for each attack type:
– the costs incurred   – the change from last year to this year

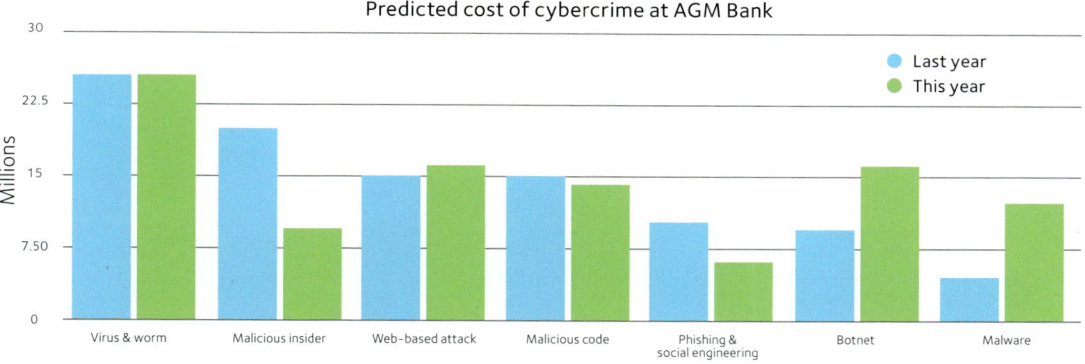

Predicted cost of cybercrime at AGM Bank

> *Useful phrases: Giving presentations, page 151; Describing graphs, page 154*

DAS KANN ICH (Unit 5)
– Firmenkunden/-kundinnen per E-Mail über Tipps gegen Internetkriminalität informieren. (Foundation)
– Über die zulässige Nutzung von Firmenrechnern und den Zugang zum Firmenportal der Ausbildungsfirma berichten. (Part A)
– Einem Kunden / Einer Kundin Sicherheitsmaßnahmen auf Englisch erklären. (Part B)
– Eine Präsentation über Kosten, die durch Internetkriminalität verursacht werden, halten. (Communication)

6 Dealing with customers

FOUNDATION: Robots for customer service

Situation: You work in the call centre at ShopArena, an online retailer that sells a wide variety of products worldwide. The office has its headquarters in San Francisco.
→ **You help a customer with a telephone enquiry.**

1 Listening about artificial intelligence (AI)

Gina Thomas, the Head of AI at ShopArena, is giving a presentation to the call centre agents about their new chatbot, Lia.

A 18)) **Listen and say whether the following statements are true or false. Correct the false statements.**

1 Lia will replace the call centre agents.
2 Customers don't need to use perfect English for Lia to understand them.
3 Lia can only provide answers about their profile and account.
4 Lia knows where a customer is, the time at their location and their name, even if they are a new customer.
5 Lia uses data about the customer to personalize interactions.
6 Lia can predict whether a customer has a complaint about a recent purchase using that customer's complaint history.

B 18)) **Complete the following short chats, then listen and check your answers.**

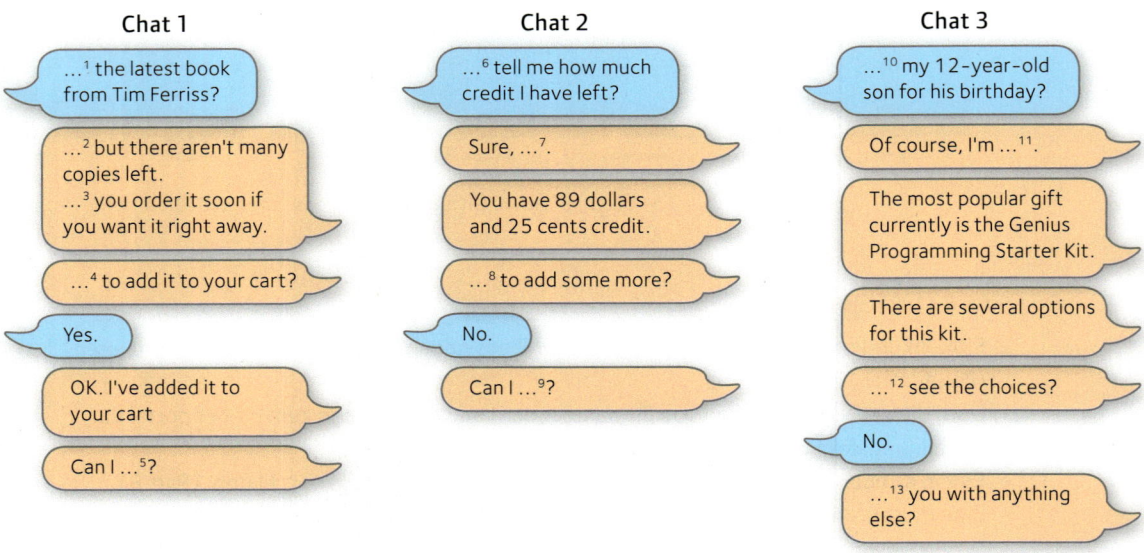

Chat 1

...¹ the latest book from Tim Ferriss?

...² but there aren't many copies left.
...³ you order it soon if you want it right away.

...⁴ to add it to your cart?

Yes.

OK. I've added it to your cart

Can I ...⁵?

Chat 2

...⁶ tell me how much credit I have left?

Sure, ...⁷.

You have 89 dollars and 25 cents credit.

...⁸ to add some more?

No.

Can I ...⁹?

Chat 3

...¹⁰ my 12-year-old son for his birthday?

Of course, I'm ...¹¹.

The most popular gift currently is the Genius Programming Starter Kit.

There are several options for this kit.

...¹² see the choices?

No.

...¹³ you with anything else?

C   👥 With a partner create two more short chats using the information below. In each chat, Lia should …

– start with a greeting.
– confirm that she can help the customer.
– offer the customer an answer or action.
– end by checking whether the interaction is finished.

1	2
Customer: Anna **Status:** existing customer **Shopping at:** 1 p.m. **Request:** delivery time for headphones?	**Customer:** Stan **Status:** existing customer **Shopping at:** 8 p.m. **Request:** update payment details?
ShopArena policy: same day delivery for orders before 2 p.m.	**ShopArena policy:** OK, but need to sign in again

INFO

Artificial intelligence (AI) refers to intelligent behaviour by machines rather than humans. Voice assistants like Siri, Samsung Bixby and Google Assistant are all examples of AI. A **chatbot** is a software program that can have a conversation with a person. It can answer questions and 'chat' in the way that a person would. Many companies use chatbots for customer service on their websites.

2   Advising a customer

If Lia is unable to help a customer to their satisfaction, she can transfer them to the call centre.

Hi, I'm Lia. I'm ShopArena's chatbot. Would you like some help with your shopping?

> Yes. I want some smart light bulbs from BriteNite.

Great. The latest model is the BN3000. It contains 6 bulbs and costs $399.

> Wow. That's too expensive.

Then how about the basic BN1000 model? It contains 4 light bulbs and costs $149.

> That's better. What features is that model missing?

You can't dim the lights using your mobile phone. There is no warm light setting.

> Oh. That's not what I had in mind. I need warm lighting.

Can I suggest another brand?

> But I hear that BriteNite are the best.

I can't answer that.

> Can I talk to a person, please?

Of course. I'm transferring you now. Thanks for shopping with ShopArena.

A   The chat above has been transferred to a call centre agent. Read it and then answer the questions.

1   Is that chat about a purchase, service or a complaint?
2   What are the names and prices of the products mentioned?
3   What reasons does the customer give for not taking the suggested products?
4   Is the chatbot able to help the customer? How does the chat end?

B   Work with a partner. **Partner A:** Look here. **Partner B:** Look at File 7 on page 136.

You are the customer service representative. Help a customer through a purchase using the information in the box.

› *Useful phrases: Advising customers, page 154*

Customer service representative
Ein Kunde / Eine Kundin braucht Hilfe beim Kauf einer externen Festplatte. Stellen Sie Fragen, um herauszufinden, welche Eigenschaften für den Kunden / die Kundin wichtig sind. Empfehlen Sie zwei Modelle:
Firebird XL, 129 $, 2 GB, 3 Jahre Garantie und Thunderbolt-Netzwerkfähigkeit
StoreRight, 99 $, 2 GB, 2 Jahre Garantie

PART A: Set-up and customization

> **Situation:** You work as a customer service representative at Culture Amp in Melbourne, Australia. Culture Amp is a software platform that creates surveys about office working conditions.
> → **You show a customer a product and how to customize it to his needs.**

1 Setting up your own data

You have a meeting next week with a new client, Rod Hamilton from SynTech. You send him the following reference material before the meeting.

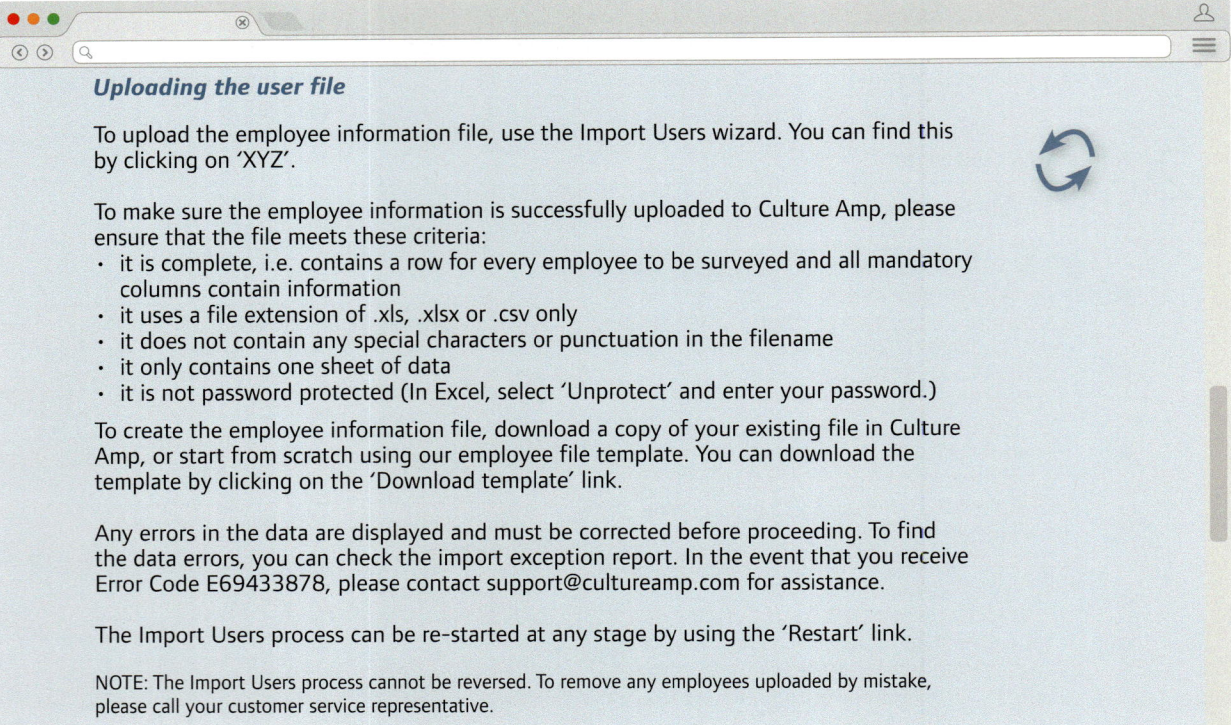

Uploading the user file

To upload the employee information file, use the Import Users wizard. You can find this by clicking on 'XYZ'.

To make sure the employee information is successfully uploaded to Culture Amp, please ensure that the file meets these criteria:
- it is complete, i.e. contains a row for every employee to be surveyed and all mandatory columns contain information
- it uses a file extension of .xls, .xlsx or .csv only
- it does not contain any special characters or punctuation in the filename
- it only contains one sheet of data
- it is not password protected (In Excel, select 'Unprotect' and enter your password.)

To create the employee information file, download a copy of your existing file in Culture Amp, or start from scratch using our employee file template. You can download the template by clicking on the 'Download template' link.

Any errors in the data are displayed and must be corrected before proceeding. To find the data errors, you can check the import exception report. In the event that you receive Error Code E69433878, please contact support@cultureamp.com for assistance.

The Import Users process can be re-started at any stage by using the 'Restart' link.

NOTE: The Import Users process cannot be reversed. To remove any employees uploaded by mistake, please call your customer service representative.

A Summarize the requirements for the Culture Amp platform set-up.

1 What does the file need for each employee in the organization?
2 What are the requirements for filenames?
3 What two reasons are given for a user to contact Culture Amp?

B How does a user do the following set-up tasks?

1 upload an employee information file
   Users upload an employee information file by using the Import Users wizard.
2 find the Import Users wizard
3 turn off password protection
4 create the employee information file
5 find import data errors
6 begin the import again
7 remove employees uploaded by mistake

> 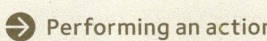 **Performing an action**
>
> You can find this **by clicking** on 'XYZ'.
> You can see data errors **by checking** the report.

› *Grammar: Gerunds, page 165*

2 Understanding standard reports

You send some further material to Rod Hamilton so that he is ready for your meeting next week.

A **Employee participation:** report shows how many of your employees submitted completed surveys for a selected data range. The number above each vertical bar shows the total number of surveys you sent out and the dark shaded area indicates how many people submitted the survey.

B **Rated questions report:** illustrates the five questions that most impact employees. Each question is displayed as a row and each column contains detailed information about the questions. The horizontal bars in the last column demonstrate how positive, neutral or negative the answers to each question were.

C **Engagement heatmap report:** This a simple yet powerful table that compares the survey results for each department. Each cell is colour shaded to indicate whether a department had a better or worse than average result. The names of the departments are in the column headings.

1

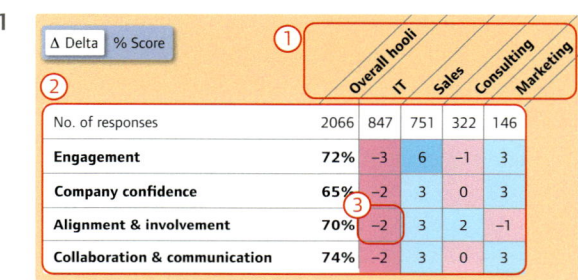

	Δ Delta	% Score	Overall hooli	IT	Sales	Consulting	Marketing
No. of responses			2066	847	751	322	146
Engagement		72%		–3	6	–1	3
Company confidence		65%		–2	3	0	3
Alignment & involvement		70%		–2	3	2	–1
Collaboration & communication		74%		–2	3	0	3

2

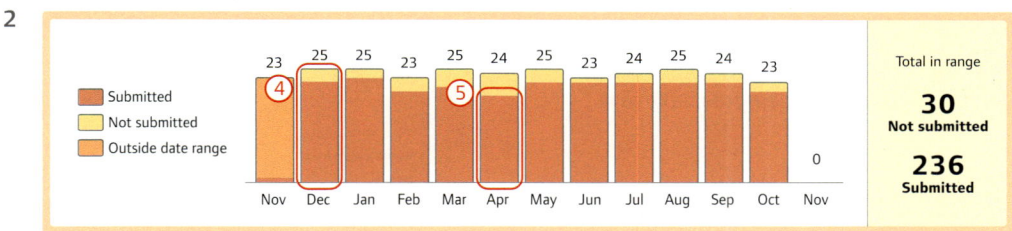

3

IMPACT	QUESTION	FACTOR	💬	FAVOURABLE SCORE
●	The leaders at Hooli have communicated a vision that motivates me	Leadership	145	74
●	I believe there are good career opportunities for me at Hooli	Learning & development	138	70
●	I have confidence in the leaders at Hooli	Leadership	158	63
●	I am given opportunities to develop skills relevant to my interests	Learning & development	132	76
●	The leaders at Hooli demonstrate that people are important to the company's success	Leadership	182	62

A   Match the reports (1–3) to their correct titles (A–C).

B   Match the highlighted words in the description to the correct part (1–8) of the reports.

 TOOLBOX

column – *Spalte*
criteria – *Kriterien*
file extension – *Dateierweiterung*

file template – *Dateivorlage*
range – *Bereich*
row – *Reihe*

shaded – *schattiert*
sheet – *Blatt*

3 Customizing reports

You and your colleague, Steven, meet with Rod Hamilton to explain how to use the Culture Amp platform.

A 19))) Listen to the dialogue and answer the following questions.

1 What does Rod say about the reports?
2 What other information does Rod want about the reports?
3 Which three reports do Rod and Steven talk about?
4 How many Culture Amp clients customize their reports? Why?

B 19))) Listen again and complete the statements from the dialogue.

- We have several options that allow you to ▄▄[1] reports.
- If you only want to see results for a specific data range, you can ▄▄[2] the date range in the results by entering a start and end date in the ▄▄[3].
- There are several options to ▄▄[4] the report.
- You can ▄▄[5] the specific department you want. If you select the column headings, you can ▄▄[6] the sort order of the results and ▄▄[7] between ascending and descending results.
- You can also ▄▄[8] your data to focus on a specific set of results using several filters.
- Let's take a look through the custom report, where you can ▄▄[9], ▄▄[10] and ▄▄[11] most of the information.

4 Explaining a survey report

You and a colleague are showing the Culture Amp custom report to another customer.

A 👥 Explain the report and what it shows using the diagram and the notes next to it.

B 👥 Now explain how to customize the report with a new filtered result using the 'Add a new data line' function. Use the phrases in the language box on the right to help you.

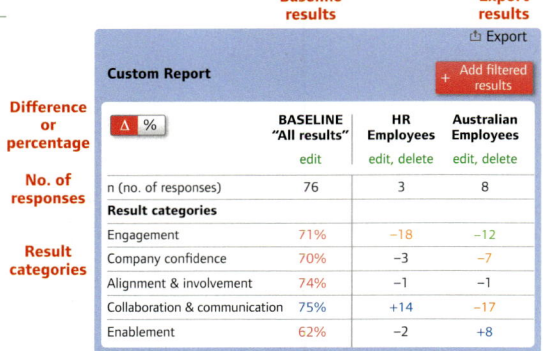

Custom Report	BASELINE "All results"	HR Employees	Australian Employees
	edit	edit, delete	edit, delete
n (no. of responses)	76	3	8
Result categories			
Engagement	71%	−18	−12
Company confidence	70%	−3	−7
Alignment & involvement	74%	−1	−1
Collaboration & communication	75%	+14	−17
Enablement	62%	−2	+8

Baseline results — Export results — Difference or percentage — Names of filtered results — No. of responses — Result categories — Filtered results

To add a new filtered result, you …

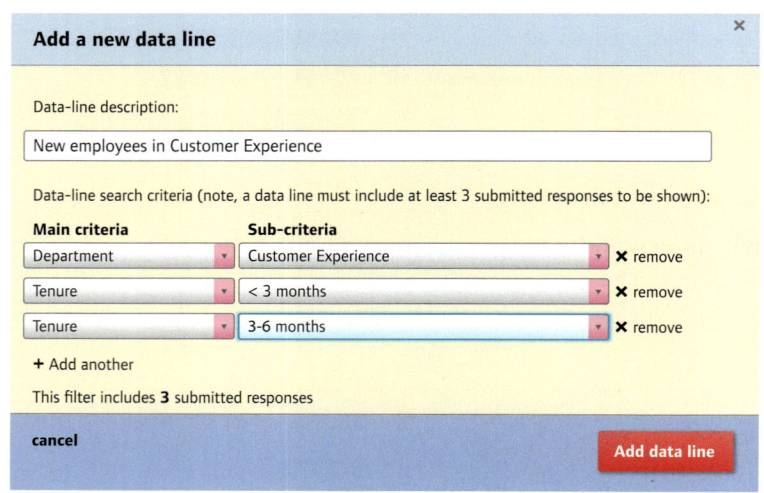

Customizing a report

- enter a new description
- choose (search) criteria for the filters
- select … from the drop-down boxes
- select a value for … from …
- add/remove filters by selecting …

› *Useful phrases: Describing processes, page 155*

PART B: Technical support

Situation: You work at Culture Amp technical support and help clients with technical questions about the Culture Amp platform.
→ **You guide a customer through a technical process.**

1 Exporting data to reports

Rod Hamilton from SynTech calls your colleague Steven. He wants to extract some raw data from the Culture Amp platform.

A   20))) **These five statements about the dialogue are false. Listen and correct them.**

1   It is a mistake that the function to extract data is disabled by default.
2   Anonymous responses do not achieve the most honest results.
3   To extract data, users need account administration or survey taker access.
4   Every user will see a warning message after they take the survey.
5   The username is the only data recorded when extracting information from the survey.

B   20))) **Listen again and match Steven's replies (A–G) to Rod Hamilton's questions (1–7).**

1   Data extraction can be enabled, right? – *Yes, exactly.*
2   OK, I can check that on my profile, can't I?
3   No, I don't have a survey ready to launch. Should I have one ready?
4   So, just to check, every user will see this warning after they take the survey?
5   And if the response rate is low because of the message, I can uncheck the check box?
6   And my details are recorded in case the data is used for the wrong reasons?
7   Have I understood that correctly?

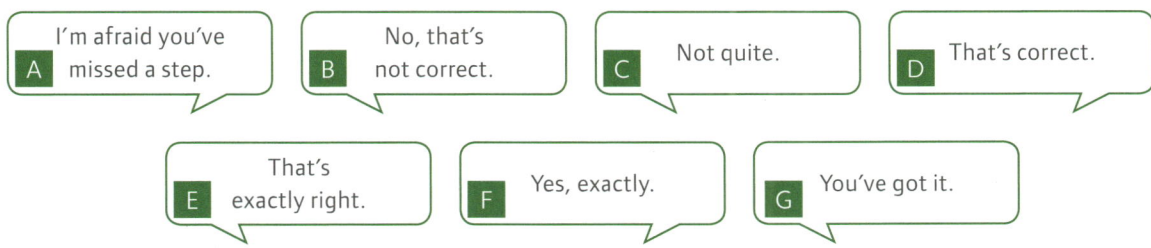

A I'm afraid you've missed a step.
B No, that's not correct.
C Not quite.
D That's correct.
E That's exactly right.
F Yes, exactly.
G You've got it.

C   👥 **Work with a partner. Which of Steven's responses to Rod's questions a) encourage(s) him or b) correct(s) him?**

TOOLBOX

analysis – *Analyse*
anonymous – *anonym*
commitment – *Engagement*

design feature – *Konstruktionsmerkmal*
to extract – *entnehmen*
raw data – *Rohdaten*

Explaining software integration

You've written a guide to help customers send their employees survey notifications via a company messaging app. The companies need to synchronize their messaging app with Culture Amp.

Integrating with Slack Messaging

We'll start at the 'Notifications' page. Click 'Add Bot to Slack'. The set-up wizard will start.

Continue by choosing whether you are an administrator or not. If you select 'I don't have admin access/I'm not sure' and click on 'Next', you'll see a message saying you need approval from your company's Slack administrator to proceed, so you'll have to send a request and wait for approval.

If you selected the wrong option, go back and select 'I'm an administrator'. Your access level will be checked. If you are confirmed to be an administrator, you'll move on to the next stage, where you authorize the integration. If not, you'll have to wait, as above.

Authorization is done by simply selecting the 'Authorize' button. Once everything is set up, you'll see a confirmation screen and can even send yourself a test message in Slack to see how your surveys will be communicated to your employees.

Once Slack integration has been successfully authorized, return to the 'Notifications' page and Slack and Culture Amp will start to synchronize automatically.

Following the first synchronization, you might see a message that some employees will not be able to receive messages via Slack.

To find these users, go to the 'Users' page. Users that cannot receive Slack messages will be highlighted. Compare the email addresses in Slack and Culture Amp and make sure they are the same.

Finally, return to the 'Sync' screen and manually synchronize by clicking the 'Resync users' button. Confirm that all users can receive Slack messages to complete the process.

Match the highlighted instructions with the letters (A-H) in the diagram.

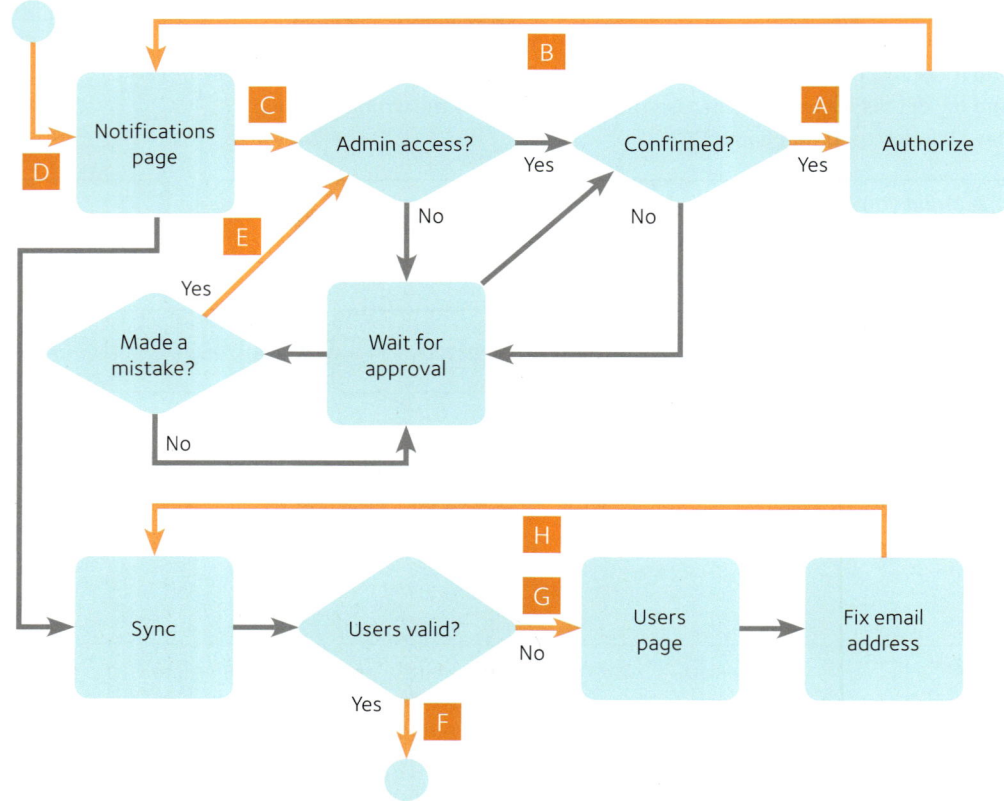

3 Guiding a customer through a process

Now you guide a new customer through a software synchronization process.

A 👥 **Use the process below to role-play a conversation where a customer is guided through the process to synchronize their HR system with Culture Amp.**

Partner A: You are the customer. Explain what you are trying to do and the problem you are having. Ask questions to check whether you understand the instructions that you are given.

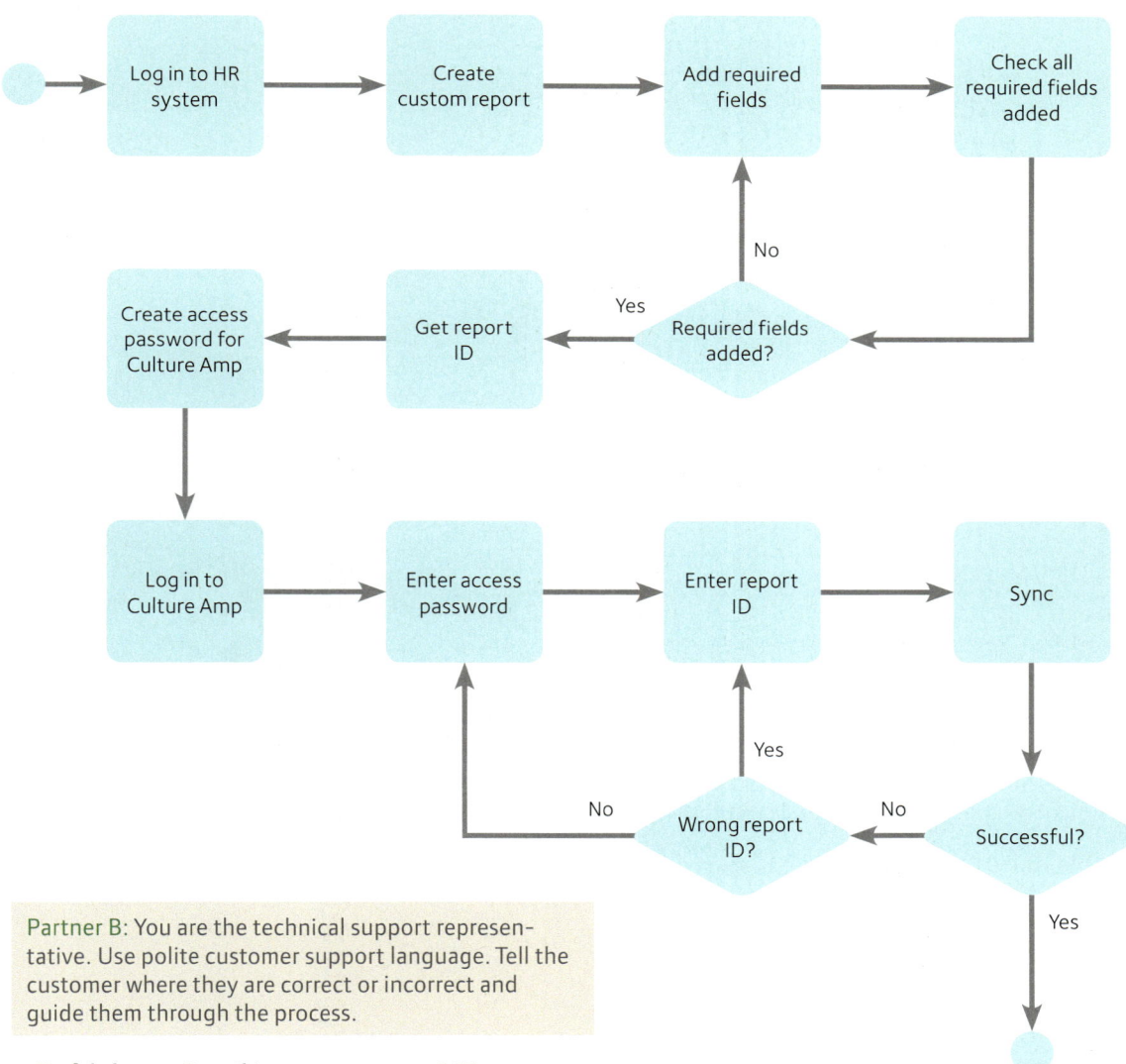

Partner B: You are the technical support representative. Use polite customer support language. Tell the customer where they are correct or incorrect and guide them through the process.

› *Useful phrases: Describing processes, page 155*

B 👥 **A friend who works in the HR department of a company in Germany is also interested in the Culture Amp platform. Explain to your friend how the synchronization process works in German.**

COMMUNICATION: Arrangements for meetings

Situation: You work at SynTech GmbH in Dusseldorf. The company is taking part in the ScotCom Trade Fair next week.

→ **You write three emails to make arrangements for meetings with customers.**

1 Setting up a meeting with a client

Paul Smith, the Head of Development at SynTech, asks you to arrange a meeting with a customer. He gives you the following instructions.

> Pls. get in touch with Mary Doyle at Software Solutions, Dublin; set up a mtg. to present our HR program. Ms Doyle wants to discuss some details before ordering.
> Suggest we meet at ScotCom in Glasgow, morning 26 April, any time (need to finish by 12.30 p.m.); or 27 April, betw. 12.30 and 6.30 p.m. Need about 3 hrs for mtg.
> Ask which day is suitable (pls. book room for mtg.).
> Thanks. Paul

> ⮕ **Telling the time in English-speaking countries**
>
> When telling the time in English, use the short forms, *a.m.* and *p.m.*
> a.m. *(ante meridiem)* = between midnight and midday
> p.m. *(post meridiem)* = after 12.00 noon
>
> In English-speaking countries the twenty-four hour clock is generally only used for timetables.

👥 **Work with a partner. Complete the email to Ms Doyle using words and phrases from the notes above.**

From:	trainee@SynTechGmbH.de
To:	m.doyle@softwaresolutions.ie
Subject:	Meeting with Paul Smith to discuss HR program

Dear Ms Doyle

Paul Smith, Head of Development at SynTech, has asked me ▭¹ with you in order to ▭² a meeting. Mr Smith would like to ▭³ our HR program and ▭⁴ with you before you place your order.

Mr Smith will be at the ScotCom Trade Fair in Glasgow next week so he ▭⁵ either of the following dates: 26 April in the ▭⁶ (Mr Smith needs to finish by 12.30 p.m.), or 27 April between 12.30 and 6.30 p.m.

He thinks that the meeting will take about ▭⁷.

Please let me know if either of these dates ▭⁸.

I hope to hear from you by tomorrow as I need time to ▭⁹ a room for the meeting.

Yours ▭¹⁰

2   Replying to the invitation to the meeting

Complete Mary Doyle's reply using words and phrases from the list.

An appointment · Best wishes · booked · invite · look forward · reserve · Thank you · We are in

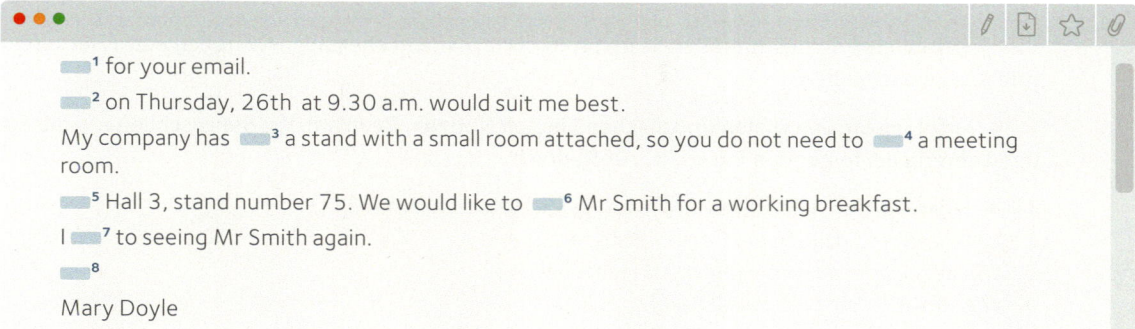

━━¹ for your email.

━━² on Thursday, 26th at 9.30 a.m. would suit me best.

My company has ━━³ a stand with a small room attached, so you do not need to ━━⁴ a meeting room.

━━⁵ Hall 3, stand number 75. We would like to ━━⁶ Mr Smith for a working breakfast.

I ━━⁷ to seeing Mr Smith again.

━━⁸

Mary Doyle

3   Changing arrangements

Paul has to set up a small presentation for Ms Doyle on Thursday morning, so he postpones a breakfast meeting with his business partner, Ian Duncan.

Write Mr Smith's email to Ian Duncan to postpone the breakfast meeting. Explain the situation and use details from the itinerary below to suggest a new date and time for a meeting, e.g. for lunch or dinner.

→ Giving dates, days and times

at 6 p.m., **at** lunchtime
at night, **at** the weekend
on Monday, **on** 21 June
in the morning, **in** January, **in** 2017

ITINERARY – **Wed 25th – Sat 28th**			
Wed 25	Flight LH 134 07.20 → Glasgow (arr. 08.40)		Dinner: Hans Treder 19.00 (Wallace Restaurant)
Thur 26	~~Breakfast: Ian Duncan 7.30 – 9.00~~ Mary Doyle (presentation) 9.30 – 12.30	Meeting: SysMet 14.00 – 16.00	
Fri 27	Stand: 10.00 – 12.00	Meeting: KL Pipes 14.00 – 18.00	
Sat 28	Meeting: Harry Jones 11.00		Flight LH 918 19.15 → Dusseldorf (arr. 21.25)

› *Useful phrases: Making arrangements, page 154*

DAS KANN ICH (Unit 6)

– Einen Kunden / Eine Kundin bei einer Anfrage telefonisch beraten. (Foundation)
– Einen Kunden / Eine Kundin beraten, wie er/sie ein Programm auf seine/ihre Bedürfnisse anpassen kann. (PartA)
– Einen technischen Vorgang einem Kunden / einer Kundin auf Englisch erklären. (PartB)
– Treffen mit englischsprachigen Kunden/Kundinnen per E-Mail organisieren. (Communication)

1 Hörverstehen: B1

Ihre Englischlehrerin hat ihren Bekannten Andy Doorbar, ein ehemaliges Mitglied eines Hackerclubs, in Ihre Klasse eingeladen.

21))) Verfolgen Sie den Dialog und machen Sie sich Notizen. Beantworten Sie anschließend die Fragen, die Ihre Lehrerin am folgenden Tag stellt, auf Deutsch.

1 Welchen Auftrag hat Andy Doorbar von der Schulleitung erhalten?
2 Welche drei Prinzipien der Hacker-Ethik zitiert Andy?
3 Wie bezeichnet Andy die Internetkriminellen?
4 Wie verdient Andy heute sein Geld?
5 Welche Sicherheitslücke hat der Chaos Computer Club aufgedeckt?
6 Warum sind die Aufladekarten elektrischer Fahrzeuge unsicher?
7 Welchen Schaden könnten Internetkriminelle damit anrichten?

2 Produktion: B1

Alexa Pawel, eine neue Mitarbeiterin im Außendienst Ihres Unternehmens, hat sich für die Aufnahme von Kundengesprächen *AudioPal* auf ihren Firmenlaptop heruntergeladen. Die Installation schlug jedoch fehl, und Ihre Kollegin erhält nun stets Fehlermeldungen.

Schicken Sie Alexa Pawel eine E-Mail auf Englisch mit folgenden Informationen:

Ursache für Fehlermeldungen:
– Kein Software- oder Hardware-Problem
– Alexa ist Standard-Nutzerin
– Ihre Zugriffsebene berechtigt sie nicht, AudioPal auf Firmenrechnern zu installieren
– AudioPal steht nicht auf der Liste überprüfter und genehmigter Software
– Nur die Zugriffsebene „*Administrator*" ist berechtigt, neue Software zu installieren

Gründe für die Einschränkung:
– Schutz der Firma und der Kunden/Kundinnen vor Schadsoftware
– Gewährleistung für die Kunden/Kundinnen, dass ihre Interviews vertraulich bleiben

Vorschlag:
– Herunterladen einer genehmigten Audiosoftware aus dem Intranet (intranet.hoffman.co.nz/itsecurity/permittedsoftware/audiomanagement.html)

3 Leseverstehen: B1/B2

Sie sollen eine Präsentation vor Kollegen/Kolleginnen Ihres Ausbildungsbetriebs über die Methoden Agile und Waterfall halten. Zur Vorbereitung werten Sie den Text auf Seite 69 aus.

Kopieren Sie die Tabelle unter dem Text auf Seite 69 und notieren Sie darin Stichwörter auf Deutsch.

Pros and cons of different software delivery methodologies

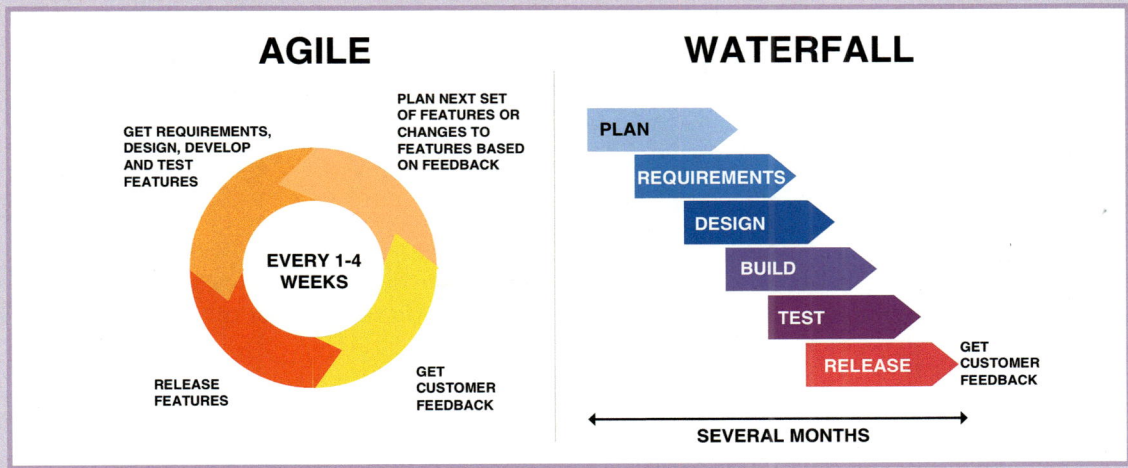

The digital team at Hillier Recruiting use an Agile Software Delivery methodology, an iterative approach that allows software to be adaptable to changing customer needs. While we prefer it over the sequential approach of traditional, Waterfall methodologies, we know that Agile is not the best choice for every project, and there are pros and cons that should be considered.

On the upside, Agile projects can get started quickly with minimal planning, however the uncertainty around scope and deadlines can make people nervous and is seen by many as a drawback. Waterfall is a more methodical approach, which many prefer.

Agile encourages close collaborative work with users of the software which brings the advantage of constant feedback on software features from actual end users. In turn, the benefit of constant feedback is that it allows for quick course correction as customer needs change. On the downside, close collaboration can mean that documentation may not be as complete as that in a Waterfall project, which requires comprehensive documentation and a structured approach to change.

Short release cycles also encourage experimentation and creativity, which can often lead to breakthrough features being discovered. However, this can also be a disadvantage as it can overcomplicate projects that have a clear scope and defined set of requirements. Waterfall approaches are more repeatable and better for solving well-known software problems.

The major plus of Agile is that the end result is higher quality software that is better suited to customer needs. This makes it the right choice for us, and we encourage other teams to give it a try.

Ihre Notizen für Ihre Präsentation:

Methodische Unterschiede der Arbeitsprozesse			
Agile		Waterfall	
Vorteile von Agile		Nachteile von Agile	
Manche Software- Entwickler bevorzugen Waterfall, weil …			

7 Communicating with colleagues

FOUNDATION: Ways of collaborating

> **Situation:** You've just joined a publishing company in Dublin to manage their collaboration software.
> → **You write an email to your team to give them information on updates to the collaboration wiki.**

1 Reading about collaboration methods

Before you start, you talk to several employees about the ways they collaborate with colleagues.

Collaboration maturity model

Individually edited work published to **private** space.	Individually edited work published to **multiple private** spaces.	Individually edited work published to a **shared** space.	Individually edited work published to a **public** space.	**Group** edited work published to a **public** space.
Desktop	**Email**	**Groupware**	**Blog**	**Wiki**

I really like using a ▦[1] because it lets everyone update the same website: we share the responsibility of keeping the site up to date. It's also very transparent when everyone can see what everyone else is working on. The downside is that you get automatic notifications when something is changed.

Most of our work stays in people's heads and on their personal ▦[3]. A lot of people learned to work this way so it is more efficient for them. However, it means that we have to have more meetings and phone calls to share information.

We still share everything via ▦[2]. I understand that this is the easiest way for most people as everyone can create office documents, but I lose track of the most recent version of documents. I don't like always having to ask someone to find the most up-to-date version.

We use ▦[4] on our network to keep documents that a few of us use. It's OK – we can all edit the same document but if we want to share it, we still have to send a link to the specific document. This is a problem because there is also no automated version control, so it's difficult to know which is the latest version.

We publish most of our shared information on our team ▦[5] – it makes the most recent information clear, because that's always at the top, and the information is always available. Of course, older information gets hidden quickly, so you have to search for it.

A   Complete the gap in each description with the correct name from the diagram.

B   👥 Work with a partner from the same training company. What tools do you use to collaborate with colleagues? What are their pros and cons? Where would you put your company on the collaboration model?

2 Collaborating on a wiki

The current administrator explains the set-up of the wiki front page to you.

Project wiki template

<Project name>

Project overview	Team
<Give a short overview of the project and its goals here.>	<List the team members and their contact details here.>

Project health	What's been happening
🟠 Budget <Explanation of why project is amber or red> 🟢 Schedule <Explanation of why project is amber or red> 🟠 Benefits <Explanation of why project is amber or red>	<List of recent things that have happened; automatically updated>

Stakeholders	Backlog
<List the stakeholders of the project here.>	<List the next things to do here.>

Important places	Related projects
< Any links to the sub-pages should be listed here. This must include a link to the: – project budget – requirements – scope – test results>	<Any projects that are similar to, adjacent to or dependent on this project should be linked to here.>

A Look at the template: which parts of the wiki page do the following refer to?

1 a list of recent events on the project
2 links to the sub-pages of the wiki
3 the status of the project
4 a short description of the project
5 a prioritized list of actions for the product
6 a list of the people within the organization impacted by the project
7 links to projects associated with the product
8 the people who are actively working on the project

B **22))) Listen to the administrator describing the Wiki template and answer the following questions.**

1 Why does the project site look different now?
   We've just updated the standard layout.
2 Why is the text on the project site bigger?
3 Why are there now two lists of people?
4 Why aren't users getting notified of updates any more?
5 Why can users now see a backlog?
6 Why can't a user see the project budget, requirements and plan on the front page?
7 Why can users see more project sites than previously?

> ➔ **Describing updates**
>
> We**'ve** just **updated** the standard layout of the wiki sites.
> We**'ve** recently **revised** the access rights to the pages.

> *Grammar: Present perfect, page 163*

3 Explaining reasons for an update

You are the new administrator. It's time to inform your team on some updates to the collaboration wiki.

Write a short email, explaining why the following points have been changed.

Update	Reasons
restrict editing rights	maintain consistency of all wiki pages
allow access to non-project members	encourage transparency of project information
limit access to project budget	keep financial information confidential
remove automated notifications	people get too many notifications

> *Useful phrases: Writing emails, page 153; Grammar: Present perfect, page 163*

PART A: Installing a new network

> **Situation:** You are a network engineer at Jupa Engineering, an engineering company in Dublin. The company is expanding and is about to move to the fourth floor of a new office building.
> → **You write an email to a colleague explaining the requirements for a new network.**

1 Explaining wireless network design to a colleague

You are on the new floor with your colleague Michael Kaeding and the project manager in charge of the move, Simon Smith. Michael is explaining some important considerations for the new network to Simon.

A **23)))** **Listen to the conversation and note down what the following numbers in the table refer to.**

Project information	
▰¹	€15,000
▰²	220
▰³	440
▰⁴	2.4 GHz 5 GHz
▰⁵	2800 m²
▰⁶	8 Mbps

B **23)))** **Listen again and complete the statements about the things the network design needs to consider.**

1 We're building a working business network, so we need ▰ the conditions that a business-grade router has to operate under.
2 Home gear isn't designed for that sort of network load, and employees need constant access to data. We need to ▰.
3 When we're building the network, we ▰ the number of connections we need now, and in five years' time.
4 One ▰ in selecting a business router is its ability to deliver rock-solid reliability under a constant load.
5 Well, if it can't deliver, productivity will be negatively impacted. Bearing ▰, I'd recommend a dual-band set-up, with 2.4 and 5 GHz.
6 We need a few spares, of course, but we need to ▰ how far apart we place the access points.
7 Placement of the access points is critical, ▰ that we need a minimum data rate of 8 Mbps.

> **➔ Taking things into consideration**
>
> We need to **take into account** the conditions that the network operates under.
> The number of access points is another **important factor**.
> **Bearing** the data rate of 8 Mbps **in mind**, we need extra access points.
> We **should consider** a dual-band set-up with 2.4 and 5 GHz.

> › *Useful phrases: Explaining requirements and consequences, page 156*

 **TOOLBOX**

access point – *Zugriffspunkt, Access Point*	interference – *Störung, Interferenz*	reliability – *Zuverlässigkeit*
bandwidth – *Bandbreite*	network load – *Netz(werk)last*	rock-solid – *(absolut) stabil*

2 Explaining consequences

Simon sends an email to you the following day, as your colleague Michael is out of the office.

From:	s.smith@jupa.ie
To:	networkservices@jupa.ie
Subject:	**Network budget estimate**

Hi

I've checked Michael's budget estimate with prices online and it looks as if the final cost is likely to be about €20,000. So we need to be able to justify the extra €5K over the current budget.

Below is a draft of what I'm going to send to Finance for approval. I've tried to explain the need for the extra money and point out the consequences of not making the investment. I think this will get their attention!

Could you add any additional information and justifications that you think are necessary?

Could you get this back to me by midday tomorrow?

Simon

– It's crucial that we purchase at least 12 access points to cover the floor area. The consequence of having fewer access points is the increased risk of slower speeds.

– Having both a 2.4 and 5 GHz band network is a high priority. Failure to invest in these mean network performance and employee productivity will suffer.

– It's vital that we invest in a wireless network that can handle the expected load increase over the next five years. Most devices only connect wirelessly and this will increase over time. It'll be cheaper to invest wisely now as we will get a bulk discount.

– As our testing equipment is quite old, we need a Wi-Fi strength measurement unit to test that the network is usable all over the floor. We'll be guessing the signal strength if we don't replace this equipment, and this could lead to coverage gaps on the floor.

A   First, read Simon's email and make notes on the points on the right.

B   👥 Work with a partner. Read the email again and point out the consequences of not investing properly in the project now. Answer your partner's questions. Change roles when you have finished.

> · What's the problem?
> · Who needs to approve?
> · How to get their attention?
> · What do I need to do?
> · By when?

1   Why can't we purchase fewer access points?
2   Can't we buy cheaper single-band routers?
3   Why can't we just buy enough to get started?
4   Can't we use our old Wi-Fi strength measurement unit?

> ➡ **Expressing consequences**
>
> We **will increase** the risk of slower speeds **if** we **don't buy** enough access points.
> **Unless** we **install** a dual-band network, employee productivity **will suffer**.

› *Grammar: Conditional sentences, page 164*

 TOOLBOX

---

consequence – *Folge*
coverage gap – *Lücke in der Netzwerkabdeckung*
draft – *Entwurf*

investment – *Investition*
measurement unit – *Messgerät*

3 Writing an email reply

You reply to your colleague Simon Smith with a few extra points to justify the amount of money you are asking for.

A For each of the requirements in the table below, make statements to express how important it is. Use the words and phrases in the list to help you.

absolutely critical • crucial • extremely important • high priority • vital

Requirements	Consequences
Four spare access points: · *access points can fail; need four spares now* · *need hardware we know works* · *need to test properly after installation to find weak signal spots*	· *lose productivity* · *can't guarantee compatibility with current network* · *need to install more access points later at a higher price*
Business-grade router: · *need shielded business-grade router* · *has to be able to handle business load*	· *corrupted data from interference* · *lower speeds and less productivity*

As access points can fail, it's vital that we buy four spare ones now.

B Now write the email, using the consequences in the list above to strengthen your arguments for extra funding.

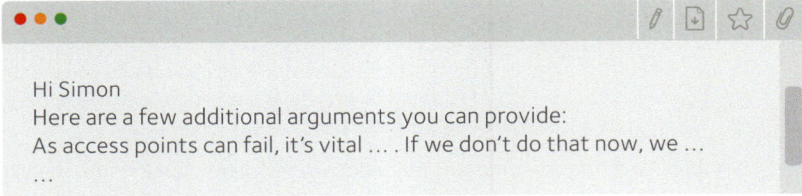

Hi Simon
Here are a few additional arguments you can provide:
As access points can fail, it's vital … . If we don't do that now, we …
…

› *Useful phrases: Writing emails, page 153*

4 Thinking about consequences

At your home or job you are likely to use a network for your computing. Both of these networks have different needs because they are used differently.

Discuss the following questions with a partner.

– Who uses your home or work network and what are they used for?
– What considerations are important when creating a network?
– What are the consequences of poor/cheap equipment?

Here are some ideas to get you started:
– How many devices do you access the network with?
– How big is your home/work area?
– How many people use the network?
– What high volume/bandwidth activities is the network used for?
– Are there many other routers around that could cause interference?

› *Useful phrases: Explaining requirements and consequences, page 156*

PART B: Local or cloud?

Situation: You are a network engineer at Jupa Engineering, an engineering company in Dublin. The company has asked you to consider using a cloud-based infrastructure.
→ **You persuade your colleagues to accept a particular option.**

1 Computer-aided design and processing

First of all, you look at how cloud-based processing would work for your company.

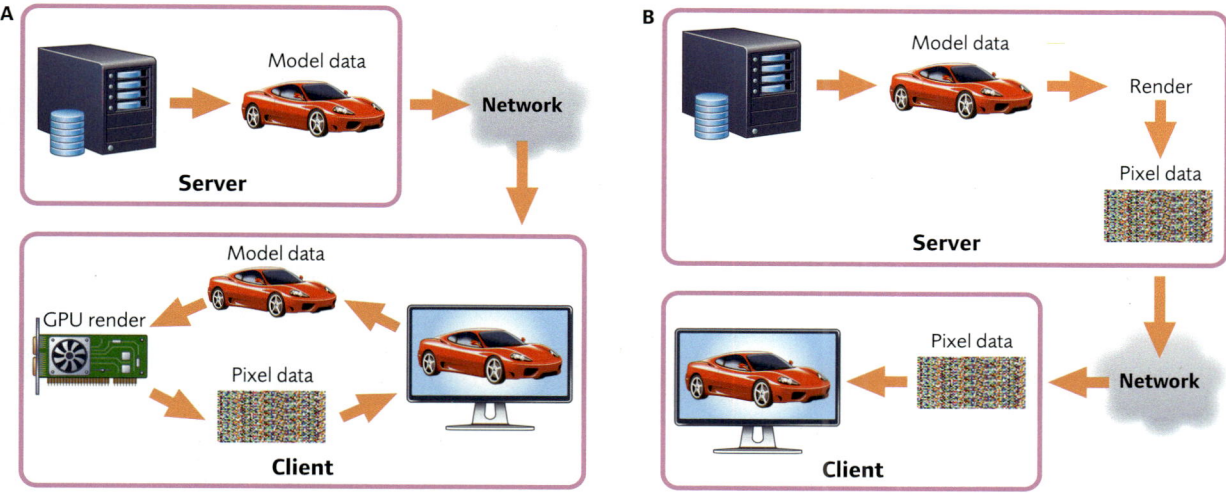

Based on a diagram by Alex Herrera, www.cadalyst.com

A The following statements describe the process flow for client-side rendering of CAD files (diagram A). Put them in the correct order.

a Finally, it is displayed on the monitor of the client computer.
b It is then converted to pixel data via the GPU.
c The model data starts on the server.
d The first step is that the model data is sent to the client machine via the network.
e Next, the model data on the client machine is sent to the GPU.

B Now describe the process flow for server-side rendering (diagram B).

C Work with a partner. Discuss the key differences between the two set-ups. Which one do you think is more …

– likely to require increased network data volume?
– likely to suffer from a slow network connection?
– secure?
– able to facilitate international collaboration?

D Exchange your ideas with another pair.

 **TOOLBOX**

client machine – *Client-Computer*   pixel – *Pixel, Bildpunkt*
GPU (graphical processing unit) – *Grafikprozessor*   to render – *berechnen, erzeugen*

2 Arguing the case for a particular option

You go online to look up some opinions on a cloud-based solution for Jupa Engineering.

A Before you read the website below, match these English expressions to their German equivalents.

1	previous solutions	**a**	(Daten-)Aufnahme
2	performance expectations	**b**	geistiges Eigentum
3	reluctance	**c**	Leistungserwartungen
4	productivity	**d**	Leistungsfähigkeit
5	intellectual property	**e**	übermäßige Latenzzeiten
6	mandatory	**f**	Widerwille
7	excessive latency	**g**	zwingend
8	uptake	**h**	bisherige Lösungen

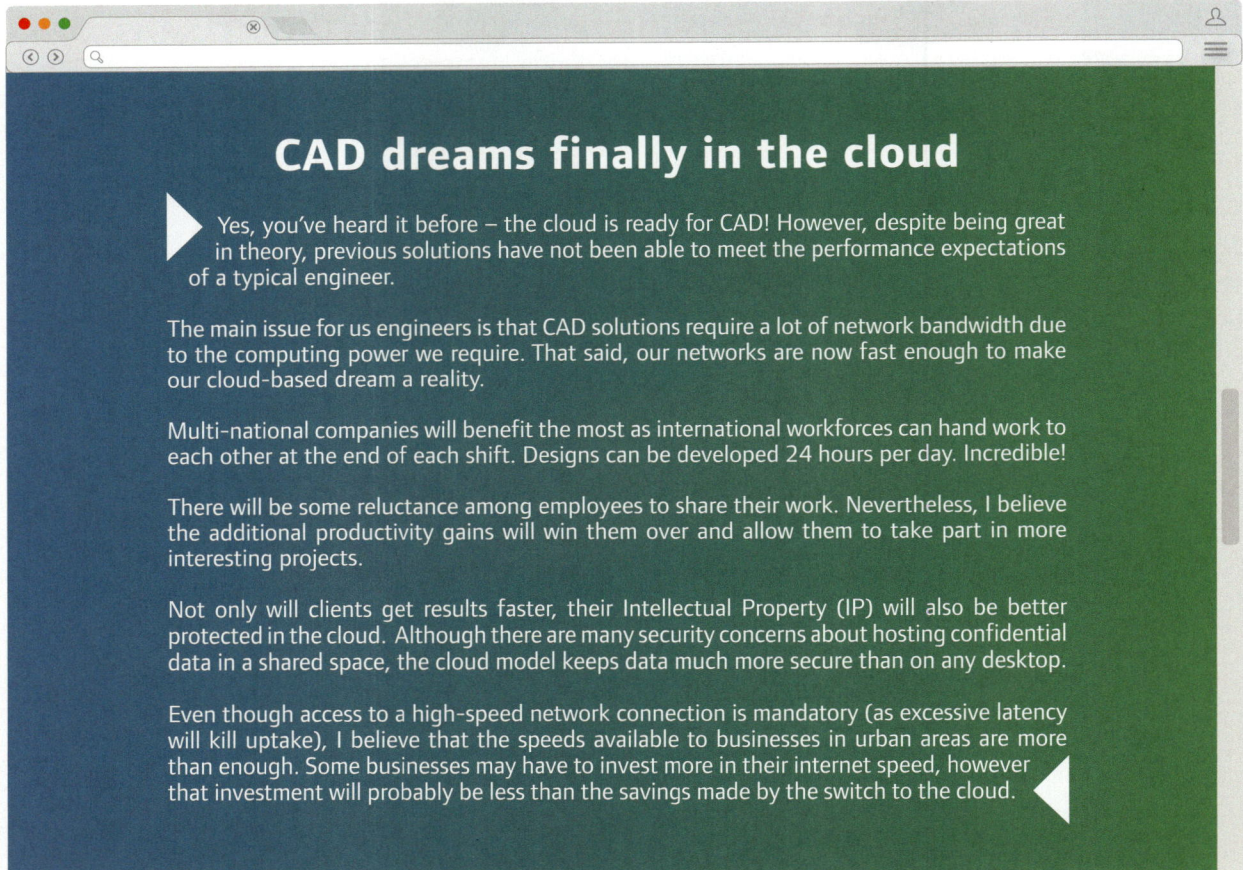

CAD dreams finally in the cloud

Yes, you've heard it before – the cloud is ready for CAD! However, despite being great in theory, previous solutions have not been able to meet the performance expectations of a typical engineer.

The main issue for us engineers is that CAD solutions require a lot of network bandwidth due to the computing power we require. That said, our networks are now fast enough to make our cloud-based dream a reality.

Multi-national companies will benefit the most as international workforces can hand work to each other at the end of each shift. Designs can be developed 24 hours per day. Incredible!

There will be some reluctance among employees to share their work. Nevertheless, I believe the additional productivity gains will win them over and allow them to take part in more interesting projects.

Not only will clients get results faster, their Intellectual Property (IP) will also be better protected in the cloud. Although there are many security concerns about hosting confidential data in a shared space, the cloud model keeps data much more secure than on any desktop.

Even though access to a high-speed network connection is mandatory (as excessive latency will kill uptake), I believe that the speeds available to businesses in urban areas are more than enough. Some businesses may have to invest more in their internet speed, however that investment will probably be less than the savings made by the switch to the cloud.

B Read the article and summarize the arguments in favour of and the concerns about cloud-based CAD. There are six pairs of arguments all together.

Cloud-based CAD	
Arguments in favour	Concerns
cloud technology is ready	*previous solutions have been disappointing*
...	*...*

C   Use the words provided to help you acknowledge the counterarguments while stating your case. The first one has been done for you

1   Even though …
    Even though previous solutions have been disappointing, cloud technology is now ready.
2   Despite …
3   Although …
4   Nevertheless, …
5   That said, …
6   Even though …

> ➤ **Acknowledging counterarguments**
>
> **Despite being** great in theory, previous solutions have not worked.
> Big companies will benefit most. **That said**, all companies can benefit.
> Solutions have come and gone. **Nevertheless**, I think the time has come for a change.

› *Useful phrases: Taking part in discussions, page 156*

3 Discussing advantages and disadvantages

Michael discusses the pros and cons of a cloud-based environment with your boss, Kieran Westing.

A   24))) ▶️ Listen to the conversation and note the advantages that Michael describes for each of the following aspects:

–   productivity (3 benefits)
–   employee satisfaction (2 benefits)
–   saving costs (2 benefits)

B   24))) ▶️ Listen again and note down Kieran's responses to the phrases that Michael uses to try and persuade him.

1   I think we have to consider them, don't we?
2   That's quite impressive, isn't it?
3   That sounds great, right?
4   The productivity gains would be amazing, right?
5   That's quite a good idea, wouldn't you agree?
6   Human Resources will be happy, won't they?
7   It's a nice benefit, don't you think?
8   I really think this looks like a great option for us, don't you agree?

C   Which of Kieran's replies confirm his agreement? Which of them express doubt?

4 Persuading your colleagues

You take part in a discussion to persuade your company to invest in a cloud-based solution.

👥 **Partner A and B:** Look at File 8 on page 137;
Partner C and D: Look at File 10 on page 138.

> ➤ **Taking part in discussions**
>
> **Looking for agreement**
> I think we have to consider it, don't we?
> That's quite impressive, isn't it?
>
> **Confirming agreement**
> I couldn't agree more.
> I'm (definitely) with you on that.
>
> **Expressing doubt**
> I'm not sure that I entirely agree.
> I partially agree, but …

› *Useful phrases: Taking part in discussions, page 156*

 **TOOLBOX**

---

heavy computation – *hohes Rechenaufkommen*   resource – *Quelle, Ressource*

COMMUNICATION: Constructive feedback

> **Situation:** Jupa Engineering in Dublin has adopted cloud infrastructure and now has different offices around the world working on the same project 24 hours a day. The company has created a set of guidelines for collaboration between its international teams.
> → **You give constructive feedback to a colleague on collaboration with other teams.**

1 Giving feedback

Kieran Westing, your project manager, has sent some feedback on the guidelines to Krystyna Galuszka, the international collaboration manager.

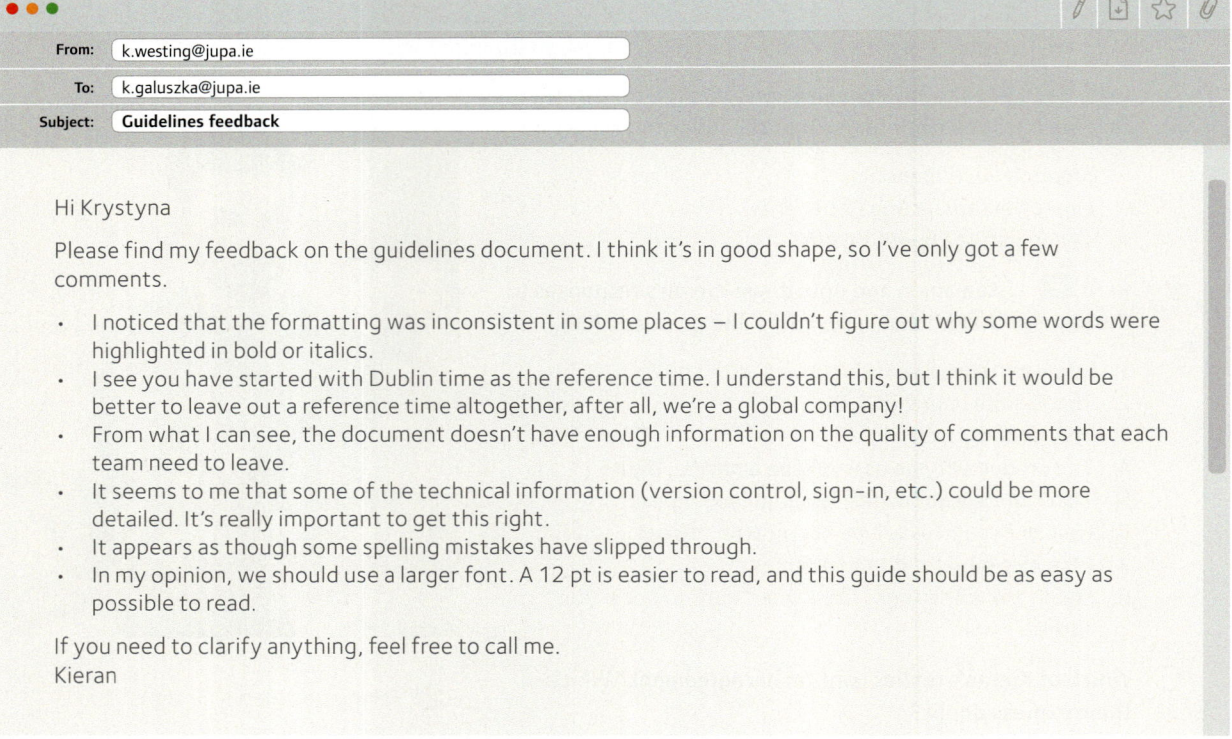

From: k.westing@jupa.ie
To: k.galuszka@jupa.ie
Subject: Guidelines feedback

Hi Krystyna

Please find my feedback on the guidelines document. I think it's in good shape, so I've only got a few comments.

- I noticed that the formatting was inconsistent in some places – I couldn't figure out why some words were highlighted in bold or italics.
- I see you have started with Dublin time as the reference time. I understand this, but I think it would be better to leave out a reference time altogether, after all, we're a global company!
- From what I can see, the document doesn't have enough information on the quality of comments that each team need to leave.
- It seems to me that some of the technical information (version control, sign-in, etc.) could be more detailed. It's really important to get this right.
- It appears as though some spelling mistakes have slipped through.
- In my opinion, we should use a larger font. A 12 pt is easier to read, and this guide should be as easy as possible to read.

If you need to clarify anything, feel free to call me.
Kieran

A Read Kieran's email and say whether these statements are true or false. Correct the false statements.

1 The quality of the guidelines is poor.
2 It's always clear why words are highlighted.
3 Reference time isn't needed.
4 There are too many technical details.
5 A 12 pt font would make the document easier to read.

 **TOOLBOX**

to be in good shape – *in gutem Zustand sein*	inconsistent – *uneinheitlich*
to figure sth out – *etw herausfinden*	sign-in – *Login*
guidelines *pl* – *Richtlinien*	

B Write a short email like Kieran's to give Krystyna the following feedback. Express your feedback from your point of view.

- *start / be more / positive*
- *introduction / need / talk more / benefits*
- *section / version control / difficult / understand*
- *too many / examples / guidelines*
- *navigation / too complicated*

In my opinion, the start should be more positive.

> 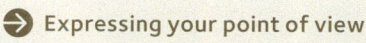 **Expressing your point of view**
>
> It seems to me (that) …
> In my opinion, …
> From what I can see, …

› *Useful phrases: Taking part in discussions, page 156*

2 Suggesting changes and improvements

Kieran Westing is giving a member of your team, Chris, some feedback about his work recently.

A **25))** Listen to both conversations: which one is more polite?

B **25))** Listen to the conversations again and complete the following polite phrases for making suggestions.

1 It ▬ for you to pay more attention to a couple of things.
2 You ▬ putting some more detail in the comments for the team in Florida to pick up.
3 ▬ spend a bit more time on them.
4 ▬ that you set aside some time at the end of every day to do so?
5 If you're uncertain about anything, you ▬ to me and ask.
6 Otherwise, ▬ checking the guidelines regularly to see if they have been updated.

C Change the following to polite feedback statements

1 You need to re-read the guidelines we published recently. (suggest) *I suggest that …*
2 You have to ask me if things aren't clear. (try)
3 You need to write more detailed comments for the team in Florida to pick up. (be a good idea)
4 You have to change them to be more descriptive. (be better)
5 You need to pay more attention to things. (perhaps)
6 You have to spend more time speaking to your colleagues. (think about)

> **Making polite suggestions**
>
> It **might be better** if you added more detail.
> It **would be a good idea** to re-read the guidelines.
> You **could think about** asking your colleagues if you're not sure.

› *Grammar: Modal verbs and their substitutes, page 167*

3 Giving constructive feedback

Now it is time for you to provide constructive feedback on collaboration to another member of your team.

Partner A: Look at File 9 on page 137; **Partner B:** Look at File 11 on page 138.

DAS KANN ICH (Unit 7)

- Englischsprachige Kollegen/Kolleginnen per E-Mail über Wiki-Updates informieren. (Foundation)
- Die Erfordernisse für ein neues Netzwerk auf Englisch erklären. (Part A)
- Englischsprachige Kollegen/Kolleginnen überzeugen, eine Cloud-Lösung einzuführen. (Part B)
- Englischsprachigen Kollegen/Kolleginnen konstruktive Rückmeldungen über die Zusammenarbeit geben. (Communication)

8 Presenting technical projects

FOUNDATION: International connection standards

Situation: You are a product engineer at LifeTech, an Australian company that makes a wide range of electronic products for the home and hobbies.
→ **You choose and present a standardized connection protocol for an electronic product.**

1 Identifying connection standards

Before you start your new job, you check your knowledge of connection types.

© by Logitech

A 👥 Work with a partner. Can you name all of the connection types in the pictures?

B 👥 What devices and appliances use each standard? What do they use each connection to do?

2 Thinking about standards

LifeTech are creating a new range of high-priced gaming keyboards and mouse devices. You do some research on different connection types.

A 👥 Work with a partner and research which connection types are open standards and which are proprietary.

B 👥 Discuss with your partner why it is important for consumers that connection types are regulated by standards. Make notes on the aspects below and add your own ideas. Then report back to the class.

- charging
- transferring data
- accessing the internet
- connecting to each other

3 Discussing open and proprietary protocols

You and your colleague, Emily Regan, are discussing the type of wireless connection you should use for the new keyboards and mouse devices with a marketing manager, James d'Amato.

A 26 ⟩⟩ Listen and say whether the following statements are true or false. Correct the false statements.

1 They are considering Wi-Fi and their own proprietary connection.
2 James is initially against the proprietary protocol.
3 The target customers are casual gamers.

B   26))) Listen again. Which of the following are key selling points according to James?

1   reliable connections   3   security   5   low power use
2   no pairing   4   high-speed data transfer   6   range

C   Match the sentence halves.

1   GameTech, …   a   who need something better than average.
2   Bluetooth is well known, …   b   which means more people can use it.
3   We have complete control, …   c   who care about security.
4   We can make the data connection more reliable d   which is better from a marketing point of view.
    so that it doesn't disconnect, …   e   which is important to everyone.
5   I don't think there are many customers …   f   which is annoying with Bluetooth.
6   The peripherals connect without pairing, …   g   who are competitors of ours, use their own
7   Don't forget that serious gamers are people …   protocol.
8   Bluetooth is built into nearly every   h   which allows us to optimize a lot of important
    computer, …   things.

4   Choosing the most appropriate protocols

LifeTech are planning a few more updates to some of their products.

A   With a partner, choose two products and decide whether they should use a standardized protocol, like
    Bluetooth and USB, or a proprietary protocol.

	Coffee machine	Fitness tracker	Vacuum robot
Purpose	programmable from anywhere in your home	a full lifestyle tracker: used to track movement, heart rate and sleep	no more vacuuming: the robot knows where and when to vacuum
Power	• plugs into wall	• rechargeable battery	• single charge covers 45m² • quick charge supported
Features	• always on • internet not required • easy set-up	• always on • wireless transfer of data to computer/ smartphone	• easy set-up • timer can be set from anywhere in the world
Target customer	• luxury market • people with large houses	• people who do some exercise, but not a lot • people who want to do more exercise	• people that care about the appearance of their home • people that are short of time

B   Present your ideas to the class, explaining
    the reasons for your decision.

> Useful phrases: Giving presentations, page 151

> Defining things more closely
>
> I'd suggest using our proprietary connection,
> **which** offers a lot of advantages.

 TOOLBOX

> Grammar: Relative clauses, page 165

---

proprietary – firmeneigen, urheberrechtlich geschützt   protocol – Protokoll   pairing – Kopplung, Pairing

PART A: Trade fairs

> **Situation:** You work for QAR Medical, an American company that provides augmented-reality software to medical companies. These educational programs help medical students and professionals learn how to use their products.
>
> → **You talk to a potential customer at your stand at a trade fair. You follow up the meeting with a telephone call.**

1 Engaging with a visitor at the booth

You are with your American boss, Julia Pasternak, at the QAR booth at the MedTech trade fair in Atlanta, Georgia.

A **27))** Listen to Julia talking to the visitors. Copy the table and complete it with the missing information about their company.

Name of company	▭
Known for	▭
Year founded	▭
Size of company	▭
Headquarters	▭
What are the visitors to their booth interested in?	▭

B **27))** Listen again and complete the sentences that Julia uses to engage the visitors and establish rapport.

1 Good afternoon, I'm Julia Pasternak from QAR. ▭ our booth. How are you today?
2 ▭ the show? It's great to see a lot of strong medical technology, ▭ ?
3 I'm ▭ that you're enjoying it.
4 ▭ who you work for?
5 MGB Health? You have a ▭ as a leader of medical instrument technology.
6 You were founded in the 1940s, in Michigan, ▭ ?
7 It also ▭ a passion for technology and helping people.
8 ▭ whether you are here looking for something in particular?
9 Great, well that's our specialty. ▭ to demonstrate our holographic anatomy program.

2 Promoting your products and services

QAR Medical has brochures describing their products, services and successes at the trade show stand. As you have to talk to customers about your company, check what you know about QAR during a coffee break.

A Read the brochure on page 83 and note down the key information about QAR Medical in German.

> · *Alter der Firma?*
> · *Kernprodukte?*
> · *Hauptkunden?*
> · *Größe der Firma?*
> · *Standort?*

 **TOOLBOX**

---

booth – *(Messe-)Stand*   specialty *(AE)* / speciality *(BE)* – *Fachgebiet*

QAR Medical
Augmenting medical specialists

Since our start just nine years ago, we've had great success in establishing a reputation as the most trusted brand in medical education.

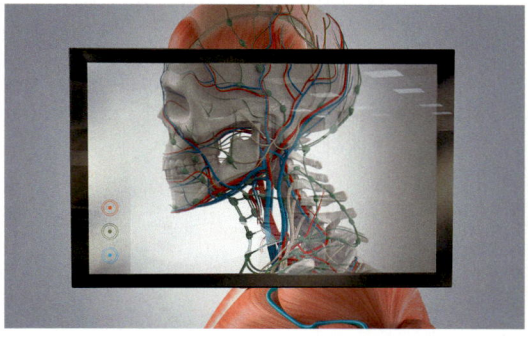

Our flagship product, HoloMedEd, combines our expertise in medical education and augmented reality and has transformed thousands of medical students into more capable professionals, confident of being able to handle the best technology in the industry.

The most respected names in medicine, such as MedTech, The Nash Institute and OnCare Instruments trust QAR Medical to deliver the educational experience to match their sophisticated products. We've helped companies achieve up to a 35 % increase in adoption of their products and helped improve the lives of countless patients.

Our educational platform is the best in the business and has been built to accompany students for their entire careers – a constant partner in development. Client testimonials tell us that we exceed expectation of delivered service over 25 % of the time.

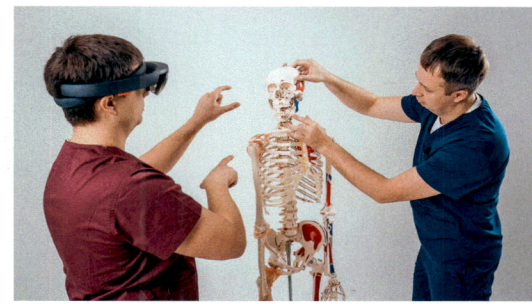

We're proud to say that students using HoloMedEd report a 94 % satisfaction rating and over 60 % say that we've helped them understand complex anatomy better than they have with any other learning material.

In that time we've grown to a company of 60 employees who are each dedicated to the future of healthcare. We're headquartered right in the heart of technology, San Francisco, with offices in Cologne and London serving our customers in Europe.

B   **Using information in the brochure, answer the questions that you receive from visitors to your booth.**

1   I haven't heard of you - what's your reputation like?
We've had great success in establishing a reputation as the most trusted brand in medical education.
2   What expertise do you have?
3   How do you benefit medical students?
4   What have you delivered for your clients?
5   How does your platform compare to others?
6   What is your delivery record like?
7   What do students think of you?

> Taking about achievements
>
> We**'ve transformed** thousands of medical students into more capable professionals.
> We**'ve helped** medical companies improve the lives of countless patients.

› *Grammar: Present perfect, page 163*

 TOOLBOX

medical procedure – *medizinischer Eingriff*   reputation – *Ruf*

3 Writing a follow-up email

Your boss, Julia Pasternak, follows up the conversation at the trade fair with an email to MGB Health.

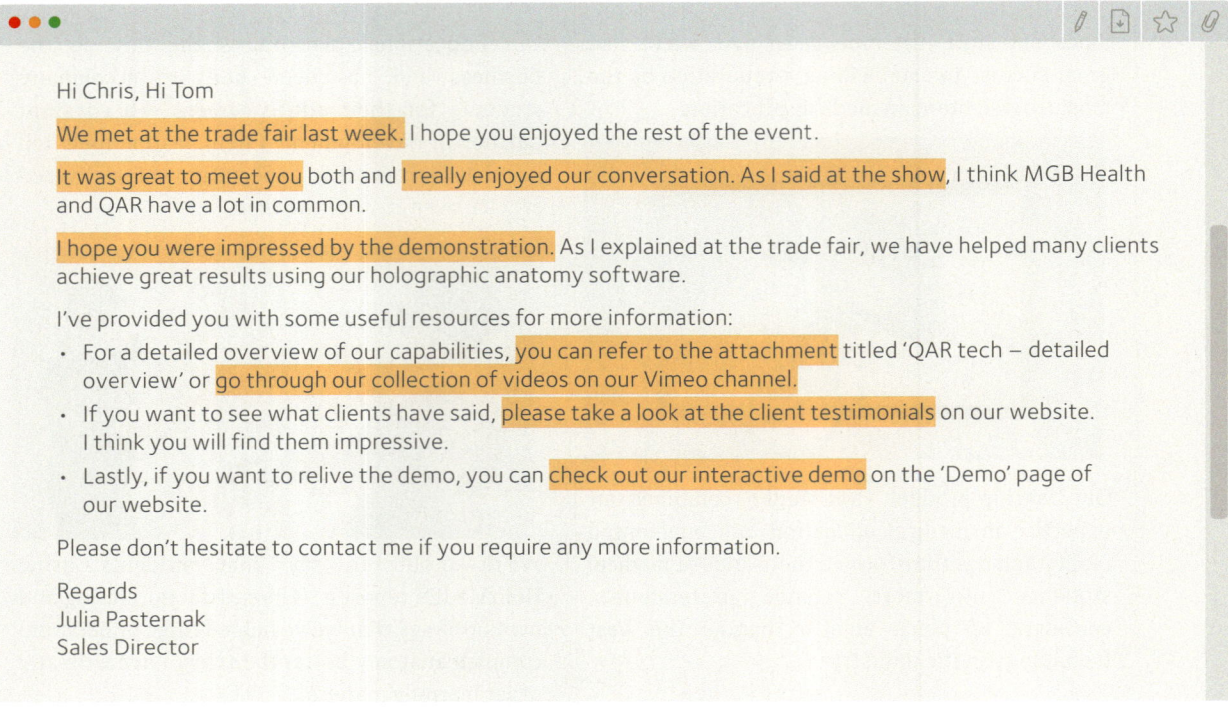

Hi Chris, Hi Tom

We met at the trade fair last week. I hope you enjoyed the rest of the event.

It was great to meet you both and I really enjoyed our conversation. As I said at the show, I think MGB Health and QAR have a lot in common.

I hope you were impressed by the demonstration. As I explained at the trade fair, we have helped many clients achieve great results using our holographic anatomy software.

I've provided you with some useful resources for more information:

- For a detailed overview of our capabilities, you can refer to the attachment titled 'QAR tech – detailed overview' or go through our collection of videos on our Vimeo channel.
- If you want to see what clients have said, please take a look at the client testimonials on our website. I think you will find them impressive.
- Lastly, if you want to relive the demo, you can check out our interactive demo on the 'Demo' page of our website.

Please don't hesitate to contact me if you require any more information.

Regards
Julia Pasternak
Sales Director

Read the email and then organize the highlighted phases into one of the following categories.

Referring to the previous meeting	Referring to information
… met	… can refer to

4 Engaging with potential customers

You are at a trade fair and engage with several customers. After the trade fair, you make some follow-up calls to offer further information about QAR Medical.

👥 Work with a partner. **Partner A:** Look here. **Partner B:** Look at File 22 on page 144.

A You work for QAR Medical. Role-play a conversation with a potential customer at a trade fair.

Engage Partner B as he/she comes into your booth.

- Establish rapport with him/her.
- Ask questions about his/her company.
- Describe your company, products and successes to him/her.

> *Useful phrases: Engaging with potential customers, page 157*

B Now make a follow-up call to Partner B. Mention the meeting you had at the trade fair and the email you sent them. Tell them where they can find more information about your company and products.

Swap roles when you have finished.

PART B: A project report for a client

Situation: QAR Medical has been selected by Modi Medical to provide training software for their medical instruments. You are the project manager from QAR who is running the project.
→ **You report on the progress of a project to a client.**

1 Planning and estimating the project

You have created a Gantt Chart to show estimates of the cost and time needed to complete each task of the project, as well as the overall cost and duration.

> **Infobox**
>
> A **Gantt chart** is a type of bar chart named after Henry Gantt (1861–1919), an American mechanical engineer and management consultant. This type of chart is used in project management to illustrate a project schedule, for example the start and finish dates of the different elements of a project. The chart is also used in information technology to represent data that has been collected.

A   **Before you look at the chart, match the words (1–5) to the correct definition (a–e).**

1	duration	a	the time that a task can be delayed without delaying other dependent tasks
2	slack	b	how much money it takes to perform a task
3	milestone	c	the date that a task is scheduled to be finished
4	due date	d	the planned time taken to perform a task
5	cost	e	completion of a phase of work

Gantt chart – Modi Medical augmented reality

Task	March	April	May	Cost
Kick-off				$6,231.00
Requirements workshops				$35,998.00
Customization analysis				$28,375.00
Augmented model creation				$47,093.00
Software customization				$35,660.00
Testing				$10,341.00
Training course creation				$5,999.00
Full delivery of AR headsets				$ –
Launch				$ –

B   **Now give estimates about the project using the Gantt chart.**

1   the duration of requirements workshops   *It will take about three weeks to complete the requirements.*
2   the cost of requirements workshops
3   the duration of customization analysis
4   the amount of slack left between customization analysis and augmented model creation
5   the due date for augmented model creation
6   the cost of software customization
7   the due date for the end of testing
8   the date of the launch milestone

> → **Giving estimates**
> We estimate that it will take **about** six weeks to …
> We've allowed for **around** four weeks …
> It will take **approximately** three days to …
> It'll cost **in the region of** $10,000.

> › *Grammar: Future with will and going to, page 164*

85

2 Reporting on the project's progress

You are giving a progress report on the project to your counterpart at Modi Medical.

Progress report – augmented-reality education
For Modi Medical Management

We've now been working for three weeks and have already had some positive results.

The team has completed some very successful and intensive requirements workshops right on time, which is great. We are due to complete writing up the requirements for your approval a day ahead of schedule and the development team have been looking at the customizations since Tuesday.

Unfortunately, we've hit some snags as well. We've come across an issue with the import of instrument specifications. Some of them can't be successfully imported via Optical Character Recognition, which is the fastest method. We can work around it, but it means that we will deliver up to two weeks later than planned.

Because of the OCR problem, the creation of the augmented models is also behind schedule. If we don't find any other unexpected issues, we only expect it to be delayed by one week.

Lastly, on a more positive note, the Modi Medical team have been working on the training plan for the first group of students for a week already, which is tracking as planned.

A Read the progress update. There are five tasks mentioned in the report. Say which ones are …

- ahead of time
- on time
- behind time (and give reasons)

B Several weeks later, you provide another progress report using the project dashboard below. Write the progress report making sure you give reasons to explain things that are behind time.

Project dashboard

Task	Started	Status	Cause	Estimated impact
Augmented models	5 weeks ago	🔴	Still behind, but have made up ground due to some hard work to get specifications imported.	< 1 week
Software customizations	4 weeks ago	🟢	Completed on Friday as planned.	–
Testing	5 weeks ago	🟡	New AR engine was released with several bugs. As a result, we have only completed 55% of tests instead of planned 80%.	2 weeks
Training plan for first group of students	4 weeks ago	🟡	Delayed slightly because one of the team members was ill.	3 days
Launch communications	1 week ago	🟢	All good.	–
Co-ordination with new client	4 days ago	🔴	Unable to contact anyone that can provide information about the first group of students.	4 days

3 Reviewing a project

When the project is finished, you organize a session to review the project and record any lessons learned.

A **28**))) **Listen to the project team reviewing the project and say whether the following statements are true or false. Correct the false statements.**

1 The software customization phase went well.
2 There were fewer customizations than wanted.
3 They rushed customization analysis because of pressure from their boss.
4 The upgrade made QAR look good.
5 The team didn't know the upgrade was coming.

> ⮕ **Giving a progress report**
>
> We **have** already **completed**.
> They**'ve been looking** at the customizations since Tuesday.

> › *Grammar: Present perfect, page 163;*
> *Present perfect progressive, page 163*

B **28**))) **Listen again and complete the phrases.**

1 ▬ , I think it went quite well.
2 The only downside was that we had to customize more than we ▬ .
3 Yes, I do. We ▬ to standardize more.
4 Modi Medical put pressure on us to deliver by a specific date, ▬ .
5 Could we also ▬ the problems caused by the new AR engine release?
6 Oh yes, you're right. ▬ , I'm surprised the Modi Medical management weren't more upset.
7 Just ▬ , do you think that we ▬ more careful in planning?
8 I think we ▬ for some extra time in the plan, in case of problems with the upgrade.

4 Giving a project progress report

Now it is time to report on a different project to a customer.

👥 **Partner A: Look here. Partner B: Look at File 12 on page 139.**

Give your partner a progress report on your project using the information in the table below.

> ⮕ **Talking about lessons learned**
>
> We **could** have been more proactive.
> We **should** have communicated better.

> › *Grammar: Modals and their substitutes,*
> *page 167*

For each phase, tell your partner:
– the original estimate and how much you have completed
– whether you are behind time, on time or ahead of time
– why certain tasks are behind time
– what dependent phases are at risk from work that is behind time

Say if there are any lessons you have learned that can be applied to future phases of the project.

Task	Planned progress	Actual progress	Comments
Requirements gathering workshops (behind)	80 %	70 %	Two sessions cancelled, due to key stakeholder illness Note: Next time allow more slack
Requirements documentation (behind – dependent)	70 %	60 %	Caused by requirements gathering workshops
Requirements sign-off (still on track, allowed some slack)	50 %	45 %	Requirements for completed scope areas are signed off. Behind due to workshop delay.
Wireframe creation (started and on track)	10 %	10 %	At risk, due to late delivery of requirements Note: Next time plan in requirements workshops

COMMUNICATION: Business trips

> **Situation:** Your company has won an award as one of the four best European start-ups of the year. You are going to the prize-giving ceremony in Amsterdam, where you will stay at the International Hotel.
> → **You do internet research to find information about people from other cultures.**

1 Checking in and checking out at a hotel

When you arrive at the hotel, there are four guests in front of you at reception. You listen to the receptionist talking to them.

1 Giovanni Rossi **2** Mary McGregor **3** Yusuf Zuabi **4** Akira Banerjee

A 29)) Copy the table. Listen to the first three guests as they check in and fill in the missing information.

	What questions do the guests ask?	What information does the receptionist give?
Giovanni Rossi	▭¹	▭²
Mary McGregor	▭³	▭⁴
Yusuf Zuabi	▭⁵	▭⁶

B Akira Banerjee is checking out. Read what she says to the receptionist. What do you think the receptionist said to the guest?

1 Good morning. I'm very well, thank you.
2 I would like to check out.
3 I was in room 207.
4 It's been great. I love Amsterdam.

5 Yes, thank you. Everything was fine. I'll definitely be back.
6 Thank you. I'm flying KLM. They're very good.

C 30)) Now listen and check your answers.

2 Role-play: At reception

👥 Work with a partner and role-play a conversation at a hotel reception desk.

Partner A: You are the hotel receptionist. Greet the guest, welcome him/her to the hotel and take down his/her details. You begin.
Partner B: You are a guest who has just arrived. Use your own personal details to check in and answer the receptionist's questions.

After that, do a second role-play and practise checking out.

› *Useful phrases: Checking in and out of hotels, page 157*

3 Chatting at breakfast

Next morning, the breakfast buffet is very full. You find a free seat at a table with another guest.

A Work with a partner. Put the dialogues in order to produce a conversation.

1 A Pleased to meet you, too. Where are you from?
   B I'm from … . What about you?
   A I'm from …
2 A I was here on holiday a few years ago.
   B Where are the best places to go?
   A If you have time, you should really go to …
3 A I'd better get ready to go now. Have a good day.
   B Thanks. See you later.

4 A Good morning. Is this seat taken?
   B No, it's not. You can sit here. Are you here for the prize-giving ceremony?
5 A Have you been to Amsterdam before?
   B No, I haven't. What about you?
6 A Yes, I am. My name's …
   B Pleased to meet you. I'm …

B Find a new partner. Add your own details then close your books and practise the dialogue.
› *Unit 1, Communication, exercise 3, page 13*

4 Cultural awareness

On the plane home, you read the following quiz about different cultures.

A Work with a partner. Complete each sentence with the best ending. When you have finished, ask your teacher for the answers and discuss which answers surprise you.

1 **Many Japanese people …**
   a always bow when they meet people for the first time.
   b bow when they meet each other, but they will shake hands with Westerners.
   c never shake hands with anyone.
2 **A lot of Irish people respect people who are …**
   a aggressive and dominant.
   b formal and quiet.
   c rich and powerful.
3 **In Italy, you should never ask people about their …**
   a families.
   b hobbies.
   c job or where they live.

4 **In the Netherlands, some people will think you are rude if you …**
   a eat cheese with a knife and fork.
   b leave a small amount of food on your plate when you've finished eating.
   c leave the table during a meal.
5 **Soon after you've been introduced, many British people will …**
   a invite you to visit them at home.
   b start to use first names.
   c want to know everything about you.
6 **Many people from the Middle East may ask to take a break during meetings so that they can …**
   a go for a walk.
   b phone home.
   c pray.

B Work in a group of four. Find information about people from other cultures on the internet. Use the information to make up a quiz like the one above. Pin your quiz on the wall and do a gallery walk with your partners. How highly does your team score on the other groups' quizzes?

DAS KANN ICH (Unit 8)

– Ein Verbindungsprotokoll für ein technisches Gerät wählen und präsentieren. (Foundation)
– Nach einer Messe Kontakt mit einem Kunden / einer Kundin per E-Mail und telefonisch aufnehmen. (Part A)
– Über den Stand eines technischen Projekts auf Englisch berichten. (Part B)
– Quizfragen über kulturelle Unterschiede auf Englisch zusammenstellen. (Communication)

1 Interaktion: B1/B2

Ihre Firma, QAR Medical, plant, ihr Flaggschiff auf einer Messe zu präsentieren. Sie und Ihre amerikanische Kollegin haben den Auftrag, die Vorbereitungen zu treffen. Sie treffen sich zu einem ersten Gespräch.

 Verwenden Sie die Rollenkarten, um ein Gespräch als Rollenspiel durchzuführen.

Partner A:

Sie fragen nach ...
- dem Messestandort
- dem Termin für die Buchung des Messestands
- den bisherigen Absprachen mit der Messeleitung
- der Ausstattung des Standes
- weiteren Vorbereitungen

Ihre Antworten und Vorschläge:
- Produktliteratur, Demos von HoloMed, Bewertung durch Kunden/Kundinnen
- Auftrag an Agentur für Catering und Servicepersonal
- Präsentation von HoloMedEd durch Dr Hill
- Einladung wichtiger Kunden per E-Mail (plus Freikarten)

Partner B:

Sie fragen nach ...
- dem Informationsmaterial für Besucher/innen
- dem Personal für Bewirtung
- dem/der Moderator/in für HoloMedEd
- Personen, die eingeladen werden sollten

Ihre Antworten und Vorschläge:
- Messestandort: Den Haag, Niederlande, Messe für Medizin
- Buchung sechs Monate vorher
- Aufnahme in Messekatalog, 20 Messeausweise
- Geräte: Beamer, Laptops, Tablets, Kopfhörer, Flaggschiff HoloMedEd
- Zahl der Stromanschlüsse ermitteln

2 Produktion: B1

Sie haben die Aufgabe, wichtige Kunden/Kundinnen zur Messe für Medizin nach Den Haag einzuladen.

Schreiben Sie zunächst eine Einladung per E-Mail an Dr Steven Milford vom Medical Research Council, London. Ihre E-Mail soll folgende Punkte enthalten:

- Höfliche Anrede
- Ort und Zeit: Den Haag MediTec, 4. März bis 8. März
- QAR Medical ist wieder Aussteller
- Einladung an Dr Milford als wichtigen Kunden zu Stand 614, Halle C
- Hinweis auf verbesserte Produkte, die Dr Milford interessieren könnten
- Erwähnung des Flaggschiffs HoloMedEd (AR-Software für die Anatomie)
- Anlage: drei Freikarten und Produktliteratur
- Sie hoffen, Dr Milford am Stand begrüßen zu können
- Dank für sein Vertrauen in QAR Medical
- Höflicher Schluss

3 Hörverstehen: B1/B2

Ihre Ausbildungsfirma hat mehrere Security-Fachleute zu einer Fortbildung eingeladen. Darunter ist auch Anne Taylor von Barclays Security, die zum Thema „How safe is your digital wallet?" spricht. Ihr Chef, Paul Höpfner, moderiert das Interview.

31 **Hören Sie das Gespräch und machen Sie sich zu folgenden Fragen Notizen auf Deutsch, um für die anschließende Diskussion gut vorbereitet zu sein.**

1 Was ist eine *digital wallet*?
2 Wo kann man Bitcoins kaufen?
3 Wie bezahlt man für Bitcoins?
4 Wie kann man am schnellsten seine Schulden mit Bitcoins begleichen?
5 Welche Vorteile hat der Zahlungsverkehr in Bitcoins im Vergleich zum Bankkonto?
6 Welche vier Sicherheitsvorkehrungen schützen vor Verlust der *digital wallet*?

4 Mediation: B1/B2

Zur Vorbereitung auf eine Präsentation, die Sie im Informatikunterricht über Wikis halten sollen, haben Sie diesen Text gefunden.

Stellen Sie die wichtigsten Informationen stichpunktartig auf Deutsch zusammen.

- Probleme mit den alten Wikis
- Prinzip des *Federated Wiki*
- Vorteile des *Federated Wiki*
- Teilnahme am *Federated Wiki*

_____ The future of wikis _____

When Ward Cunningham, the architect of the first wiki, was asked in a 2006 why he had never had the wiki concept patented, he explained that the idea "just sounded like something that no one would want to pay money for". Ten years later, on the occasion of Wikipedia's 15th anniversary, he outlined the future of his invention in an interview. He was disappointed with the development of the old wikis because they had been "turned into a mess". The people who write for Wikipedia, for example, need to spend a tremendous amount of energy correcting misuses.

That is why he has been working for the last five years on what he calls the "Federated Wiki". To join the federation of wikis, you put up a wiki on your own server. So two users, for example Tim and Tom, both write on their individual wikis. Anything Tim writes, Tom is welcome to take via Creative Commons and make changes to, edit or add his own ideas. And when Tim revises Tom's new, changed document, he puts it on his wiki, not back on Tom's wiki. Both users can give something away and still own it. Thus the Federated Wiki allows a community to share their data and keep their originals. Cunningham calls it a kind of collective ownership. In 2016 there were already more than 800 sites.

Federated Wikis won't have the problems the authors who write for Wikipedia are struggling with. They won't need to waste time and energy correcting abuses. The Federated Wiki solves that problem because when you put something on your wiki server, people are free to use it, but they can't change or edit your pages.
There are two ways of joining a Federated Wiki. One possibility is to go to a wiki website or a Federated Wiki provider, to create an account and start using it. Another option is be a provider yourself; just install the software and run it on a server.

9 Enquiries and offers for IT services

FOUNDATION: A video conferencing system

Situation: You work for the German subsidiary of a Maltese firm that is interested in installing a video conferencing system.
→ **You write a report on a suitable system for your supervisor.**

1 Listening to a phone call

The owner of the firm in Malta would like to discuss the conferencing system with your supervisor, Claudia Weber. He has sent an email describing what he wants from the system.

A 👥 **Work with a partner. Match the items in James Camilleri's email (1–4) with the list of suggestions Claudia Weber would like to make (a–f). There are two extra suggestions.**

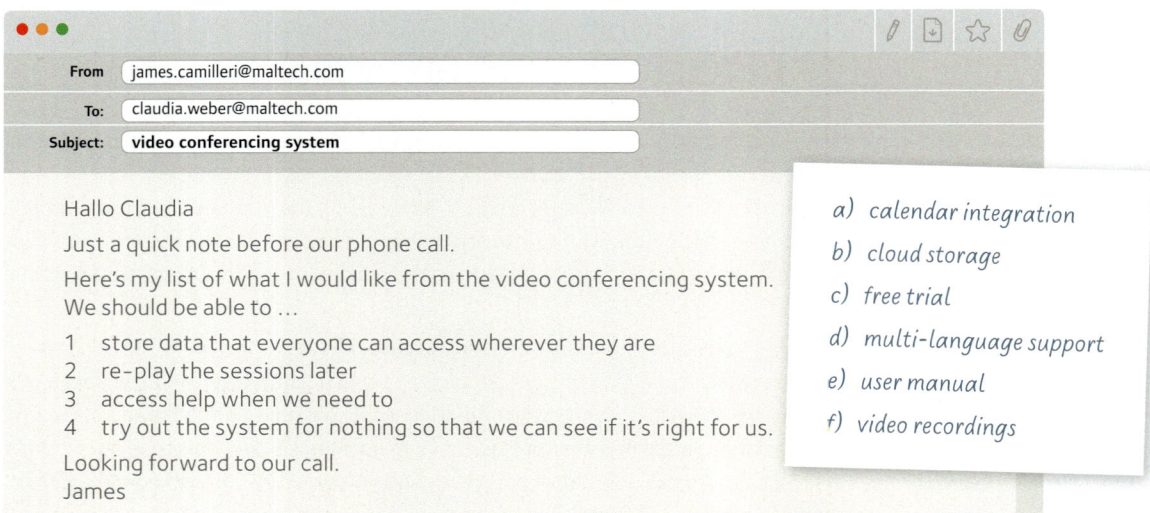

From: james.camilleri@maltech.com
To: claudia.weber@maltech.com
Subject: video conferencing system

Hallo Claudia
Just a quick note before our phone call.
Here's my list of what I would like from the video conferencing system. We should be able to …
1 store data that everyone can access wherever they are
2 re-play the sessions later
3 access help when we need to
4 try out the system for nothing so that we can see if it's right for us.
Looking forward to our call.
James

a) calendar integration
b) cloud storage
c) free trial
d) multi-language support
e) user manual
f) video recordings

B 32))) ▶ **Listen to the telephone conversation and check your answers to exercise 1A. Does James Camilleri agree or disagree with the extra items Claudia Weber suggests?**

> ➡ **Comparing items**
>
> This is **the cheapest** system.
> This is **the most/least expensive** system.
> good > **best**   bad > **worst**   little > **least**

> › *Grammar: Comparatives and superlatives, page 166*

2 Comparing video conferencing systems

You find an overview of video conferencing systems online.

A Study the chart below and choose the system you think is best.

B 👥 Work with a partner. Compare your ideas and agree together on the system which is best for the company. Make notes on the advantages of the system you have chosen. Make notes on the other systems so that you can argue against them.

C 👥 Work with another pair. Discuss all the options and decide on the best system for the company.

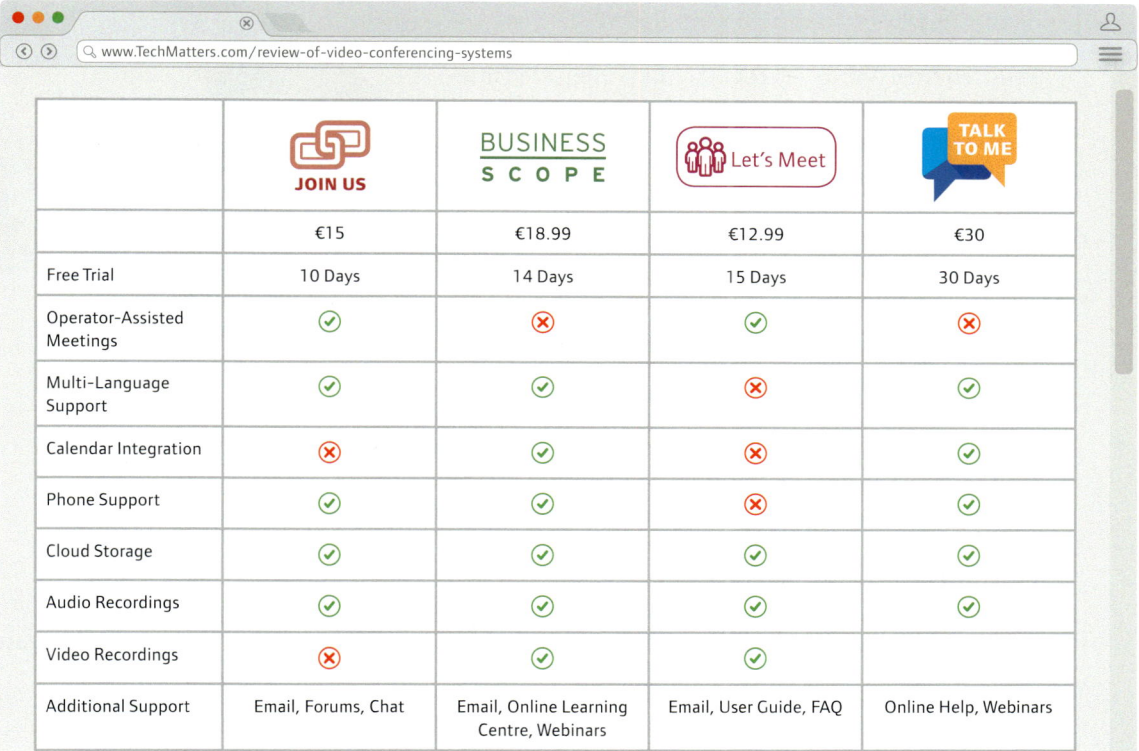

	JOIN US	BUSINESS SCOPE	Let's Meet	TALK TO ME
	€15	€18.99	€12.99	€30
Free Trial	10 Days	14 Days	15 Days	30 Days
Operator-Assisted Meetings	✓	✗	✓	✗
Multi-Language Support	✓	✓	✗	✓
Calendar Integration	✗	✓	✗	✓
Phone Support	✓	✓	✗	✓
Cloud Storage	✓	✓	✓	✓
Audio Recordings	✓	✓	✓	✓
Video Recordings	✗	✓	✓	
Additional Support	Email, Forums, Chat	Email, Online Learning Centre, Webinars	Email, User Guide, FAQ	Online Help, Webinars

3 Writing a report

Now you write the report on the system you have chosen for Claudia Weber and James Camilleri.

👥 Work with a partner. Write your report on the video conferencing system using the following structure.

Introduction	– State the purpose of the report. – Give a short description of your research.	*This report will explain how we …* *We searched the internet and found …*
Main part	– Give the names of the systems. (The system you are going to suggest should come last on the list.) – Say which system you have chosen and explain why.	*We have chosen the … (name of the system) because …* *The system features …* *It does not feature …*
Conclusion	– Sum up and make recommendations.	*For these reasons, we believe that …* *In conclusion, we suggest …*

PART A: Customer requirements

Situation: You are a sales representative at CollectThoughts.com, an American company providing a cloud-based platform that enables teams to upload, store and collaborate on documents.

→ **You discuss a customer's requirements and make him/her an offer.**

1 Asking the right questions

Your colleague Sebastian Heinz is meeting with Chris Petersen from Astrus Telecom. Astrus is interested in a new document management system and Sebastian wants to make sure he understands exactly what they need.

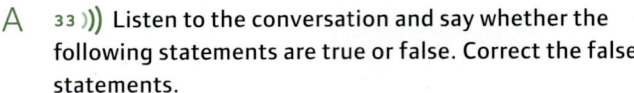

A 33))) **Listen to the conversation and say whether the following statements are true or false. Correct the false statements.**

1 Chris Petersen's team is a project management office.
2 The team manages project documents for part of the company.
3 The team has to run reports across all the project documents.
4 Chris Petersen's team doesn't need to do a lot of collaboration between many locations.
5 They can collate all of the emails and feedback in real time.
6 The team has a document management system that is difficult to use.
7 Most of the employees use the document management system.
8 The team needs a central place to search for all of the documents, feedback, etc.

B 33))) **Listen again and complete the questions that Sebastian uses to find out more from Chris Petersen.**

1 ▰ what responsibilities your team has?
2 Can you explain ▰ to manage?
3 ▰ some more details?
4 And could you ▰ how conference calls are used?
5 Could you tell me ▰ your current environment ▰?
6 ▰ most of your colleagues feel?
7 ▰ elaborate?
8 Can you tell me ▰ you?
9 ▰ an easy-to-use solution ▰?
10 ▰ a bit further?

C **Which questions in exercise 1B ask for ...**

a a yes/no answer? **b** specific information? **c** more information?

 **TOOLBOX**

to collate – *(Dokumente) zusammentragen, abgleichen*	to elaborate – *ins Detail gehen*
document management – *Dokumentenverwaltung*	essential – *unbedingt erforderlich*

2 Matching features to requirements

Sebastian has summarized the requirements from the meeting with Astrus Telecom and asks you to explain how CollectThoughts meets all these requirements.

A   First match the key requirements with the relevant CollectThoughts features.

Key requirements	CollectThoughts feature
1 remote working, with or without internet access	A support for all popular file formats such as .pdf, .doc, .xls, images and videos
2 data security	B user-friendly interface and simple uploading and sharing of information
3 simple collation of feedback	C allows online/offline access to information, and supports remote working
4 automated version control	D allows multiple users to provide simultaneous feedback
5 storage and viewing of information in many different formats	E industry-standard TLS/SSL encryption and two-step verification
6 high usage from non-technical people	F automatically manages versions and allows reversion to older versions with a few clicks

B   Demonstrate the unique selling proposition of CollectThoughts. Create statements using the requirements and features from exercise 2A and the words provided.

1   support remote working / by   *Supports remote working by allowing online and offline access to information.*
2   protect data security / using
3   simplify collation of feedback / by
4   reduce complexity of version control / by
5   make it easy to store and view information in different formats / with
6   increase usage from non-technical employees / via

3 Writing a follow-up email to a potential customer

Sebastian asks you to write a follow-up email to a potential customer in Germany.

Using the information in exercise 2, write a German email to follow up a meeting that you had with a potential customer in Germany. The customer has the following key requirements:

– data security
– automated version control
– viewing and storage of information from many sources and in many formats
– simple and immediate collation of feedback

4 Role-play: Finding out a customer's requirements

Now it is time for you to talk to a potential customer and find out their requirements.

 Partner A: Look at File 13 on page 139. **Partner B:** Look at File 14 on page 140.

› *Useful phrases: Advising customers, page 154; Asking for advice, page 155*

 TOOLBOX

TLS = Transport Layer Security   version control – *Versionsverwaltung*

PART B: A contract for cloud-based services

Situation: You are a sales representative at CollectThoughts.com, an American company that provides cloud-based platforms and software solutions.
→ **You negotiate the details of a contract with a customer and write an email to summarize the details of the agreement.**

1 Starting negotiations

Your colleague Sebastian Heinz receives an email from Astrus Telecom (see Part A) that details the next steps to agreeing a contract.

A **First match the following phrases to their German equivalents.**

1	affect the price	a	Nutzungsbedingungen
2	begin negotiations	b	den Preis beeinflussen
3	legally-binding agreement	c	ein Angebot überprüfen
4	reach an agreement	d	einen schriftlichen Vertrag unterzeichnen
5	review a proposal	e	Punkte auflisten
6	set out points	f	rechtsverbindliche Vereinbarung
7	sign a written contract	g	sich einigen
8	terms and conditions	h	Verhandlungen aufnehmen

B **Now complete the email with suitable English phrases from exercise 1A. Make any other changes that are necessary.**

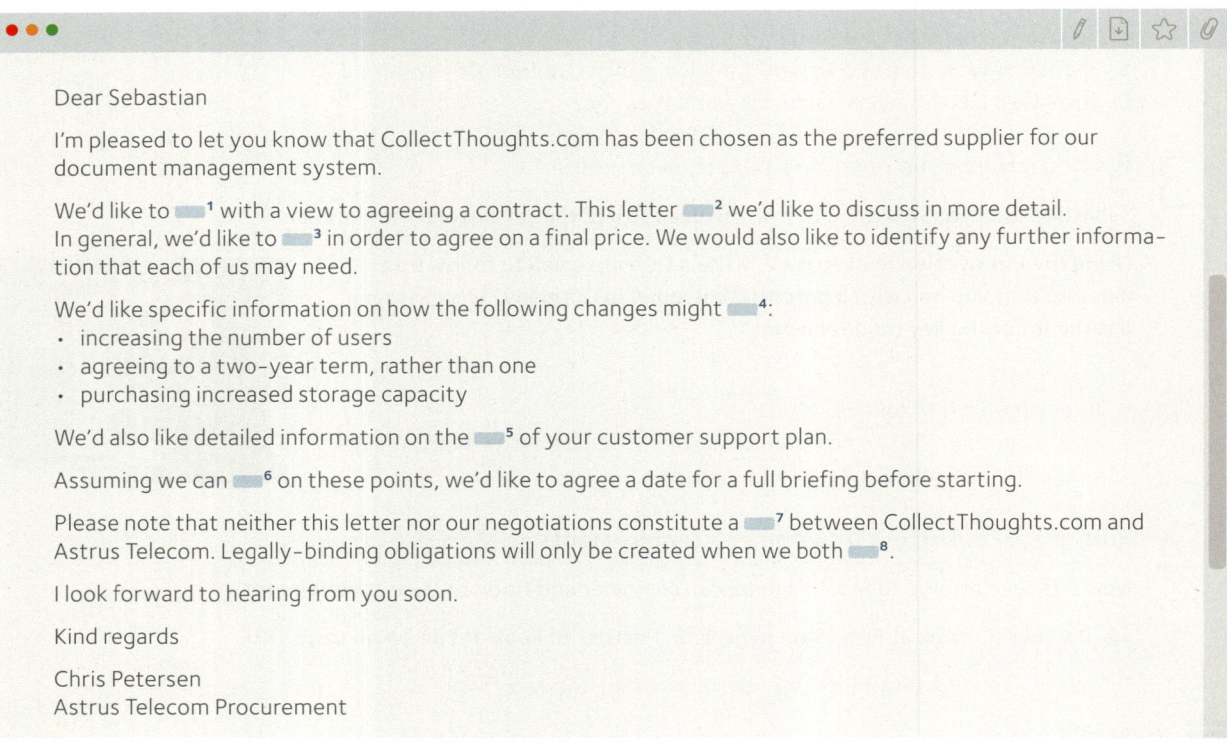

Dear Sebastian

I'm pleased to let you know that CollectThoughts.com has been chosen as the preferred supplier for our document management system.

We'd like to ▭¹ with a view to agreeing a contract. This letter ▭² we'd like to discuss in more detail. In general, we'd like to ▭³ in order to agree on a final price. We would also like to identify any further information that each of us may need.

We'd like specific information on how the following changes might ▭⁴:
- increasing the number of users
- agreeing to a two-year term, rather than one
- purchasing increased storage capacity

We'd also like detailed information on the ▭⁵ of your customer support plan.

Assuming we can ▭⁶ on these points, we'd like to agree a date for a full briefing before starting.

Please note that neither this letter nor our negotiations constitute a ▭⁷ between CollectThoughts.com and Astrus Telecom. Legally-binding obligations will only be created when we both ▭⁸.

I look forward to hearing from you soon.

Kind regards

Chris Petersen
Astrus Telecom Procurement

C **Read the email and explain the stages of the negotiation process to your partner.**

2 Negotiating the details of an agreement

Sebastian from CollectThoughts and Chris from Astrus Telecom are meeting to negotiate terms.

A   34))) **Listen to the negotiation and match the numbers (1–6) to what they refer to (a–f).**

1	10	a	discount offered on original number of licences
2	30	b	discount for purchasing an annual subscription
3	15	c	number of support calls per month
4	7%	d	increased storage capacity
5	20%	e	recommended number of extra licences
6	70	f	number of times clients usually call per month

B   34))) **Listen again. Complete what Sebastian replies when Chris makes the following requests using phrases from the language box below.**

1 Seeing as we are new customers, we were hoping that you would upgrade our customer support plan.
   › ▬▬ an upgrade to the premium support plan. … › ▬▬ upgrade the number of calls to 35.

2 Could you also do a better price on the support plan?
   › ▬▬ The extra support calls I'm offering are as good as unlimited, even for a team of your size.

3 Given we have so many users, could you give us a discount on that?
   › ▬▬ But you'll have to buy 15 extra licences.

4 And is a discount available if we purchase an annual licence?
   › ▬▬ If you pay annually instead of monthly, we'll give you a further 20% discount.

5 Could you give us a bit more of a discount?
   › ▬▬

6 Would you give us more storage capacity as a starting bonus, too?
   › ▬▬ How about a 40% increase from 50 GB to 70 GB?

> **Negotiating**
>
> **Accommodating changes to the offer**
> I have some room to move.
> OK. I'm prepared to offer you that.
> Yes, I think we can do that for you.
>
> **Refusing what the client asks for**
> I'm sorry, but the price that I quoted you is the best I can do.
> No. I'm afraid I can't do that.
> Well, I can't offer you … . But what I can do is …

› *Useful phrases: Negotiating, page 158*

3 Role-play: Negotiating the terms of an offer

Now it is time for you to negotiate the terms of an offer with a business partner and summarize what you have agreed on in a follow-up email.

A   👥 **Partner A:** Look at File 16 on page 141. **Partner B:** Look at File 18 on page 142.

B   **When you have finished negotiating, write an email to your partner confirming the agreements made.**

 TOOLBOX

preferred supplier – *bevorzugter Anbieter/Lieferant*

COMMUNICATION: The layout of business letters

> **Situation:** You work at Berlin Medical Systems, a company that manufactures computer hardware for clinics and hospitals. This week, you are helping out in the Sales department.
> → **You write an offer to a new customer in the UK.**

1 Reading an English business letter

Your supervisor gives you a letter of enquiry from a new customer.

Study the layout and match the parts (1–11) of the letter on page 99 to the labels below (a–k).

a address	**d** copies	**g** inside address	**j** signature
b body of the letter	**e** date	**h** reference initials	**k** subject line
c complimentary close	**f** enclosure	**i** salutation	

2 Writing an English business letter

Your supervisor asks you to write an offer to Ms Lambert at the Dryden Clinic.

A Complete the letter with suitable words and phrases from the list.

confirmation · deal with · delivery · discount · enclosing · enquiry · guaranteed · look forward to · offer · packed · price · this date

---

Thank you for your ▬▬¹ about operating theatre monitors. We are pleased to send you the following ▬▬²:

One (1) 32" OT-HD monitor. ▬▬³: €2700.00.

We can deliver within two weeks of ▬▬⁴ of your order. Terms of ▬▬⁵ are DAP your clinic.

This offer is valid for two weeks from ▬▬⁶. If you place your order within one week, we can also offer a 2% ▬▬⁷. All of our monitors are ▬▬⁸ for two years.

We will ▬▬⁹ your order carefully and quickly. The monitor will be ▬▬¹⁰ in a wooden packing crate.

I am ▬▬¹¹ a copy of our latest catalogue and price list and ▬▬¹² future orders.

> › *Useful phrases: Writing offers, page 159*

B Write the complete offer, using the correct layout for a business letter, a suitable salutation and complimentary close, today's date, etc. Use the addresses from the letter on page 99.

> › *Useful phrases: Writing business letters, page 158*

➜ Salutation and complimentary closes in letters

	Salutation	Complimentary close
to a firm	Dear Sir or Madam	Yours faithfully (BE)
		Yours very truly / Cordially yours (AE)
to a person	Dear Mr Brown	Yours sincerely (BE)
	Dear Sharon	Sincerely yours / Best personal regards (AE)

TOOLBOX

---

confirmation of an order – *Auftragsbestätigung*
terms of delivery and payment – *Liefer- und Zahlungsbedingungen*

trade magazine – *Fachzeitschrift*
trial order – *Probebestellung*

1 Dryden Clinic
17 Dryden Street
London SE9 2BS
+44 (0)20 129546783
info@drydenclinic.com

2 29 April 20..

3 Our ref: LL/DC

4 Berlin Medical Systems
Rudower Straße 250
12489 Berlin
GERMANY

5 Dear Sir or Madam

6 **Enquiry about operating theatre monitors**

7 We have seen your advertisement in this month's editon of the trade magazine "Medical Business". We see that your company sells medical hardware.

We are a large outpatient clinic in London. We are planning to update our operating theatres and are interested in high-definition operating theatre monitors. We would like to place a trial order for one 32" OT-HD monitor. If the product is suitable, we may place further orders.

Please note that the housing of the monitor should be completely sealed and DIN EN60601 certified dust- and waterproof.

Please let us have details of your terms of delivery and payment. We would also like to know what type of packaging you use to protect the monitor during transport.

Many thanks for your attention to our enquiry. We look forward to hearing from you soon.

8 Yours faithfully

9 *Linda Lambert*
Linda Lambert
Clinic Manager

10 cc Dr Alice Black

11 Enc: Information pack "Dryden Clinic"

DAS KANN ICH (Unit 9)

– Einen Bericht über ein neues Videokonferenzsystem auf Englisch schreiben. (Foundation)
– Die Bedürfnisse eines Kunden / einer Kundin besprechen und ein Angebot auf Englisch formulieren. (Part A)
– Die Details eines Verkaufsvertrags mit einem Kunden / einer Kundin aushandeln und in einer E-Mail festhalten. (Part B)
– Ein Angebot auf Englisch erstellen. (Communication)

FOUNDATION: Technology for the disabled

Situation: You are getting work experience at AccessAble Ltd, a British company that sells materials and designs for 3D printers. The company's products allow people to print low-cost prosthetics at home.

→ **You call a customer and confirm an order by email.**

1 Reading about the product

To help you prepare for a phone call to a customer, you read the company website and note down the advantages and properties of AccessAble materials.

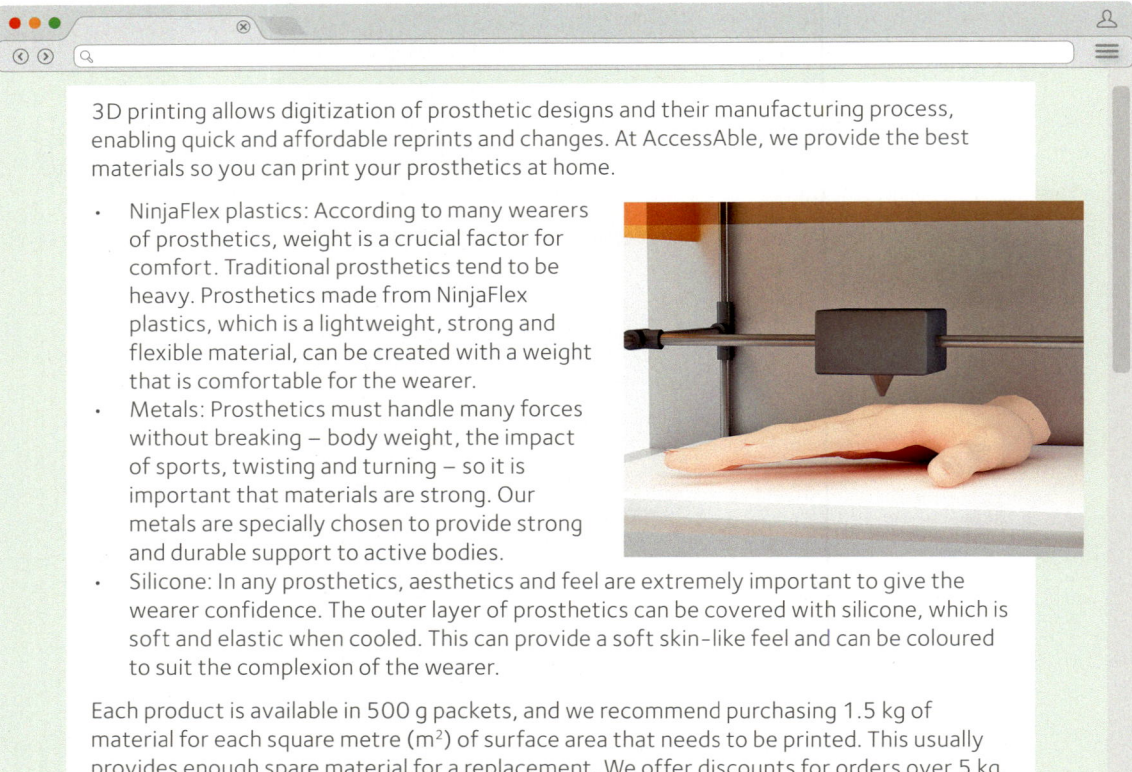

3D printing allows digitization of prosthetic designs and their manufacturing process, enabling quick and affordable reprints and changes. At AccessAble, we provide the best materials so you can print your prosthetics at home.

- NinjaFlex plastics: According to many wearers of prosthetics, weight is a crucial factor for comfort. Traditional prosthetics tend to be heavy. Prosthetics made from NinjaFlex plastics, which is a lightweight, strong and flexible material, can be created with a weight that is comfortable for the wearer.
- Metals: Prosthetics must handle many forces without breaking – body weight, the impact of sports, twisting and turning – so it is important that materials are strong. Our metals are specially chosen to provide strong and durable support to active bodies.
- Silicone: In any prosthetics, aesthetics and feel are extremely important to give the wearer confidence. The outer layer of prosthetics can be covered with silicone, which is soft and elastic when cooled. This can provide a soft skin-like feel and can be coloured to suit the complexion of the wearer.

Each product is available in 500 g packets, and we recommend purchasing 1.5 kg of material for each square metre (m²) of surface area that needs to be printed. This usually provides enough spare material for a replacement. We offer discounts for orders over 5 kg. You can also sign up to our subscription service that delivers an agreed amount every month at a reduced price.

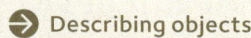 With a partner, discuss the advantages of the materials on the AccessAble website and make notes that you can use when talking to the customer. Copy and complete the table below to sort your notes.

Material	Properties	Advantages for wearer
Ninjaflex	▬	▬
Metals	▬	▬
Silicone	▬	▬

> **Describing objects**
>
> Our products **are made** from Semiflex plastics.
> Our metals **are** specially **chosen** to provide strong and durable support.
> The outer layer of prosthetics **can be covered** with silicone.

› *Grammar: Passive forms, page 164*

2 Role-play: Calling a customer

Your supervisor tells you that a prospective customer, Chris Young, would like some information before placing an order. He asks you to call the customer.

Partner A: Look here. **Partner B:** Look at File 17 on page 141.

Partner A
Read the website on page 100 (exercise 1) again and prepare to answer the customer's questions.

- Ring Chris Young, introduce yourself and explain why you are calling.
- Answer his/her questions using the information on the website and your notes.
- Suggest that s/he selects the sports plastics package and the sports metal package and explain the reasons why. Add that silicone is also advisable.
- Explain the discounts available and the subscription service.
- Say that you will confirm his/her order by email.

Swap roles when you have finished.

› *Useful phrases: Telephoning, page 152; Advising customers, page 154*

3 Confirming the order

Your supervisor asks you to confirm the customer's order by email.

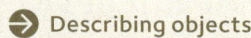 Work with the same partner as in exercise 2. Write an email to Chris Young using the prompts and information below.

- refer to your telephone conversation
- confirm the order
- summarize the weight of the order including protective packaging (300g)
- give the expected delivery time
- confirm delivery by insured registered post
- provide a receipt confirming discount
- attach a product catalogue & price list

› *Useful phrases: Writing emails, page 153*

 TOOLBOX

complexion – *Teint, Hautfarbe*
confidence – *Selbstvertrauen*

durable – *strapazierfähig*
prosthetic – *Prothese*

PART A: Health devices

> **Situation:** You've just started working for FitNext, a company in Melbourne, Australia, that provides smartwatches and wristbands as well as software services to help customers achieve their health goals.
> → **You find out about a customer's needs and recommend a product.**

1 Understanding the services

As a new employee, you take the company's online induction course. You are directed to the intranet page that explains the basic technologies in FitNext smartwatches.

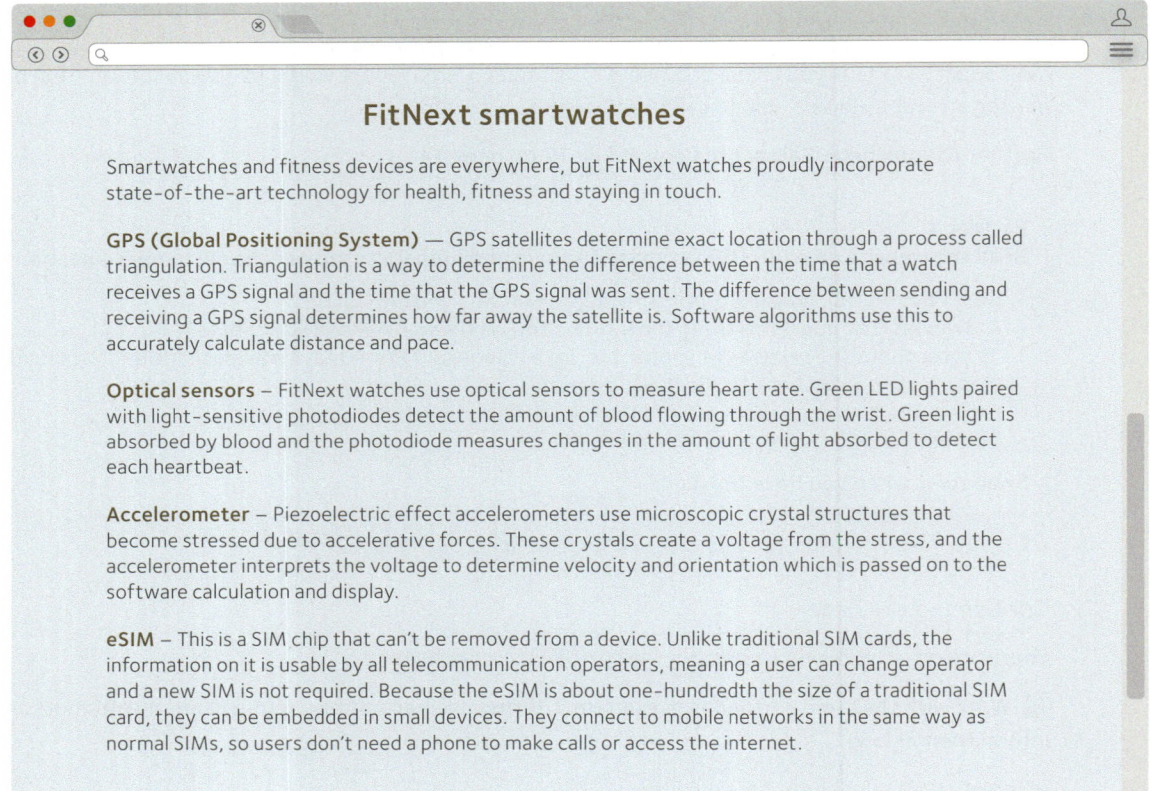

FitNext smartwatches

Smartwatches and fitness devices are everywhere, but FitNext watches proudly incorporate state-of-the-art technology for health, fitness and staying in touch.

GPS (Global Positioning System) — GPS satellites determine exact location through a process called triangulation. Triangulation is a way to determine the difference between the time that a watch receives a GPS signal and the time that the GPS signal was sent. The difference between sending and receiving a GPS signal determines how far away the satellite is. Software algorithms use this to accurately calculate distance and pace.

Optical sensors – FitNext watches use optical sensors to measure heart rate. Green LED lights paired with light-sensitive photodiodes detect the amount of blood flowing through the wrist. Green light is absorbed by blood and the photodiode measures changes in the amount of light absorbed to detect each heartbeat.

Accelerometer – Piezoelectric effect accelerometers use microscopic crystal structures that become stressed due to accelerative forces. These crystals create a voltage from the stress, and the accelerometer interprets the voltage to determine velocity and orientation which is passed on to the software calculation and display.

eSIM – This is a SIM chip that can't be removed from a device. Unlike traditional SIM cards, the information on it is usable by all telecommunication operators, meaning a user can change operator and a new SIM is not required. Because the eSIM is about one-hundredth the size of a traditional SIM card, they can be embedded in small devices. They connect to mobile networks in the same way as normal SIMs, so users don't need a phone to make calls or access the internet.

A Read the article and make notes on which technology achieves each of the following results – and how.

1 determine distance and pace
2 measure heart rate
3 detect velocity and orientation
4 connect to the internet

B 👥 Work in groups. Do internet research on the following technologies found in smartwatches. Explain to the group how they work and what function they perform in smartwatches.

– altimeter   – thermometer   – compass

 **TOOLBOX**

orientation – *Orientierung, Ausrichtung*	velocity – *Geschwindigkeit*
pace – *Tempo*	voltage – *(elektrische) Spannung*

2 Comparing different devices

You study three of the most popular models from FitNext. You need to fully understand the capabilities of each model as you are starting work in the store tomorrow as part of your induction course.

Model	Sirius 3	Runner 5X	FitnessMate
Image			
Lens material	sapphire crystal	strengthened glass	strengthened glass
Case material	stainless steel or titanium	polymer	plastic
Strap material	silicone, steel, titanium	silicone	silicone
Physical size	49 x 49 x 15 mm	47 x 47 x 13.9 mm	35.5 x 40.7 x 13.3 mm
Weight	steel & silicone band: 96 g, steel & steel band: 186 g, titanium & silicone band: 76 g titanium & titanium band: 112 g	49 g	37.3 g
Display size	1.2" (30.4 mm) diameter	1.0" (25.4 mm) diameter	23.5 x 23.4 mm
Display resolution	218 x 218 pixels	240 x 240 pixels	128 x 128 pixels
GPS	Yes	Yes	No
Heart rate monitor	Yes	Yes	Yes
Barometric altimeter	Yes	No	No
Compass	Yes	Yes	No
Accelerometer	Yes	Yes	Yes
Thermometer	Yes	No	No
Waterproof	Yes to 50 m	Yes to 10 m	Rain and splash only
Colour display	Yes	Yes	No
Battery life	Up to 24 hours	Up to 40 hours	Up to 18 hours
Connectivity	Bluetooth, Wi-Fi, eSIM	Bluetooth, Wi-Fi, eSIM	Bluetooth, USB
Price	$999	$499	$99

 Rate each of the watches as best, second best or worst in each of the following categories. Go online if you need to. Give reasons for your ratings as some of them will be subjective.

- scratch resistance?   - fashionable?   - comprehensiveness?
- lightweight?   - practicality?   - ease of reading information?

🧰 TOOLBOX

polymer – *Polymer, Kunststoff*   strap – *Armband*
sapphire crystal – *Saphirglas*   titanium – *Titan*

3 Answering customer questions

When you start work in the store, you overhear a conversation between a colleague and a customer.

A 35))) ▶ **Listen and state whether the following are true or false. Correct the false statements.**

1 The customer wants to get better at running.
2 She already has a smartwatch.
3 She doesn't spend time in water.
4 Leaving her phone at home while running very important.
5 She lives in a flat area.
6 She intends to wear it to work.

B **Work with a partner. Decide together which model you would recommend to the customer. Present your recommendation and explain your reasons to the class.**

4 Recommending a smartwatch to a customer

You are now working in the FitNext store. You ask a customer questions so that you can recommend an appropriate smartwatch.

Work with a partner and role-play a sales conversation.
Partner A: Find out what the customer needs and recommend a suitable product from the list in exercise 2.
Partner B: Ask questions about the different technologies and why they are important.

Swap roles when you have finished.

When you are the customer, you can choose from one of the customer profiles below or choose to be yourself.

Customer 1	Customer 2
Age: 43	**Age:** 37
Job:	**Job:**
– manager at large company	– freelance writer
Lifestyle:	**Lifestyle:**
– semi-active	– very active; lives for sport
– jogs every now and then	– young family
– goes to gym occasionally	– runs marathons 4 times per year
– rides bike casually (less than 10 km)	– does triathlons 2–3 times per year
– no water sports	– surfs every week
– fashion-conscious	– hikes
Why interested:	– prefers T-shirts to shirts
– wants to improve health; having a monitor on wrist will help motivation	**Why interested:**
– curious about own energy use	– needs a new smartwatch after previous one broke
	– needs to be on call for family

› *Useful phrases: Asking for advice, page 155; Advising customers, page 154*

PART B: Software as a service

> **Situation:** You have now joined the IT Support department of FitNext, a company in Melbourne, Australia that provides smartwatches and armbands. They are considering moving their internal office software to a subscription payment model.
> → **You order cameras and cloud storage for your office security system.**

1 Comparing payment models

Your supervisor asks you to compare payment models for office software. You compare two options: purchasing the software or subscribing to the software.

	One-time purchase	Subscription payments
Payments	Pay a single, one-time fee	Pay a recurring small monthly fee OR Save by paying for a full year up front
Software version	Most recent version of the application	Most recent version of the application
Feature updates	Security updates included; upgrades to major releases aren't included	Latest features and updates available, including major upgrades to newer versions
Number of installations	One-time purchases are designed for a single operating system	Applications can be installed on up to 5 desktops, which may include different operating systems; can be shared with other household members
Mobile devices	Basic editing features available via browser versions of tablet or smartphone software	Full version of software can be installed on up to 5 tablets and 5 smartphones
Extra online storage	Not included	1 TB of cloud storage per user, for up to 5 users
Technical support	Technical support is included for initial installation only	Technical, subscription and billing support available throughout subscription at no extra cost
Duration of software use	Unlimited after purchase	Access to software available only as long as monthly access fee is paid
Cancellation policy	None	Monthly subscription can be cancelled at any time Annual subscription can only be cancelled after contract expires
Cost	$119	$7.99 per month (annual purchase) $9.99 per month (monthly subscription)

A Work with a partner. Discuss which payment model you would choose for the following types of company software.

1 software that is extremely important to the company – it should always provide the most up-to-date features
2 software that is only used a few times a year
3 software that is important, but that doesn't need to be the latest version
4 software used by three employees that work on mobile devices as well as desktops; it only requires basic editing and doesn't need to be the latest version

B Work in groups and list the software that you pay a monthly subscription for and which you pay for up front. Explain why you choose one way of payment over another. Is there any subscription software you wish you could pay for up front? What about vice-versa?

2 Ordering software online

The IT Support department has decided that the company's graphic design software should be a subscription purchase. You look at an online order form to determine the upfront and recurring costs.

KreateSoftware.com			Your order
[1]	[2]	[3]	[4]
DreamKreate Bundle	3	$29.99 per month per user	✕
2 TB cloud storage	3	$9.99 per month per user	✕
Training video access	3	$4.99 per month per user	✕
1 day trainer	1	$1,499.00 one off	✕
[5] **(15% off training)**		$224.86	
[6] **(paid now)**		$1409.06	
[7] (monthly)		$134.91	
12 months [8]			

Place order

TOOLBOX

annual – *jährlich*
cancellation policy – *Kündigungsbedingungen*
to expire – *auslaufen*

one-time purchase – *einmaliger Kauf*
subscription – *Abonnement*

A   First match the German words (1–8) with the correct English terms (a–h).

1	Einzelpreis	a	discount
2	erste Zahlung / Anfangszahlung	b	initial payment
3	löschen/entfernen	c	item
4	Menge/Stückzahl	d	minimum commitment
5	Mindestvertragslaufzeit	e	price per item
6	Artikel	f	quantity
7	Rabatt	g	recurring payment
8	wiederkehrende/turnusmäßige Zahlung	h	remove

B   Now match the correct English terms (a–h) above to the numbers on the online order form on page 106.

C   Your supervisor calls and asks you about the cost of graphic design software. Give him a quick summary of the following information:

– what you suggest purchasing
– what it will cost
– what you will save
– what your commitment will be

3 Ordering security software and hardware

You are talking to your company's telecommunications provider. This company also offers cameras and cloud storage options for your office security.

👥 Work with a partner and create a sales dialogue, using the prompts below.

Partner A	Partner B
You are from FitNext and want security equipment for the FitNext offices.	You are the salesperson in the store.
– The offices are on three floors of 80m² each. – You need to store at least 2 years of data. – You want high-resolution cameras. – You expect a significant discount.	– All of your security packages come with cameras and storage and are paid monthly, with a minimum 2-year commitment. – The most suitable camera is the HS model; it films in high resolution and allows for high zoom. – They need 12 cameras to cover their offices. – Recommend a storage option of 10 TB immediate access and 100 TB archived files. This is about 3 years of storage.

Swap roles when you have finished.

› *Useful phrases: Asking for advice, page 155; Advising customers, page 154*

COMMUNICATION: Enquiries, offers and orders

Situation: You are getting some work experience at AccessAble Ltd, a British company that sells materials and designs for 3D printers. The company's products allow people to print low-cost prosthetics at home.

→ **You write an enquiry and an order to a supplier; then you write an offer to a customer.**

1 Checking language for enquiries

You check that you know suitable English phrases for writing a letter of enquiry.

Match the phrases and sentences from a German letter of enquiry (a–i) to the English equivalents (1–9).

TIP

You will find similar phrases in the model letter on page 99.

a Wir haben Ihre Anzeige … gesehen.
b Wir sind ein/eine … in Deutschland.
c Wir haben vor, …
d Wir interessieren uns …
e Wir möchten eine Probebestellung … aufgeben.
f Wenn das Produkt / die Dienstleistungen Ihrer Firma unsere Voraussetzungen erfüllen, …
g Bitte nennen Sie uns Einzelheiten …
h Die … Bank wird Ihnen gerne Referenzen zukommen lassen.
i Wir freuen uns, bald von Ihnen zu hören.

1 If the product is suitable …
2 … *(name of bank)* will be happy to supply references.
3 Please let us have details …
4 We are a … *(type of firm)* in Germany.
5 We are interested in …
6 We are planning …
7 We have seen your advertisement …
8 We look forward to hearing from you soon.
9 We would like to place a trial order …

2 Writing an enquiry for calibration equipment

AccessAble Ltd is looking for a supplier of calibration equipment. Jane Ruby, the Quality Control Manager, asks you to write a letter of enquiry to a manufacturer. She gives you the following details.

👥 **Work with a partner. Write a letter of enquiry to MCE using the notes on the right. Add today's date and your own reference numbers. Remember to use the correct salutation and complimentary close.**

› *Useful phrases: Writing enquiries, page 158*

TIP

The letter on page 99 will help you with the layout.

Enquiry to MCE – Medical Calibration Equipment, Silverbank Industrial Estate, B5, Ferry Road, Edinburgh EH4 2EF
I found their details online.

· Tell them who we are and what we do.
· Say that we're extending the Quality Control Department and we need more calibration equipment.
· Ask about a trial order for one calibration machine.
· Say that if the trial order is OK, we'll place another order.
· Ask for terms of delivery / payment.
· Give Barclays Bank, Manchester as a reference.
· Sign it with your name and let me have a copy.

Thanks,
Jane

 **TOOLBOX**

calibration equipment – *Kalibriergerät*

3 Writing an order for calibration equipment

Neil McCain, the sales manager from Medical Calibration in Edinburgh, has replied to your enquiry. Jane Ruby is happy with the offer and asks you to write the order.

Write the complete order using Jane Ruby's notes.

> · Thank Mr McCain for his reply to our letter of enquiry.
> · Confirm the trial order for one calibration machine.
> · The price we agreed is £ 362 including VAT.
> · Agree to the terms: delivery on payment.
> · Thank Mr McCain for his attention to our order.
> · Say that if the product is suitable, we will place a second order.

Start like this and end with a suitable complimentary close.

Dear Mr McCain
Thank you for your reply to our letter of enquiry.
We would like to confirm …

› *Useful phrases: Writing orders, page 159*

4 Writing an offer for wheelchairs

Your supervisor took a call from a customer earlier today. She gives you her notes and asks you to write an offer.

Read your supervisor's notes then write the offer following the scheme below.

– Thank customer for the enquiry (give today's date).
– Thank for the interest in your company's products.
– Give details of terms of delivery and payment.
– Say that you are enclosing a price list and catalogue as requested.
– Express hope that you will hear from Ms Smith soon.

› *Useful phrases: Writing offers, page 159*

> Call from Ms Alana Smith, 25 Westways Road, Manchester M13 4PG;
> email: smithalana22@gmail.com
>
> Re: 1 AAXS 3D printer   £ 299.00
>   2 kg NinjaFlex   £ 49.90 / kg
>   2 kg Metals   £ 35.90 / kg
>   2 kg Silicone   £ 29.90 / kg
>
> Terms: delivery on payment
> Delivery: insured post, within 2 working days of payment
> Discount for new customer: 5 %
> Would like a current price list and catalogue

DAS KANN ICH (Unit 10)

– Einen Kunden / Eine Kundin telefonisch beraten; eine Bestellung per E-Mail bestätigen. (Foundation)
– Ein Kundenberatungsgespräch auf Englisch führen. (Part A)
– Eine Bestellung für ein neues Sicherheitssystem aufgeben. (Part B)
– Eine Anfrage und eine Bestellung auf Englisch schreiben; ein Angebot erstellen. (Communication)

1 Hörverstehen: B2

Sie arbeiten in der IT-Abteilung eines großen Klinikkonzerns. Der Einkaufsleiter schickt Ihnen den Link zu einem Podcast über intelligente Teppiche. Er bittet Sie, ihm folgende Fragen zu beantworten.

36))) Hören Sie das Interview und machen Sie sich Notizen zu den Fragen auf Deutsch.

1 Wo wurden intelligente Teppiche entwickelt?
2 Welche Personendaten kann der Teppich sammeln? Welche nicht?
3 Warum kann der Teppich zwischen Männern und Frauen unterscheiden?
4 Beschreiben Sie den Datenfluss vom Teppich zum Monitor.
5 Welche praktischen Anwendungen gibt es?

2 Produktion: B1

Sie absolvieren ein Praktikum in einem Klinikum in Berlin. Die kaufmännische Leiterin bittet Sie, sich bei einem Anbieter von Hotel- und Krankenhausausstattung über intelligente Teppiche zu erkundigen.

Schreiben Sie eine Anfrage in englischer Sprache an EVW Hotel & Clinic Requisites unter Berücksichtigung folgender Punkte:

– **Absender:** Paracelsius Klinikum, Potsdamer Straße 250, 12345 Berlin
– **Anschrift:** EVW Hotel & Clinic Requisites, Dryden Street, London SE9 2BS
– **Bezug:** Artikel in *Medical Business* über intelligente Teppiche
– **Grund der Anfrage:** Auslegung eines Korridors mit einem intelligenten Teppich; Farbe blau
– **Anforderungen:** Orientierungshilfe für Patienten im Dunkeln
– **Auftrag:** Probebestellung für einen Korridor; bei Erfüllung der Anforderungen Folgeaufträge
– **Bitte:** Preisauskunft pro Quadratmeter, Zusendung der Zahlungsbedingungen und Lieferzeiten
– Angemessener Schlusssatz

3 Leseverstehen: B1/B2

Sie arbeiten in der Technikzentrale eines deutschen Klinikums. Ihr Kollege soll eine Präsentation über ein neues bildgebendes Verfahren für die Anatomie halten. Er gibt Ihnen einen englischen Text über Mixed Reality (MR) und bittet Sie, ihm bei den Fragen zu helfen.

Beantworten Sie die Fragen zum Text auf Seite 111 stichwortartig auf Deutsch.

1 Welche zwei Möglichkeiten des Einsatzes von MR beschreibt der Text?
2 Welche Nachteile hat die traditionelle Ausbildung von Anatomiestudenten?
3 Warum heißt die neue Technologie „Mixed Reality"?
4 Welche Vorteile hat der Einsatz von HoloLens in der Anatomie? Nennen Sie einige Beispiele.
5 Welchen Nachteil haben traditionelle bildgebende Verfahren?
6 Wie können Chirurgen mit den Hologrammen interagieren?
7 Wie profitiert die Entwicklung neuer chirurgischer Methoden von MR?

Mixed Reality (MR) in modern medicine

For centuries, medical students have explored the anatomy of the body using animal and human cadavers. However, dead bodies are not the same as living humans: colours change as the lungs stop functioning and the textures are not the same. Moreover, the chemicals used to keep the bodies in good condition can cause allergies, and the laboratories are expensive to maintain. But masks, chemicals, scalpels and the expensive storage of cadavers might soon belong to the past. With new technology, students won't have to use scalpels to get to the inside of a body. Mixed reality will save time and money, and will become the ideal tool for training and educational purposes.

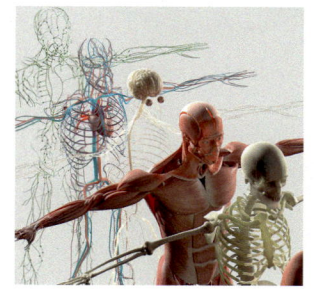

This new technology is called mixed reality because it combines virtual reality, augmented reality and holographic imaging. Combining a HoloLens headset with an anatomy app, both developed by Microsoft, provides students with an experience that goes beyond virtual reality and augmented reality. Let us explore one of its uses in medical education. Professional actors are filmed simulating real-world conditions and the video images are transformed into holograms that can be placed into any environment. Students in the real world are able to walk around the holographic models, study them, and make a diagnosis. They see all the different structures in three dimensions from whatever perspective they choose: With a tap they can strip layer after layer from the body and navigate through the skin, muscle, veins, arteries, and organs to the skeleton below. They can turn the heart around and see how it pumps blood around the body, and where each of the veins and arteries leads to.

HoloLens will also benefit patients who are going to have a complicated operation. Up to now, teams performing operations have used images created by computer tomography (CT) and magnetic resonance imaging (MRI) before and during the operation. These scanners provide detailed views of the patient's body. However, they present these images only in the form of two-dimensional slices. When a doctor puts on the HoloLens headsets, they can create 3D models of their patient using the data collected by their scanners. HoloLens displays this information while they are performing the operation. They can, for example, zoom in and rotate a 3D model of an organ in the patient they are operating on. Using air tap and voice commands, they can interact with the holograms. Another advantage is that the surgeon can share their opinion either locally or via videoconference with colleagues or students, which makes the technology an ideal tool for quality control and for the presentation of new surgical techniques.

4 Interaktion: B1/B2

Die Leitung eines Klinikums in London möchte eine Präsentation von *HoloLens-Anatomy* organisieren.

 Führen Sie mit Ihrem Partner / Ihrer Partnerin ein Gespräch anhand der Rollenkarten, um diese Präsentation vorzubereiten.

Partner A: Look here. **Partner B:** Look at File 19 on page 142.

Sie sind Angestellte/r in der IT Support-Abteilung des Klinikums und sollen die Präsentation organisieren. Sie begrüßen den Vertreter / die Vertreterin von HoloMed Ltd in Ihrem Büro.

Ihre Fragen:	Ihre Auskünfte:
– möglicher Termin für die Präsentation?	– Grund für die Präsentation: fehlgeschlagener Versuch, ein Labor zu simulieren; Touchscreens nur zweidimensional
– Kosten der Präsentation?	
– Headset für alle Teilnehmer?	– Vorführraum: kleiner Hörsaal (*lecture hall*)
– Wie sehen Studenten die Hologramme ohne Headset?	– Teilnehmerzahl: 30 Studenten, 5 Ärzte
	– große Leinwand
– Lieferzeit ab Auftragserteilung?	– Bestellung von drei Systemen, falls Anforderungen erfüllt

11 Problems and complaints

FOUNDATION: Technology and the environment

Situation: You work in the Sustainability department of an international computer manufacturer.
→ **You reply to a comment about technology and the environment on a web forum.**

1 Reading about environmental issues

You attend a workshop on information technology and sustainability. To start you off, the trainer asks your group to brainstorm the influence IT has on the environment.

<u>Sustainability</u>
· development of non-harmful materials and technologies
· replacing harmful materials

Consumption
- non-renewable resources are used to produce technological equipment
- resources used to generate electricity for technology
- some renewable resources being used faster than they can renew

Waste
· manufacturing technology causes climate change
· pollution through used computers and electronic waste
· special disposal requires a lot of energy use

Research
· experts from all fields and locations can share research
· better, smarter solutions for disposing of waste and feeding the planet
· improved understanding of medical problems
· access to huge amounts of data from anyone, anywhere at anytime

Health hazards
· toxic materials in computers & smartphones = health hazard
· people addicted to their smartphones
· technology addiction leads to obesity and physical problems

Paperless
· email and online payments reduce the amount of trees used
· office printing often not needed

Disrupting ecology
- animal habitats destroyed by data centres / manufacturing plants
- pollution contaminates the food chain
- CO_2 consumption contributes to climate change

Intelligence
- smarter technologies respond to how we use them
- adjust themselves to reduce climate change
- we understand that we have an impact on climate change

 TOOLBOX

consumption – *Verbrauch*
pollution – *(Umwelt-)Verschmutzung*
renewable resources *pl* – *erneuerbare Rohstoffe*

sustainability – *Nachhaltigkeit*
toxic – *giftig*
waste – *Abfall, Müll*

A 👥 With a partner, organize the headings into positive and negative impacts.

B Describe in your own words how the following areas are being influenced by IT:

– health   – ecology   – climate

C 👥 In groups, discuss whether IT has a positive or negative effect on our health and the environment.

2 Understanding a presentation

The trainer talks about how much energy some everyday technologies consume.

A Before you listen, match the German words (1–6) to the English words (a–f) in the list.

1	Akku	4	CO_2-Fußabdruck	a	battery	d	dissolve
2	(sich) auflösen	5	in Zahlen bestimmen	b	carbon dioxide	e	greenhouse gas
3	CO_2	6	Treibhausgas	c	carbon footprint	f	quantify

B 37)) ▶ Read the statements below. Then listen to the presentation and complete the notes.

The energy used by a single email can multiply quickly:
– an ordinary email uses ▬[1] of CO_2.
– a 1 MB attachment pushes CO_2 emission up to ▬[2].
– the forwarding and storage of the attachment could use as much as ▬[3] of CO_2.
– A traditional 4-page letter, sent by post, generates roughly ▬[4] of CO_2.
According to Netflix, the average customer has a carbon footprint of ▬[5] per year, which is about ▬[6] of the typical American household use.
Televisions are using more energy due to larger screen sizes. Per hour …
– an old 32-inch CRT television used ▬[7] of CO_2.
– a 15-inch LCD TV uses ▬[8] of CO_2.
– a 42-inch plasma TV uses ▬[9] of CO_2.
Streaming an album ▬[10] times uses the same amount of energy as producing and shipping a CD.

3 Suggesting improvements

The trainer asks you to discuss what technology providers could do to improve their record on environmental issues. She writes some points on the board.

👥 Talk in groups. Expand on the suggestions for dealing with environmental issues related to the manufacture of technology. Add your own ideas.

> *use clean energy sources / offer recycling programmes at no cost / turn off rather than stand-by mode / cut down on packaging / build in cooler areas / use recycled materials / create better materials / put limits on usage / make services more expensive*

4 Replying to a comment on a forum

At the end of the workshop, the trainer points out the following comment on a forum. She asks you to write a reply.

"So many people complain about the effects of technology on our surroundings. Why don't people understand that we can't produce technological equipment without damaging the environment?"

Give your opinion on the topic. Mention the pros and cons you have discovered and discussed on these pages to give examples to illustrate your opinion.

PART A: Cyberattacks

Situation: You are a customer service representative at SkillUpU.com, a company that offers online business-related courses, as well as in-house training courses at various locations around England.
→ **You reply to a customer complaint.**

1 Reading an email of complaint

SkillUpU accepts online payments for its courses and requires students to create an account with their payment details. You receive an email of complaint from a student.

From:	elario.morrison@samail.co.sa
To:	customerservice@SkillUpU.co.uk
Subject:	**Account hacked!**

Your security is a FAIL – my account has been hacked!

I received three emails this morning saying that I booked courses last night – while I was asleep! Conveniently, they are three of your most expensive courses – a total amount of £3600!

Sure enough, I checked my credit card and there are three entries, all with today's date, with SkillUpU as the payment recipient.

How could this happen given the amazingly secure encryption SkillUpU advertises??? You know what – your security is not amazing. In fact, you've got major problems with your security!

I'm really angry about this – I demand a full refund!

You'd better fix this immediately!

Elario Morrison

A Read the email of complaint and do the following tasks.

1 Summarize the problem and how it was discovered.
2 Describe the tone of the email.
3 Do you think that this is the right way to write a complaint in this situation?

B Change the following complaints to make them more polite. Use the phrases from the language box.

1 I'm telling you loud and clear that I'm very disappointed about the security measures.
2 You'd better get back to me by the end of the day.
3 You have a big problem with your customer account security.
4 I demand that you refund the amount of these purchases in full.
5 I'm angry about wasting my time to deal with this.
6 Your security has failed – my account has been hacked!
7 I'm telling you to fix this ASAP.

> **➔ Making a complaint**
>
> I'm afraid I've got a complaint (about) …
> I request that …
> I'm sorry to say this but …
> There could be a problem with the …
> Can I ask that you …
> I would appreciate it if you'd …
> I'm not happy about …

› *Useful phrases: Making complaints, page 160*

C   Write a more polite version of the email of complaint in exercise 1A.

D    Discuss the differences between the polite and impolite ways of complaining.

– Which style of complaining do you hear most often? Which do you use?
– When would you use each style?

2   Replying to a complaint

You pass the complaint on to the IT Security team at SkillUpU. In the meantime, you reply to the customer.

A   Complete the email using phrases from the language box below.

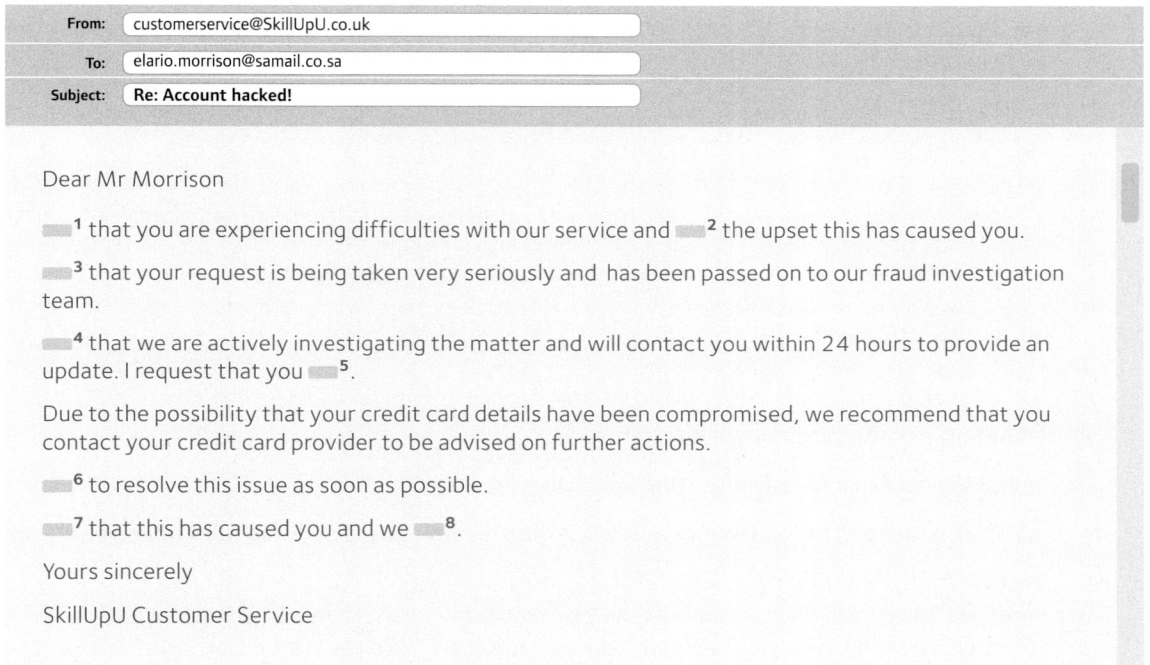

From:	customerservice@SkillUpU.co.uk
To:	elario.morrison@samail.co.sa
Subject:	Re: Account hacked!

Dear Mr Morrison

▬▬ [1] that you are experiencing difficulties with our service and ▬▬ [2] the upset this has caused you.

▬▬ [3] that your request is being taken very seriously and has been passed on to our fraud investigation team.

▬▬ [4] that we are actively investigating the matter and will contact you within 24 hours to provide an update. I request that you ▬▬ [5].

Due to the possibility that your credit card details have been compromised, we recommend that you contact your credit card provider to be advised on further actions.

▬▬ [6] to resolve this issue as soon as possible.

▬▬ [7] that this has caused you and we ▬▬ [8].

Yours sincerely

SkillUpU Customer Service

> → **Replying to a complaint**
>
> I can assure you (that) …   Please be assured (that) …
> I'm very sorry to hear (that) …   We are doing everything we can (to) …
> I would like to apologize for …   We regret any inconvenience (that) …
> Please bear with us in the meantime.   We thank you for your patience.

> › *Useful phrases: Dealing with complaints, page 160*

B   Answer the following questions.

– How are SkillUpU handling the complaint?
– What actions has Elario been asked to take?

🧰 TOOLBOX

to compromise sth – *(Daten) unberechtigt nutzen, gefährden*   to investigate – *untersuchen*
fraud – *Betrug*   to resolve sth – *etw klären*

3   Replying to a complaint about credit card management

The customer service team receives a further complaint about credit card management.

Write a reply to Brian Jenson and cover the following points:

- apologize for the difficulties
- you are aware that the process is confusing for many users
- provide a link to the instructions for changing an expired credit card
- advise him that you will follow up in 24 hours to check his progress
- you will ensure that the service is not disrupted
- conclude with an appropriate message

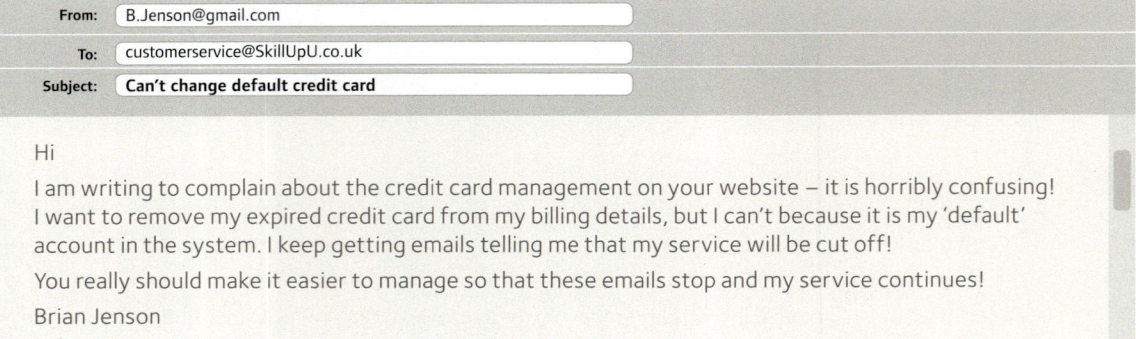

From:	B.Jenson@gmail.com
To:	customerservice@SkillUpU.co.uk
Subject:	Can't change default credit card

Hi

I am writing to complain about the credit card management on your website – it is horribly confusing!
I want to remove my expired credit card from my billing details, but I can't because it is my 'default'
account in the system. I keep getting emails telling me that my service will be cut off!

You really should make it easier to manage so that these emails stop and my service continues!

Brian Jenson

4   Handling a complaint from a customer

Now it is time to handle customer complaints face-to-face.

 Work with a partner and role-play an over-the-counter complaint. Swap roles when you are finished.

Partner A

While you are out shopping at the weekend your mobile phone shuts down and won't react when you try to turn it on. You need your phone for your work and personal life, so you want it working as soon as possible. Frustrated, you go into the mobile phone store and complain to the customer service staff.
Keep your complaint as polite as possible.

Partner B

You are part of the customer service staff in a mobile phone store. It is your job to handle customers' complaints professionally.

- Make the customer feel that you take them seriously.
- Check that they are a customer.
- Confirm that you will help them.
- Suggest that they try holding the side button on their phone for 10 seconds to reset.
- Ask them to leave their phone with you for an hour if they have time.
- Explain the process you follow if you can't fix it in an hour.

Attempt to fix in-store within hour. ▶ Send to technical support. Attempt to fix within 48 hours. ▶ Replace device.

PART B: A dispute over an invoice

Situation: SkillUpU are upgrading the rooms in their London building. You are part of the project team that is responsible for the purchase of new computer hardware and furniture.
→ **You negotiate a settlement to a dispute over an invoice.**

1 Pointing out mistakes

The supplier, EduTech, sends you an invoice for the equipment.

EduTech Ltd
234 Pine Street
London SE23 4JG

Date: 31 May 20..
Invoice number: 0008762

Invoice to:
SkillUpU.com Ltd
34 Hornacre Road
London NW1 2AB

Model	Item	Quantity	Price/item	Discount	Total
	Consulting fee (hours)	75	£184.00		£13,800.00
RT333	Wireless extenders	7	£459.08		£3,213.56
SS9384	Monitors 50"	4	£1,195.08	10%	£4,302.29
FDG323	Tablets	8	£624.68		£4,997.44
CC2343	Cabling and charging	1	£919.08		£919.08
MNT988	Mounts	8	£36.80		£294.40
PI993	Desks	30	£460.00		£13,800.00
BC34	Chairs	120	£183.08	10%	£19,772.64
SSP	Premium Service & Support (12 months)	1	£9,200.00	20%	£7,360.00
	Installation charge				£2,000.00
	Delivery charge				£392.00
	Subtotal				£70,851.41
	VAT (20%)				£14,170.28
	Total Price				**£85,021.69**

Note that a 25% deposit payment is required in advance.

We thank you for your prompt payment.

Look at the invoice, then do the tasks on page 118.

A Match the English words (a–g) to the correct German terms (1–7).

1	Anzahlung		a	delivery charge
2	Gesamtpreis		b	deposit
3	Zustellgebühr		c	installation charge
4	Mehrwertsteuer		d	invoice number
5	Einrichtungs- und Montagekosten		e	subtotal
6	Rechnungsnummer		f	total price
7	Zwischensumme		g	VAT

B You have compared the invoice to your previous conversations with Robyn Callahan at EduTech Ltd and have written down the following six items that you think are incorrect.

Write a letter of complaint to point out the mistakes that you think they have made. Use the language box on page 114 to help you.

> – 20% discount on monitors agreed
> – 30% discount on cabling and charging missing
> – only 20 desks ordered
> – 25% discount on Service & Support agreed
> – delivery charge on invoice not discussed
> – total price almost 10% higher!

➜ **Pointing out mistakes**

A few mistakes **have been made**.
The discount **was left off**.
A delivery charge **wasn't discussed** at any stage.

› *Grammar: Passive forms, page 164*

> Dear Robyn
>
> I've just taken a look at the invoice that you sent and I'm sorry to say …
>
> …
>
> We are only two weeks away from starting courses in the London office, so …

2 Renegotiating an invoice

A day later, you and your boss call Robyn Callahan from EduTech to discuss the mistakes in the invoice.

A 38))) Listen to your boss talking to Robyn about the invoice and note down which items she agrees to change – and what the changes are.

1 discount on monitors
2 discount on cabling & charging
3 discount on Service and Support
4 the delivery charge
5 number of desks
6 any other items

B 38))) Listen again and complete the following sentences.

1 I think there ▬ that I'd like to clear up.
2 I'd ▬ if you could rectify these mistakes quickly.
3 I'm sure you're right. I ▬ for that. I'll make sure that it's ▬ immediately.
4 20% is the maximum discount we ever offer. I'm ▬ to discount it any further as we'd lose money on it.
5 OK. I'm prepared to ▬ on that. However, one thing I'm ▬ at any stage is the delivery charge on the invoice.
6 But, as this is your first order and we've made a few mistakes, ▬ the delivery charge.
7 I ▬ these misunderstandings and the bad impression they make.
8 ▬ we reduce our consulting fee?

3 Role-play: Negotiating a disputed invoice

The boardroom at SkillUpU has been upgraded with new teleconferencing equipment. You have received an invoice for the upgrade work from BoardRoomTech, but you believe the invoice has some mistakes.

Partner A: Look here. **Partner B:** Look at File 20 on page 143.

Compare the invoice with your notes and highlight where you believe the invoice has some mistakes. Then call your partner (who works for BoardRoomTech) to come to an agreement over the final invoice.

BoardRoomTech Ltd

24 Wanderers Way
London NE23 7PH

Date: 13 August 20..

Invoice number: 000837629

Code	Item	Quantity	Item price	Discount	Price
ST948	Speaker – Set of 8	1	£2639.12		£2,639.12
PP993	Projector – 4K	1	£6,195.08	5%	£5,885.33
DM394	Desk microphones	20	£128.44	10%	£2,311.92
VC394	Desk-mounted video cameras	16	£239.34		£3,829.44
CC992	Cabling	1	£1,080.00		£1,080.00
SSP	Basic Service & Support (12 months)	1	£823.00	10%	£740.70
	Consultation (hours)	15	£90.00		£1,350.00
	Installation charge				£999.00
	Delivery charge				£199.00
	Subtotal				£19,034.51
	VAT	20%			£3,806.91
	TOTAL				**£22,841.41**

Your notes from the meeting:

Speaker – set of 8
Projector 4K – 10% discount
Desk microphones – 20 pieces @ 15% discount
Desk-mounted video cameras – 20 pieces @ 15% discount
Cabling – 10% discount
Basic Service & Support (12 months)
Consultation – 1 person for 1 day
Installation charge – approx. £1000
Total with VAT – approx. budget of £20,000

COMMUNICATION: A telephone complaint

> **Situation:** You work at World Medical, a company that manufactures medical equipment.
> → **You deal with a telephone complaint.**

1 Dealing with complaints on the telephone

Your supervisor gives you a list of phrases for dealing with complaints and tells you to keep it by the phone.

Match the headings (1–5) to the phrases (a–j). There are at least two phrases for every heading. Some phrases match more than one heading.

1	Apologizing	a	Can I just check with you that I've understood everything?
2	Asking for information	b	Could you tell me what it's about, please?
3	Reacting to information	c	Could you give me the order number, please?
4	Action	d	I'll have a replacement sent out as soon as possible.
5	Ending the call	e	I'm sorry to hear that.
		f	Is there anything else I can do for you today?
		g	Just a moment while I write that down.
		h	Oh, no. That doesn't sound at all good.
› *Useful phrases: Dealing with*		i	Thank you for your call. Once again, I'm sorry that there was a problem.
complaints, page 160		j	We're prepared to replace the goods at our expense.

2 Dealing politely with customers

A new customer, Jerzy Adamczyk, calls to complain about a trial order of X-ray machines. Your colleague, Melissa Wolf, takes the call. She is not very polite.

A 39))) 👥 **With a partner, listen to the phone call and decide together how you would improve it. Make a list.**

B 40))) 👥 **Now listen to how Melissa should have dealt with the phone call with Jerzy Adamczyk. Which (if any) of your improvements does she make?**

> **TIP**
>
> **Making / Dealing with complaints on the phone**
> Give your name clearly at the start of the call and write down the name of the person you are speaking to immediately. If necessary, check the spelling of the name.

3 Complaining to a supplier

World Medical ships their orders in special containers made by Sheffield Metal, a company in England. The latest consignment has not arrived, so your supervisor phones to complain about the delay in delivery. Jeanette Hogg answers the phone.

A 👥 **Work with a partner. Look at the phrases (a–h) below and decide who says what – the caller or the person taking the call. (There are four phrases for each speaker.)**

a	delivery was promised	e	the exact details
b	How can I help you?	f	the order number?
c	I will do my best	g	to enquire about my order
d	it's an order for	h	We can't fulfil our orders

B   **When you have finished, match the phrases (a–h) with the gaps (1–8) in the text to complete the transcript of the phone call.**

Jeanette	Good morning. Sheffield Metal, Sales Department. Jeannette Hogg speaking.
Max	Good morning. This is Max Jahn from World Medical in Germany.
Jeanette	Good morning, Mr Jahn. ▭¹
Max	I'm calling ▭² for containers for medical equipment. The order was sent almost one month ago, on 18 April, and ▭³ by 3 May but, so far, nothing has arrived.
Jeanette	Oh. I'm sorry to hear that. Could you give me ▭⁴
Max	Yes. It's DF54736.
Jeanette	DF54736. Just a moment, please. I'll check. I'm sorry, Mr Jahn. I don't seem to have any record of your order. Can I just check that I've understood everything? The order number is DF54736 and you ordered the containers on 18 April. Could you give me ▭⁵ of the order, please?
Max	Yes, ▭⁶ your aluminium containers for medical equipment.
Jeanette	Aluminium containers for medical equipment. Mr Jahn, I'll have to speak to my colleague to find out what the problem is. Can I get back to you later?
Max	Well, yes. But I hope it won't take long. ▭⁷ until we have your containers.
Jeanette	Yes. I realize that, Mr Jahn. I'm very sorry about this and ▭⁸ to get back to you as soon as possible.
Max	Many thanks for your help, Ms Hogg.

C   **41))) Now listen and check your answers.**

4   Role-play: Making a complaint by telephone

Now it is time to practise dealing with telephone complaints.

A   **Work with a partner and role-play a telephone complaint using the prompts below.**

PARTNER A	PARTNER B
You work for the supplier. You take a call from a customer who makes a complaint. Before you begin, check your knowledge of phrases for dealing with complaints (exercise 1).	You are the customer. Before you begin, make some notes as follows: – the name of your firm – the order number – the date of delivery – the problem (e.g. damaged/wrong goods, delay in delivery) – what you hope from Partner A

› *Useful phrases: Telephoning, page 152; Making complaints, page 160; Dealing with complaints, page 160*

B   **When you have finished the phone call, change roles and do it again using different details.**

DAS KANN ICH (Unit 11)

– Einen Kommentar zu einem Beitrag in einem Webforum auf Englisch schreiben. (Foundation)
– Eine Antwort auf die Beschwerde eines Kunden / einer Kundin auf Englisch schreiben. (Part A)
– Verhandlungen über eine strittige Rechnung auf Englisch führen. (Part B)
– Mit telefonischen Beschwerden auf Englisch richtig umgehen. (Communication)

12 A job application

FOUNDATION: Where do I go from here?

Situation: You are thinking about applying for a work placement abroad. You start to think about what you have learned in your apprenticeship and where you might work when you have qualified.
→ **You write a description of your apprenticeship for a European job agency.**

1 Listening to newly-qualified IT technicians

You listen to an interview with three newly-qualified technicians. They are talking about the jobs they do and where they would like to find a permanent position.

1	Maren

IT assistant

2	Garry

IT helpdesk technician

3	Delon

IT network administrator

A 42))) **Listen and say what the speakers liked best about their apprenticeship.**

1 Who enjoyed the "hands-on" aspect of the job?
2 Who liked the mixture of going to college and working in the company?
3 Who enjoyed the fact that the work is varied?

B 42))) **Listen again and complete the table. What are the speakers' plans for the future?**

Name	What I do at work	I'd like to become …
Maren	I ▬▬¹ data and process it. I also ▬▬² data and make sure it's not become ▬▬³.	▬▬⁴
Garry	I work with people ▬▬⁵. After every job, I write a short ▬▬ ⁶ for my manager.	▬▬⁷
Delon	I install ▬▬⁸ systems, update ▬▬⁹ and run ▬▬¹⁰. I also ▬▬¹¹ problems.	▬▬¹²

2 Thinking about your skills

You think about the skills you have learned during your apprenticeship.

A What do you enjoy most about your apprenticeship? What skills are you learning? How do you learn and develop these skills. First make notes on your own.

B 👥 Now talk to a partner about the skills you are learning.

C 👥 Now compare your ideas with another pair and make a list of the skills you are all learning, for example, scanning and capturing data, installing software, etc. (Keep this list; you will need it for Part A, exercise 2B, page 125.)

D Report your ideas to the class. In class, make a list in English of the different job titles in your field, e.g. installation technician. How can you use the skills you are learning in your preferred area of work?

> ➡ **Talking about skills; thinking about possibilities**
>
> I **can** diagnose and repair computer problems.
> We**'re able to** update the databank without any help.
> They **might be able to** get a job in the UK.
> You **could** look for work in the IT sector.

> › *Grammar: Modals and their substitutes, page 167*

3 Doing internet research

You search the internet for job opportunities in Europe.

A 👥 Work with a partner. Do internet research to find suitable career prospects in Europe. Make a poster showing job offers and companies in your sector. Present your ideas to the class.

B When you have finished, pin your poster to the wall and do a gallery walk. Rank the posters using the categories below. Give points from 1–5 for each category.

headline · design · photos/pictures · content · overall effect

4 Reading about the Europass

While you are doing your research online, you come across the European Skills Passport (Europass). You decide to use it to collect your own personal details for applications and your CV.

Download the Europass and start to complete it with your details. (Your teacher has the correct URL.)

5 Describing your apprenticeship

You have contacted an EU job agency asking for help in looking for work experience in Europe. The agent for Germany asks you to write a short description of your apprenticeship in English for the agency file.

Write a short description of your apprenticeship. Before you begin, think about the aspects you should include, e.g. type of training, skills you learned, qualifications you gained, and make notes.

INFO

The European Skills Passport (Europass)
This is a standardized CV and language document that can be created online or on your own computer. Potential employers throughout Europe can clearly see your skills and qualifications.

The following sections might be of particular interest to you:
– **Language Passport** – a self-assessment tool for language skills and qualifications;
– **Europass Mobility** – a record of skills acquired during a learning experience in a European country;
– **Certificate Supplement** – a description of skills acquired by holders of vocational training certificates.

PART A: Job adverts and applications

> **Situation:** You would like to gain some work experience abroad.
> → **You study some job adverts online and write an application for one of them.**

1 Analysing a job advertisement

You have found some information online about job opportunities abroad.

Study the advertisement below and say …

1 in which sector the employer is active.
2 what the company is looking for.
3 what the job requirements are.
4 what benefits are offered.
5 how to apply for the job.
6 what happens if the application is shortlisted.

IT OPPORTUNITIES

Recruiter: Top-Tech Recruitment Agency

Fields: database administration, network administration, web development, IT security
Sector: IT systems

Region: London
Salary: Negotiable
Job Type: Renewable contracts

The UK is facing a chronic skills shortage in the IT sector and trained workers from abroad are in high demand. We are a leading UK recruitment agency that is looking to recruit suitably qualified IT personnel.
If you are interested in applying for a position, please complete our application form.

We are looking for:
- Reliability, commitment to the job and the willingness to work hard.
- The ability to work as part of a team.
- Strong personal drive and the ability to use your own initiative.
- The ability to work under pressure.
- Recognized qualifications and at least 2 years' experience in your field.
- Good spoken and written English.

What's on offer:
- Contracts of 6 months, renewable.
- Starting salary £18 per hour minimum.
- Learning on the job from experienced staff.
- Opportunities for overtime.
- Starting date: Immediately

If your application is shortlisted, you will be asked to send your CV together with a covering letter.

Initial interviews will be conducted by telephone.

🧰 TOOLBOX

---

commitment – *Engagement*
drive – *Tatendrang, Motivation*
in high demand – *sehr gefragt*
initial – *erste/r/s*

negotiable – *verhandelbar*
overtime – *Überstunden*
recognized qualifications – *anerkannte Qualifikationen*
renewable – *verlängerbar*

2 Discussing job advertisements

You study some job advertisements and discuss them with your colleagues.

A   Work in groups of three. **Partner A:** Look here. **Partner B:** Look at File 15 on page 140. **Partner C:** Look at File 21 on page 144.

Read the job advertisement below and be ready to answer your partners' questions about it. Ask your partners questions about their job adverts. Find out …

1   about the type of employer.
2   what the job is.
3   what the requirements are.

4   the salary and benefits.
5   how to apply.
6   what happens if the application is shortlisted.

IT Assistant

Data Services Ltd, Cambridge, UK

We are a successful software services company with a vacancy for a newly-qualified IT assistant. You will support the scanning and data capture department to capture, enter, validate and process data using database management applications. This permanent vacancy offers the opportunity to become a project manager.

We are looking for someone who has …
– IT experience as an IT assistant,
– good organizational and problem-solving skills,
– advanced experience with Microsoft Word, Excel, Access and SQL.

Skills required: knowledge of database functions, document management application skills, data entry skills.

Job Type: full-time, Monday to Friday, 9 a.m. to 5 p.m.; 24 days paid holiday, plus public holidays.
Salary: £20–25,000 p.a.
Required education: Vocational College Certificate or equivalent.

Use this link to apply with your CV, qualifications and references.
If your application is shortlisted, we will contact you to arrange a time for a telephone interview.

B   Discuss the job offers in your group. Say which position interests you. Explain why you are (or are not) qualified for the position. Use the list of skills that you developed in Foundation, exercise 2C (page 123) to support your answer.

> **Expressing your wishes**
>
> **I'd** (= I would) **like** a job as a web developer.
> **I'd** (= I would) **love** to work for … (company) / to work in … (sector).

3 Writing an application

You are going to apply to one of the advertisements you read in exercise 2 above. Choose the one which you think suits you best.

A   Read the tips for writing a CV on page 128. Then write your own CV, using the model on page 129 and any appropriate words and phrases from the model.

› *Unit 12, Communication, pages 128–129*

B   Read the tips for writing a covering letter on page 130. Then write a covering letter for the job advertisement you have chosen, using the model on page 131 and any appropriate words and phrases.

› *Unit 12, Communication, pages 130–131; Useful phrases: Writing covering letters, page 161*

PART B: Job interviews

Situation: You have been shortlisted for a job in the UK.
→ You prepare for and practise a telephone interview and a face-to-face interview.

1 Handling telephone interviews

You and a colleague have decided to practise telephone interviews together.

👥 With your partner, read the text below and decide which sentences (1–8) fit the gaps (A–F) in the text. There are two more sentences than you need.

YOUR TELEPHONE INTERVIEW

One short phone call is all it takes to get you to the next level in your job application process. Here are some tips to help you get that job.

Be prepared!
Gather the following documents and lists the day before the interview:
- a copy of the job description;
- a copy of your letter of application, your CV and your references;
- a list of questions you want to ask the interviewer;
- a list of your strengths and weaknesses.

So that the interviewer doesn't get irritated by the sound of you flicking through papers, ▬ A ▬ .

On the day of the call
- Place a notebook and a couple of pens beside the phone ▬ B ▬ .
- Make sure the room you are in is quiet.
- Switch off your computer and disconnect all social media.
- If possible, use a landline. If you use your mobile phone, make sure it is fully charged ▬ C ▬ .
- Get the interviewer's phone number in case you get disconnected.

Dress for the job
You should dress as you would for a face-to-face interview. Strange as it sounds, ▬ D ▬ .
Remember to smile: You can't sound bored or uninterested if you have a smile on your face.
To keep your voice sounding good, ▬ E ▬ .

During the call
Concentrate and stay focused. Listen carefully and reply to the interviewer appropriately.
Be professional and polite. At the end of the call, you can ask, "Do my qualifications meet the company's needs?" However the interview goes, always end with "Thank you for your call." The last few words of a conversation are often the ones that people remember ▬ F ▬ .

1 and that you take the call in a place where reception is good
2 ask the interviewer how many candidates he/she has spoken to today
3 pin these documents and lists to the wall so that you can check them during the call
4 please hang on while I think of the answer
5 so always leave a good impression at the end
6 so that you can take notes during the interview
7 swallow a teaspoon of honey just before the call
8 you're more likely to feel and sound professional if you look the part

2 Practising a telephone interview

Now it is time to practise a telephone interview together.

A 👥 Work with a partner. Study the list of common questions for interviews and how to answer them in File 23 on page 145.

B 👥 With your partner, prepare a dialogue and role-play a telephone interview.

> ➔ **Asking for clarification**
>
> I'm sorry, could you say that again?
> So, if I understand you correctly …
> I don't quite understand what you mean by …

› *Useful phrases: Telephoning, page 152*

3 Preparing for a face-to-face interview

You listen to a podcast in which an expert gives tips about how to handle face-to-face job interviews.

A 👥 What is the expert likely to say? With a partner, brainstorm a list of expressions you might hear and make notes under the headings below.

Here are a few expressions from the podcast to start you off.

Stage 1: Greetings and introductions
arrive at the interview on time

Stage 2: Small talk
talk about the weather

Stage 3: The main part of the interview
talk about yourself

Stage 4: Questions from the candidate
do background research into the company before the interview

Stage 5: Further arrangements and the end of the interview
ask when you can expect to hear from the company again

B 43))) ▶ Now listen and check. How many of your expressions did you hear?

4 Practising for an interview

You and your colleague decide to practise the main part of an interview together.

A First of all, study the list of common interview questions (File 23 on page 145) and how to answer them.

B 👥 Work with a partner.

Partner A: Choose one of the job advertisements you read in Part A (page 125, File 15 or File 21) and tell your partner which one you have chosen. Think about the questions the interviewer might ask and how you might answer. Make notes.

Partner B: Study the job advertisement your partner has chosen. Make a list of questions you might ask.

C 👥 When you are both ready, role-play the job interview. When you have finished, change roles if you wish.

COMMUNICATION: A CV and a covering letter

Situation: You find out online about the documents which you will need for job applications.
→ **You study an English CV and covering letter and tips on how to prepare them.**

1 Reading a website about CVs

You find an interesting website with tips, but the headings have got mixed up.

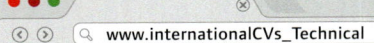 **Work with a partner. Read the tips (1–9) and match them to the headings (a–i).**

a Education and training	**d** Personal details	**g** Work experience
b Hobbies and interests	**e** References	**h** Contact details
c Personal statement	**f** Key skills	**i** Further skills

www.internationalCVs_Technical

⇒ TIPS for writing your CV

International CVs

Your CV is a summary of your abilities, work experience, education and qualifications. There is no set format for a British CV but you should keep it short, using clear headings to guide the reader.

1 Give your name and address, telephone number(s) (home/mobile) and email address.

2 This should be a short message that grabs the attention of the reader. Use note form. This helps to keep your CV focused and direct, for example: *Motivated electronic technician with experience in German engineering industry.*

3 Here you can summarize your skills and experience which are relevant to the job for which you are applying.

4 As a general rule, CVs should be in reverse chronological order, listing the most recent position first. For each position held you should provide the dates of the start and end of employment, the employer's name and address, the job title, the main duties and responsibilities and achievements.

5 Give a brief description of qualifications (school, academic and/or professional). Give the names of schools or colleges in reverse chronological order.

6 Here you should write about common skills gained throughout your education and work experience, such as languages, IT skills, good maths skills or a full, clean driving licence. These skills are of interest for any employer.

7 This feature is optional, but could provide something more personal to discuss at an interview. Be careful about what you write; a dangerous sport or *socializing with friends* may not be what an employer wants to hear!

8 Write your date of birth and nationality under this heading.

9 Due to data protection laws, candidates should not provide referees' names, addresses or any other contact details on CVs, but should state that details are available on request. Always ask your referees' permission before you give someone their contact details.

2 Analysing a CV

You also find an example of a British-style CV online.

Study the CV below. What differences can you find between this CV and a German CV?

MARTIN BIENEK
Am Kattenkamp 236, 33611 Bielefeld, Germany
Landline: (+49) 521 394677
Mobile: (+49) 176 3628419
Email: martin.bienek43@gmx.com

PERSONAL STATEMENT
A qualified and motivated young IT professional with business experience supporting various users in a busy computing environment. Currently looking for an opportunity to develop and widen work experience abroad.

KEY SKILLS
Experienced at updating computerized support systems
Strong technical and interpersonal communication
Excellent spoken and written English
Good spoken and written Russian

WORK EXPERIENCE
Since 20..   Experience during apprenticeship in preparing new company workstations, answering the telephone to internal customers and company suppliers
20..   Two-week placement at ComputerMacher GmbH (local computer hardware specialist) doing maintenance and repairs of customer desktop computers

EDUCATION AND TRAINING
Since 20..   Three-year apprenticeship in IT Support Department, Schmidt Anlagentechnik GmbH and Vocational Training College for Economy and Administration in Bielefeld, Germany
June 20..   BKFH (final examination equal to GNVQ)
                  Main subjects: Physics, Computer Studies
20..–20..   Primary and secondary education in Bielefeld

FURTHER SKILLS
Team-working course, database management
Full driving licence
First aid certificate

HOBBIES AND INTERESTS
Athletics, football
Training local junior football team

PERSONAL DETAILS
Date of birth: 06 April 20..
Nationality: German

REFERENCES
Available on request

3 Analysing a covering letter

Martin has applied for a job as an IT assistant at an electrical engineering company in Ireland.

Read Martin's covering letter on the opposite page and match the parts (1–5) with explanations from the list.

a asking the employer to invite you for an interview
b reference to details on your CV
c reference to the position
d saying why the applicant is applying for the position
e stating why the applicant is the best person for the job

4 Mediation: Writing a covering letter

Your supervisor gives you the following text and asks you to make notes on the contents in German for the apprentice file.

Read the text and make notes in German for the file.

Writing your covering letter

A covering letter is a formal letter with a standard structure. Do not use the same letter for all companies and all jobs but include a different covering letter with your CV for each job you are applying for. Your covering letter should be one page long. Try to avoid having too many sentences beginning with "I".
In the letter you should …

1 refer to the position for which you are applying; give the source of the employer's address;

2 give details of your education and training; explain what you are doing at the moment;

3 explain why you are applying for the position;

4 explain what you can offer the employer;

5 close politely, referring to enclosures (attachments in the case of online applications) and asking the employer to invite you for an interview.

Here are some things to remember:
» After "Dear …" all letters and emails then start with a capital letter.
» If you start a letter / an email with a personal name (*Dear Anne, Dear Ms Green*), you finish it with "Yours sincerely".
» If you begin a letter / an email with no personal name (*Dear Sir or Madam*), you always finish it with "Yours faithfully".

› *Useful phrases: Writing covering letters, page 161*

Am Kattenkamp 236, 33611 Bielefeld, Germany
Phone: (+49) 521 394677, Mobile: (+49) 176 3628419
Email: martin.bienek43@gmx.com

20 April 20..

Scott Electrics Ltd
Silverbank Industrial Estate
DUBLIN
D11 D4E2
IRELAND

Attn. Mr Haig, Human Resources Director

Dear Mr Haig

IT assistant

1 With reference to your advertisement Ref. No. 17673 on the internet, I would like to apply for the post described.

2 I am very interested in the job you are offering as I feel sure it will give me the opportunity to develop both personally and professionally. I am particularly keen to work where I can apply my skills on a daily basis.

3 By June of this year I will have completed the final year of a three-year apprenticeship in the IT Support Department of Schmidt Anlagentechnick GmbH with theoretical instruction at the Vocational Training College for Economy and Administration in Bielefeld, Germany. I will then be a fully-qualified management assistant for IT systems.

4 As I have practical skills and experience, am flexible and mobile and speak fluent English, German and Russian, I believe I will be a strong member of any team I join and will benefit your company.

5 My CV is enclosed and I am available for an interview at short notice.

I would very much appreciate it if you would consider my application and hope that you will grant me an interview.

I look forward to hearing from you soon.

Yours sincerely

M. Bienek

Martin Bienek

Encl.

DAS KANN ICH (Unit 12)

– Eine Beschreibung meiner Ausbildung auf Englisch verfassen. (Foundation)
– Englische Stellenanzeigen analysieren und mich darauf bewerben. (Part A)
– Mich auf ein Bewerbungsgespräch auf Englisch gut vorbereiten. (Part B)
– Bewerbungsunterlagen auf Englisch richtig verfassen und gestalten. (Communication)

1 Leseverstehen: B1

Ihr Ausbildungsbetrieb plant, staubsaugende Roboter in die Produktpalette aufzunehmen. Sie erhalten von Ihrem Chef eine E-Mail mit Fragen zu einem englischen Text. Er bittet Sie, ihn bei der Vorbereitung für eine Besprechung über dieses Thema zu entlasten.

Beantworten Sie die Fragen zum Text auf Deutsch in Stichworten.

1 Wer ist die Zielgruppe für staubsaugende Roboter?
2 Wie viel muss man je nach Leistung der Roboter investieren?
3 Warum sind sie ideal für das Saugen unter Sofas und Kommoden?
4 Für welche Bodenbeläge sind sie geeignet?
5 Welche Technologien nutzen die Roboter, um sich im Raum zu orientieren?
6 Wie kann verhindert werden, dass die Roboter Möbel beschädigen oder den Raum verlassen?
7 Welche Zusatzfunktionen haben Roboter mit Wi-Fi?

The intelligent vacuum cleaner

Do you care about the appearance of your home, are you short of time, and do you hate to clean the floor after your party guests have gone home? Then you belong to the target group of robot vacuum cleaners. But before deciding whether to purchase such a vacuum cleaner, you might be interested in learning more about these clever little helpers.

Weighing in at between three to five kilos, these robots are not any heavier than your ordinary vacuum cleaner. Depending on how intelligent they are programmed to be, they can cost anything between 200 and 1000 euros. A cheaper robot vacuum cleaner can easily cover a surface area of 45 square metres with a single charge, can find its way back to the base station for a quick recharge whenever needed, and then – if necessary – carry on cleaning. Because they are only ten centimetres high, they can glide under a couch or a cupboard and reach edges and corners you can't normally reach with an ordinary vacuum cleaner. That is, unless you lie flat on your stomach.

You can set the room and the time using a remote control, letting the robot know where and when to clean each day. It quickly adapts to almost any floor surface thanks to its artificial brain. Its sensors recognize hardwood floors and carpets and handle them accordingly. Some more expensive robots both vacuum and mop tiles, ensuring a dust-free home every day. And some models not only clean your home's floors, but they also disinfect them using UV light to kill bacteria.

How does the robot find its way round the obstacles in the room? Unlike the traditional ultrasound-based models, the new robots use laser-vision or a 360-degree camera mounted on top, which takes dozens of pictures per second and creates a map of every room in your house. Some models scan the room and develop the map before they start cleaning, more sophisticated ones perform this while cleaning, using a technology called Visual Simultaneous Localization and Mapping (VSLAM). To manoeuvre round the legs of tables and chairs, or the cat, they are equipped with obstacle sensors or light touch bumpers. If you are worried that the robot might damage your antique chest of drawers, or leave the room it's supposed to be cleaning, you can create virtual walls to screen off such areas. Models featuring Wi-Fi also allow you to check whether the robot is doing its job while you are on vacation, at the same time as using the camera as a home-security device. You'll find plenty of YouTube videos showing happy customers, and demonstrating that not only homemakers benefit, but that cats and babies can also have fun riding across the living-room floor on top of a robot vacuum cleaner.

2 Hörverstehen: B1

Sie sind Auszubildende/r bei Spearhead Models International. Zu Trainingszwecken werden Gespräche mit Kunden/Kundinnen, die ihr Einverständnis geben, aufgezeichnet. Sie hören den Mitschnitt eines Telefongesprächs zwischen Larry Maham und dem Kunden Charles Baxter.

44))) Hören Sie das Interview und fertigen Sie eine Telefonnotiz an. Nutzen Sie folgende Aspekte:

- Name und persönliche Daten des Kunden
- Grund der Beschwerde
- Name des beanstandeten Produkts
- Problem des Kunden
- Grund für nicht erfolgte Lieferung
- Verbesserungsvorschläge des Kunden
- Angebote an den Kunden

3 Mediation: B2

Ihr Freund ist in Offiziersausbildung bei der Bundeswehr. Er soll eine Präsentation über die Strava App für Fitnessbänder halten. Weil sein Englisch nicht so gut ist, bittet er Sie, ihm bei diesem Text zu helfen.

Fassen Sie die wichtigsten Informationen auf Deutsch zusammen. Berücksichtigen Sie dabei Folgendes:

- Zielgruppe von Strava App
- gesammelte Daten in Strava Heatmap
- Maßnahme des Pentagons 2013
- Informationen über Nathan Ruser
- Beispiele für Sicherheitsproblem mit Strava App
- Vermeidung des Risikos

The Strava Heatmap for fitness trackers

A popular app created by Strava for runners, cyclists and even swimmers is available for many fitness trackers. This includes devices like smartphones, Fitbit, Android Wear, Samsung's Galaxy Gear, and other health tracking devices. Using GPS, athletes can share their running routes with friends. The app allows Strava to create and publish a heatmap that shows details about their activities worldwide. Tiny light markers highlight popular running routes in and around major cities, or show joggers in more remote areas. According to Strava, this global heatmap is "a direct visualization of Strava's global network of athletes." The latest version has been built from "one billion activities, some three trillion points of data, covering 27 billion km of distance run, jogged, swum or covered by car."

In 2013, the Pentagon, the U.S. Department of Defense, was interested in the fitness of their soldiers and distributed Fitbit trackers to their troops. Like other athletes, the soldiers have been wearing their fitness trackers to measure their total number of steps. Clearly the Pentagon was not aware of the security risks when it encouraged the military personnel to wear the Fitbits.

In January 2018, Nathan Ruser, a 20-year-old Australian studying international security at the Australian National University came across the Strava heatmap while browsing a cartography blog. He noticed that the thin lines of light markers appeared in regions of Syria and the Sahara which were not inhabited by civilians. Furthermore, he realized that these lines seemed to connect military bases, and could therefore trace the routes used by American forces. "If a soldier wearing a fitness tracker goes out on patrol," wrote Ruser in a blog, "his data is integrated within the Strava heatmap. If several soldiers are doing the same thing, you can see not only military sites but also routes that are frequently patrolled."

What started as a tool to help people keep fit has become a matter of national security. The Strava heatmap might motivate terrorists to scan it for sensitive information about military installations worldwide. This shows that unless the GPS function is de-activated, smartphones or fitness trackers could lead to serious consequences for both athletes enjoying sports as a hobby, and military personnel alike.

FILE 1: Unit 2, Communication, exercise 5

Partner A and Partner B

Partner A: You work for your training company. (Use your own name and the name of your company.)
Partner B: You work for Trent IT Equipment Ltd in Stoke. (Make up an English name for yourself.)

Role-play a telephone call and taking a message. Partner A starts:
Good morning, (name of company). (Your name) speaking. ...

Partner A

Answer the phone. Introduce yourself and ask how you can help.

Say that Mr Schmidt is out of the office at the moment.

Say that Ms Wendlinger is in a meeting. Ask if the caller would like to leave a message.

Ask the caller for his/her contact details.

Say that you will pass on the message.

Thank Partner B for calling.

Partner B

Introduce yourself and ask to speak to Mr Schmidt in the Purchasing department.

Ask to speak to Ms Wendlinger.

Say that the monitors the company ordered are not available. Ask for somebody to call you back to discuss an alternative.

Give your contact details.

Thank Partner A and end the call politely.

› *Useful phrases: Telephoning, page 152; Taking telephone calls, page 152*

FILE 2: Unit 3, Communication, exercise 1C

Partner A

Dictate these email addresses to Partner B. Check B's answers.

1 DavidMcCarthy+list@net.us
2 sergei-nikitin@com.ru
3 your own email address
4 the email address of your firm or another email address you often write to

FILE 3: Unit 4, Part A, exercise 3

Partner B

A Ask your partner questions to find out the following information:

– the progress of the patches released in the week up to 22 October
– the percentage success rate of the XLerate patch
– the main reasons for failure for the XLerate patch
– if there is dependent software that is causing problems

B Answer your partner's questions about the patch releases using the report below.

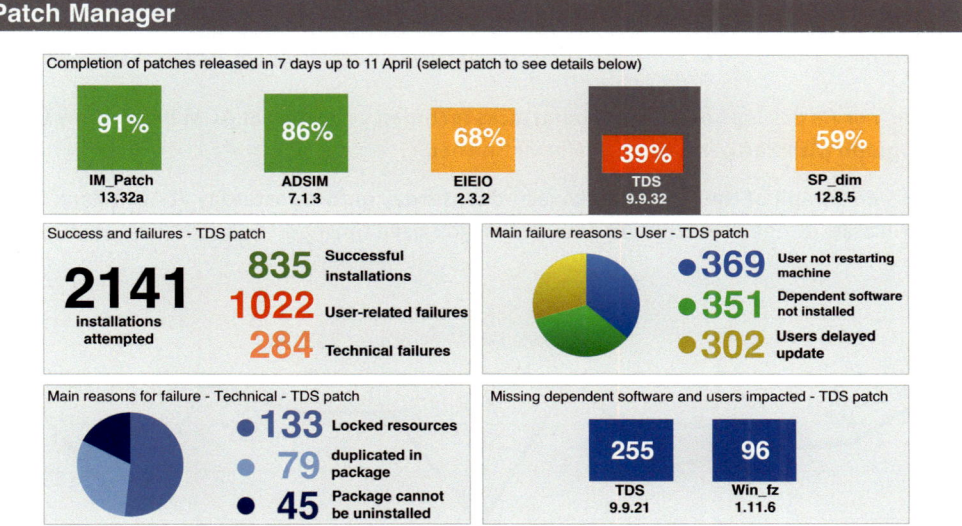

FILE 4: Unit 5, Communication, exercise 2

Partner A

A Describe this line graph of the cyberattacks recorded yesterday at AGM Bank to Partner B. Partner B will draw it. Check Partner B's graph when you have finished.

› *Useful phrases: Describing graphs, page 154*

B Listen to Partner B's description of the cyberattacks recorded the day before yesterday at AGM Bank. Draw the line graph. Check your graph with Partner B when you have finished.

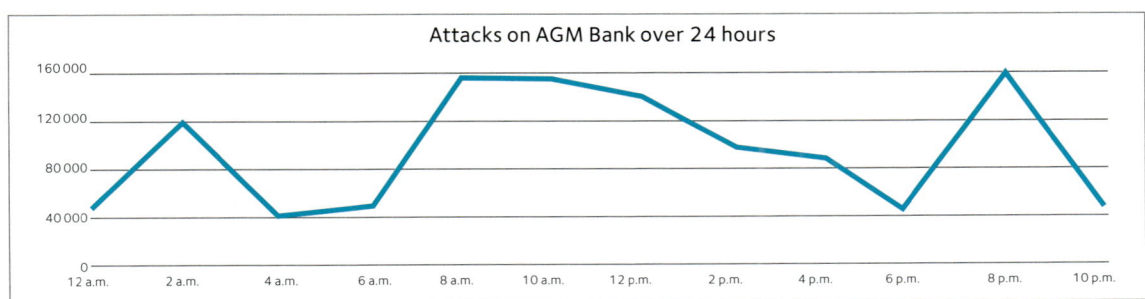

FILE 5: Unit 3, Communication, exercise 1C

Partner B

Dictate these email addresses to Partner A. Check A's answers.

1 beatrice-kuhn@berlin_tools.de
2 Hamish.MacPherson@net.uk
3 your own email address
4 the email address of your firm or another email address you often write to

FILE 6: Unit 5, Communication, exercise 2

Partner B

A   Listen to Partner A's description of the cyberattacks recorded yesterday at AGM Bank. Draw the line graph. Check your graph with Partner A when you have finished.

B   Describe this line graph of the cyberattacks recorded the day before yesterday at AGM Bank to Partner A. Partner A will draw it. Check Partner A's graph when you have finished.

> *Useful phrases: Describing graphs, page 154*

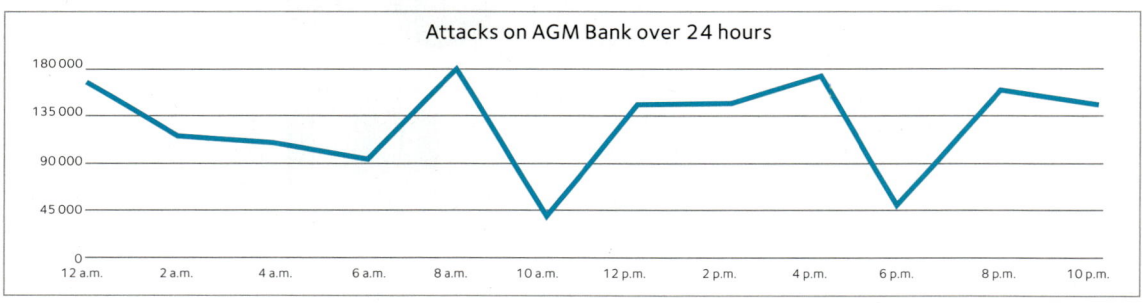

FILE 7: Unit 6, Foundation, exercise 2B

Partner B

You are a customer. Ask the customer service representative questions to make a purchase.

> **Customer**
>
> Sie brauchen Hilfe beim Kauf einer externen Festplatte.
> Sie wissen nicht ganz genau, wie viel Speicherplatz Sie benötigen. Sie möchten Familien-
> fotos und Videos von Ihrem Smartphone darauf speichern.
> Sie nehmen ungefähr 20 Videos pro Monat auf.
> Die Geschwindigkeit ist Ihnen nicht so wichtig.

> *Useful phrases: Advising customers, page 154; Asking for advice, page 155*

FILE 8: Unit 7, Part B, exercise 4

Partner A and B

Role-play a discussion about investment in a new cloud-based solution for your company. Make sure to demonstrate that you have done your research and that you have considered potential counter-arguments. Try to gain agreement from the others in your group and express doubt where appropriate.

Partner A:
You are a company executive.
– You want 24-hour productivity.
– You want to offer your employees flexible working times.
– You want to move to a more secure data environment.

Partner B:
You are a CAD engineer and live 90 minutes from the office.
– You would like to work from home.
– You would like to have flexible hours.
– You want to work on designs with other people because it leads to better ideas.

› *Useful phrases: Taking part in discussions, page 156*

FILE 9: Unit 7, Communication, exercise 3

Partner A

Your team have been using some new collaboration software and have agreed on a set of guidelines.

Give Partner B some polite and constructive feedback and make suggestions for improving the collaboration between team members. Use these ideas to help you:

– leaving documents signed out for too long
– not suggesting improvements to colleagues as often as they should
– still saving too much work on his/her desktop
– not leaving detailed comments to describe the changes
– emailing documents too often
– not using the same formatting as agreed

› *Useful phrases: Giving feedback, page 157*

Swap roles when you have finished.

FILE 10: Unit 7, Part B, exercise 4

Partner C and D

Role-play a discussion about investment in a new cloud-based solution for your company. Make sure to demonstrate that you have done your research and that you have considered potential counter-arguments. Try to gain agreement from the others in your group and express doubt where appropriate.

Partner C:

You are an older employee at the company.

– You don't want to have to work late shifts.

– You are worried that your intellectual property will not be safe in the cloud.

– You don't like sharing your work with others – they always mess it up!

Partner D:

You are a project manager.

– You want to have your team in one place, in the office.

– You are worried about performance of the network and lost productivity.

– You don't want to deal with your team complaining about the international offices.

› *Useful phrases: Taking part in discussions, page 156*

FILE 11: Unit 7, Communication, exercise 3

Partner B

Your team have been using some new collaboration software and have agreed on a set of guidelines.

Partner A will give you some feedback and make suggestions for improving the collaboration between team members. Reply politely to Partner A's suggestions, using the phrases in the language box.

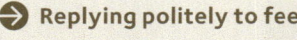

➜ Replying politely to feedback

Can you give me some examples?
Is there something I have missed?
How can I improve … ?
OK. You may have a point there.
Sure. I'll do that (in future).
Thanks. I will.

Swap roles when you have finished.

FILE 12: Unit 8, Part B, exercise 4

Partner B

Give your partner a progress report on your project using the information in the table below.

For each phase, tell your partner:
- the original estimate and how much you have completed
- whether you are behind time, on time or ahead of time
- why certain tasks are behind time
- what dependent phases are at risk from work that is behind time

Say if there are any lessons you have learned that can be applied to future phases of the project.

Task	Planned progress	Actual progress	Comments
User acceptance testing	65%	60%	Lack of resources Note: Next time allow for Easter break
System integration testing	55%	58%	
Data migration	33%	23%	Data quality worse than expected Note: Next time allow time to improve data quality
User instructions	60%	50%	Many changes to screens have put us a few days behind Note: Next time allow more slack

FILE 13: Unit 9, Part A, exercise 4

Partner A

You work for the CloudNote, the most secure document collaboration site on the internet. A potential customer has called you about using CloudNote for their business and wants to know how it could help them.

Ask questions about their company and the problems they are trying to solve. After you've found out all the information you need, explain the features of CloudNote that can solve the user's problems.

You can start your questions using the two topics that most callers are interested in:
- collaboration between teams
- security of information

Your product CloudNote offers the following features:
- feedback can be attached directly to documents
- clean user-friendly interface
- CloudNote can search handwritten notes
- all file formats shareable
- generous space limits in shared spaces
- single sign-on integration means that when an employee leaves the company, they are automatically denied CloudNote access
- online and offline access to documents

FILE 14: Unit 9, Part A, exercise 4

Partner B

You are talking on the phone to a salesperson from CloudNote, whose product you are interested in. You want to find out whether their product is appropriate for your problems.

Think of some reasons why the following problems occur and answer the questions that your partner asks you.

- an ex-employee used the company login to steal documents
- teams still prefer to use email to share documents
- low usage rate of existing tool
- training videos cannot be shared

Listen as your partner tells your about the CloudNote platform and let them know whether the product features sound appealing to you.

FILE 15: Unit 12, Part A, exercise 2A

Partner B

Read the job advertisement below and be ready to answer your partners' questions about it. Ask your partners questions about their job adverts. Find out ...

1 about the type of employer.
2 what the job is.
3 what the requirements are.
4 the salary and benefits.
5 how to apply.
6 what happens if the application is shortlisted.

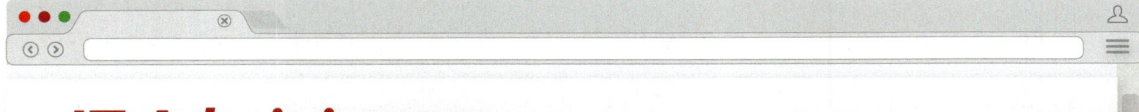

IT Administrator

Office Resources Ltd, Nottingham

We are an office services supplier based in Nottingham and are currently recruiting for a full-time IT administrator. Your duties will include general administration, data entry, working with Excel spreadsheets, IT support, user creation, password re-setting, email account set-up.

The ideal candidate will ...
- be competent in Excel
- have good communications skills
- have good attention to detail
- be reliable and show good initiative

If you feel you are suitable for this role, please apply with your CV and a covering letter to Office Resources Ltd, Unit 7, Sheffield Road Industrial Estate, NG2 7JY, UK.

Successful candidates will be invited to a preliminary interview at a local assessment centre.

Job type: full-time; 25 days paid holiday
Salary: depending on experience
Required education: vocational school qualification

FILE 16: Unit 9, Part B, exercise 3A

Partner A

Your company is interested in buying in-company feedback software from a supplier (Partner B's company). You need the software to create surveys about working conditions in your company.

Try to negotiate better conditions from Partner B for the points listed below. Make notes of what you agree on during your negotiation.

> **Price:**
> Internal Feedback Surveys $15.99 per month per user + $5.95 support per user
> *(aim: to reduce)*
>
> **Inclusions:**
> Document management
> Number of surveys per month: 20 *(aim: to increase)*
> Number of questions per survey: 50 *(aim: to increase)*
>
> **Support**
> Number of questions raised via chat: Unlimited *(OK)*
> Number of total support calls per month: 5 *(aim: to increase)*

› *Useful phrases: Negotiating, page 158*

FILE 17: Unit 10, Foundation, exercise 2

Partner B

You are Chris Young and are a prosthetics wearer. You have a 3D printer of your own and are printing your own prosthetics for the first time. An employee at AccessAble (**Partner A**) is going to phone you to give you information about the right materials you require to print your prosthetics. You are not sure about what you want, so you may need to ask the caller to repeat information.

Before you start, read the prompts below carefully. You start the conversation by answering the phone:

Hello, Chris Young speaking. ...

- Explain that you would like some information about materials for prosthetics before you order.
- You would like to know:
    - the recommended materials to print prosthetics for the activities you perform: dancing, playing football, everyday use
    - how much material is needed
    - whether the materials can be ordered in bulk
    - what discounts are offered
- Say that you would like to place a bulk order for the recommended products.
- Ask for a copy of the latest catalogue and price list.
- Thank the caller for his/her help and say you look forward to receiving confirmation of the order.
- End the phone call politely.

Swap roles when you have finished.

› *Useful phrases: Telephoning, page 152; Asking for advice, page 155*

Partner B

Your company offers in-company feedback software. Partner A's company is interested in buying this software from you.

Try to protect the offer you have made (below) to Partner A. Keep in mind that you can only compromise on the areas highlighted below. Make notes of what you agree on during your negotiation.

Price:
Internal Feedback Surveys $15.99 per month per user + $5.95 support per user
(can drop support price by $2 per user/month)

Inclusions:
Document management
Number of surveys per month: 20 *(no increase)*
Number of questions per survey: 50 *(can go up to 100)*

Support
Number of questions raised via chat: Unlimited *(OK)*
Number of total support calls per month: 5 *(can increase if training purchased)*

> *Useful phrases: Negotiating, page 158*

Partner B

Sie sind Vertreter/in von HoloMed Ltd, UK, und besprechen mit Partner A die Einzelheiten der geplanten Präsentation.

Ihre Fragen:	Ihre Auskünfte:
– Grund für die Präsentation?	– Termin: erste Augustwoche 20..
– Vorführraum?	– Kosten der Präsentation: 3.500 €
– Zahl der Teilnehmer/innen?	– Headset nur für Moderator
– verfügbare TV-Geräte oder Leinwände?	– Spezialkameras mit Bewegungs- und
– etwaige Bestellungen bei Erfüllung der	Lagesensoren; Projektion der 3D-Hologramme
Anforderungen?	– Lieferzeit ab Bestellung drei Wochen

FILE 20: Unit 11, Part B, exercise 3

Partner B

You work at BoardRoomTech and have helped SkillUpU with the upgrade of the video conferencing equipment in their board room. You receive an email from SkillUpU asking for a phone call to discuss some issues with the invoice.

Compare the invoice with your notes below and highlight where you believe the invoice has some mistakes. Then take a call from your partner and come to an agreement over the final invoice.

BoardRoomTech Ltd
24 Wanderers Way
London NE23 7PH

Date: 13 August 20..

Invoice number: 000837629

Code	Item	Quantity	Item price	Discount	Price
ST948	Speaker – set of 8	1	£2639.12		£2,639.12
PP993	Projector – 4K	1	£6,195.08	5%	£5,885.33
DM394	Desk microphones	20	£128.44	10%	£2,311.92
VC394	Desk-mounted video cameras	16	£239.34		£3,829.44
CC992	Cabling	1	£1,080.00		£1,080.00
SSP	Basic Service & Support (12 months)	1	£823.00	10%	£740.70
	Consultation (hours)	15	£90.00		£1,350.00
	Installation charge				£999.00
	Delivery charge				£199.00
	Subtotal				£19,034.51
	VAT	20%			£3,806.91
	TOTAL				**£22,841.41**

Your notes from the meeting:

Speaker – set of 8 – no discount
Projector – 4K – 10% discount
Desk microphones – 20 pieces @ 10% discount
Desk-mounted video cameras – 16 pieces @ 10% discount
Cabling
Basic Service & Support (12 months)
Consultation – 1 person for 1 day + 1 day of office work
Installation charge – approx. £1000
Delivery charge – approx. £200

Partner C

Read the job advertisement below and be ready to answer your partners' questions about it. Ask your partners questions about their job adverts. Find out …

1 about the type of employer.
2 what the job is.
3 what the requirements are.

4 the salary and benefits.
5 how to apply.
6 what happens if the application is shortlisted.

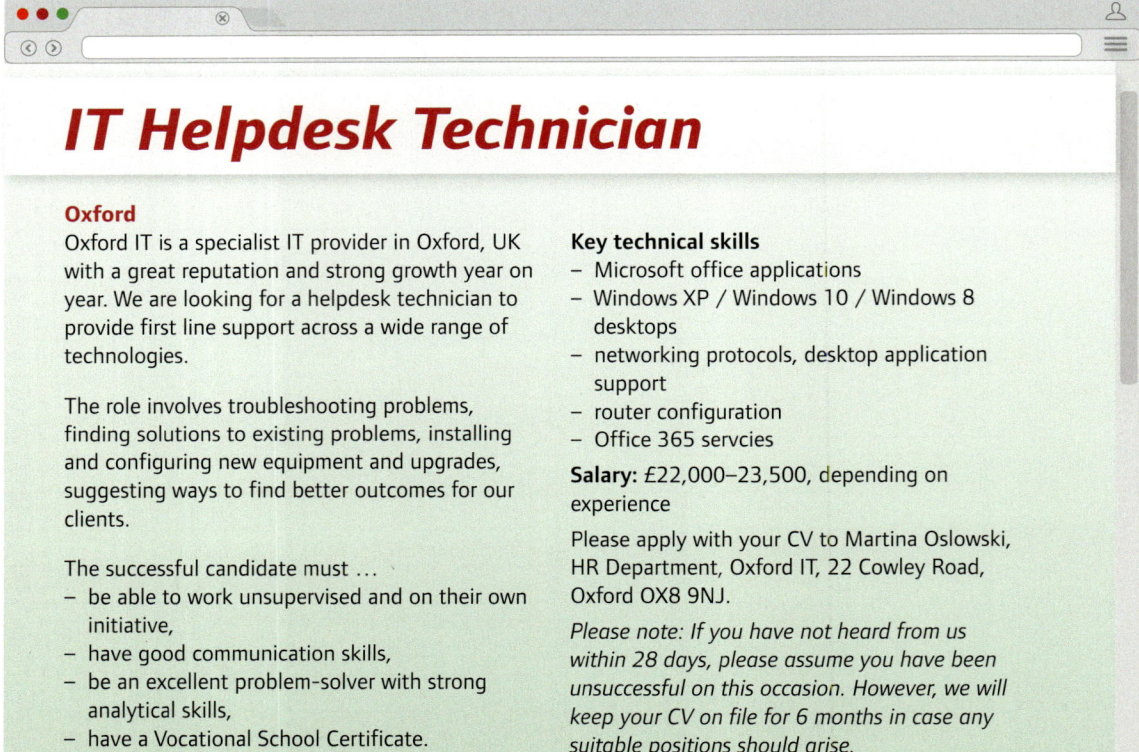

IT Helpdesk Technician

Oxford

Oxford IT is a specialist IT provider in Oxford, UK with a great reputation and strong growth year on year. We are looking for a helpdesk technician to provide first line support across a wide range of technologies.

The role involves troubleshooting problems, finding solutions to existing problems, installing and configuring new equipment and upgrades, suggesting ways to find better outcomes for our clients.

The successful candidate must …
– be able to work unsupervised and on their own initiative,
– have good communication skills,
– be an excellent problem-solver with strong analytical skills,
– have a Vocational School Certificate.

Key technical skills
– Microsoft office applications
– Windows XP / Windows 10 / Windows 8 desktops
– networking protocols, desktop application support
– router configuration
– Office 365 servcies

Salary: £22,000–23,500, depending on experience

Please apply with your CV to Martina Oslowski, HR Department, Oxford IT, 22 Cowley Road, Oxford OX8 9NJ.

Please note: If you have not heard from us within 28 days, please assume you have been unsuccessful on this occasion. However, we will keep your CV on file for 6 months in case any suitable positions should arise.

Partner B

A **You work for White Medical Institute and visit the QAR Medical booth at a trade fair. React to Partner A.**

– Establish rapport with Partner A.
– Describe your company to him/her.
– Find out more about QAR Medical.

B **Now you answer a follow-up call from Partner A. React to Partner A and ask where you can get more information about QAR and their products.**

Swap roles when you have finished.

FILE 23: Unit 12, Part B, exercise 4

Common interview questions	Tips
… about yourself – Tell us about yourself. – How would you describe yourself? – What are your strengths and weaknesses? – What are your hobbies? – Tell us about a mistake you made in the past and how you handled it. – What question would you not like us to ask you?	– Be honest. Show that you are able to use your strengths and indicate that you are working on your "weaknesses". – Be positive. Even if a mistake was made, remember to say that you learned from it. – Say that you hope they do not ask you about a particular department / task as you do not yet have much experience in that department/area. Keep it simple and say something positive.
… about your education, work experience and skills – Why did you choose to train at vocational college? – What responsibilities did you have / do you have during the work placement? / at work? – Please tell me about your present job. – What have you learned in your present job that you think will help you in the position you're applying for with us?	– Talk about the aspects of your education, work experience and skills that are relevant for the job in question. – Talk about a particular project or task which you did successfully.
… about what you know – What languages do you speak? – What computer software are you familiar with?	– Answer honestly. – Be honest. Don't say you know MS Office if you only learned Word, PowerPoint and Excel.
… about your motivation – Why did you apply for this job? – Why do you want to work for this company? – Why do you think you would be a good candidate for this job? – What would you like to achieve in the next five/ten years?	– Show that you have researched the company and know what the job is about. – Stress the positive aspects of the company and the job. – Talk about realistic goals and describe how you would like to progress with your career.
Questions you can ask the interviewer	
– I would like to continue improving my skills. What courses does the company offer? – What kind of training is given to new employees? – Who would I report to? – What are the prospects for promotion? – What are the next stages of the selection process? – When could I start?	

Schriftliche Prüfung

Zeit:	120 Minuten
Hilfsmittel:	allgemeines zweisprachiges Wörterbuch
Maximale Punktzahl:	100 Punkte

Im Rahmen der schriftlichen Prüfung werden die Aufgabenanteile für die drei Kompetenz-bereiche wie folgt gewichtet:

Rezeption	40 %
Produktion	30 %
Mediation	30 %.

Im Folgenden werden vier Aufgaben vorgelegt, die Sie bearbeiten sollen. Die erste und die zweite Aufgabe beziehen sich auf Ihre Fähigkeit, englische Texte (gesprochene und geschriebene) zu verstehen = **Rezeption**. Bei der dritten Aufgabe wird von Ihnen erwartet, dass Sie ein Schriftstück erstellen = **Produktion** eines englischen Textes. In der vierten Aufgabe sollen Sie Texte von der deutschen oder englischen in die jeweils andere Sprache übertragen = **Mediation**.

Die Prüfung beginnt mit der Hörverständnisaufgabe. Alle weiteren Aufgaben können in beliebiger Reihenfolge bearbeitet werden.

Rezeption I: Hörverstehen   **20 Punkte**

Sie machen ein Praktikum in der Abteilung „Service & Support" des Autohauses Schneider. Sie hören zu Ausbildungszwecken ein telefonisches Kundengespräch zwischen Brian Hemming und dem Kunden Sven Forsberg mit.

45))) Übertragen Sie das Formular in Ihr Notizbuch. Füllen Sie es stichwortartig in deutscher Sprache aus, während Sie das Gespräch zweimal anhören.

Name des Kunden / der Kundin:	▭
Kfz-Modell des Kunden:	▭
Grund des Anrufs / Problem des Kunden / der Kundin:	▭
Diebstahlsicherung des Kundenfahrzeugs:	▭
Schwächen von Keyless-Go:	▭
Ausrüstung der Kfz-Diebe:	▭
Vorgehen der Kfz-Diebe:	▭
Versicherung des Fahrzeugs:	▭
Empfohlene Sicherheitsmaßnahme bei Keyless-Go:	▭
Angebot an Kunden/Kundin:	▭
Dauer der Inanspruchnahme des Leihwagens:	▭
Funktion der Sicherheitsausstattung der Leihwagen:	▭

Rezeption II: Leseverstehen   20 Punkte

Sie sind Auszubildende/r bei Adler Network Components in Duisburg und sollen eine Präsentation auf Deutsch über künstliche Intelligenz halten. Sie haben einen Text im Internet gefunden und bereiten sich mithilfe dessen vor.

Machen Sie sich stichwortartige Notizen auf Deutsch zu folgenden Punkten:

Leistungen, für die Alan Turing weltbekannt wurde:	▭
Kurze Beschreibung des Turing-Tests:	▭
Turings Prophezeiung:	▭
Anforderungen an die Gewinner eines Loebner-Preises:	▭
Kritik am Turing-Test:	▭
Programmierung/Funktionsweise von DeepBlue:	▭
Programmierung/Funktionsweise von AlphaGo:	▭
Programmierung/Funktionsweise von Libratus:	▭
Grenzen der künstlichen Intelligenz:	▭

Can computers think?

Alan Turing was a brilliant mathematician who became famous for cracking the 'Enigma' code used by the German armed forces to send secret messages to their troops during the Second World War. This task was extremely difficult as the code changed daily. It has been estimated that the efforts of Turing shortened the war by more than two years and saved more than 14 million lives.

In 1950, in a paper entitled *Computing Machinery and Intelligence* Turing asked the following questions "Can machines think?" And if a computer could think, "How could we tell?" He suggested a test, known as the Turing Test: A human judge has a chat via a keyboard with a computer program and with a human being. The computer passes the test if, after five minutes, the judge cannot tell which is the computer and which is the human. Turing predicted that by the year 2000 the average judge would not have more than a 70 per cent chance of making the right identification.

In 1990 Hugh Loebner set up a prize of $4,000 for the first chatbot to pass the original text-based Turing Test. He also donated another prize of $25,000 for the creators of the first chatbot that the judges consider to be human-like, and he also set up a reward of $100,000 for the first program that judges cannot distinguish from a real human in a 30-minute Turing Test that includes understanding text, visual and voice input. This annual competition in artificial intelligence will only come to an end once the $100,000 has been won: as the main prize hasn't been awarded to anyone so far, the competition is still going on.

Steve Worswick's Mitsuku, possibly the world's best conversational chatbot, is a three-time winner of a Loebner medal. In 2017, after four rounds of chat sessions, it received the top ranking among the four competitors and was awarded the Loebner bronze medal in the annual Turing Test. When one judge asked: "What did you learn today?" Mitsuki answered: "I learned a bit more about human behaviour and relationships." Still the question remains whether the Turing Test is an adequate test of intelligence. Are the prize-winning chatbots nothing other than cleverly-coded pieces of software programmed to fool the judges, as some scientists think?

In the years since Turing, more artificially-intelligent machines have been created that are smart enough to defeat the best players in games of logic and skill. In 1997, IBM's DeepBlue was able to beat Garry Kasparov, the world chess champion. AlphaGo played thousands of games against itself before it was able to beat the world champion in 2001. In 2017, Libratus, a computer poker program, beat the world's top poker players by a margin of $1.2 million.

DeepBlue defeated Kasparov mainly thanks to its immense computing power. It had learned and analysed thousands of master games, and between games its developers were allowed to fine-tune the program. AlphaGo and Libratus are more intelligent. AlphaGo learned by reinforcement. It played a large number of games against itself and learned from experience based on feedback from previous games. Libratus does not have a fixed built-in strategy, but an algorithm that decides on its moves step by step.

However, all these artificially-intelligent computers cannot think the way humans think. They are programmed to do just one particular task. As long as we do not fully understand how our brain works, we will not be able to build machines that learn new things the way a clever child can.

Produktion

Sie absolvieren ein Praktikum in einem Reisebüro in Crawley, UK. Judith Eichner, eine neue Mitbewohner-in Ihrer WG, hat ein Problem mit einem Drucker, den Sie bei Hastings Appliance, 40b Devonshire Road, Hastings TN34 1NF, gekauft hatte. Da sie sich eine schriftliche Reklamation nicht zutraut, erklären Sie sich bereit, in ihrem Namen eine E-Mail an die Firma zu schreiben.

Ihre E-Mail sollte die folgenden Punkte enthalten:

- höfliche Anrede
- Kauf: vor zwei Monaten am 15. September
- Problem: zwei Wochen nach Kauf schwarze horizontale Linien quer über das Dokument; schwarze Druckerpatrone leckt

- Bitte um Mitteilung der Ursache
- Garantie des Druckers noch vorhanden
- Einsendung oder Reparatur vor Ort
- höflicher Briefschluss

Mediation

Sie sind Auszubildende/r bei einer Logistikfirma. Ihr Chef gibt Ihnen den Brief der Nuyotashi Service Division über die Rückrufaktion von Elektro-Vans. Er bittet Sie, die Informationen auf die Webseite Ihrer Firma zu stellen, um die Fahrer/innen zu informieren.

Fassen Sie die wichtigsten Informationen auf Deutsch stichwortartig zusammen unter Berücksichtigung folgender Punkte:

- Grund der Rückrufaktion
- Angebot des Herstellers

- zeitlicher Aufwand für die Inspektion
- Nachricht an etwaige Käufer von Gebraucht-wagen der Firma

Recall MEVCX 2018/120742; Vehicle identification number MEVCX 7278196702

Dear Sir or Madam

Recently there have been rumours about software problems with one electronic control unit (ECU) in our Multi EVanCX (2018 models). The rumours that a control unit might malfunction in hotter regions and affect the Electronic Stability Control (ESC) or the Adaptive Cruise Control (ACC) interface have not been confirmed by any of our dealers. Nor have any accidents caused by ECU failures been reported so far.

If you have not experienced problems with your van so far, you can be certain that your MultiEVanCX is safe to drive. Should you have any questions or concerns, please contact the service manager of your authorized retailer.

However, we take the issue very seriously and advise you to call your local dealer without delay to request a service date for Recall MEVanCX 2018/120742. Please provide your dealer with the VIN of your vehicle which is printed at the beginning of this letter.

We have authorized our dealership to check and service the software of the electronic control units. This is free of charge (including parts and labour). The inspection is estimated to take three hours. We have instructed our dealers to provide you with a van of similar design in case the inspection cannot be completed the same day.

This offer also extends to other 2017 model Multi EVanCX vehicles in your possession which you might have bought second-hand. In case you have sold the above-mentioned vehicle (VIN MEVCX 7278196702), please inform the new owner of our offers.

We apologize for any inconvenience this precautionary measure may cause you and thank you for your atten-tion to this important matter.

Sincerely

James Usinto

Nuyotashi Service Division Europe

Mündliche Prüfung

Die mündliche Prüfung ist eine Tandem- oder Gruppenprüfung, bei der Sie Gespräche persönlichen und fachlichen Inhalts in der Fremdsprache führen sollen. Sie dauert pro Kandidat/in ca. 25 Min. Zur Vorbereitung haben Sie 20 Minuten Zeit.

Phase I: Sie werden gebeten, sich zu persönlichen oder beruflichen Themen (z. B. Vorstellung des eigenen Werdegangs, der Firma und des Aufgabengebietes) zu äußern. Die Kandidaten/Kandidatinnen werden im Wechsel befragt.

Phase II: Im zweiten Teil sollen Sie zusammen mit einem/einer anderen Kandidaten/Kandidatin ein Rollenspiel durchführen. Dazu erhalten Sie vom Prüfer / von der Prüferin Rollenkarten, auf denen eine Situation beschrieben ist, die Sie vorspielen sollen.

Hilfsmittel: allgemeines zweisprachiges Wörterbuch

Interaktion   **30 Punkte**

Ihre Aufgaben für Phase I könnten wie folgt lauten:

Geben Sie Auskünfte über sich anhand folgender Stichworte:

Ihr beruflicher Werdegang:	• Ausbildung, Abschlüsse, Praktika usw. • Gründe für diese Berufswahl
Ihre Ausbildungsfirma:	• allgemeines Geschäftsfeld / Spezialisierungsbereiche • Anzahl der Beschäftigten, Arbeitsbedingungen usw.
Ihr Arbeitsalltag in der Firma:	• Verwaltungsaufgaben (Beispiele) • verwendete Hard- und Software (Beispiele) • Vorlieben/Abneigungen

Ihre Aufgaben für Phase II könnten wie folgt lauten:

Sie arbeiten in einer englischen Firma für Gebäudesicherung. Ihre Chefin teilt Ihnen und Ihrem Kollegen / Ihrer Kollegin mit, dass Sie nach Malta fliegen dürfen, um Vorgespräche mit dem Leiter eines Pharmakonzerns zu führen. Es geht um die Schließanlagen für die nuklearen Hochsicherheitsbereiche der Laboratorien und die Zugangsberechtigungen.

Sie klären vor der Reise gemeinsam folgende Punkte:

– was Sie über Malta wissen / noch nicht wissen
– wer die Flüge und wer das Hotel bucht
– welche Geräte, Muster und Anschauungsmaterialien Sie mitnehmen
– welche Fragen Sie dem Kunden stellen müssen
– welche Fragen Ihnen der Kunde stellen könnte
– mögliche Vor- und Nachteile von Transpondern für den Kunden
– Vor- und Nachteile von RFID-Implantaten für den Kunden
– Vor- und Nachteile von RFID-Implantaten für die Angestellten

Transponder
Vorteile: sicher, kostengünstig, programmierbar, Berechtigte erkennbar
Nachteile: Verlust, Diebstahl, Missbrauch durch Dritte

RFID-Implantat
Vorteile: programmierbar, sicher, Missbrauch ausgeschlossen …
Nachteile: Berechtigte nicht erkennbar, *wireless theft*; Bedenken der Mitarbeiter: körperlicher Eingriff, Überwachung der Privatsphäre

Describing companies   Unit 1

– We are a start-up / medium-sized company in the IT sector.	– *Wir sind ein Start-up(-Unternehmen) / ein mittelständisches Unternehmen in der IT-Branche.*
– The company is based in …	– *Das Unternehmen hat seinen Sitz in …*
– We produce/manufacture hardware components for the … industry.	– *Wir produzieren/fertigen Hardwarekomponenten für die …-Industrie.*
– We supply/provide software systems for customers in the … sector.	– *Wir liefern Softwaresysteme für Kunden in der …-Branche.*
– Our products are used in …	– *Unsere Produkte werden in … eingesetzt.*
– We install/manufacture/export …	– *Wir installieren/fertigen/exportieren …*
– The company maintains / carries out …	– *Das Unternehmen hält … instand / führt … aus.*

Making introductions   Unit 1

Greeting people you do not know

– Good morning/afternoon/evening. I'm …	– *Guten Morgen/Tag/Abend. Ich bin …*
– How do you do? My name is …	– *Freut mich. Mein Name ist …*
– Nice/Pleased to meet you.	– *Es freut mich, Sie kennen zu lernen.*
– Nice to meet you, too.	– *Ganz meinerseits.*
– Excuse me. Are you … ?	– *Entschuldigung. Sind Sie … ?*
– Yes, I am. / No, I'm not. I'm …	– *Ja, das bin ich. / Nein, das bin ich nicht. Ich heiße …*
– Welcome to …	– *Herzlich willkommen bei/in …*
– Thank you. It's nice to be here.	– *Dankeschön. Es ist schön, hier zu sein.*

Introducing people

– This is … . / These are my colleagues, John and Mary.	– *Das ist … . / Das sind meine Kollegen, John und Mary.*
– I'd like to introduce … from the … department.	– *Darf ich Ihnen … aus der …-Abteilung vorstellen?*

Showing visitors around the company   Unit 1

Giving a tour of the company

– Let's start by visiting …	– *Lassen Sie uns mit dem Besuch der/des … beginnen.*
– Here we have the … department.	– *Hier ist die …-Abteilung.*
– On the left/right, you can see …	– *Zu Ihrer Linken/Rechten sehen Sie …*
– This is where we make/assemble …	– *Hier stellen wir … her / bauen wir … zusammen.*

Asking for and giving directions

– Could you tell me the way to …, please?	– *Könnten Sie mir bitte sagen, wie ich nach/zur/zum … komme?*
– Yes, certainly.	– *Ja, selbstverständlich.*
– Go down the corridor until you get to …	– *Gehen Sie den Flur entlang, bis Sie zur/zum … kommen.*
– Take the first/second/last door on your right.	– *Nehmen Sie die erste/zweite/letzte Tür rechts.*
– Turn right at the end of the corridor.	– *Biegen Sie am Ende des Flures rechts ab.*

Offering help/refreshments

– Can I take your coat?	– *Möchten Sie Ihren Mantel ablegen?*
– Would you like something to drink?	– *Darf ich Ihnen etwas zu trinken anbieten?*
– Would you like some tea/coffee/water?	– *Möchten Sie Tee/Kaffee/Wasser?*

Describing jobs and responsibilities — Unit 1, Unit 2

– I work in a team of software testers.	– *Ich arbeite in einem Team von Software-Testern.*
– I install/test/replace/inspect …	– *Ich installiere/teste/ersetze/kontrolliere …*
– I maintain/repair network systems.	– *Ich warte/repariere Netzwerksysteme.*
– I troubleshoot/diagnose software problems.	– *Ich behebe Software-Probleme / stelle Software-Probleme fest.*
– I make sure our software products get to our clients.	– *Ich stelle sicher, dass unsere Software-Produkte unseren Kunden/Kundinnen geliefert werden.*
– I am responsible for maintaining our database.	– *Ich bin dafür verantwortlich, die Datenbank zu pflegen.*
– I report directly to the project manager.	– *Ich erstatte direkt dem/der Projektmanager/in Bericht.*
– I work fixed hours / a 39-hour week / shifts.	– *Ich habe feste Arbeitszeiten / eine 39-Stunden-Woche / arbeite Schicht.*
– I do a lot of overtime.	– *Ich mache viele Überstunden.*

Giving presentations — Unit 2

Introduction

– My name is … and this is my partner, …	– *Mein Name ist … und das ist meine/e Partner/in, …*
– We are apprentices at … in Germany.	– *Wir sind Auszubildende bei … in Deutschland.*
– This morning, I'm / we're going to talk about …	– *Heute Morgen werde(n) ich/wir über … sprechen.*
– Our topic today is …	– *Das heutige Thema lautet …*

Structure

– I've divided my presentation into three main parts, as follows: …	– *Ich habe meine Präsentation in drei Hauptteile unterteilt, und zwar …*
– First/Firstly, … ; Second/Secondly, … ; After that / Then …	– *Erstens … ; Zweitens … ; Anschließend/Dann …*

Signposts

– To begin with, …; Next, …; Now …	– *Zuerst …; Als Nächstes …; Jetzt …*
– The next topic I'm going to talk about is …	– *Das nächste Thema, das ich behandeln möchte, lautet …*
– Now I'd like to move on to …	– *Jetzt möchte ich zum Thema … übergehen.*

Handouts

– I've prepared a few things/handouts for you to take away.	– *Ich habe etwas/Handouts für Sie zum Mitnehmen vorbereitet.*
– I hope you'll find these copies of the graphics useful.	– *Ich hoffe, dass Sie diese Ausdrucke der Grafiken nützlich finden.*

Conclusion

– Before I finish my presentation, I'd just like to mention …	– *Bevor ich meinen Vortrag beende, möchte ich kurz … erwähnen.*
– I'd like to go over the main points again.	– *Ich möchte die Hauptpunkte nochmals kurz darlegen.*
– Finally / In conclusion / In summary, …	– *Zum Schluss / Abschließend / Zusammenfassend …*

Questions / Thanking the audience

– Are there any questions?	– *Gibt es / Haben Sie noch Fragen?*
– We have time for a few questions / one last question.	– *Wir haben noch Zeit für ein paar Fragen / eine letzte Frage.*
– Well, that's the end of my presentation.	– *Damit bin ich am Ende meiner Präsentation angelangt.*
– Thank you for your attention / for listening.	– *Vielen Dank für Ihre Aufmerksamkeit / fürs Zuhören.*

Identifying yourself
- Good morning. My name's ...
- Good afternoon. This is ... from ... (company).
- Good evening. I work for ...

– Guten Morgen. Ich heiße ...
– Guten Tag. Hier spricht ... von ... (Firma).
– Guten Abend. Ich arbeite bei ...

Explaining the reason for your call
- I'm enquiring about ...
- I'd like some information on ...

– Ich wollte mich nach ... erkundigen.
– Ich hätte gern nähere Informationen zu ...

Asking for a person/department
- I'd like to speak to Mr/Ms ...
- Could you put me through to the ... department, please?

– Ich hätte gern (mit) Herrn/Frau ... gesprochen.
– Könnten Sie mich bitte zur ...-Abteilung durchstellen?

Saying what you want to do
- Can I leave a message?
- I'll call again later.
- Could you ask Mr/Ms ... to call me back?

– Kann ich eine Nachricht hinterlassen?
– Ich rufe später noch einmal an.
– Könnten Sie Herrn/Frau ... bitten, mich zurückzurufen?

Ending the call
- Thank you for your help/assistance.
- You're welcome.
- Goodbye.
- Have a nice day/evening.

– Vielen Dank für Ihre Hilfe/Unterstützung.
– Gern geschehen. / Bitte sehr.
– Auf Wiederhören.
– Einen schönen Tag/Abend noch.

| Taking telephone calls | Unit 2 |

- Who's calling, please?
- Could you spell your name, please?
- I'm sorry, I didn't understand. Could you repeat that, please?
- I'll put you through.
- I'm trying to connect you.
- Please hold the line.
- I'm afraid the line is engaged.
- I'm sorry, ... (name) is unavailable at the moment.
- Would you like to speak to someone else?
- Would you like to leave a message?

– Wie ist Ihr Name bitte?
– Könnten Sie bitte Ihren Namen buchstabieren?
– Ich habe das nicht verstanden. Könnten Sie das bitte wiederholen?
– Ich stelle Sie durch.
– Ich versuche, Sie zu verbinden.
– Bleiben Sie bitte dran.
– Der Anschluss ist leider besetzt.
– Es tut mir leid, ... (Name) ist im Moment nicht da.
– Möchten Sie mit jemand anderem sprechen?
– Möchten Sie eine Nachricht hinterlassen?

| Giving instructions | Unit 3 |

- Turn off your laptop.
- Make sure that ...
- Check that/if ...
- Disconnect the power cable.
- Take the bottom off the laptop case.
- It should come off fairly easily, but you may need to lightly force it.
- Be careful not to ...
- You mustn't ...

– Schalten Sie Ihren Laptop aus.
– Stellen Sie sicher, dass ...
– Überprüfen Sie, dass/ob ...
– Ziehen Sie das Stromkabel heraus.
– Entfernen Sie die untere Laptop-Abdeckung.
– Es sollte recht leicht abgehen, aber es kann sein, dass Sie ein wenig Kraft anwenden müssen.
– Achten Sie darauf, nicht zu ...
– Sie dürfen nicht ...

Writing emails | Unit 3

Salutation
- Dear Sir or Madam (*formal*)
- Dear Mr/Ms Smith (*formal*)
- Dear Paul (und Paula)
- Good morning, Paul (*less formal*)
- Hi/Hello Paula (*less formal*)

- *Sehr geehrte Damen und Herren,*
- *Sehr geehrte/r Herr/Frau Schmidt,*
- *Lieber Paul(, Liebe Paula)*
- *Guten Morgen, Paul,*
- *Hallo Paula,*

Complimentary close
- Yours faithfully (*formal*)
- Regards / Best regards / Best wishes / Yours sincerely (*formal*)

- Regards / Best regards / Best wishes
- All the best (*less formal*)

- *Mit freundlichen Grüßen*
- *Mit freundlichen Grüßen / Freundliche Grüße*

- *Viele Grüße / Freundlichen Grüße*
- *Alles Gute / Herzliche Grüße*

Opening sentence
- I'm just writing to ... (*formal*)
- Just a quick note/message to ... (*less formal*)

- *Ich schreibe Ihnen, ... zu ...*
- *Nur eine kurze Mitteilung/Nachricht, ... zu ...*

Conclusion
- I look forward to your reply / to hearing from you. (*formal*)
- Many thanks in advance. (*formal*)
- I hope to hear from you soon. (*less formal*)

- *Ich freue mich auf Ihre Antwort.*

- *Vielen Dank im Voraus.*
- *Ich freue mich, bald von Ihnen/Dir zu hören.*

Navigating GUIs | Unit 4

- Tap once on the symbol and you will see the information you require.
- Place two fingers together on the screen and then spread them.
- Double tap the place you want to zoom into on the screen.
- Place two fingers on the screen and then pinch to control the zoom.

- To scroll slowly, touch the screen and drag your finger in any direction.
- To scroll quickly, touch the screen and swipe up or down, left or right.

- *Drücken Sie einmal auf das Symbol, und Sie werden die benötigten Informationen sehen.*
- *Platzieren Sie zwei Finger zusammen auf dem Bildschirm und spreizen Sie sie dann.*
- *Doppelklicken Sie auf die Stelle auf dem Bildschirm, die Sie vergrößern möchten.*
- *Mit Auf- und Zuziehen von zwei Fingern auf dem Bildschirm können Sie (Inhalte) vergrößern bzw. verkleinern.*
- *Um langsam zu scrollen, berühren Sie den Bildschirm und ziehen Sie Ihren Finger in eine beliebige Richtung.*
- *Um schnell zu scrollen, berühren Sie den Bildschirm und wischen Sie nach oben oder unten, links oder rechts.*

Installing software | Unit 4

- Make sure you have sufficient privilege to perform the installation.
- Choose 'Add new extension' under the 'Extensions' menu.
- Enter the URL provided in your licence confirmation email.
- Click on 'View components' and then select 'Continue'.
- To confirm that the package installed successfully, check that it is visible in the 'Active extensions' menu.

- Take additional steps to verify your specific settings.

- *Stellen Sie sicher, dass Sie ausreichende Berechtigungen haben, um die Installation auszuführen.*
- *Wählen Sie „Neue Erweiterung hinzufügen" unter dem Menüpunkt „Erweiterungen".*
- *Geben Sie die URL ein, die in Ihrer Lizenzbestätigungsmail angegeben ist.*
- *Klicken Sie auf „Komponenten ansehen" und wählen Sie dann „Fortfahren".*
- *Um zu bestätigen, dass das Paket erfolgreich installiert worden ist, prüfen Sie, dass es im Menü „Aktive Erweiterungen" sichtbar ist.*
- *Führen Sie weitere Schritte aus, um Ihre anwenderspezifischen Einstellungen zu überprüfen.*

Explaining access requirements

– You are (not) allowed/permitted to install software from the internet.	– *Sie haben (k)eine Erlaubnis/Berechtigung, Software aus dem Internet zu installieren.*
– You do (not) have permission to download videos.	– *Sie haben (k)eine Berechtigung, Videos herunterzuladen.*
– There are a number of options to gain access to the company network.	– *Es gibt mehrere Optionen, um Zugang zum Firmennetzwerk zu erhalten.*
– Clients do (not) have access to the company intranet.	– *Kunden/Kundinnen haben (k)einen Zugang zum Intranet.*
– To access your email you need a smartphone, tablet or desktop computer.	– *Um Ihre Mails abzurufen, benötigen Sie ein Smartphone, Tablet oder einen PC.*
– Authentication via a soft token requires a smartphone or tablet with the app installed.	– *Die Authentifizierung mittels Software-Token erfordert die Installierung der App auf einem Smartphone oder einem Tablet-PC.*

Describing graphs

– The graph/chart shows/presents …	– *Die Grafik / Das Diagramm zeigt … / stellt … dar.*
– The horizontal/vertical axis has a scale from … to …	– *Die waagerechte/senkrechte Achse hat eine Skala von … bis …*
– The x axis / The y axis is divided into … units/sections each representing …	– *Die X-Achse / Die Y-Achse ist unterteilt in … Einheiten/Abschnitte, die … darstellen.*
– The number of cyberattacks decreased slightly last month.	– *Die Zahl der Cyberangriffe ging letzten Monat leicht zurück.*
– The number of attacks jumped sharply in June.	– *Die Zahl der Angriffe nahm im Juni stark zu.*
– They reached their peak in August, then levelled off towards the end of the year.	– *Sie erreichten ihren Höhepunkt im August und blieben dann bis zum Ende des Jahres gleich.*
– Phishing accounted for about/roughly/approximately one third of all cyberattacks.	– *Phishing machte etwa/annähernd/ungefähr ein Drittel aller Cyberangriffe aus.*
– Malware made up just over/under one tenth of web-based attacks.	– *Schadsoftware machte etwas über/unter ein Zehntel der netzbasierten Angriffe aus.*

Advising customers

Greeting

– Good morning/afternoon. How can I help you?	– *Guten Morgen/Tag. Wie kann ich Ihnen helfen?*

Showing the product

– This is our latest model.	– *Das ist unser neuestes Modell.*
– How about this hard disk?	– *Wie wäre es mit dieser Festplatte?*
– This one has some interesting features.	– *Dieses (Modell) hat interessante Funktionen.*
– There's a five-year guarantee.	– *Es gibt fünf Jahre Garantie.*

Making suggestions

– I wouldn't recommend that one.	– *Ich würde dieses dort nicht empfehlen.*
– You could try this one instead.	– *Sie könnten stattdessen dieses hier ausprobieren.*
– It might be better to take this model.	– *Vermutlich wäre es besser, dieses Modell zu nehmen.*

Asking for advice	Unit 6

Explaining what you need

– I'm looking for a/an …	– *Ich suche ein/eine/einen …*
– I need a/an … for my …	– *Ich brauche ein/eine/einen … für mein/meine/ meinen …*

Asking about the product

– How much storage space does it have?	– *Wie viel Speicherplatz hat es?*
– Will I need to buy a new graphics card?	– *Werde ich eine neue Grafikkarte kaufen müssen?*

Accepting/rejecting suggestions

– Yes, I think that's the right one for me.	– *Ja, ich denke, dass dies das Richtige für mich ist.*
– Good. I'll take it/them.	– *Gut, ich nehme ihn/sie/es.*
– Sorry, I don't think that's what I had in mind.	– *Das ist leider nicht das, was ich mir vorgestellt habe.*
– I'm afraid that's not really what I'm looking for.	– *Ich fürchte, das ist nicht das, wonach ich suche.*

Describing processes	Unit 6

– There are several options that allow you to customize software.	– *Es gibt mehrere Optionen, die Ihnen ermöglichen, die Software anzupassen.*
– The first step in any installation/customization is to …	– *Der erste Schritt bei jeder Installation/Anpassung ist …*
– If you want to …, you can …	– *Wenn Sie möchten, können Sie …*
– We start by …-ing …	– *Wir beginnen mit der/dem …*
– After that, / Then / Next we …	– *Im Anschluss / Dann / Als Nächstes … wir …*
– Once that is done, we …	– *Sobald dies getan ist, … wir …*
– If you selected the wrong option, go back / return to the 'Options' menu.	– *Wenn Sie die falsche Option wählen, gehen Sie zum Menüpunkt „Optionen" zurück.*
– Authorization is completed by selecting the 'Authorize' button.	– *Die Berechtigung wird abgeschlossen, indem man auf „Erlauben" klickt.*
– The final stage of the installation is to …	– *Der letzte Schritt der Installation ist …*

Making arrangements	Unit 6

Inviting somebody to a meeting

– Ms Smith would like to invite you to a meeting on … (day) at … (time).	– *Frau Smith möchte Sie zu einem Treffen am … (Tag) um … (Zeit) Uhr einladen.*
– I would like to invite you to lunch/dinner.	– *Ich möchte Sie zum Mittagessen/Abendessen einladen.*
– The meeting will take place at my office / our premises in … (place/city).	– *Das Treffen findet in meinem Büro / in unseren Räumlichkeiten in … (Ort/Stadt) statt.*

Accepting/Declining the invitation

– Thank you for your invitation to meet you at … (place).	– *Vielen Dank für Ihre Einladung für das Treffen in … (Ort).*
– I am pleased / We are delighted to accept your invitation/offer.	– *Gern nehme(n) ich/wir Ihre Einladung / Ihr Angebot an.*
– I'm sorry, but I'm … (reason) on that date / at that time.	– *Es tut mir leid, aber ich kann an diesem Tag / zu dieser Zeit nicht, da … (Grund).*

Making an alternative suggestion

– How about meeting on … (day) at … (time) instead?	– *Wie wäre es, wenn wir uns stattdessen am … (Tag) um … (Uhrzeit) treffen?*

Conclusion

– I look forward to your reply. (*formal*)	– *Ich freue mich auf Ihre Antwort.*
– I hope to hear from you soon. Many thanks.	– *Ich hoffe, von Ihnen bald zu hören. Besten Dank.*

Explaining requirements and consequences

Taking things into consideration
- We need to take into account the conditions that the network operates under.
- The number of access points is another important factor.
- Bearing the data rate in mind, we need extra access points.
- We should consider a dual-band set-up with 2.4 and 5 GHz.

Expressing consequences
- We will increase the risk of slower speeds if we don't buy enough access points.

- Unless we install a dual-band network, employee productivity will suffer.
- As access points can fail, it's vital that we buy four spare ones now.

- *Wir müssen die Bedingungen berücksichtigen, unter denen das Netzwerk betrieben wird.*
- *Die Zahl der Access Points ist ein anderer wichtiger Faktor.*
- *Wenn man die Datenrate berücksichtigt, benötigen wir zusätzliche Access Points.*
- *Wir sollten ein Dualband-Netzwerk mit 2,4 und 5 GHz in Betracht ziehen.*

- *Wir werden eine langsamere Geschwindigkeit riskieren, wenn wir nicht genügend Access Points kaufen.*
- *Wenn wir kein Dualband-Netzwerk installieren, wird die Produktivität der Mitarbeiter darunter leiden.*
- *Da Access Points ausfallen können, ist es wichtig, dass wir nun vier Ersatz-Access Points kaufen.*

Taking part in discussions

Asking for opinions
- What do you think about ...?
- What's your opinion of / view on ...?

Expressing a point of view
- It seems to me (that) ...
- In my opinion, ...
- From what I can see, ...

Looking for agreement
- I think we have to consider it, don't we?
- That's quite impressive, isn't it?

Confirming agreement
- I couldn't agree more.
- I'm (definitely) with you on that.

Disagreeing politely
- Oh, I don't agree. / (Well,) As a matter of fact, ...
- Actually, / In fact, I think (that) ...

Partially agreeing with an argument
- I'm not sure that I entirely agree.
- I partially agree, but ...
- There's some / a lot of truth in what you say. However, ...
- I see what you mean, but ...
- I'd go along with a lot of that, but ...

- *Was denken Sie über ...?*
- *Was ist Ihre Meinung zu ... ?*

- *Mir kommt es so vor, dass ...*
- *Meiner Meinung nach ...*
- *Soweit ich sagen kann, ...*

- *Ich denke, dass wir dies berücksichtigen müssen, oder?*
- *Dies ist recht eindrucksvoll, oder?*

- *Ich stimme voll und ganz zu.*
- *Ich stimme Ihnen diesbezüglich (absolut) zu.*

- *Oh, das sehe ich anders. / Tatsächlich ...*
- *Eigentlich / Vielmehr denke ich, dass ...*

- *Ich bin mir nicht sicher, ob ich vollkommen zustimme.*
- *Ich stimme teilweise zu, aber ...*
- *Da steckt etwas / viel Wahrheit in dem, was Sie sagen. Jedoch ...*
- *Ich verstehe, was Sie meinen, aber ...*
- *Ich würde dem zustimmen, aber ...*

Giving feedback	Unit 7

Making polite suggestions
– It might be better if ...	– Es könnte besser sein, wenn ...
– It would be a good idea to ...	– Es wäre eine gute Idee, zu ...
– You could think about ...	– Sie könnten über ... nachdenken.
– Why don't you try ...-ing?	– Warum versuchen Sie nicht, zu ... ?

Reacting politely to feedback
– Can you give me some examples?	– Können Sie mir Beispiele nennen?
– Is there something I have missed?	– Habe ich etwas übersehen?
– How can I improve ... ?	– Wie kann ich ... verbessern?
– OK. You may have a point there.	– Okay. Darin mögen Sie Recht haben.
– Sure. I'll do that (in future).	– Sicher. Ich werde dies (in Zukunft) tun.

Engaging with potential customers	Unit 8

Establishing rapport
– Good afternoon, I'm ... (name) from ... (company). Welcome to our booth/stand. How are you today?	– Guten Tag, ich bin ... (Name) von ... (Firma). Willkommen an unserem Messestand. Wie geht es Ihnen?
– How are you enjoying the trade fair?	– Wie gefällt Ihnen die Messe?
– It's great to see a lot of strong technology, don't you agree?	– Es ist toll, so viel leistungsstarke Technologie zu sehen, finden Sie nicht?
– May I ask who you work for?	– Darf ich fragen, bei wem Sie arbeiten?
– You have a great reputation as a leader of IT technology.	– Ihnen eilt ein großartiger Ruf als Spitzenreiter innerhalb der IT-Technologie voraus.
– Can I ask whether you are looking for something in particular?	– Darf ich Sie fragen, ob Sie etwas Bestimmtes suchen?
– That's our speciality. I'd be happy to demonstrate our ... program.	– Das ist unser Spezialgebiet. Ich würde mich freuen, Ihnen unser ...-Programm zu zeigen.

Following up a first meeting by phone/email
– We met last week at the trade fair.	– Wir haben uns letzte Woche auf der Messe kennengelernt.
– I really enjoyed our conversation.	– Ich habe mich sehr gerne mit Ihnen unterhalten.
– As I said at the show, ...	– Wie ich bei der Vorführung sagte, ...
– You can refer to the attachment.	– Sie können sich auf den Anhang beziehen.
– You can check out our interactive demonstration on the 'Demo' page of our website.	– Sie können unsere interaktive Vorführung auf der Demoseite unserer Homepage ausprobieren.

Checking in and out of hotels	Unit 8

Checking in
– Good morning. My name is ... . I have a reservation.	– Guten Morgen. Mein Name ist ... . Ich habe reserviert.
– The reservation may be under the name of my company, ...	– Die Reservierung kann unter dem Namen meiner Firma ... sein.
– I would like to check in. I booked a room on the ground floor, with wheelchair access.	– Ich würde gerne einchecken. Ich habe ein barrierefreies Zimmer im Erdgeschoss gebucht.
– Where can I park my car?	– Wo kann ich mein Auto parken?
– What time is breakfast?	– Wann gibt es Frühstück?

Checking in
– I'm going home today, so I would like to check out.	– Ich reise heute ab und würde gerne auschecken.
– Could I have the bill, please?	– Könnte ich bitte die Rechnung bekommen?
– The bill is being paid by / should be sent to ...	– Die Rechnung wird beglichen von ... / sollte an ... gesandt werden.

Negotiating Unit 9

Accommodating changes to the offer
- I have some room to move.
- OK. I'm prepared to offer you that.
- Yes, I think we can do that for you.

Refusing what the client asks for
- I'm sorry, but the price that I quoted you is the best I can do.
- No. I'm afraid I can't do that.
- Well, I can't offer you … . But what I can do is …

– Ich habe einigen Spielraum.	
– In Ordnung. Ich biete Ihnen dies gerne an.	
– Ja, ich denke, dass wir dies für Sie tun können.	
– Es tut mir leid, aber der Preis, den ich genannt habe, ist das Äußerste, das ich Ihnen anbieten kann.	
– Nein, ich kann dies leider nicht tun.	
– Ich kann Ihnen kein/e … anbieten. Ich kann jedoch …	

Writing business letters Unit 9

Salutation
- Dear Sir or Madam (*to a firm*)
- Dear Mr/Ms Brown
- Dear Sharon

Complimentary close
- Yours faithfully (*BE: to a firm*)
- Yours very truly / Cordially yours (*AE: to a firm*)
- Yours sincerely (*BE*)
- Sincerely yours / Best personal regards (*AE*)

– *Sehr geehrte Damen und Herren,*	
– *Sehr geehrte/r Herr/Frau Brown,*	
– *Liebe Sharon,*	
– *Mit freundlichen Grüßen*	
– *Mit freundlichen Grüßen*	
– *Mit freundlichen Grüßen*	
– *Mit freundlichen Grüßen / Beste Grüße*	

Writing enquiries Unit 10

Source of address
- We saw your advertisement/brochure/catalogue in …
- We visited your stand/presentation at the trade fair in …

About your firm
- We are a small/medium-sized company in the IT sector.
- We are interested in your … (products).

What you require
- Please send us samples of your … / your latest catalogue.
- Please give us / let us have a quotation for … / details of all discounts.
- Full details of your terms of delivery and payment would be appreciated.

References
- References can be obtained from … (name of bank/ company).

Polite ending
- If your products find our customers' approval, … .
- … we will be able to place a sizeable order very soon.

- We look forward to hearing from you soon / receiving your offer within the next few days.

– *Wir haben Ihre/n Anzeige/Prospekt/Katalog in … gesehen.*	
– *Wir haben Ihren Stand / Ihre Präsentation auf der Messe in … besucht.*	
– *Wir sind ein kleiner/mittelständischer Betrieb in der IT-Branche.*	
– *Wir interessieren uns für Ihre … (Produkte).*	
– *Bitte schicken Sie uns Muster/Proben Ihrer … / Ihren aktuellen Katalog zu.*	
– *Bitte schicken Sie uns ein Angebot für … / informieren Sie uns zu allen Einzelheiten Ihrer Rabatte.*	
– *Wir würden uns freuen, genaue Informationen zu Ihren Versand- und Zahlungsbedingungen zu erhalten.*	
– *Referenzen können von … (Name der Bank/Firma) angefordert werden.*	
– *Sollten Ihre Produkte unseren Kunden zusagen, … .*	
– *… werden wir in naher Zukunft eine größere Bestellung in Auftrag geben.*	
– *Wir würden uns freuen, bald von Ihnen zu hören / Ihr Angebot in den nächsten Tagen zu erhalten.*	

Writing offers	Unit 9, Unit 10
Reference to enquiry	
– Many thanks for your letter of … (date) enquiring about … (*general enquiry*)	– *Vielen Dank für Ihren Brief vom … (Datum) mit Ihrer Anfrage bzgl. …*
– We refer to your enquiry of … (date) for … (*specific enquiry*)	– *Wir beziehen uns auf Ihre Anfrage vom … (Datum) bzgl. …*
Reference to information, samples, etc.	
– Enclosed (please find) our latest brochure / catalogue / price list.	– *Anbei finden Sie unsere(n) aktuelle(n) Prospekt/ Katalog/Preisliste.*
– We are sending you a selection of samples.	– *Wir übersenden Ihnen eine Auswahl an Mustern/ Proben.*
Terms	
– We would like to point out that our prices are quoted DAP / EXW / …	– *Wir möchten darauf hinweisen, dass sich unsere Preise DAP / EXW / … verstehen.*
– We draw your attention to the fact that our guarantee / warranty period extends over … / is valid for …	– *Wir möchten Sie darauf hinweisen, dass unser Garantie-/Haftungszeitraum … beträgt / gültig ist.*
– Terms of payment: we offer a …% cash discount for payment within … days.	– *Zahlungsbedingungen: Bei Zahlung innerhalb von … Tagen gewähren wir … % Skonto.*
– For orders over … we offer a discount of …%.	– *Für Bestellungen über … räumen wir einen (Mengen-) Rabatt von … % ein.*
Further information	
– Our delivery date is approximately … days/weeks after receipt of your order.	– *Die Lieferung erfolgt etwa … Tage/Wochen nach Eingang Ihrer Bestellung.*
– Delivery time is about … weeks/months.	– *Der Lieferzeitraum beträgt etwa … Wochen/Monate.*
– We can guarantee immediate delivery.	– *Wir können Ihnen eine sofortige Lieferung garantieren.*
Polite ending	
– We look forward to receiving your order and assure you that we will give it our prompt and careful attention.	– *Wir freuen uns auf Ihre Bestellung und sichern Ihnen eine zügige und gewissenhafte Abwicklung zu.*

Writing orders	Unit 10
– Thank you for your quotation of …	– *Vielen Dank für Ihr Angebot für …*
– Many thanks for your quotation.	– *Vielen Dank für Ihr Angebot.*
– We agree to your terms and are pleased to give you an order for …	– *Wir stimmen Ihren Bedingungen zu und freuen uns, Sie mit einer Bestellung über … zu beauftragen.*
– We enclose / are enclosing order no. …	– *Wir fügen Bestellnr. … bei.*
– We understand that all prices are DAP / EXW / … / include VAT.	– *Wir sind uns bewusst, dass sich alle Preise DAP / EXW / … / inklusive Mehrwertsteuer verstehen.*
– Payment will be made by … (method of payment) on delivery of the goods.	– *Die Zahlung erfolgt durch … (Zahlungsmethode) bei Lieferung der Ware(n).*
– Payment will be made within … days of receipt of the goods.	– *Die Zahlung erfolgt innerhalb von … Tagen nach Eingang der Ware(n).*
– Please acknowledge this order by return of post.	– *Bitte bestätigen Sie diese Bestellung postwendend.*
– We look forward to receiving the goods as soon as possible.	– *Wir würden uns freuen, die Ware(n) sobald wie möglich zu erhalten.*
– We trust you will give this order your prompt/careful attention.	– *Wir erwarten eine zügige/gewissenhafte Abwicklung dieser Bestellung.*

Situation

- With reference to our order number ... which arrived / was due on ... (date), ...
- I'm sorry to have to inform you that ...
- When we opened the boxes we discovered/saw that ...
- ... some/all of the items/parts were broken/ damaged/missing.
- While testing the equipment we saw that it was not working properly / it became apparent that it was not up to standard.

– Mit Bezug auf unsere Bestellnummer ..., die am ... (Datum) eingetroffen ist / fällig war, ...
– Leider müssen wir Ihnen mitteilen, dass ...
– Beim Öffnen der Behälter bemerkten/sahen wir, dass ...
– ... einige der / alle Artikel/Teile kaputt/beschädigt waren / fehlten.
– Beim Testen des Geräts / der Geräte stellten wir fest / stellte sich heraus, dass es/sie nicht funktionierte(n) / es/sie den Anforderungen nicht entsprach(en).

Request

- Please investigate the matter as soon as possible.

- Please let us know what can be done to solve this problem.
- Could you please explain (why) ... ?
- I would appreciate it if you would ...
- Can I ask that you ...

– Bitte untersuchen Sie diese Angelegenheit so schnell wie möglich.
– Bitte teilen Sie uns mit, welche Maßnahmen getroffen werden können, um dieses Problem zu beheben.
– Könnten Sie bitte erklären (warum) ... ?
– Ich wäre dankbar, wenn Sie ...
– Kann ich Sie bitten, ...

Reason

- We have a large order from a regular customer, which we have to fill quickly.
- We are unable to continue production until we have the equipment.
- If we do not receive the goods within the next ... days, we will have to stop production.

– Wir haben eine große Bestellung eines Stammkunden, die wir schnell ausführen müssen.
– Wir können mit der Produktion nicht fortfahren, solange die Geräte nicht da sind.
– Wenn wir die Ware nicht innerhalb der nächsten ... Tage erhalten, müssen wir die Produktion einstellen.

Polite ending

- We hope to receive your answer / an explanation immediately / without delay / by ... (date).
- We must point out that our further business relationship will depend on a satisfactory solution to the problem.

– Wir hoffen auf Ihre sofortige Antwort/Erklärung / bis zum ... (Datum).
– Wir müssen darauf hinweisen, dass unsere weitere Zusammenarbeit von einer zufriedenstellenden Lösung des Problems abhängt.

Polite opening

- We are very sorry (to hear) that the goods arrived damaged/broken/late.
- We are very sorry (to learn) that you have received faulty/damaged / the wrong goods.
- Please accept our sincere apologies.
- We apologize for the inconvenience caused.

- We regret any inconvenience that this has caused you.

– Wir bedauern sehr, dass die Ware bei Ihnen beschädigt/kaputt/verspätet eingetroffen ist.
– Es tut uns sehr leid, dass Sie mangelhafte/ schadhafte / die falsche Ware erhalten haben.
– Wir bitten vielmals um Entschuldigung.
– Wir entschuldigen uns vielmals für die entstandenen Unannehmlichkeiten.
– Wir bedauern, dass dies Ihnen Unannehmlichkeiten verursacht hat.

Reason

- Unfortunately, there was a mix-up in our sales department.
- We are sorry to say that one of our staff was ill and could not complete the order.

– Leider ist es in unserer Vertriebsabteilung zu einer Verwechslung gekommen.
– Leider war eine/r unserer Mitarbeiter/innen krank und konnte daher die Bestellung nicht bearbeiten.

- The damage was caused by bad handling in transit / a problem with the packing.

- We have had some problems with new software but these have now been solved.

Action taken
- We have sent a replacement consignment by courier / by express delivery which you will receive by … at the latest.

Polite ending
- We hope that we can continue our successful business relationship, despite this problem.
- We assure you that we will make every effort to ensure there are no problems in the future.

- We hope that this solution solves your problem to your satisfaction.
- Don't hesitate to contact us again if you have any further difficulties.

- *Der Schaden ist durch mangelhafte Abfertigung während des Transports / ein Problem bei der Verpackung entstanden.*
- *Wir hatten einige Probleme mit der neuen Software, aber diese konnten behoben werden.*

- *Wir haben Ihnen per Kurierdienst/Expressversand eine Ersatzlieferung geschickt, die Sie spätestens bis … erhalten werden.*

- *Wir hoffen sehr, dass wir trotz dieses Problems unsere erfolgreiche Zusammenarbeit fortsetzen können.*
- *Wir möchten Ihnen versichern, dass wir alles tun werden, um derartige Probleme in Zukunft zu vermeiden.*
- *Wir hoffen, dass diese Lösung das Problem zu Ihrer Zufriedenheit behebt.*
- *Bitte kontaktieren Sie uns, sollten Sie weitere Schwierigkeiten haben.*

Writing covering letters	**Unit 12**

Opening phrases
- With reference to your advertisement in … (newspaper) of … (date), …
- I would like / wish to apply for the above-mentioned position/post of … (job).

Education, training, present employment
- I attended … (school/college) for … (length of time).
- I studied … (subjects) at vocational school in … (town/city) from … (date) to … (date).
- At present I am working for a/an… (type of company) as a/an… (job).
- I will complete my period of training on … (date).

Closing paragraph
- I enclose / Enclosed is my CV (*BE*) / résumé (*AE*) / a list of my qualifications and experience.
- I am available for interview at your earliest convenience.
- I hope you will consider my application favourably and …
- … (I) look forward to hearing from you in the near future.

- *Bezugnehmend auf Ihre Ausschreibung in … (Zeitung) vom … (Datum), …*
- *Hiermit möchte ich mich für die oben genannte Stelle als … (Berufsbezeichnung) bewerben.*

- *Von … bis … (Jahr) besuchte ich (Schule/Hochschule).*
- *An der Berufs(fach)schule in … (Ort) lernte/belegte ich … (Fächer) von … (Datum) bis … (Datum).*
- *Zurzeit arbeite ich für eine / bei einer … (Firmenbezeichnung) als … (Berufsbezeichnung).*
- *Am … (Datum) werde ich meine Ausbildung abschließen.*

- *Anbei finden Sie meinen Lebenslauf / eine Übersicht meiner Qualifikationen und Erfahrungen.*
- *Für ein Vorstellungsgespräch stehe ich Ihnen jederzeit gern zur Verfügung.*
- *Über eine positive Antwort freue ich mich sehr und …*

- *… (ich) freue mich darauf, von Ihnen bald zu hören.*

Grammar

Simple present

1 I **work** in the IT department of an engineering company. I **maintain** and **repair** computer networks.
2 The company **produces** components for the automobile industry.
3 My laptop **doesn't start up** when you switch on the power.

- Das *simple present* wird für wiederholte, oft regelmäßige Handlungen in der Gegenwart verwendet.
- Signalwörter: *regularly, sometimes, often, always, normally* usw.
- Manche Verben, die keine Handlung, sondern einen Zustand ausdrücken (*need, like, want, hate, love, know, believe* usw.), stehen (fast) ausschließlich im *simple present*.
- In der 3. Person (*he, she, it, Peter, the firm* usw.) wird ein *-s* angefügt (2).
- Verneinungen werden mit *doesn't/don't* + Infinitiv (ohne *to*) gebildet (3).

Present progressive

1 One of our customers **is** currently **having** a problem with new software.
2 The project managers **are looking** at the plans on their laptop right now.

- Das *present progressive* wird gebraucht, wenn man gerade ablaufende oder noch nicht abgeschlossene Handlungen beschreibt.
- Signalwörter: *at the moment, (right) now, just, currently* usw.

Questions and short answers

1 **Do** you **use** mobile apps often? – Yes, I **do**. / No, I **don't**.
2 **Did** you **create** the app yourself? – Yes, I **did**. / No, I **didn't**.
3 **Can** you **use** it on your smartphone? – Yes, you **can**. / No, you **can't**.
4 **Is** it freeware? – Yes, it **is**. / No, it **isn't**.
5 **When/Why/How did** you **change** the password?

- Fragen im *simple present* werden mit *do/does* gebildet (1).
- Fragen im *simple past* werden mit *did* gebildet (2).
- In Sätzen mit Hilfsverben (*is/have/can/will/should/…*) bildet man Fragen, indem man das Hilfsverb des Aussagesatzes vor das Subjekt stellt (3, 4).
- Kurzantworten bestehen aus *yes/no* + Personalpronomen + Hilfsverb (+ *n't*) (1–4).
- Fragewörter stehen immer am Anfang des Fragesatzes (5).

Imperatives

1 **Keep** your passwords safe at all times.
2 **Take** the elevator up to level 1 and **go** to the end of the corridor.
3 **Do not / Don't use** use public access wireless networks.
4 **Never touch** a live power cable.

- Man verwendet den Imperativ für Hinweise, Befehle, Warnungen und Erklärungen.
- Der Imperativ ist die Grundform (= Infinitiv) des Verbs. Man verwendet die gleiche Form, wenn man zu einer oder mehreren Personen spricht.
- Negativformen werden mit *do not* bzw. *don't* gebildet (3).
- Bei Negativformen mit *never* entfällt *don't* (4).

Simple past

1   I **talked** to my supervisor about the job last week.
2   Yesterday I **created** a database on my laptop.
3   I **didn't finish** my project until late in the afternoon.
4   What time **did** you **start** work?
5   My first day at work **was** a disaster.

- Das *simple past* verwendet man, um zu sagen, wann etwas geschehen ist (1, 2, 3), oder um über Vergangenes zu berichten (5).
- Signalwörter: *yesterday, last week, two days ago, in 1998, When ...?* usw.
- Bei den regelmäßigen Verben wird im *simple past* in allen Personen meist *-ed* angehängt.
- Verneinungen und Fragen werden in allen Personen mit *did/didn't* + Infinitiv (ohne *to*) gebildet.
- Eine Liste der unregelmäßigen Verben befindet sich auf S. 231.

Past progressive

1   I **was working** in the Customer Services department last week.
2   I **was talking** to a customer when a colleague **bumped** into me and I **dropped** the phone.

- Das *past progressive* wird mit *was/were* + *-ing*-Form gebildet.
- Mit dem *past progressive* drückt man aus, dass eine Handlung oder ein Vorgang zu einer bestimmten Zeit in der Vergangenheit gerade im Verlauf war (1).
- Es beschreibt oft eine Handlung, die gerade im Verlauf war, als eine zweite Handlung einsetzte. Die zweite Handlung steht im *simple past* (2).

Present perfect

1   We**'ve** just **updated** the layout of the wiki sites.
2   We**'ve** recently **revised** the access rights to the pages.
3   We **haven't found** the source of the virus yet.
4   **Have** you **been able to** replace the graphics card?

- Das *present perfect* wird mit *have/has* + Partizip Perfekt (3. Verbform) gebildet.
- Mit dem *present perfect* sagt man, dass (nicht: wann!) etwas geschehen ist. Man drückt damit auch aus, seit wann oder wie lange ein Zustand schon andauert.
- Signalwörter (Zeitadverbien): *for two years, this week, since 1998, already, just, recently, yet* usw.

Present perfect progressive

1   They**'ve been looking** at the customization **since** Tuesday.
2   **How long has** the team **been working** on the project?

- Das *present perfect progressive* wird mit *have/has been* + *-ing*-Form gebildet.
- Das *present perfect progressive* drückt aus, dass eine Handlung oder ein Vorgang in der Vergangenheit begonnen hat und bis (oder fast bis) in die Gegenwart andauert. Dabei wird die Dauer des Geschehens betont.
- Signalwörter: *all day, all night, the whole afternoon, since ... , for ...* sowie Fragen mit *How long ... ?*

Future with *will* and *going to*

1 I think the software installation **will take** about two hours.
2 **I'll (will) order** the new monitors this afternoon.
3 We **won't (will not) need** the new monitors until next week.
4 We**'re going to replace** all our laptops next month.
5 This old computer **is going to break down** soon.

  – *Will* wird verwendet, um Vorhersagen zu machen oder Vermutungen über die Zukunft auszudrücken (1).
  – *Will* wird für spontane Entscheidungen, Angebote und Versprechen verwendet (2).
  – Im gesprochenen Englisch lautet die Verneinung *won't*, ansonsten *will not* (3).
  – *Be going to* (+ Infinitiv des Verbs) wird verwendet, um über Pläne oder Absichten zu sprechen (4), oder wenn die Gewissheit (oder ein Anzeichen dafür) besteht, dass etwas geschehen wird (5).

Passive forms

1 The wireless access points **are mounted** on the walls.
2 The new router **was installed** on Tuesday morning.
3 The cables **have** already **been laid**.
4 The testing equipment **could be bought** from a local supplier.
5 The software **will be installed by** the company as part of their customer service.

  – Das Passiv wird oft verwendet, wenn man auf eher unpersönliche Art und Weise über Fakten, Vorgänge und Zahlen berichtet.
  – Das Passiv wird mit der entsprechenden Form von *be* + Partizip Perfekt (3. Verbform) gebildet. Es können alle Zeiten gebildet werden.
  – Passivsätze mit modalen Hilfsverben werden mit einem modalen Hilfsverb + *be* + Partizip Perfekt (3. Verbform) gebildet (4).
  – „Von" und „durch" werden in Passivsätzen durch *by* ausgedrückt (5).

Conditional sentences

1 Type 0: **If** it **trips** the switch, it **turns** on the alarm.
2 Type 1: **If** you **click on** 'Next', you**'ll receive** a notification message.
3 **Unless** we **install** a dual-band network, employee productivity **will suffer**.

  – Bedingungen, die allgemeingültig sind bzw. die immer eintreffen, werden mit einem *if*-Satz des Typs 0 ausgedrückt. Hier sind beide Satzteile im *simple present* (1).
  – Ein *if*-Satz des Typs 1 drückt eine Bedingung aus, die der Sprecher für durchaus möglich oder wahrscheinlich hält. Der damit verbundene Hauptsatz drückt eine Vorhersage aus, die je nach Situation als Warnung, Versprechen o. ä. zu verstehen ist (2). Meist steht im *if*-Satz das *simple present* und im Hauptsatz das *will-future* oder ein modales Hilfsverb + Infinitiv.
  – Steht der *if*-Nebensatz an erster Stelle, wird er durch ein Komma vom Hauptsatz abgetrennt (1, 2).
  – *Unless = if + not* …: *If we don't install a dual-band network, …* (3).

Verb + *to*-infinitive or *-ing* form

1 I enjoy **working** in a team.
2 I expect **to qualify** as a network administrator in June.
3 I love **repairing / to repair** old computers.
4 I'd prefer **to work** from home more often.
5 I'm interested in **getting** some work experience abroad.

  – Auf eine Gruppe von Verben folgt immer die *-ing*-Form (1). Zu diesen Verben gehören *dislike, enjoy, finish, give up, imagine, involve, keep, mind, miss, practise, recommend, risk, stop, suggest.*
  – Auf eine zweite Gruppe von Verben folgt immer ein *to*-Infinitiv (2). Zu diesen Verben gehören *agree, arrange, choose, decide, expect, hope, learn, offer, manage, plan, promise, want.*
  – Auf eine dritte Gruppe von Verben kann sowohl die *-ing*-Form als auch ein *to*-Infinitiv folgen (3). Zu diesen Verben gehören *begin, continue, hate, like, love, prefer, start.*
  – Nach *would hate, would like, would love* and *would prefer* (Kurzform *'d like* usw.) steht nur der *to*-Infinitiv (4).
  – Nach einer Präposition kommt immer die *-ing*-Form (5).

Gerunds

1 **Working** with different customers means there is a lot of variety in my job.
2 Do you like **being** on standby at the weekends?
3 My work consists **of installing** new software.
4 You can see data errors by **checking** the report.

  – Das Gerundium (= *-ing*-Form des Verbs) kann die Rolle eines Nomens übernehmen.
  – Das Gerundium kann als Subjekt (1), Objekt (2) oder nach Präpositionen (3, 4) verwendet werden.

Relative clauses

1 Serious gamers are people **who/that care about IT security**.
2 The peripherals **(which/that) they are using** connect without pairing.
3 GameTech, **which is our biggest competitor,** uses its own connection protocol.

  – Relativpronomen leiten Relativsätze ein.
  – Es gibt den notwendigen und den nicht notwendigen Relativsatz. Notwendige Relativsätze sind für das Verständnis des Satzes unbedingt erforderlich (1, 2) und stehen ohne Komma. Nicht notwendige Relativsätze geben lediglich Zusatzinformationen und werden durch Kommata getrennt (3).
  – In notwendigen Relativsätzen kann das Relativpronomen wegfallen, wenn es Objekt ist, d. h. wenn im Relativsatz ein Subjekt steht (2).

Adjectives and adverbs

1 Repairing the laptop is an **easy** job.
2 We need it to be fixed **quickly**.
3 It's **really** easy to customize the software.
4 Can it be installed **easily**?
5 I don't speak German very **well**.

– Man verwendet Adjektive, um Personen oder Sachen näher zu beschreiben (1).
– Adverbien beziehen sich auf Verben (2, 4, 5) oder Adjektive (3).
– Adverbien haben in der Regel eine andere Form als Adjektive. Man fügt normalerweise die Endung -ly an das Adjektiv an (2, 3). Endet das Adjektiv auf -y, wird die Endung zu -ily (4).
– Das Adverb von good lautet well (5).

Comparatives and superlatives

1 The new laptop is **harder/easier** to use.
2 It's **more expensive than** the other laptop.
3 It's the **simplest** and **cheapest** laptop, but not the **best**.
4 This software is the **most flexible** solution.
5 The company spent **less** money on software last year.
6 The new app is**n't as easy** to update **as** the old one.

– Einsilbige Adjektive und zweisilbige Adjektive, die auf -y enden, steigert man mit -er/-est (1).
– Zweisilbige Adjektive, die nicht auf -y enden, und mehrsilbige Adjektive werden mit more/most gesteigert (2).
– Unregelmäßig sind: good – better – best, bad – worse – worst, little (wenig) – less – least, far – farther/further – farthest/furthest (3, 5).
– Vergleiche bildet man mit than und (not) as ... as (2, 6).

Much, many, a lot (of)

1 How **much** time do you spend answering emails?
2 How **many** text messages do you get at work every day?
3 I get **a lot of** text messages. **Lots of** them are instructions from my supervisor.
4 We have **too many** meetings at work. We waste **too much** time on them.

– Much verwendet man nur bei nicht-zählbaren Nomen, z.B. time (1).
– Many verwendet man nur bei Nomen im Plural (2).
– Much und many werden meist in verneinten Aussagesätzen und in Fragen verwendet. In bejahten Aussagesätzen ist a lot of bzw. lots of gebräuchlicher (3).
– Nach too, so, as, very und how werden immer much und many verwendet (4).

Modals and their substitutes

1 I **can** work from home two days a week.
2 I **could** work longer hours in the office if I lived closer.
3 This survey **must** be carried out anonymously.
4 You **will be able to** create the survey with the new software.
5 We **won't be allowed to** install the new software on our own.
6 We **should** compare the costs of both systems.
7 The mouse was broken and **had to** be replaced.
8 You **mustn't** switch this computer back on again.
9 I **would** like a job as a network supervisor.

- Modale Hilfsverben wie *can, could, may, would* usw. drücken eine Fähigkeit, eine Erlaubnis, eine Empfehlung, ein Verbot oder einen Wunsch aus.
- Modale Hilfsverben haben in allen Personen die gleiche Form; bei der Verneinung gibt es zusammen-gezogene Kurzformen.
- Modale Hilfsverben stehen normalerweise in der Gegenwartsform, manche auch in der Vergangenheit. Ersatzverben (*substitutes*) werden verwendet, um alle übrigen Zeiten zu bilden.

Hilfsverb	Ersatzverb
can	*be able to*
could	
may	*be allowed to*
might	
must	*have to*
need not	*don't have to*
shall	
should/ought to	
must not	*not be allowed to*

T Transcripts

Track 2: Unit 1, Foundation, exercise 2

1   OK. I'll start. The company I work for is called BCC Electronics. We manufacture electronic equipment. The head office is in London. It's a medium-sized company.
2   I'm a trainee at International Solutions. It's an IT company. The head office is in Berlin. It's a start-up.
3   I'm an apprentice at Nilsson Construction. It's a Swedish building company. The head office is in Stockholm, in Sweden. You've probably heard of it. It's a big multinational.
4   I work for a company called Han Gao. It's a metal dealer. The Head office is in Hong Kong. It's a global company.
5   Right. I'm doing an apprenticeship at Jahn Services. We're in the automotive sector. The head office is in Minden. It's a large company.
6   The name of my company is Aikon. We manufacture medical equipment. The head office is in Stuttgart. It's a small firm.

Track 3: Unit 1, Part A, exercise 2

We'll start our tour on the second floor. There are two teams located on this floor. The first team, Quality Assurance, have several rooms on this floor. The door just in front of us leads to the Quality Assurance team. We also have the Hardware Support team. It's important that you know where they are located because you'll need to visit them when you have computer problems. You can find them by going along this corridor and through the door at the end. The elevators are located in the middle of each floor. You can also find the toilets in this area. Don't forget: you'll need your security pass to get through the security doors, so it's best to carry it with you all the time.

Now, I'd like you to follow me up the stairs to the third floor. As you can see, the third floor is an open-plan office so, before we go on, could I ask you to please keep quiet so we don't disturb the teams. There are two teams on this floor, Software Development takes up about three quarters of the floor. The team extends from this wall, all the way over to the far wall and around the corner as well.

Let's continue. If we walk straight ahead along the walkway, … we'll be able to see the Research and Development team. … They are located over there in the corner.

Lastly, I'll show you to the fourth floor, which is the top floor. After that, we'll take the elevator to the first floor to get some coffee in the cafeteria.

Track 4: Unit 1, Part B, exercise 1

Starting from the top, the Chief Executive Officer, or CEO as most people say, is Stephanie Sullivan. It's her responsibility to set the overall company goals and strategies and to manage the company. The Chief Information Officer, or CIO, and Chief Technology Officer, or CTO, are our company's top technological people.

Our CTO, Chris Turner, reports directly to the CEO. He deals with system architecture, platforms, data processing, system analysis, and so on.

The CIO, Mark Young, is responsible for deciding how we use technology in Accensys to maximize benefit to the company and clients. He also reports to the CEO.

Chloe Russell is our Chief Digital Officer. She plays a key role in making sure that we make the most of digital technology in everything we do. She works directly for the CEO as well.

The Head of the project management Office, or PMO, Lilian Lee, supervises a large team of project managers. She liaises with all of the software teams to make sure we deliver our projects on time. This is one of four roles that report to the CIO.

Naree Partridge reports to the CIO in the role of Head of Software Engineering and is responsible for software products getting to our clients.

Our Head of Quality Assurance, Bharath Raghu, manages a team of Quality Assurance Managers. His testing teams make sure that we release high quality software products to our clients.

And finally, Andrew Burke, our Head of IT Operations, is in charge of the team that keeps our hardware and software platforms running, so that both we and our clients can perform our daily tasks. A team of Product Managers reports to him. Both Andrew and Bharath report to the CIO as well.

Track 5: Unit 1, Communication, exercise 1A

Martyna	Hello. I'm Martyna Nowak. I'm 42. I was born in Poland. I'm a product manager.
Halil	Good morning. My name is Halil Özdemir. I'm 29 years old. I was born in Germany. I'm a training supervisor.
Deema	Good afternoon. My name is Deema Mansour. I'm 19. I was born in Syria. I'm a trainee IT administrator.
Robert	Hello. I'm Robert Klein. I'm 21. I was born in Austria. I'm a quality assurance tester.
Canan	Hello. I'm Canan Tolon. I'm 25 years old. I was born in Turkey. I'm a business analyst.
Alexei	Good morning. My name is Alexei Melnyk. I'm 39 years old. I was born in Ukraine. I'm a software developer.

Track 6: Unit 2, Foundation, exercise 2

1: Making a quick decision

David	OK. The supervisor is going to a meeting about improving internal communication in the company and he'd like us to tell him what internal communication we use, what we use it for, what we like, what we don't like and so on. Where are we going to start? Marta, you always have good ideas …
Marta	Well, it might be a good idea to think about situations where we need internal communication and start from there. Hmm? Come on, you guys. Janek, what do you think?
Janek	Right. What about when we have to make a quick decision on something?
Marta	OK. Well, I think a face-to-face meeting is good when you want to make a quick decision. And when you need to sort out a problem, a face-to-face meeting is always best.
David	Yes, but if the other person isn't around, you can't have a face-to-face meeting. When I'm out on a job and I need a quick decision from my supervisor, I phone him.
Janek	I agree with David, the phone's good for a quick decision. There are some situations when I want to have my supervisor's decision in writing, though, so I'd say that when you want a quick decision in writing, it's better to send a message.

Marta	Uh-hu. I see what you're getting at, Janek.
David	Yes. So, what are we going to say, then? When we need to make a quick decision, a face-to-face meeting is a good option. Other good options for making a quick decision are using the telephone for a phone call or a text. Is that what we're going to say?

2: Sharing information

David	Is that what we're going to say?
Marta	Yes. I think that's fine. What next? What about sharing information? I use emails a lot of the time. I like emails because you can write them in a couple of minutes and send them in a second. Sometimes my emails just contain text, but a lot of the time I attach documents or drawings. The really big advantage for me, though, is that I can copy in so many people, so I only have to write the email once.
Janek	Yes, but one of the things I really dislike about emails is that you get so many of them. My personal favourite is the intranet. The big advantage over email is that an intranet is structured, so it's easy to find the information you're looking for.
David	Sorry, but I have the same problem with the intranet as I have with face-to-face meetings. You need to be at work to access the intranet. I work all over the place so I need to have access to information wherever I am. I think cloud storage is better. You can access cloud storage from anywhere and, it's not just that you can share information, you can also synchronize files. I wish we used cloud storage here.
Marta	You can share selected information with clients on the cloud, too, can't you? Maybe we should mention that to the supervisor?
Janek	Hey. That's a good idea. Let's tell the supervisor that we use emails and the intranet, but we feel that using the cloud might be more useful. Yes? And, of course, the advantage of using the cloud is that the company can share information with clients. He can bring that up at the meeting.

3: Discussing a project

Janek	He can bring that up at the meeting.
David	Oh, yes. The meeting. That's another type of internal communication, isn't it? In this case, they're discussing the project. I'm glad I don't have to go to a lot of meetings. Meetings take up too much time. I'd rather be out doing my job.
Marta	Me, too. I hate meetings. Especially when somebody stands up and reads things from slides.
Janek	I can only agree with you there. When they're full of writing, slides are a real waste of time. When it's written information, a hand-out is always better.
David	Right, well, I think we have enough now. Face-to-face meetings, phone calls and text messages for making quick decisions; emails and intranet for sharing information, and a suggestion that the company might consider cloud storage.
Marta	And, don't forget to mention that, at meetings, slides should only be used for graphic images and not for a lot of text. If it's written information, we'd rather have a hand-out.

Track 7: Unit 2, Part A, exercise 1A/B

Here at Hillier Recruiting, we're big believers in providing a work-life balance that suits each employee, so we try to offer flexible working conditions.

For example, you get 20 days of paid annual leave and can take up to 10 days of paid sick leave ... only if you need it, of course. We also allow you to take an additional two weeks of unpaid leave each year and save up to six weeks of leave if you like longer holidays. You can work remotely if you choose to, which means that you don't have to be in the office every day but you must co-ordinate the days that you work from home with your boss.

Although we offer flexible start and finish times, you can't start and finish at any time of day and have to be working between 10 a.m. and 3 p.m. In addition, you may not be in the office after 8 p.m. without permission. You may take up to one hour for lunch.

In the office you don't have to wear formal clothing, but your clothes have to be neat. You can wear jeans and a clean T-shirt, if you like – the IT department is quite casual – but you mustn't wear shorts.

Track 8: Unit 2, Part B, exercise 3

Justin	Hello everyone, and thanks for coming. As I mentioned in the invite to this meeting, we are running three weeks behind our schedule, and we need to think of ways to improve our productivity. So, first, I'd like to discuss the pros and cons of the locations of the team members and remote working. Kenny, what do you think?
Kenny	OK, well, I think we need to separate the development team from the rest of the team. We still feel that we are being interrupted too often, which is a disadvantage for all of us.
Justin	What about you, Jessica?
Jessica	I agree with Kenny. I know everyone has tried, but we still aren't getting the time we need to solve problems. I get interrupted by a question or just the noise on the floor at least once an hour. You agree with me, don't you Kenny?
Kenny	Yes I do. As a solution, I think the development team should move into a separate meeting room but stay on this floor.
Justin	Good idea. That would also remove the drawback of distraction from the other teams on the floor. It does get pretty loud when the customer support team are busy.
Jessica	I agree – the noise level is a real downside to our open-plan floors. What's your opinion, Dave?
Dave	Actually, I have another idea. I think the software developers should be able to work from home more often. The major plus in working from home is that there are no distractions. I get my best thinking done when I work from home.
Kenny	But on the downside, we can't come and ask you a question. When you work from home, Dave, you seem to be offline most of the time.
Dave	That may be a negative for you, but for me it's a huge benefit. I turn off instant messaging and close my email.
Justin	But if we all worked from home and turned off our IM and email, it would be a disaster.
Dave	Would it really? I think having high-quality code is a huge upside.
Jessica	Well, I agree that we don't have to be available to respond to a question instantaneously at all times. But it's definitely an advantage if there are no distractions.

Justin	OK, let me just summarize here. We have two suggestions …
Kenny	… that the development team should move into a separate meeting room but stay on this floor …
Dave	… and that the software developers should be able to work from home more often.
Justin	Those sound like good ideas. Let me talk to …

Track 9: Unit 2, Communication, exercise 4

Julie	Fischer Digital Ltd. Julie Matthews speaking.
Liam	Can I speak to Martin Brown in Hardware Support, please?
Julie	Who's calling please?
Liam	This is Liam Donnelly.
Julie	I'm sorry, could you spell your name, please?
Liam	It's L I A M D O double-N E double-L Y. I'm calling from Adler Network Components in Manchester. It's about the cables Mr Brown ordered.
Julie	Thank you, Mr Donnelly. I'll try Mr Brown for you. Please hold the line.
Liam	Thank you.
Julie	Mr Donnelly. I'm sorry, Mr Brown is unavailable at the moment. Would you like to speak to someone else?
Liam	Yes. All right. Anyone in Hardware Support will do.
Julie	Thank you. I'll put you through.
Julie	I'm sorry, Mr Donnelly. I'm afraid the line is engaged. Would you like to leave a message for Mr Brown?
Liam	Yes, please. Would you tell Mr Brown that the cables he ordered aren't available and ask him to call me to discuss an alternative. My telephone number is 161 839 5005 and the extension is 822.
Julie	I'm sorry. I didn't understand. Could you repeat that, please?
Liam	Sure. It's 161 839 5005, extension 822.
Julie	Thank you, Mr Donnelly. I'll make sure that Mr Brown gets the message.

Track 10: Unit 3, Foundation, exercise 3

Colleague	First of all let's talk about what you need. Where will you be working?
Customer	I'll mostly be working at my desk on my laptop, but I'd also like to be able to move around the room when I'm talking or when I'm coming up with ideas. Music also helps me to be creative.
Colleague	OK. Do you take calls on your computer?
Customer	Yes, I do.
Colleague	Right, so if you want to talk hands-free on a headset, get a Bluetooth version and pair it with your computer. It's very easy and convenient. You can also connect them to your smartphone if you need to.
Customer	OK. And what about listening to music on speakers while I'm working?
Colleague	I'd say you should connect via the normal 3.5mm jack because the audio quality is better.
Customer	I'd like a large monitor, too. I want something that I can easily plug into and work with two screens.
Colleague	Do you have USB-C connectors?
Customer	Yes, I do.
Colleague	Then I'd recommend this monitor. You only need one USB-C cable to link the monitor to your computer and charge it as well. It's really simple. It means that you don't need a separate cable for power. It also comes with an adapter in case someone else needs to plug into your monitor via their HDMI port.
Customer	I'll also need an external hard drive. At least one terabyte.
Colleague	OK. This one is really fast. It also only needs one USB cable to connect and get power. You can even stick the cable into this monitor so you don't have to plug and unplug it from your computer.
Customer	OK. How about printing? I just want a simple printer in case I need it. All of my work is for websites and social media.
Colleague	This one is the simplest one to use. You can hook it into your Wi-Fi network and print from your computer and smartphone. The print quality is good for the price too. You can also plug it into a USB port if you want to.
Customer	Why would I want to do that?
Colleague	It can be more reliable. It also means that you have a backup way to print if you have Wi-Fi problems.
Customer	My Wi-Fi connection is really good.
Colleague	That's great … but if you do have problems with it, you can also connect your modem via Ethernet cable.
Customer	OK, that's good to know. I think I have everything now is there anything else I need to get …

Track 11: Unit 3, Part B, exercise 2

We have three computer configurations that we give to employees here at DIY Hardware based on what we think they need, which is often different to what they think they need. We have a budget to stick to, so not everybody gets the computer they want.

We had a new guy start in Sales last week. Now, being in Sales, he attends a lot of meetings with clients, so he's on the road a lot. Of course, this means that a desktop is not fit-for-purpose and a laptop is the most appropriate computer for him. He needs good wireless and hardware connectivity so he can access our mail servers as well as connect to clients' projectors or screens to give his presentations. Something with a lot of connection options is suitable. He'll probably spend three full days per week out of the office, too, so portability is very important. Light-weight and a long-lasting battery are spot on for his needs.

Now, he doesn't need a lot of storage space, so a 128 GB hard disk is more than enough. Likewise, an overly fast processor isn't advisable due to cost, but a solid-state drive is appropriate, as he does need documents and videos to load quickly in front of clients. He asked for a powerful graphics card, but I told him that it would be inappropriate given his needs. As I said, not everybody is happy with what they are given.

Of course, he also needs a good-looking computer to impress the clients. All things considered, configuration 1 is the best fit for him.

Track 12: Unit 3, Communication, exercise 1B

Supervisor	I'll just give you my email address. It's t m dot martin at hardware underscore house dot co dot uk.
Mary-Anne	Sorry, could you repeat that please?
Supervisor	No problem. t m dot martin at hardware underscore house dot co dot uk. You can reach me directly with that address.
Mary-Anne	Thank you. Well, my email address is mary hyphen anne hyphen brown at five plus five services dot net. The fives are written as numbers. Oh, and my first name, Mary-Anne – Anne is written with an e.
Supervisor	OK. I'll just read that back to you. Mary hyphen anne hyphen brown at five plus five services dot net. Mary-Anne with a hyphen, the fives written as numbers and Mary-Anne written with an e at the end of Anne.
Mary-Anne	Yes. That's correct.

Track 13: Unit 4, Part B, exercise 2

Gavin	There are pros and cons whichever way we configure software installations. On the one hand, if we minimize the options that users have, we will have a clean, secure software environment. On the other hand, if we allow them to control when their updates are installed, we will get fewer complaints.
Boss	So we need to find the right balance.
Gavin	Yes ... but in my opinion, we should restrict what they can control if we want to do our job properly. We should force updates.
Boss	Of course, the benefits of that are clear – less risk, more stability of our systems, better reliability for users. The downside with forced updates is that the users may not be able to use their computers when they need to and that leads to a LOT of complaints.
Gavin	I know, but the problem with allowing users control is that it's very likely that updates will never be installed.
Boss	Yes, but it's also our job to allow users to do their work efficiently. If we want a good balance, allowing them to delay installation is a good idea. The upside of this is that user flexibility and IT security are both considered. The advantage of allowing limited delay is that it gives users the impression of control.
Gavin	How about this – if we want them to have control, we could tell them how many times more they can delay an install?
Boss	I'm not sure that's a good idea. The major disadvantage of that is confusion for users. There are usually multiple releases at any one time. We can't tell them that they have 4 delays left for install A and 2 left for install B. If we do that, we will get more complaints.
Gavin	OK. Couldn't we email them? If we send them an email to explain how important installs are, they'll be less likely to delay.
Boss	Most users won't read the communications I'm afraid. They are all as busy as we are.
Gavin	What about installing on startup?
Boss	The main problem is that many users don't turn their computers off for weeks, sometimes months, which means that the restart can take an extremely long time because of all of the updates it tries to process. They'll call and complain about the slow startup if their battery goes flat in the middle of the day.

Track 14: KMK Exam practice 2, exercise 1, Hörverstehen

Kevin	Good morning. Can I be of help? You seem to be interested in these smartwatches.
Susan	Well, I'm not sure. I'm just looking for a present. It's for my husband. They look nice, but why would he need a smartwatch?
Kevin	OK ... First of all, most things you do on your smartphone you can do on these watches and a lot more. Answering messages, replying to texts by voice, streaming Apple Music, using the Maps app for directions and ...
Susan	That's all very well, but we both have iPhones. We can do all these things without these watches, can't we?
Kevin	Yes and no. Just imagine your phone is ringing right now. What do you do? You fumble around in your bag and if you're lucky, you find it just in time. With a smartwatch you can leave your phone at home, listen to music and still be connected.
Susan	I see ... Well, that's something my husband might be interested in. He doesn't like to carry his phone while he's jogging, and I can't get hold of him when he's out.
Kevin	Exactly. It's best to leave your iPhone at home when you're out jogging. Do you have a minute? I could show you a few of the things you can't do on your phone.
Susan	OK, go ahead.
Kevin	Now, look, I'm wearing one myself. This is a watchOS 3. Let's start with the basics. You have a Dock, of course, to keep all your favourite apps. You choose which apps go in your Dock and you choose the order they appear.
Susan	And how do you bring up your Dock?
Kevin	I just press the side button and – ta-da – there we are. Now I can swipe through my apps one at a time or put my finger on the dots at the bottom of the screen and fly through my Dock to get to any app. All the apps in my Dock are live. So I can get a quick glance at information without even launching one and I can ...
Susan	Well, I'm familiar with all that. But what are these coloured rings? What do they do?
Kevin	Well, they're really great. These are the Activity Rings. They help me track my workouts. They show me how active I am every day. This ring tells me if I've been sitting too much. Look here! This one shows how active I've been today ... Uh-ho, not much to be proud of there. The idea is to close all the rings every day and that motivates me to get more exercise. By the way, there are about 40 specially designed fitness apps that work with Apple Health.
Susan	Apple Health? That sounds interesting. Does it show your blood pressure?
Kevin	Not yet, but they're working on it. At the moment, it can use the built-in monitor to work out my heart rate. It's a bit on the high side at the moment. Moreover, a motion sensor tracks how many steps I've taken and figures out how many calories I've burned. All these apps have been redesigned to put me within one tap of the things I most want to know. It has GPS and an altimeter, so it has all the features you need to take your run to the next level. It uses an eSimcard that is a hundred times smaller than an ordinary one, and ...

| Susan | Thanks, that sounds really great. But tell me, is it waterproof? |
| Kevin | Yes, it's swim-proof, so your husband can take a dip in the pool after his run. But he shouldn't go scuba diving with it. Now maybe you'd like to … |

Track 15: Unit 5, Foundation, exercise 1

… so we need to be careful in future. Now I'd like to take you through each of the hacks and viruses that we've looked at and tell you which ones we think are the most likely to have been used to gain access to our customer accounts. I must say that the findings are disappointing, as they show that our employees don't seem to pay attention to our warnings about cybercrime.

We started with phishing, which is very common. Phishing is usually an email pretending to be from a trustworthy organization like a bank or an auction site, like eBay. The email contains links to websites that are infected with malware. It seems likely that one of our employees visited a malware site using a link in an email. This is frustrating as we send an information email to employees each month. I can only repeat what we say there: Beware of phishing!

Next, we checked for worms, which are a type of virus that copy themselves and spread to other computers on a network and then send sensitive information to the hackers. Worms usually use up bandwidth, and we can confirm that our usage is about 15 per cent higher than usual, so it seems that a worm was downloaded from an infected website and gained access to the account records. Our network monitoring team continues to keep an eye out for worms.

We then checked for backdoors that provide hackers access to a network by bypassing normal authentication. When they hide in an inactive state, they are very difficult to detect. We continually watch out for communications that are going to unidentified locations and we haven't found anything yet, so it seems unlikely.

We also looked for man-in-the-middle attacks, where software is used to monitor communication between a user and the network they are using. As you know, many of our staff work remotely, sometimes in cafés, even though they have been told to make sure they use secure networks.

We then checked for injection attacks, which exploit flaws in databases. They happen when employees open files that seem to be trustworthy but install software code with hidden commands, or 'injections', instead. These are hard to detect, so we ask employees to pick up on anything that just doesn't look right. We haven't found any injections yet, so that's good news.

Finally, we checked for social engineering which exploits weaknesses in people, not software. A caller pretends to be a real customer and they persuade employees to open an email which contains malware. We have found more than one employee that opened an email that a caller asked them to open. Our employee training contains lessons on how to guard against social engineering – we might want to think of another way to make our point. Now I'd like to move on to …

Track 16: Unit 5, Part A, exercise 1

Colleague	Good morning, Hoffman IT Security. How can I help you?
Esther	Hi. This is Esther Smith from the Corporate Auditing team.
Colleague	Hi, Esther. Before we start, could you give me your employee number, please?
Esther	Sure. It's D8773893.
Colleague	Thanks. … How can I help you, Esther?
Esther	I've downloaded AudioMan audio management software onto my computer. It downloads successfully, but it looks like I'm not allowed to install it.
Colleague	Are you getting an error message?
Esther	Yes, when I try to install it I get a message that says "You don't have permission to install this application".
Colleague	OK, I can see that the access level on your profile is 'Standard User'. Unfortunately, this means that you are not permitted to install any new programs, except those that IT has pre-approved. Only users with administrator access have permission to install applications on their laptops.
Esther	OK. So AudioMan is not on the pre-approved list?
Colleague	That's right.
Esther	Can you add it to the list? I record some of the interviews that I do with clients and want to sync them to the AudioMan app on my phone.
Colleague	I'm afraid I can't do that, for a few reasons. Users are permitted to install only a limited set of software, so we can protect the company from software that can damage our systems. We have three approved software applications to manage audio files.
Esther	OK. What are the other reasons?
Colleague	The main reason is that the interviews with clients are considered confidential information, which means that they are not permitted to be shared on personal devices. Synchronizing them with your smartphone means that the audio files are out of our control and could end up in the wrong hands. Employees are only allowed to manage interviews via the approved audio management applications.
Esther	Right, of course. Thank you for the clarification – could I ask you to send me a link to the audio management program that I have access to install?
Colleague	Of course I can.

Track 17: Unit 5, Communication, exercise 1

Good morning everyone. We have a lot to get through today, so I'd like to get straight into it. We'll start our session with a look at last year. In general, the number of attacks detected rose steadily last year, with some peaks and troughs midway through the year. In January, there were 19.08 million attacks and then, as you can see, they declined slightly in February, as they tended to do in previous years. In March, they increased sharply to 28.13 million then they remained steady in April and stayed the same in May.

In June, attacks climbed significantly again and that was the peak for the year at 39.75 million. Strangely, they fell drastically the next month to only 9.76 million. We can't really be certain of the reason for this as the fluctuations in attacks each month appear to be somewhat random, meaning we always need to be aware of the possibility of threats.

Following that trough in July, the number of attacks jumped sharply in August to 22.3 million and then decreased marginally in September. The number of attacks then grew gradually over the last quarter of the year, then stayed the same from November to December, where we had 25.2 million attacks. Overall this represents an increase of 44.65 per cent from January to December.

Track 18: Unit 6, Foundation, exercise 1A/B

Gina   Hi everyone. After many months of hard work by our artificial intelligence team, we're pleased to introduce you to our chatbot, who will help you to serve our customers better. Her name is Lia.

Lia is a natural language chatbot, meaning that customers don't have to use perfect English when asking her questions, which is great for people like me! She can understand and interpret everyday English to provide customers with answers about their profile and account, advise them about our products and even engage in conversation with them. Sounds great, right? Let's take a look!

When you start a session on our website, Lia pops up and offers you a greeting, for example: "Good morning Gina, I'm Lia the chatbot. How can I help you?"

Now, I'd like to show you what she can do, so I'd like to ask you all to suggest some questions to ask her. Who wants to start?

Voice 1   Do you have the latest book by Tim Ferriss?

Gina   For those that can't read the screen, I'll read her response. She says "Yes, we do, but there aren't many copies left. I suggest that you order it soon if you want it right away. Would you like me to add it to your cart?"

And I'll type in "Yes".

And Lia replies with "OK. I've added it to your cart. Can I do anything else for you?"

Can someone ask another question?

Voice 2   Are you able to tell me how much credit I have left?

Gina   Lia says "Sure, I can do that. You have 89 dollars and 25 cents credit. Would you like to add some more?"

And I'll type in "No".

And she'll check again and say "Can I be of further assistance?"

I'll take one more question.

Voice 3   What should I get my 12-year-old son for his birthday?

Gina   Good question – I think Lia can help. Lia says "Of course, I'm happy to help. The most popular gift currently is the Genius Programming Starter Kit. There are several options for this kit. Would you like to see the choices?"

And, again, I'll type in "No" ... And again, she'll check and ask "Can I help you with anything else?" Isn't that great!?

Lia knows where a customer is, the time of day at their location and, if they have previously shopped with us, she knows their name. If a customer is shopping on our website after work, Lia might say "Good evening Tim, my name is Lia. Can I assist you with anything today?" and if it's a Saturday afternoon she'd say "Hi Ben! Good afternoon and welcome back. What can I do for you today?" It's a very personalized interaction because it uses data we know about the customer.

Lia also goes further than that. She knows what a customer has bought from us in the past, their likes and dislikes from reviews they've given and if there is anything they've returned. She knows almost everything about a customer's past with ShopArena and uses this to help them make better purchase decisions. She can also predict whether they are contacting us about a problem with a recent purchase because she knows about complaints other customers have made.

Track 19: Unit 6, Part A, exercise 3

Steven   So Rod, that's everything we have to say about the standard reports. Do you feel comfortable with them?

Rod   Yes, I'm very happy with them. I think the standard reports are easy to understand and I can see that we will get a lot of useful information from them.

Steven   I'm pleased to hear that. Do you have any other questions?

Rod   Yes, I do. First of all, I'd like to know how we can customize the reports. I'm sure we'll need to do this at some point.

Steven   Of course, I'd be happy to take you through it. We have several options that allow you to customize reports. Shall we start with the employee participation report?

Rod   Sure.

Steven   If you only want to see results for a specific data range, you can choose the date range in the results by entering a start and end date in the filter.

Rod   I see. Thanks. What about the rated questions report?

Steven   Well, there are several options to tailor the report. You can select the specific department you want. If you select the column headings, you can change the sort order of the results and toggle between ascending and descending results. You can also refine your data to focus on a specific set of results using several filters.

Rod   Excellent. I can see that that will be useful.

Steven   Lastly, let's take a look through the custom report, where you can add, remove and edit most of the information on the report.

Rod   Great – before you do, can I ask out of interest, how many of your clients customize reports?

Steven   To be honest, not many of them. Most of them customize the surveys but not the reports. The standard reports are very powerful and contain enough information for most of our clients.

Track 20: Unit 6, Part B, exercise 1A/B

Steven   Thanks for calling Culture Amp. My name's Steven. How can I help you?

Rod   Hi, Steven. This is Rod Hamilton from SynTech.

Steven   Hi, Rod. Nice to hear from you again. How are things?

Rod   Things are working really fine. But I'd like to extract our raw data so we can do some of our own analysis. The problem is that the function isn't enabled.

Steven   Oh, OK ... well, that isn't a mistake. It's a design feature of the software. Data extraction is disabled by default.

Rod   I see. Could you explain why that is?

Steven   Sure. We have a commitment to keeping survey responses anonymous, as we think that anonymous surveys are the best way to get honest answers.

Rod   OK. That makes a lot of sense and is a great idea, but we trust each other here at SynTech. Data extraction can be enabled, right?

Steven   Yes, exactly. Would you like me to walk you through the steps to enable data extraction?

Rod   Yes, please.

Steven   To start with, confirm that you have either account administration or survey administrator access.

Rod   OK, I can check that on my profile, can't I?

Steven   That's correct.

Rod   OK. I have survey administrator access.

Steven Great. Now, the next step is to check the raw data extract checkbox.

Rod I can't see the checkbox.

Steven Do you have a survey ready?

Rod No, I don't have a survey ready to launch. Should I have one ready?

Steven I'm afraid you've missed a step. Sorry, I should have checked. Can I ask you to create one quickly so that I can explain how to enable raw data extraction?

Rod Sure. Hang on. … OK. I've created a dummy survey.

Steven Thanks. Now let's go back and check the raw data extract checkbox.

Rod OK. I've done that. It's checked.

Steven Thanks. Checking that box means that a warning message will be displayed to every user that takes the survey. It tells them that the survey will not be anonymous.

Rod So, just to check, every user will see this warning after they take the survey?

Steven Not quite. The message will display before the users take the survey … as well as throughout the whole survey.

Rod OK. And if the response rate is low because of the message, I can uncheck the check box?

Steven No, that's not correct. The check box can't be changed once the survey is launched.

Rod OK.

Steven Finally, before you extract the data, you'll also need to acknowledge that your user details will be tracked when you click extract.

Rod And my details are recorded in case the data is used for the wrong reasons?

Steven That's exactly right. Your username and the date and time of the extract.

Rod OK. So to play it back: if I want to extract raw data, I can see the responses and the people that gave the responses. To protect users, they are warned that the surveys are not anonymous and there is also a record of who has exported the data. Have I understood that correctly?

Steven You've got it. Is there anything else I can help you with?

Track 21: KMK Exam practice 3, exercise 1, Hörverstehen

Gaby … so you used to be a member of a hacker club, didn't you, Andy? Tell us, would you be able to hack into our school network and … let's say … steal the exam papers? How long would that take you?

Andy Well, first of all, that's right: I used to be a member of a hacker club, and your headmaster has asked me to have a look at your network. I'm going to check if there's a gap in your security, and if there is, I'll show you how to improve security. But to answer your question, a top hacker would get access to your network before you can say Jack Robinson. Yet he wouldn't steal any exam papers. Crackers might do that, but honest hackers have a common bond to the Chaos Computer Club and share their hacker ethics.

Gaby What are the ethical principles of hacking? Can you give us a few examples?

Andy Well, to mention just three: Firstly, we don't litter other people's data; secondly, we make public data available, and thirdly, we protect private data. We're the White Hats. Crackers are the bad guys – we call them Black Hats. You see, it's just like in the old Western movies.

Gaby I see. But tell us some more about how you protect private data.

Andy We do it by offering our hacker know-how to organizations and companies. For example, the car manufacturer I work for hired me to test their security systems for flaws. … That reminds me, Gaby, didn't your husband mention the other day that you were thinking of buying an electric car?

Gaby Yes, we are. How come? Is there anything wrong with electric cars?

Andy Well, if I were you, I'd think twice before making a decision. People from the Chaos Computer Club have just discovered that the convenient charging cards for electric cars are so insecure that it's not advisable to use them.

Gaby Oh no! Why is that? Could you explain in some more detail?

Andy Well, a number is stored on these charging cards. The providers need the numbers to identify you. Some hackers from the Chaos Computer Club have found out that the numbers are what they call "public" and can be copied as often as they see fit. Therefore, it's possible to clone a charging card. An attacker, for example, could link their costs to your account, and you would have a hard time proving that that wasn't you. And what's more, he could make charging cards for other people at no extra cost. It could be weeks before the theft of a charge card number is noticed.

Gaby Unbelievable! Do the providers know about the problem? Surely they must be doing something about it?

Andy Of course they know about it. But I'm afraid they won't take action – not until the scandal is reported in the media and they're forced …

Track 22: Unit 7, Foundation, exercise 2B

… let's look at the wikis in detail, shall we? So, the wiki sites that you'll be managing have a pretty simple hierarchy, there's a main site for each of the projects that we run and each has a series of sub-pages. You're joining us at a good time as we've just updated the standard layout of the wiki sites.

The wiki is set up for full collaboration, so anyone on the team can update it. The most up-to-date information is kept on these sites, so everyone can refer to a single document. However, we've limited the editing rights, so that all the wiki pages are consistent.

The main wiki page has been redesigned to be easier to read. At the top of the page is the 'Project overview' section, which describes the project and what it's trying to achieve.

Next to that is the 'Team' section, which we've recently separated from the stakeholder section. We wanted to make it clear who is working on the project and who is impacted by it.

The next section is the 'Project health' section, which shows how the project is performing as far as budget, schedule and benefits are concerned. We use red, amber and green so that the project health is easy to understand quickly.

Next to that is a section that we call 'What's been happening?', which is an automatically-generated list of the most recent changes to the wiki. We used to send automated notifications, but we have removed those because people were getting too many.

The 'Stakeholders' list, which I mentioned earlier, shows the people impacted by the project. On the right of that is the 'Backlog' section, which we've recently added because so many people wanted a simple list of upcoming tasks.

The 'Important places' section contains the links to the sub-pages for each app, typically these are project budget, project requirements and the project plan. We used to have these on the front page, but we've moved them to make the front page clearer. Lastly, we have the 'Related projects' section, which is a list of projects that are related to, or impacted by, this project. Links to each project site are kept here.

We've also just revised the access rights to make all of the wikis public access, so anyone in the company can see them. The only exception is the project budget page, which we've limited to the project manager only.

Track 23: Unit 7, Part A, exercise 1

Michael ... OK, so here we are on the floor. Just remind me what our budget is again, please, Simon.

Simon About €15,000 has been set aside.

Michael OK. That's a bit less than ideal. An unlimited budget would be better ...

Simon So it's not as simple as going to a computer store, buying a few off-the-shelf routers and plugging them in?

Michael We could, but we wouldn't have a very good network. We're building a working business network, so we need to consider the conditions that a business-grade router has to operate under.

Simon Such as?

Michael Well, for starters, how many people will be working on this floor?

Simon About 220.

Michael Right, and they probably have at least two devices each, including mobile phones?

Simon Yes, probably ...

Michael So that's 440 connections all happening at the same time. Home gear isn't designed for that sort of network load, and employees need constant access to data. We need to take that into account.

Simon That's a good point.

Michael When we're building the network, we should consider the number of connections we need now, and in five years' time. We could have more people on the floor or simply more devices connecting. One important factor in selecting a business router is its ability to deliver rock-solid reliability under a constant load.

Simon ... and what happens if it doesn't?

Michael ... Well, if it can't deliver, productivity will be negatively impacted. Bearing this in mind, I'd recommend a dual-band setup, with 2.4 and 5 GHz.

Simon Why is that?

Michael Well, there's more bandwidth in the 5 GHz band making it great for business environments. The significant advantage of the 2.4 GHz frequency band is that it does have a better range. It's critical to have the best of both worlds. ... How big is the floor again?

Simon About 2800 square metres.

Michael OK, a bit smaller than upstairs. Good to know. Twelve access points should cover it.

Simon Do we need to get a few more to ensure performance?

Michael Not necessarily. We need a few spares, of course, but we need to keep in mind how far apart we place the access points. Access points all interfere with one another, so having them too close together could actually reduce the number of devices supported and decrease network performance.

Simon Oh. I didn't realize that – at least that will keep the budget down!

Michael That's true. The interference acts as noise and can lead to lower data speed. Placement of the access points is critical, considering that we need a minimum data rate of 8Mbps to ensure employees have a painless experience.

Simon That's a lot to think about.

Michael There's more – we'll need to take a look at the materials used in the construction of the floor to help us determine where we place the access points. We'll also need some new test equipment to help us check that the network is usable all over the floor too.

Simon Uh-oh ... I can already see the budget going up ...

Track 24: Unit 7, Part B, exercise 3 A/B

Kieran ... OK, so let's move on to talk about cloud-based servers.

Michael We've always had a local server-based network at Jupa because the computing power we need for the CAD software is so high. However, given that several cloud-based options claim to achieve the performance that we need, I think we have to consider them, don't we?

Kieran I couldn't agree more. I've thought about the advantages that cloud-based services offer and I'm quite open to it.

Michael Great. Now, some of the biggest players in the industry – like AMD, Intel and Microsoft – have been investing in cloud-based solutions. As you can see from the diagram here, these solutions move the data, heavy computation and rendering away from company desktops and place them in a central resource hosted in the cloud. The only thing that gets transferred is the pixels. That's quite impressive, isn't it?

Kieran Yes, it is. It sounds like a good idea.

Michael So, as you know, everything is stored and processed centrally in the cloud. This means that we could make some great gains in productivity. For example, our engineers could be on the road but still be contributing to the same designs as their team in the office. That sounds great, right?

Kieran I'm not sure that I entirely agree. What if they're somewhere in the middle of nowhere with a poor internet connection and have a terrible time trying to work?

Michael OK. I see your point – network speed is obviously an issue. That said, how about our international engineers picking up processing when our local teams go home in the evening? We're only a medium-sized company, but we might be able to have almost 24 hours of work being done per day if we co-ordinate well. The productivity gains would be amazing, right?

Kieran Yes, I completely agree with that. The gains would be incredible.

Michael Also, in terms of employee satisfaction, we could give employees the chance to work from home. So we could offer them more flexibility and a better work-life balance. That's quite a good idea, wouldn't you agree?

Kieran I agree to a point. Working from home is great, but the ability to work at home on ADSL speeds, which is what most people have, is still a concern.

Michael Sure, that's a valid concern. We could also offer flexible office hours – our early starters could do 6 a.m. to 2 p.m., while the night-owls, especially the younger team members, could choose to work from 1 p.m. to 9 p.m., or something like that. I think giving them these options would be great for employee satisfaction – Human Resources will be happy, won't they?

Kieran   I'm not sure about that. Most of our team have families and I don't think we want to tell people to work until 9 p.m. However, I can see that the younger engineers might like the option of starting and working later.

Michael Yes, I think they might too. Now, there are other benefits. In terms of saving costs, we don't need to invest in high-powered desktops and we can run thin client machines, potentially saving quite a bit of money on hardware. It's a nice benefit, don't you think?

Kieran   I'm definitely with you on that.

Michael Great. I really think this looks like a great option for us, don't you agree?

Kieran   I partially agree, but we also need to talk about the drawbacks. As I said, the network performance is a concern, both here and …

Track 25: Unit 7, Communication, exercise 2A/B

Conversation 1

Kieran   Right, Chris. I've looked at how you're working with the international colleagues. Can we talk about it?

Chris   Sure.

Kieran   So, to start, you clearly haven't understood the guidelines we published.

Chris   Really? What do you mean?

Kieran   Where do I start? You need to pay more attention to a lot of things.

Chris   Can you give me some examples?

Kieran   For starters, you need to write useful comments for the team in Florida to pick up.

Chris   How are they not useful?

Kieran   You have to change them to be more descriptive. They've clearly been rushed.

Chris   OK – you may have a point there.

Kieran   And why haven't you been signing in your models before you go home? No one can make changes unless the models are signed in.

Chris   Sorry, I thought I had been. No one has mentioned it to me until today.

Kieran   Well, I'm telling you now – you need to sign them in every day. It's unacceptable not to.

Chris   I'll do that.

Kieran   You have to ask if things aren't clear.

Chris   Right.

Kieran   And you need to read the guidelines regularly to keep up with the changes.

Conversation 2

Kieran   Right, Chris. I've looked at how you're working with the international colleagues. Can we talk about it?

Chris   Sure.

Kieran   So, to start, can I ask whether everything in the guideline document is clear?

Chris   Yes, I think so … is there something that I've missed?

Kieran   It would be a good idea for you to pay more attention to a couple of things.

Chris   Can you give me some examples?

Kieran   Sure. You could try putting some more detail in the comments for the team in Florida to pick up.

Chris   Oh, they aren't detailed enough? How can I improve them?

Kieran   Perhaps you could spend a bit more time on them. Clear comments really help the team in Florida.

Chris   OK.

Kieran   It's nothing you can't handle. They sometimes seem a little rushed, which I can appreciate given your train only leaves once an hour.

Chris   OK – you may have a point there.

Kieran   Now, I also noticed that you'd forgotten to sign your models in a few times.

Chris   Yes, I am aware of doing that once or twice.

Kieran   Again, I'm sure it's because of the rush to get out of the office at the end of a long day. Can I suggest that you set aside some time at the end of every day to do so?

Chris   Sure. I'll do that.

Kieran   If you're uncertain about anything, you could come to me and ask.

Chris   Thanks. I will.

Kieran   Otherwise, maybe think about checking the guidelines regularly to see if they have been updated.

Chris   OK, I will. Is there anything else … ?

Track 26: Unit 8, Foundation, exercise 3A/B

Emily   … so the thing is, we're still trying to decide between Bluetooth and our proprietary wireless protocol for the new range.

James   Well … Bluetooth is well known, which is better from a marketing point of view.

Emily   Agreed, but there are also advantages to using our own protocol.

James   Does anyone not use Bluetooth?

Emily   GameTech, who are our main competitors, use their own protocol.

James   OK. So why would we use our own?

Emily   We have complete control, which allows us to optimize a lot of important things.

James   Such as?

Emily   We can make the data connection more reliable so that it doesn't disconnect, which is important to everyone.

James   Yes, I agree. Reliability is really important. We can't have our most expensive items connecting badly. OK, what else?

Emily   We can also make it so that the peripherals connect without pairing, you know, when you have to find a device, connect to it, confirm the connection and so on, which is annoying with Bluetooth.

James   Yes, that is a selling point. Easy to set up. I'm starting to like our proprietary protocol. What else?

Emily   We can also optimize things that enhance security.

James   Well, given that we're only talking about keyboards and mice, I don't think there are many customers who care about security. It isn't a key concern.

Emily   OK. How about optimization for high-speed data transfer?

James   I agree that high-speed data sounds great, but how fast does the data transfer need to be? It's not like we are transferring media that requires a high data rate.

Emily   It might not be a lot of information, but don't forget that serious gamers are people who need something better than average. I think it's really important to them.

James	Yes – you're right. OK, any other reason why we shouldn't use Bluetooth?
Emily	We can reduce the power that the peripherals use.
James	Is low power usage important for gaming peripherals?
Emily	Yes, serious gamers play for hours and hours. You don't want to tell them to stop after a few hours because there is no battery.
James	Hmmmm. OK, I agree – that is important. Anything else?
Emily	We can also do more to increase the distance over which they can communicate. But I guess that's not so important.
James	No, it isn't. Will using a proprietary connection limit our market? I imagine using something standardized like Bluetooth allows a device to connect to anything – like plug and play?
Emily	That's true. If we use our own, we have to include a wireless dongle that plugs into a USB port.
James	And Bluetooth is built into nearly every computer, which means more people can use it. OK, just let me summarize …

Track 27: Unit 8, Part A, exercise 1

Julia	Good afternoon, I'm Julia Pasternak from QAR. Welcome to our booth. How are you today?
Tom	Well, thanks.
Julia	How are you enjoying the show? It's great to see a lot of strong medical technology, don't you agree?
Chris	We're enjoying it a lot, it's a very strong showing this year. There are a lot of great products and services on the floor. We must have visited 25 booths and been impressed with most of them.
Julia	I'm glad to hear that you're enjoying it.
Chris	Yes, absolutely. As most companies do, we have a few things that we want to improve, and it's great that there are so many options to help us.
Julia	May I ask who you work for?
Tom	We work for MGB Health.
Julia	MGB Health? You have a great reputation as a leader of medical instrument technology.
Tom	Thanks – we like to think so.
Julia	You were founded in the 1940s, in Michigan, isn't that right? Even then the company provided the latest instruments to help patients.
Chris	Yes, you're right. We were founded in 1944, to be precise, and had 3 employees. Now we have 1,800 employees that are crazy about technology and helping patients. We're still headquartered in Michigan though.
Julia	That sounds like a great place to work. It also sounds like we share a passion for technology and helping people. Can I ask whether you are here looking for something in particular?
Tom	Yes, we are very interested in how augmented reality can be used to educate staff in using our instruments in medical procedures.
Julia	Great, well that's our specialty. I'd be happy to demonstrate our holographic anatomy program. You can choose from any of the major headset manufacturers – we support all of them.

Track 28: Unit 8, Part B, exercise 3

Justin	Let's take a look at the software customization phase. Anthony, you were involved in this, can you give us your thoughts on how this went?
Anthony	Sure. In hindsight, I think it went quite well. The requirements workshops allowed us to get an early start and we delivered on time. The only downside was that we had to customize more than we would've liked. Don't you agree, Chuck?
Chuck	I agree with Anthony. We should've tried to standardize more. I understand that Modi Medical put pressure on us to deliver by a specific date, if I recall correctly. This meant we rushed through the customization analysis a bit too quickly.
Anthony	I agree, and think this is a good lesson. Could we also reflect on the problems caused by the new AR engine release?
Chuck	Oh yes, you're right. Looking back now, I'm surprised the Modi Medical management weren't more upset. It didn't make QAR look very good.
Justin	Just thinking about it again, do you think that we could've been more careful in planning?
Chuck	We knew that the upgrade was coming and I think we should've allowed for some extra time in the plan, in case of problems with the upgrade.
Anthony	Yes, I think that is a good lesson for other projects.

Track 29: Unit 8, Communication, exercise 1A

1

Receptionist	Good morning. Welcome to the International Hotel.
Guest	Good morning. My name is Rossi – Giovanni Rossi. I have a reservation.
Receptionist	Here we are. Giovanni Rossi.
Guest	Yes. From Rossi Technology, Rome.
Receptionist	Thank you. You're in room 303, on the third floor.
Guest	What time is breakfast served?
Receptionist	We serve a buffet breakfast in the dining room between 8 and 10 a.m.
Guest	Eight till 10? Can I have a swim before breakfast?
Receptionist	Yes, of course. The swimming pool is open from 6 a.m. till 10 p.m.
Guest	That's great. Thank you.
Receptionist	You're welcome. Enjoy your stay, Mr Rossi.

2

Receptionist	Good morning. Welcome to the International Hotel.
Guest	Good morning. I have a reservation under McGregor, McGregorRobotics.
Receptionist	Mary McGregor, from Glasgow.
Guest	Yes. That's right. I booked a room on the ground floor, with wheelchair access.
Receptionist	Yes, that's correct. You're in room 15, on this floor.
Guest	Does the dining room have wheelchair access?
Receptionist	Yes, it does. All of our rooms and facilities have wheelchair access.
Guest	Good. Thank you.
Receptionist	Let me know if you need any extra towels or pillows.
Guest	That's very kind of you.
Receptionist	My pleasure. Have a good stay, Ms McGregor.

3

Receptionist	Good morning. Welcome to the International Hotel.
Guest	Thank you. I would like to check in.
Receptionist	Of course. What name is the reservation under?
Guest	My name is Yusuf Zuabi.
Receptionist	Could you spell your surname, please?
Guest	Yes. It's Z U A B I, "Zuabi", with a Z. The reservation may be under the name of my company, Tech Solutions.
Receptionist	Thank you. Ah, yes, here it is, Tech Solutions, Berlin, Mr Yusuf Zuabi. You're in room 201, on the second floor. Here's your key. The buffet breakfast is served in the dining room between 8 and 10 a.m.
Guest	Thank you. I have a question. Where can I park my car?
Receptionist	There's a secure car park at the back of the hotel. The man at the gate will let you in.
Guest	Good. Thank you.
Receptionist	No problem. Enjoy your stay.

Track 30: Unit 8, Communication, exercise 1C

Receptionist	Good morning, Ms Banerjee. How are you this morning?
Guest	Good morning. I'm very well, thank you.
Receptionist	How can I help you?
Guest	I'm going home today so I would like to check out.
Receptionist	Of course. What room were you in?
Guest	I was in room 207.
Receptionist	Did you have a nice time in Amsterdam?
Guest	It's been great. I love Amsterdam.
Receptionist	Was everything OK for you in the hotel?
Guest	Yes, thank you. Everything was fine. I'll definitely be back.
Receptionist	I'm pleased to hear that. Have a good trip home.
Guest	Thank you. I'm flying KLM. They're very good.

Track 31: KMK Exam practice 4, exercise 3, Hörverstehen

Paul	… and although Bitcoins have been around for quite a few years now, many people have questions about them, just like I do. Take my wallet, for example, could I put some Bitcoins in it?
Anne	I'm afraid you can't, Paul – at least not in your physical wallet. But you can create a digital wallet. It's like a personal database that you store on your computer or smartphone or in the cloud. However, I wouldn't advise you to keep your wallet in the cloud. There's always a high risk of it being stolen.
Paul	OK, I'll remember that. So how do I fill up this digital wallet with Bitcoins when I need some? Can I go to Barclays and buy them?
Anne	Well, we're working on it. Presently you can buy Bitcoins either from brokers, or directly from other people via market places. You can pay for them in a variety of ways, ranging from hard cash to a credit card, or even with other cryptocurrencies, depending on who you are trading with.
Paul	Now let's take another example. Suppose I've got some Bitcoins in my digital wallet to pay you for this interview. How do we go about it?

Anne	Very well. All I need to do is to display the Quick Response Code in my wallet app and let you scan my mobile, or touch our two phones together. It's the simplest way to exchange money from one personal wallet to another at a very low cost. There are no extra fees for making an international transfer, no banks to make you wait three business days, and no limitations as to the amount you can send.
Paul	What about security? You mentioned that the cloud is not the safest place for my savings. What about my laptop? Wouldn't a hacker be able to hack into my digital wallet?
Anne	Well, it's like in the real world with lost property, pickpockets and burglars. It all depends on how careful you are. If your digital wallet is only on your smartphone and you break it or lose it, it's simply gone forever. Or if you lose your wallet's hard drive data or even your wallet password, your wallet's contents are gone forever.
Paul	You're a security specialist, Anne. What would you advise us to do?
Anne	Well, there are three things you mustn't forget to do. First of all, you need to back up your wallet on a regular basis. Next, you should use different hardware for the backups, like USB sticks and CDs. And, last but not least, encrypting any backup that is on your network is always good security practice. Before I forget, Paul, think about your will. Your Bitcoins could be lost forever if you don't have any family involved. If the location of your wallet or your password aren't known by your family when you're gone, there's no chance that your funds will ever …

Track 32: Unit 9, Foundation, exercise 1B

Claudia	Good morning, Mr Camilleri. It's Claudia here. You wanted to talk about the video conferencing system?
Mr Camilleri	Ah. Hello there, Claudia. Thanks for calling. How's the weather there in Berlin? It's a beautiful day here in Valletta.
Claudia	You're lucky. It's raining here.
Mr Camillari	Oh, dear. Well, never mind. Perhaps it will be nice tomorrow. Do you have my email there?
Claudia	Yes, I do.
Mr Camilleri	Good. Let's start. First of all, I'd like to be able to store data that everyone can access wherever they are. What do you think of that idea?
Claudia	It's a good idea. We'll need cloud storage.
Mr Camilleri	Cloud storage? Oh, yes. I've heard of that. Fine. And I'd like the system to let us re-play the sessions later.
Claudia	So, we'll need a video recording function.
Mr Camilleri	Right. That makes sense. It's a video conferencing system, so it should be able to make video recordings.
Claudia	Yes, that's right.
Mr Camilleri	Of course. Right, well, only two more things. Will the makers supply a guide that helps us to use the system?
Claudia	A user manual? Yes. Probably. If not, there will be some other kind of help available.
Mr Camilleri	Oh. All right. Then, the last thing is, will they let us try out the system for nothing so that we know if it is the right one for us?
Claudia	Sure. Most of them offer a free trial.

Mr Camilleri	Good. Well, I think that's it. I'd like you to get started on that today.
Claudia	I'll do that, Mr Camilleri, but I wanted to suggest two other functions.
Mr Camilleri	Oh. All right. You're the expert. What else do you suggest?
Claudia	Hmm. I wondered about multi-language support.
Mr Camilleri	Why would we need that?
Claudia	Hmm. Just in case someone doesn't speak good English?
Mr Camilleri	Oh, no. I don't think we need that. What was the other thing?
Claudia	Well, some video conferencing systems have calendar integration so that you can schedule more meetings. I think you'll want to arrange more meetings.
Mr Camilleri	Well, yes, but my secretary, Maria, does that for me.
Claudia	Oh, of course. I just thought it might be useful.
Mr Camilleri	All right. I'll probably never use it, but you can add the calendar thing to the other items we discussed.
Claudia	Very well, Mr Camilleri. I'll get on with it right away.
Mr Camilleri	Thanks, Claudia. Goodbye.

Track 33: Unit 9, Part A, exercise 1A/B

Sebastian	Could I ask you to start by telling me about your team?
Chris	Sure. Our team is a project management office.
Sebastian	Thanks. Could you tell me what responsibilities your team has?
Chris	We manage project documents for the entire organization.
Sebastian	Now, you mentioned that you are having problems with your document management system – is that correct?
Chris	Yes it is.
Sebastian	Can you explain what you need to manage?
Chris	Our team has to run reports across all the project documents to show which ones are up to date and being used. There is a large set of stakeholders that rely on these documents.
Sebastian	Can you give me some more details?
Chris	Sure – we've got a few offices around the country, so we need to do a lot of collaboration via conference call or video conference.
Sebastian	Thanks. And could you tell me more about how conference calls are used?
Chris	In the video conference, we often talk about one of the documents and have participants provide feedback. People usually write their own notes and send them via email later, which means that we have to collate all of the emails and feedback after the call. It's annoying and time-consuming.
Sebastian	Could you tell me what your current environment is like?
Chris	Well, we have our documents stored in an electronic document management system that's quite old, so it's complex and difficult to use. It's also horrible to look at – like it's from the 90s.
Sebastian	Is that how most of your colleagues feel?
Chris	Yes!
Sebastian	Can you elaborate?

Chris	People don't like using it, so they don't. They continue to keep their feedback and meeting notes on their hard drives. If anyone wants to see them, they need to ask for an email.
Sebastian	Can you tell me what problems this causes you?
Chris	It means that our information is practically impossible to find and co-ordinate. A lot of information is lost as some people have left the organization; so we waste time recreating this lost work.
Sebastian	Can I ask what you think the best solution is?
Chris	It's quite obvious, I think. We need an easily-accessible and centralized place for all of the documents, feedback, meeting notes and so forth.
Sebastian	Is an easy-to-use solution important for you?
Chris	Yes, of course.
Sebastian	Could you explain a bit further?
Chris	People are used to nice interfaces. It's absolutely key to this being successful. If it's easy to use, people are more likely to use it. If it's nice to look at, that's even better, although it's not essential.
Sebastian	Great – is there anything else you'd like to mention?
Chris	Well, the other thing is …

Track 34: Unit 9, Part B, exercise 2

Chris	Right, shall we get down to business?
Sebastian	Sure. Let's start.
Chris	Seeing as we are new customers, we were hoping that you would upgrade our customer support plan.
Sebastian	Well, I can't offer you an upgrade to the premium support plan. Let's see. You're currently on 10 support calls per month. What I can do is upgrade the number of calls to 35. Is that acceptable?
Chris	It's a start. Could you also do a better price on the support plan?
Sebastian	I'm sorry but the price that I quoted you is the best I can do. The extra support calls I'm offering are as good as unlimited, even for a team of your size. Most of our clients of your size call about 30 times per month and that number is reducing.
Chris	If that's the case, then I think we can live with it. Speaking of our team size, given we have so many users, could you give us a discount on that?
Sebastian	Yes, I think we can do that for you. But you'll have to buy 15 extra licences. This will bring your overall price down by 7% over the current price. You're also ready for growth.
Chris	And is a discount available if we purchase an annual licence?
Sebastian	OK. I'm prepared to offer you that. If you pay annually instead of monthly, we'll give you a further 20% discount.
Chris	Could you give us a bit more of a discount?
Sebastian	No. I'm afraid I can't do that.
Chris	Would you give us more storage capacity as a starting bonus, too?
Sebastian	Hmm. I have some room to move. How about a 40% increase from 50 GB to 70 GB? That will be plenty of space.
Chris	That sounds OK, yes.

Track 35: Unit 10, Part A, exercise 3A

Customer	So I've heard that a smartwatch can be a good motivator for getting better at sports – is that true?
Colleague	Yes. I know a lot of people that get motivated by having something remind them that they want to get healthier. What sports do you want to improve?
Customer	I run a few times per week and want to get up to doing a marathon later this year. I also ride my bike to and from work, and I surf occasionally.
Colleague	Great. Well, as you're looking to improve to marathon standard, I won't recommend the FitnessMate because I think you'll need GPS.
Customer	Why do I need GPS?
Colleague	You need it if you want to accurately determine the distance you run, your speed and pace.
Customer	Oh, OK. That makes sense. I have an activity tracker that just records my steps. It doesn't tell me those things.
Colleague	Right. Now, you said you surf occasionally. Do you want to be able to get notifications while surfing?
Customer	Hmm. I like being away from everything when I surf, so that's not a priority.
Colleague	How about when you're running?
Customer	Actually that *is* important. I hate taking my smartphone with me when I run. Can these watches let me make calls?
Colleague	Yes. Since that seems important I'd say an eSIM is a good feature for you. Can I ask how important it is for you to know things like your altitude and the temperature around you?
Customer	I live in a flat area not far from the coast, so altitude isn't important. Temperature would be handy to know, but it's not essential.
Colleague	OK. Now do you do any scuba-diving?
Customer	No.
Colleague	In that case, you only need water resistance to 10 metres because you don't need to go deeper than a few metres under the water. Now, last question. Do you want to wear it aside from exercise – like to work or socially?
Customer	No. I only intend to wear it while doing sports.
Colleague	OK. That being the case, it doesn't sound like you need options for different straps and materials.

Track 36: KMK Exam practice 5, exercise 1, Hörverstehen

Host	Welcome back to our weekly series "Unbelievable but True". I'm your host Brian Spears and today's guest in the studio is Peter Forbes. Peter is a science journalist who writes for several magazines. Now Peter, what have you brought us today? Looks like a piece of carpet, doesn't it?
Peter	Thank you for inviting me, Brian. And to answer your question, yes, it *is* part of a carpet and it can do some very astonishing things.
Host	Are you going to tell us it can fly like a magic carpet?
Peter	Not yet, but they're working on it. But joking apart, it was developed at the National Institute of Advanced Industrial Science and Technology in Japan …
Host	In Japan! Where else? Sorry for interrupting. Please go on.
Peter	Well, Brian, if you walked on a carpet like this here in the studio, it could tell us some things you might not like to share with your audience. For example, it could display, or even speak, your age and sex when you walk across it.
Host	No problem! I'm quite willing to share that information with anybody. Or is there more to come?
Peter	What about your weight, Brian? Would you like your boss to know that you put on five kilos in the last three weeks, as you told me before we went on air?
Host	Uh-ho!
Peter	… And the carpet could tell us even more about you. It distinguishes between people in their 20s or 60s with almost 100% accuracy. And how does it do this, you'll ask? By collecting and analysing your foot size, your stride, and your walking speed.
Host	Unbelievable! Is there anything the carpet can't do? For example, tell us which university I went to?
Peter	I'm afraid that's something it can't do. Nor will it be able to reveal your skin or hair colour in the near future. But it would know that you're not a woman because you've got larger feet and a longer stride and your centre of gravity is different.
Host	That's really amazing! Now, can you explain the technology behind it?
Peter	I was just coming to that. The carpet has a layer of plastic optical fibres that bend under the pressure of your foot and transmit light according to your weight. They are combined with a number of rather large sensors and a software called guided-path tomography. They send the data to a display that shows the position and footfall of a person walking on the carpet in real time together with all the information I've mentioned before.
Host	That's all very well, but who would buy a carpet like this? Is there really a market for it?
Peter	Obviously there is a market. Otherwise the German carpet maker *Vorwerk Teppichwerke* and semiconductor company Infineon Technologies wouldn't have developed their own model. Starwood and Marriott are considering installing similar carpets in their hotels.
Host	How would they and their guests benefit from these carpets?
Peter	A night trip to the bathroom is made much easier by the carpet sensors that guide you in the dark. They also automatically switch on the lights via the Radio-Frequency-Identification. Suppose a guest is lying motionless in some dark corridor of the hotel. Reception can detect and track their footprints and call an emergency service or …
Host	Sorry, Peter, but our time's up. I'm pretty sure that many a scatter-brained boss who can't remember the age, weight and gender of his employees will soon have this amazing piece of technology laid in his office … Thank you all for joining us.

Track 37: Unit 11, Foundation, exercise 2B

Many researchers have looked into the carbon footprint of these types of technology – meaning the amount of greenhouse gas produced to support the activity – to measure the impact they have on the environment. This is commonly expressed in the volume of carbon dioxide. Using more energy tends to increase greenhouse gas emissions, but using alternative forms of energy that don't burn greenhouse gases can reduce a technology's carbon footprint.

I'd like to take you through some surprising figures about services that we all use but may not consider when we talk about the impact of technology on the environment.

I'll start with email. An ordinary email that you click on, open, forward or reply to emits 4 grams of CO_2. If that email has an attachment of, for example 1 MB, the CO_2 goes up to 19 g, and if that attachment is then forwarded or filed, the footprint for that one email could be as high as 50 g! Every email has a unique footprint that reflects its size and the number of times it is moved around. A traditional 4-page letter sent by post, generates roughly 30 g of CO_2 when delivered to a location 400 km away.

Let's move on to streaming video … now Netflix has put the average customer's carbon footprint at 300 g per year, which only includes the energy used to deliver the service itself. According to Netflix, this amounts to approximately 0.007% of the carbon footprint of the average American household. Another study found that a shift to streaming instead of renting DVDs would save enough energy in one year to power 200,000 homes.

Given that a lot of Netflix is consumed on family TVs, the power consumption, and carbon footprint, of televisions must also be taken into account.

Interestingly, televisions are using more energy now than previously due to the increased sizes of our screens. An hour of television viewing on an old 32-inch CRT – that's cathode-ray tube – television uses about 84 g of CO_2 per hour, while a 15-inch LCD television generates 37 g. However, a 42-inch plasma television generates the most with 240 g of CO_2 per hour.

Lastly, I'd just like to mention music streaming. This is very difficult to specify, but it's been estimated that streaming an album 27 times uses up the same amount of energy as producing and shipping a CD. So if you wonder whether streaming an album is better for the environment than buying it on CD, it depends on how often you listen to that album.

In every case, the question of how much CO_2 an activity produces may depend on which company you're using. Several companies, including Apple, Google and Netflix, have committed to using clean sources of energy for their data centres – and, in many cases, are increasing the percentage of clean energy they're using for their services each year.

Track 38: Unit 11, Part B, exercise 2

John	Thanks for taking the time to discuss the invoice with me, Robyn. I think there may have been some misunderstandings that I'd like to clear up.
Robyn	Yes, OK. I have the invoice in front of me and I'm happy to discuss it with you. Could you tell me which specific items you have issues with?
John	Yes. Well, first of all, there are a few discounts that we discussed that haven't been granted fully, or have been left off the invoice altogether. I'd be grateful if you could rectify these mistakes quickly.
Robyn	I'll do my best to help, of course. Which discounts are you referring to?
John	I believe you mentioned a 20% discount on monitors. The invoice only has a 10% discount applied.
Robyn	I'm sure you're right. I sincerely apologize for that. I'll make sure that it's corrected immediately.
John	Thanks. Next, I thought we'd agreed on a 30% discount on cabling & charging.
Robyn	That sounds possible – what does the invoice say? Oh, nothing at all. I'm sorry about that. I'll also have that changed.

John	Thank you. Now, I also recall a 25% discount on Service & Support for the first 12 months. The invoice only says 20%.
Robyn	That's not my recollection, John. 20% is the maximum discount we ever offer. I'm not willing to discount it any further as we'd lose money on it. The first year of support is break-even for us. I don't believe that I would have offered more.
John	OK. I'm prepared to take your word on that. However, one thing I'm sure wasn't discussed at any stage is the delivery charge on the invoice.
Robyn	No, it wasn't discussed, but a delivery charge for any hardware is quite normal as we have to hire a courier company to deliver it. But, as this is your first order and we've made a few mistakes, I'm happy to waive the delivery charge.
John	Thank you. Finally, I also need you to change the number of desks ordered to 20, not 30. We have 5 rooms and each room needs 4 desks.
Robyn	Yes, that's right. That must have been a typing error. I'm sorry about that. We'll get it changed, of course.
John	I hope this isn't a sign of things to come, Robyn. I'm disappointed that there are so many problems with this first invoice.
Robyn	Yes, I know, John. I really regret these misunderstandings and the bad impression they make. Look, we appreciate your business and we want to continue our relationship: how about we reduce our consulting fee? I think I could cut the hours from 75 to 70.
John	Thank you. I appreciate that. OK, that's settled then. You'll send us the revised invoice and let me know when you can start …

Track 39: Unit 11, Communication, exercise 2A

Melissa	Wolf.
Jerzy	Oh. Hello. Erm. Do you speak English?
Melissa	Yes.
Jerzy	Oh. Good. This is Jerzy Adamczyk calling from the Denta Dental Clinic in Warsaw. Is that the sales department?
Melissa	Yes.
Jerzy	And, erm, who am I speaking to, please?
Melissa	Wolf.
Jerzy	Ah. Ms Wolf. Erm. Is, erm, are you the correct person to take a complaint about a delivery?
Melissa	What's the problem?
Jerzy	It's about my order for X-ray machines. Both of the X-ray machines were damaged. One of them – the glass on one of the machines is scratched and the other machine is dented. I mean, the metal casing is dented. I think that …
Melissa	What's the order number?
Jerzy	942761.
Melissa	OK. I can't do anything at the moment. I'll get it sorted after lunch.
Jerzy	So, will you phone me back? My phone number is …
Melissa	It's here on the display.
Jerzy	0048 129 546 783?
Melissa	Yes.
Jerzy	And my name is Adamczyk. You will be sure to look into this? Well, thank you very much.

Track 40: Unit 11, Communication, exercise 2B

Melissa	*Guten Morgen. Verkaufsabteilung. Melissa Wolf am Apparat.*
Jerzy	Oh. Hello. Erm. Do you speak English?
Melissa	Yes, of course. How can I help you?
Jerzy	Oh. Good. This is Jerzy Adamczyk calling from the Denta Dental Clinic in Warsaw. Is that the sales department?
Melissa	Yes, this is the sales department. My name's Melissa Wolf.
Jerzy	Ah. Mrs, erm, Ms Wolf. Hmm. Is, erm, are you the correct person to take a complaint about a delivery?
Melissa	It depends on what it's about. Could you give me some details?
Jerzy	It's about my order for X-ray machines. Both of the X-ray machines were damaged. One of them – the glass on one of the machines is scratched and the other machine is dented. I mean, the metal casing is dented. I think that there was a problem during transport.
Melissa	Oh, I'm sorry to hear that. Could you give me the order number, please?
Jerzy	It's 942761.
Melissa	Just a moment, please. Right. 942761. I have it here. Two X-ray machines. And you say that both of them are damaged?
Jerzy	That is correct. I am sorry, but I have to say that I am disappointed about this business. This is a trial order, but I had to complain last week because the equipment did not arrive on the date we agreed. Now the machines are here and I can't use them.
Melissa	Oh, dear. I'm extremely sorry to hear that you've had so much trouble. I'm sure my superior would like to discuss this with you. Can I ask her to phone you when she comes in to work tomorrow?
Jerzy	Yes. All right. I'll be at home all day tomorrow so she should call me there. The number is 0048 129 546 993.
Melissa	0048 129 546 993. Yes. You'll get a call from my superior tomorrow, Mr Adamczyk.
Jerzy	Could you tell me her name, please?
Melissa	It's Mia Richter.
Jerzy	Mia Richter. Good. Thank you very much, Ms Wolf.
Melissa	You're welcome, Mr Adamczyk. Thank you for calling.
Jerzy	Goodbye.

Track 41: Unit 11, Communication, exercise 3C

Jeanette	Good morning. Sheffield Metal, Sales Department, Jeanette Hogg speaking.
Supervisor	Good morning. This is Max Jahn from World Medical in Germany.
Jeanette	Good morning, Mr Jahn. How can I help you?
Supervisor	I'm calling to enquire about my order for containers for medical equipment. The order was sent almost one month ago, on 18 April, and delivery was promised by 3 May but, so far, nothing has arrived.
Jeanette	Oh. I'm sorry to hear that. Could you give me the order number?
Supervisor	Yes. It's DF54736.
Jeanette	DF54736. Just a moment, please. I'll check. I'm sorry, Mr Jahn. I don't seem to have any record of your order. Can I just check that I've understood everything? The order number is DF54736 and you ordered the containers on 18 April. Could you give me the exact details of the order, please?
Supervisor	Yes, it's an order for your aluminium containers for medical equipment.
Jeanette	Aluminium containers for medical equipment. Mr Jahn, I'll have to speak to my colleague to find out what the problem is. Can I get back to you later?
Supervisor	Well, yes. But I hope it won't take long. We can't fulfil our orders until we have your containers.
Jeanette	Yes. I realize that, Mr Jahn. I'm very sorry about this and I will do my best to get back to you as soon as possible.
Supervisor	Many thanks for your help, Ms Hogg.

Track 42: Unit 12, Foundation, exercise 1

1 Maren

Presenter	Hello, and welcome to this week's podcast. This week, we're talking to a group of people who have recently gained their IT qualifications. Let's start with you. Would you like to introduce yourself?
Maren	Sure. I'm Maren and I've just completed my apprenticeship as an IT assistant in a wholesale electronics company.
Presenter	What did you enjoy most about your apprenticeship?
Maren	I liked the fact that the work is varied.
Presenter	OK. What do you do at work?
Maren	Mainly, I'm involved in data processing. I scan and capture data and process it using database management applications. I also have to back up data each day and make sure that any data that's been saved has not become corrupted. Sometimes, I have to install new hardware or software to keep up with an organization's changing data storage and communication needs.
Presenter	What about the future?
Maren	I'd like to become a project manager in a similar kind of company.

2 Garry

Presenter	Hi. What's your name and what do you do?
Garry	My name's Garry and I'm an IT helpdesk technician for a computer software company.
Presenter	OK. What did you enjoy most about your apprenticeship, Garry?
Garry	I really enjoyed the "hands on" aspect of the job and working out the problems in a logical way.
Presenter	Right. What do you do specifically?
Garry	Well, I take calls from private users or business clients who need assistance with their software. I deal with people on the phone and online. You have to find the best way to communicate solutions to both technical and non-technical individuals. I don't usually have problems doing that but when I do, I pass on the call to my manager. After every job, I write a short report for my manager.
Presenter	OK. So, where do you go from here? What are your plans?
Garry	Well, I'd like to become a helpdesk technician manager.

3 Delon

Presenter	Hello. Can you tell us your name and something about your apprenticeship?
Delon	Yes. My name's Delon and I've just qualified as an IT network administrator at a large insurance company.

Presenter	What did you like best about your apprenticeship?
Delon	I liked the mixture of going to vocational school and working in the company.
Presenter	That's good. So … what do you do in your job?
Delon	Basically, I provide systems support for the firm I work for. I install network and computer systems, update software and run virus checks. I also diagnose and repair problems.
Presenter	Hmm. OK. One last question, Delon. Now that you're qualified, what would you like to do in the future?
Delon	I'd like to stay at the insurance company I already work for and work my way up to become a supervisor.

Track 43: Unit 12, Part B, exercise 3B

Presenter	Thanks for coming along to talk to us today, Pat.
Pat	My pleasure. It's nice to be here.
Presenter	Good. Now, today you're going to give us advice about how to prepare for an interview.
Pat	Correct. I'm going to go through each of the five stages of a job interview and talk about how candidates can prepare themselves. So, stage one, greetings and introductions. That's perhaps the easiest part of the interview but it still needs some preparation. First of all, you should find out where the interview location is and how to get there so that you arrive in good time. Try to give yourself enough time to relax and calm down. You should also make sure that you're wearing appropriate clothes.
Presenter	First impressions count. Would you advise people to buy new clothes specially for the interview?
Pat	No, not particularly. Your clothes need to be appropriate for the job, clean and smart, that's all. They don't have to be new.
Presenter	Right. What about body language at the start of the interview?
Pat	Body language is important. Walk into the room as confidently as possible, shake hands and make eye contact. Don't be shy. Look directly at the interviewer or interviewers. You'll be asked to take a seat, and there will be a bit of small talk.
Presenter	Talking about the weather, your journey, that kind of thing?
Pat	That's right. There might also be a question about where you live or your hobbies.
Presenter	Some people find it difficult to make small talk, even in their own language. What advice can you give us there, Pat?
Pat	I think the best thing to do is to simply get into the habit of making small talk in English with a colleague or a friend.
Presenter	That's a good idea. Practise making small talk whenever you can.
Pat	That's it. Now, let's move on to the main part of the interview. You'll be asked questions by one or more interviewers.
Presenter	The interview might be conducted by more than one person?
Pat	That's correct. Sometimes there's a panel of interviewers. Now, preparation for this part is extremely important. Think about the questions you might be asked and make a list. You'll definitely be

	asked to talk about yourself. Perhaps the interviewer will ask you about your strengths and weaknesses. Write down the questions – and think about how you're going to answer. And always remember to relate your answers to the job on offer.
Presenter	Yes, that's important. Keep focused on the job. What should a candidate do if he or she doesn't understand a question?
Pat	If you don't understand a question, ask the interviewer to clarify. You can say: "Could you explain what you mean by … ?" – whatever it is. A good interviewer will ask the question again in a slightly different way.
Presenter	Hmm. I hope so. Now, earlier you mentioned questions from the candidate. I remember my very first interview. I had no idea what to ask.
Pat	Oh, dear. Some preparation would have helped. It's important to do some background research into the company before you go for the interview. Find out about the company's most recent developments and the future prospects of the company you hope to work for. Go to the firm's home page on the internet, read the business section of your newspaper, or look through business magazines. As you're doing your research, note down any questions that occur to you concerning the company. You should also, of course, prepare some questions about the job itself. Then, when you're asked if you have any questions, this is your chance to show your interest in the company and the job.
Presenter	Right. Be prepared with questions about the company and the job! And that's the end of the interview and you can say goodbye.
Pat	Well, not quite. Before the interview comes to an end, the interviewer usually says when the candidate can expect to hear from the company or if there's to be a further interview or a test – hmm – say, in the form of an assessment centre evaluation. So, only after these arrangements have been made, then your last task as a candidate is to say thank you and goodbye. Again, a good, firm handshake and a smile, and that's it.
Presenter	Well, thank you, Pat, for these very helpful interviewing tips. I'm sure our listeners have learned a lot today and that they'll be able to put your tips to good use in their interviews. Now, next week's podcast is about …

Track 44: KMK Exam practice 6, exercise 2, Hörverstehen

Larry	Spearhead Models International. Good morning, Larry Maham speaking. How can I help you?
Charles	My name's Baxter, Charles Baxter. I ordered two of your racing boats three weeks ago … they haven't arrived yet.
Larry	I apologize for the inconvenience this has caused you. I'm a hobby skipper myself, so I can imagine your disappointment, Mr Baxter.
Charles	No, I don't think you can. I'm a competitor in the National Model Speedboat Championships. The thing is, I'll lose the chance to compete in the first race if the boats don't arrive this week.

Larry	Oh, I'm sorry to hear that you're having problems, sir. Let me just check your order. Could you give me the order number, please?
Charles	It's 648-A. And by the way, I sent an email to your customer service a week ago and got a friendly reply saying they'd look into the matter, but nothing has happened so far.
Larry	I'm awfully sorry to hear that. Please hold the line, Mr Baxter. Order number 648-A, … Here we are. Two boats of the Spearhead Lightning series … including the radio controls. And …
Charles	Anything wrong? I hope you didn't send them by water, down the Thames.
Larry	Certainly not, Mr Baxter, but I'm afraid there seems to be a slight hitch. Well, to cut a long story short – there's good news and bad news for you. The bad news is that we're holding the Spearhead Lightning back. We've had a customer complaint that there's something wrong with the on-board software. Our engineers are working on it right now.
Charles	It's no good working on the software. Isn't it the same software in all your boats? There's never been a problem with the electronics. Take some advice from an expert and get your engineers working on the radio link between the transmitter and the on-board receiver. Believe me … my Spearhead Shark once stopped in the middle of Lake Windermere, and I had a lot of trouble restarting it. Tell your people it's always the receiver. It simply needs a better antenna. That's why I ordered the Lightning.
Larry	Yes, sir. I'll pass that information on.
Charles	OK, so what's the good news?
Larry	The good news is that I can offer you our flagship, the new Spearhead Flash. It has been specially designed for competitive racing and reaches fifty miles per hour and believe me – this boat has amazing acceleration.
Charles	Hmmm … Fifty miles per hour, you say? What about the radio link? Have they improved on that as well?
Larry	Our people in the R&D department have come up with a new type of radio link that features more frequencies. This allows you to run three boats at a time. All the components are state of the art.
Charles	That sounds interesting … what do they cost?
Larry	The price for one Spearhead Flash is £830, including the radio link. But in your case, I can grant you a 20 per cent discount.
Charles	OK, it's a deal, then, I'll cancel my order and take two of your Spearhead Flash. And please send them by FedEx Premium.
Larry	That's fine, Mr Baxter. I'll get those sent out to you as soon as possible. Don't hesitate to call again should you have any questions …

Track 45: KMK Mock exam: Rezeption I, Hörverstehen

Brian	*Autohaus Schneider. Guten Morgen. Sie sprechen mit Brian Hemming. Was kann ich für Sie tun?*
Sven	*Mein Name ist Sven Forsberg.* Excuse me, your name sounds English, so your English might be better than my German.
Brian	I'm not sure about that, but my mother is English. What can I do for you, Mr Forsberg?
Sven	Well, I bought this SUV, an MXQuadro from your company two years ago, and now it's gone – stolen. And your salesman assured me that this model was theft-proof and that it was equipped with state-of-the-art security electronics. Obviously the doors don't lock properly.
Brian	I'm very sorry to hear that, Mr Forsberg. But it's very unlikely that there was something wrong with the doors. Are you sure that it was stolen? Could it be that you forgot where you parked it?
Sven	That's impossible. I left it in the car park at a supermarket and when I came back it was gone … and yes, I've reported the theft to the police … and the officer there told me that they had about a dozen similar cases on their desk.
Brian	Let me check our customer files … Here we go. I see that your car is equipped with a Keyless-Go like many of our vehicles. The truth is Keyless-Go is no longer 100% safe. Car thieves have started using wireless theft gadgets to bypass the anti-theft devices. Unfortunately, anyone can buy them online.
Sven	Wireless theft devices? I've never heard of them before. How do they work?
Brian	My guess is that someone bumped into you, or got close to you, while you were going into the supermarket. With a little device they probably captured the signal from your Keyless-Go. Whoever it was could have sent the signal via smartphone to an accomplice in the car park who was then able to open your car and drive away.
Sven	I can't believe it! Well, fortunately my car has comprehensive insurance. But the reason for my call was actually to ask you if you could let me have a replacement car for three days.
Brian	I don't think that should be a problem. That's the least we can do to make up for your inconvenience.
Sven	Thanks, that's some good news at least. So, tell me, what I can do to stop this from happening again.
Brian	Well, the best way to prevent wireless theft is to put the key in a small Faraday cage. It's a bit inconvenient but it blocks any electronic signal. We'll provide you with one when you pick up the replacement vehicle, Mr Forsberg.
Sven	A Faraday cage? You're not serious, are you? A nineteenth-century device to protect twenty-first-century electronics! Isn't there anything more sophisticated than that?
Brian	Well, we advise our customers to fit a GPS tracking box to their cars. It triggers off the alarm if your car is stolen and it records its speed and exact location.
Sven	That's all very well. But how do I find out where my car is?
Brian	In case of theft, you'll get an SMS notification in real time with the speed and current location of the vehicle … and then the police can follow its route on the smartphone. All our models in the upper price range are equipped with tracking devices and your replacement car will be too. When would you like to pick it up, by the way? Would the day after tomorrow be convenient for you?
Sven	Thank you, that's very kind of you. And if my car fails to turn up again, I'll buy my next SUV from you, Mr Hemming.
Brian	I'm glad to hear that you'll continue doing business with us, Mr Forsberg, in spite of your bad luck and if …

Dieses Wörterverzeichnis enthält alle neuen Wörter aus *IT Matters – 3rd Edition* in der Reihenfolge ihres Erscheinens (Seitenzahlen sind angegeben). Nicht angeführt sind die Wörter aus dem Grundwortschatz (vgl. **Handreichungen für den Unterricht**). Wörter aus den Hörverständnisübungen sind mit einem **T** (Transkript) und Wörter aus den *Partner files* mit einem **P** gekennzeichnet. Die Zahl am linken Rand gibt die Seitenzahl an.

Abkürzungen	AE = amerikanisches Englisch	jdm = jemandem	pl = plural noun
	BE = britisches Englisch	jdn = jemanden	sb = somebody
	etw = etwas	jds = jemandes	sth = something

UNIT 1

6	foundation [faʊnˈdeɪʃn]	Grundlage	
	company [ˈkʌmpəni]	Unternehmen	
	profile [ˈprəʊfaɪl]	Porträt, Beschreibung, Profil	
	apprentice [əˈprentɪs]	Auszubildende/r, Lehrling	
	IT administrator [aɪ ˌtiː ədˈmɪnɪstreɪtə]	IT-Kaufmann/-frau	
	trainee [treɪˈniː]	Auszubildende/r, Praktikant/in	
	from abroad [frəm əˈbrɔːd]	aus dem Ausland	
	network [ˈnetwɜːk]	Netzwerk	
	component [kəmˈpəʊnənt]	Bauteil, Bauelement	
	producer [prəˈdjuːsə]	Hersteller, Produzent	
	device [dɪˈvaɪs]	Gerät, Apparat	
	connection [kəˈnekʃn]	Verbindung, Anschluss	
	head office [ˌhed ˈɒfɪs]	Zentrale, Hauptsitz	
	to found [faʊnd]	gründen	
	family business [ˈfæməli bɪznəs]	Familienunternehmen	
	to run [rʌn]	(Unternehmen usw.) führen	
	structure [ˈstrʌktʃə]	Aufbau, Struktur	
	chairman [ˈtʃeəmən]	Vorsitzende(r)	
	board [bɔːd]	Aufsichtsrat	
	(general) partner [ˈpɑːtnə]	Gesellschafter/in, Teilhaber/in	
	finance [ˈfaɪnæns]	Finanz, Finanzen	
	purchasing [ˈpɜːtʃəsɪŋ]	Einkauf	
	sales [seɪlz]	Verkauf, Vertrieb	
	to employ sb [ɪmˈplɔɪ]	jdn beschäftigen	
	including [ɪnˈkluːdɪŋ]	einschließlich	
	to develop [dɪˈveləp]	entwickeln	
	to manufacture [ˌmænjuˈfæktʃə]	fertigen, herstellen	
	cable [ˈkeɪbl]	Kabel	
	connector [kəˈnektə]	Verbinder, Stecker	
	mechanical engineering [mɪˌkænɪkl ˌendʒɪˈnɪərɪŋ]	Maschinenbau	
	factory [ˈfæktəri]	Fabrik, Werk	
	automation [ˌɔːtəˈmeɪʃn]	Automatisierung, Automation	

	data processing [ˌdeɪtə ˈprəʊsesɪŋ]	Datenverarbeitung	
	industrial electronics [ɪnˌdʌstriəl ɪlekˈtrɒnɪks]	Industrieelektronik	
	telecommunication(s) [ˌtelɪkəˌmjuːnɪˈkeɪʃn]	Fernmeldetechnik, Telekommunikation	
	vocational training [vəʊˌkeɪʃənl ˈtreɪnɪŋ]	Berufsausbildung	
	apprenticeship [əˈprentɪʃɪp]	Lehre, Ausbildung	
	role [rəʊl]	Rolle, Funktion	
	headline [ˈhedlaɪn]	Überschrift	
7	according to [əˈkɔːdɪŋ tə]	gemäß, entsprechend, zufolge	
	multinational (company) [ˌmʌltiˈnæʃnəl]	inter-/multinationaler Konzern	
	well-known [ˌwelˈnəʊn]	bekannt	
	production [prəˈdʌkʃn]	Produktion, Fertigung, Herstellung	
	sector [ˈsektə]	Bereich, Branche, Sektor	
	grid [grɪd]	Raster	
	size [saɪz]	Größe	
	medium-sized [ˈmiːdiəm saɪzd]	mittelgroß, mittelständisch	
	solution [səˈluːʃn]	Lösung	
	construction [kənˈstrʌkʃn]	Bau	
	building [ˈbɪldɪŋ]	Bauwesen	
	service [ˈsɜːvɪs]	Dienst, Dienstleistung	
T	equipment [ɪˈkwɪpmənt]	Geräte, Ausstattung	
	dealer [ˈdiːlə]	Händler/in	
	training [ˈtreɪnɪŋ]	Ausbildung	
	automotive [ɔːˈtɒməʊtɪv]	Automobil-	
	medical [ˈmedɪkl]	medizinisch, Medizin-	
	to cover [ˈkʌvə]	(Thema) behandeln	
	employee [ɪmˈplɔɪiː]	Angestellte/r, Beschäftigte/r	
	target group [ˈtɑːgɪt gruːp]	Zielgruppe	
	competitor [kəmˈpetɪtə]	Wettbewerber/in, Konkurrent/in	
	on one's own [ɒn wʌnz ˈəʊn]	alleine	
	to structure [ˈstrʌktʃə]	aufbauen, strukturieren	

	prepared [prɪˈpeəd]	bereit, vorbereitet
	audience [ˈɔːdiəns]	Publikum
8	layout [ˈleɪaʊt]	Raumaufteilung, Plan
	subsidiary [səbˈsɪdiəri]	Niederlassung
	induction [ɪnˈdʌkʃn]	Einführung, Einarbeitung
	training company [ˈtreɪnɪŋ kʌmpəni]	Ausbildungsbetrieb
	premises pl [ˈpremɪsɪz]	(Betriebs-)Gelände, Räumlichkeiten
	introductory course [ɪntrəˌdʌktəri ˈkɔːs]	Einführungsseminar
	to explain [ɪkˈspleɪn]	erklären, erläutern
	legal department [ˌliːgl dɪˈpɑːtmənt]	Rechtsabteilung
	Human Resources (HR) [ˌhjuːmən rɪˈsɔːsɪz]	Personalabteilung
	R&D (Research & Development) [ˌɑːr ən ˈdiː]	Forschung und Entwicklung
	development [dɪˈveləpmənt]	Entwicklung
	support [səˈpɔːt]	Hilfe, Unterstützung, Betreuung, Kundendienst, Support
	quality assurance [ˈkwɒləti əʃʊərəns]	Qualitätssicherung
	customer service [ˌkʌstəmə ˈsɜːvɪs]	Kundendienst
	reception [rɪˈsepʃn]	Empfang, Rezeption
	elevator AE [ˈelɪveɪtə]	Aufzug, Lift
	ground floor [ˌgraʊnd ˈflɔː]	Erdgeschoss
9	to promote sth [prəˈməʊt]	für etw Werbung machen
	to increase sth [ɪnˈkriːs]	etw steigern, etw erhöhen
	to make sure [ˌmeɪk ˈʃʊə]	sicherstellen, gewährleisten
	to meet standards [miːt ˈstændədz]	Normen erfüllen
	to recruit [rɪˈkruːt]	(Personal) einstellen
	to interview sb [ˈɪntəvjuː]	mit jdm ein Vorstellungsgespräch führen
	benefits pl [ˈbenɪfɪts]	Zusatzleistungen, Sozialleistungen
	internal [ɪnˈtɜːnl]	intern
	external [ɪkˈstɜːnl]	extern
	legal issues pl [ˌliːgl ˈɪʃuːz]	juristische Fragen, Rechtsangelegenheiten
	to maintain [meɪnˈteɪn]	warten, instand halten
	company-owned [ˌkʌmpəni ˌəʊnd]	firmeneigen
	to create [kriˈeɪt]	(Software) erstellen, (Produkt) gestalten
	to document [ˈdɒkjumənt]	dokumentieren
	to debug [diːˈbʌg]	Fehler beseitigen, debuggen
	innovative [ˈɪnəveɪtɪv]	innovativ
	existing [ɪgˈzɪstɪŋ]	bestehend, existierend
	method [ˈmeθəd]	Art, Weise, Methode
	to reply to sth [rɪˈplaɪ tə]	etw beantworten, auf etw antworten
	complaint [kəmˈpleɪnt]	Beschwerde, Reklamation

	guided tour [ˌgaɪdɪd ˈtʊə]	Führung
	tour [tʊə]	Rundgang
T	to be located [bi ləʊˈkeɪtɪd]	sich befinden
	to lead [liːd]	führen
	corridor [ˈkɒrɪdɔː]	Flur, Gang
	security pass [sɪˈkjʊərəti pɑːs]	Firmenausweis, Zugangskarte
	security doors pl [sɪˈkjʊərəti dɔːz]	Sicherheitsschleuse, Sicherheitstüren
	stairs pl [steəz]	Treppe
	open-plan office [ˌəʊpənplæn ˈɒfɪs]	Großraumbüro
	to keep quiet [ˌkiːp ˈkwaɪət]	sich ruhig verhalten
	to disturb [dɪˈstɜːb]	stören
	to take up sth [ˌteɪk ˈʌp]	etw ausmachen, etw in Anspruch nehmen
	to extend [ɪkˈstend]	sich erstrecken, sich ausdehnen
	to continue [kənˈtɪnjuː]	weitermachen, fortfahren
	straight ahead [ˌstreɪt əˈhed]	geradeaus
	walkway [ˈwɔːkweɪ]	Gang, Weg
	lastly [ˈlɑːstli]	schließlich, zum Schluss
	directions pl [dəˈrekʃnz]	Wegbeschreibung
	to give directions [ˌgɪv dəˈrekʃnz]	den Weg beschreiben
	to swap [swɒp]	tauschen
	to show sb around [ˌʃəʊ əˈraʊnd]	jdn herumführen
	floor plan [ˈflɔː plæn]	Grundriss, Lageplan
10 T	CEO (Chief Executive Officer) [ˌtʃiːf ɪgˈzekjətɪv ɒfɪsə]	Vorstandsvorsitzende/r, Geschäftsführer/in
	responsibility [rɪˌspɒnsəˈbɪləti]	Aufgabe, Zuständigkeit, Verantwortlichkeit
	overall [ˌəʊvərˈɔːl]	Gesamt-, allgemein
	goal [gəʊl]	Ziel
	strategy [ˈstrætədʒi]	Strategie
	to report to sb [rɪˈpɔːt tə]	jdm unterstehen
	to deal with sth [ˈdiːl wɪð]	sich um etw kümmern
	system architecture [ˌsɪstəm ˈɑːkɪtektʃə]	Systemarchitektur
	platform [ˈplætfɔːm]	Plattform
	system analysis [ˌsɪstəm əˈnæləsɪs]	Systemanalyse
	to maximize [ˈmæksɪmaɪz]	maximieren
	benefit [ˈbenɪfɪt]	Nutzen, Vorteil(e)
	client [ˈklaɪənt]	Kunde/Kundin
	to make the most of sth [ˌmeɪk ðə ˈməʊst əv]	etw (bestmöglich) nutzen
	to supervise [ˈsuːpəvaɪz]	führen, leiten, vorgesetzt sein
	to liaise with sb [liˈeɪz wɪð]	mit jdm zusammenarbeiten
	on time [ɒn ˈtaɪm]	rechtzeitig, pünktlich

software engineering [ˈsɒftweər ˌendʒɪˈnɪərɪŋ]	Softwareentwicklung	
testing [ˈtestɪŋ]	Prüfung, Erprobung	
to release [rɪˈliːs]	veröffentlichen, herausgeben	
to be in charge of sth [bi ɪn ˈtʃɑːdʒ əv]	für etw zuständig/ verantwortlich sein	
to perform [pəˈfɔːm]	*(Tätigkeit)* ausführen	
daily [ˈdeɪli]	täglich, Alltags-	

11	**to join sth** [dʒɔɪn]	bei etw mitmachen, zu etw stoßen
	billing [ˈbɪlɪŋ]	Abrechnung, Rechnungs- stellung
	to analyse [ˈænəlaɪz]	analysieren
	requirements *pl* [rɪˈkwaɪəmənts]	Anforderungen, Bedürfnisse, Wünsche
	senior [ˈsiːniə]	leitend
	to integrate with one another [ˈɪntɪɡreɪt wɪð]	ineinandergreifen
	input [ˈɪnpʊt]	Idee(n), Anregung(en)
	lead [liːd]	Chef-, Haupt-
	developer [dɪˈveləpə]	Entwickler/in
	Regards [rɪˈɡɑːdz]	*(Brief:)* Mit freundlichen Grüßen
	to highlight [ˈhaɪlaɪt]	hervorheben
	to include [ɪnˈkluːd]	einbeziehen, aufnehmen
	organization chart [ˌɔːɡənaɪˈzeɪʃn tʃɑːt]	Organigramm
	job title [ˈdʒɒb taɪtl]	Stellenbezeichnung
	member [ˈmembə]	Mitglied
12	**introductions** *pl* [ˌɪntrəˈdʌkʃnz]	Bekanntmachen, Vorstellen
	...-based [beɪst]	mit Sitz in ...
	engineering [ˌendʒɪˈnɪərɪŋ]	Technik, Ingenieurwissen- schaft, Maschinenbau
	supervisor [ˈsuːpəvaɪzə]	Ausbildungsleiter/in, Abteilungsleiter/in, Vorgesetzte/r
	colleague [ˈkɒliːɡ]	Kollege/Kollegin
	computerized [kəmˈpjuːtəraɪzd]	Computer-
	personnel [ˌpɜːsəˈnel]	Personal
	personnel file [ˌpɜːsəˈnel faɪl]	Personalakte
	place of birth [ˌpleɪs əv ˈbɜːθ]	Geburtsort
	job description [ˈdʒɒb dɪskrɪpʃn]	Stellenbeschreibung
13	**formal** [ˈfɔːml]	formell, förmlich
	suitable [ˈsuːtəbl]	geeignet, passend
	to avoid [əˈvɔɪd]	vermeiden
	illness [ˈɪlnəs]	Krankheit
	politics [ˈpɒlətɪks]	Politik
	journey [ˈdʒɜːni]	Fahrt, Anreise
	pay [peɪ]	Bezahlung, Gehalt
	response [rɪˈspɒns]	Antwort, Reaktion
	to be based in ... [bi ˈbeɪst ɪn]	seinen Sitz in ... haben, in ... sein
	fantastic [fænˈtæstɪk]	phantastisch, toll

view [vjuː]	Aussicht, Blick	
in fact [ɪn ˈfækt]	tatsächlich, eigentlich	
Excuse me. [ɪkˈskjuːz mi]	Verzeihung./Entschuldi- gung.	
to hold up sb [ˌhəʊld ˈʌp]	jdn aufhalten	
to keep sb waiting [kiːp ˈweɪtɪŋ]	jdn warten lassen	
refreshment [rɪˈfreʃmənt]	Erfrischung	

UNIT 2

14	**workplace** [ˈwɜːkpleɪs]	Arbeitsplatz
	to carry out sth [ˌkæri ˈaʊt]	etw durchführen
	measure [ˈmeʒə]	Maßnahme
	survey [ˈsɜːveɪ]	Umfrage
	means of communication [ˌmiːnz əf kəmjuːnɪˈkeɪʃn]	Kommunikationsmittel
	improvement [ɪmˈpruːvmənt]	Verbesserung
	to rank [ræŋk]	einstufen, (in einer Rang- liste) bewerten
	to get a message across [get ə ˌmesɪdʒ əˈkrɒs]	eine Botschaft vermitteln

15	**and so on** [ənd ˈsəʊ ɒn]	und so weiter
T	**face-to-face** [ˌfeɪs tə ˈfeɪs]	persönlich
	to sort sth out [ˌsɔːt ˈaʊt]	etw klären, etw in Ordnung bringen
	in writing [ɪn ˈraɪtɪŋ]	schriftlich
	text (message) [ˈtekst mesɪdʒ]	SMS
	to get at sth [ˈget ət]	auf etw hinauswollen
	to attach [əˈtætʃ]	*(E-Mail:)* anhängen
	to copy in sb [ˌkɒpi ˈɪn]	jdn auf CC in den Verteiler setzen
	structured [ˈstrʌktʃəd]	strukturiert
	to access sth [ˈækses]	auf etw zugreifen
	all over the place [ɔːl ˌəʊvə ðə ˈpleɪs]	überall (in der Welt- geschichte)
	access (to sth) [ˈækses]	Zugriff (auf etw)
	storage [ˈstɔːrɪdʒ]	(Daten-)Speicherung
	to synchronize [ˈsɪŋkrənaɪz]	abgleichen, synchronisieren
	to select [sɪˈlekt]	auswählen
	to mention (sth to sb) [ˈmenʃn]	(etw jdm gegenüber) erwähnen
	to bring up sth [ˌbrɪŋ ˈʌp]	etw zur Sprache bringen
	to take up time [ˌteɪk ˈʌp taɪm]	Zeit beanspruchen
	slide [slaɪd]	*(Präsentation:)* Folie
	waste of time [ˌweɪst əf ˈtaɪm]	Zeitverschwendung
	hand-out [ˈhændaʊt]	Arbeitsblatt, Informations- blatt, Merkblatt
	to consider sth [kənˈsɪdə]	etw in Betracht ziehen, über etw nachdenken
	graphic image [ˌɡræfɪk ˈɪmɪdʒ]	Grafik

to **brainstorm** ['breɪnstɔːm]	Ideen sammeln	
quantity ['kwɒntəti]	Menge, Anzahl	
instruction [ɪn'strʌkʃn]	Anweisung	
to **record** [rɪ'kɔːd]	aufzeichnen, festhalten	
attachment [ə'tætʃmənt]	(E-Mail:) Anhang	
16 **recruitment** [rɪ'kruːtmənt]	Personalvermittlung	
headquarters pl [ˌhed'kwɔːtəz]	Zentrale, Hauptsitz	
aspect ['æspekt]	Gesichtspunkt, Aspekt	
condition [kən'dɪʃn]	Bedingung	

T
to **be big believers in sth** [bi ˌbɪg bɪ'liːvəz ɪn]	fest von etw überzeugt sein
balance ['bæləns]	Gleichgewicht
to **suit sb/sth** [suːt]	(zu) jdm/etw passen
flexible ['fleksəbl]	variabel, flexibel
annual leave [ˌænjuəl 'liːv]	Jahresurlaub
sick leave ['sɪk liːv]	Krankentage
unpaid leave [ʌnˌpaɪd 'liːv]	unbezahlter Urlaub
to **work remotely** [ˌwɜːk rɪ'məʊtli]	von zu Hause aus arbeiten, ortsungebunden arbeiten
to **co-ordinate** [kəʊ'ɔːdɪneɪt]	(aufeinander) abstimmen, koordinieren
in addition [ɪn ə'dɪʃn]	außerdem
permission [pə'mɪʃn]	Genehmigung, Erlaubnis
clothing ['kləʊðɪŋ]	Kleidung
neat [niːt]	sauber, ordentlich
casual ['kæʒuəl]	zwanglos, locker

17 **functionality** [ˌfʌŋkʃə'næləti]	Funktionen	
applicant ['æplɪkənt]	Bewerber/in	
to **look sth up** [ˌlʊk 'ʌp]	etw nachschlagen, etw nachlesen	
graduate ['grædʒuət]	mit Abschluss	
to **work closely with sb** [ˌwɜːk 'kləʊsli wɪð]	eng mit jdm zusammen- arbeiten	
test data pl ['test deɪtə]	Prüfdaten	
to **test** [test]	prüfen, testen	
defect ['diːfekt]	Mangel, Fehler	
user ['juːzə]	Benutzer/in, Anwender/in, User/in	
creative [kri'eɪtɪv]	kreativ	
finish ['fɪnɪʃ]	Ende	
commute [kə'mjuːt]	Fahrt zur Arbeit	
update (on sth) ['ʌpdeɪt]	aktuelle Informationen (zu etw)	
to **raise sth** [reɪz]	etw ansprechen, auf etw aufmerksam machen	
to **remove** [rɪ'muːv]	entfernen, aus dem Weg räumen	
roadblock ['rəʊdblɒk]	Hindernis	
to **slow sb down** [ˌsləʊ 'daʊn]	jdn aufhalten, jdn bremsen	
to **affect sb/sth** [ə'fekt]	sich auf jdn/etw auswirken	
to **force** [fɔːs]	zwingen	

relationship [rɪ'leɪʃnʃɪp]	Beziehung, Verhältnis	
easily understandable [ˌiːzəli ʌndə'stændəbl]	leicht verständlich	
detailed ['diːteɪld]	ausführlich, genau	
comment ['kɒment]	Kommentar	
productive [prə'dʌktɪv]	produktiv	
to **separate** ['sepəreɪt]	trennen	
18 to **ensure** [ɪn'ʃʊə]	dafür sorgen, sicherstellen	
obstacle ['ɒbstəkl]	Hindernis	
to **fix** [fɪks]	(etw) in Ordnung bringen, reparieren	
to **update** [ˌʌp'deɪt]	auf den neuesten Stand bringen	
standard ['stændəd]	üblich, normal	
timeline ['taɪmlaɪn]	Zeitschiene	
report [rɪ'pɔːt]	Bericht, Meldung	
interface ['ɪntəfeɪs]	Schnittstelle, Interface	
specification [ˌspesɪfɪ'keɪʃn]	technische Anforderung(en)	
test plan ['test plæn]	Prüfplan	
likes and dislikes pl [ˌlaɪks ən 'dɪslaɪks]	Vorlieben und Abneigungen	
to **pin** [pɪn]	(mit einer Nadel) befestigen, anheften	
gallery walk ['gæləri wɔːk]	Galerierundgang	
19 **phase** [feɪz]	Stadium, Phase	
feedback ['fiːdbæk]	Rückmeldung(en)	
conversation [ˌkɒnvə'seɪʃn]	Gespräch	
to **propose** [prə'pəʊz]	vorschlagen	
guideline ['gaɪdlaɪn]	Richtlinie, Leitfaden	
output ['aʊtpʊt]	Arbeitsergebnis(se)	
request [rɪ'kwest]	Wunsch, Bitte	
stand-up ['stænd ʌp]	im Stehen	
even though ['iːvn ðəʊ]	obwohl	
agenda [ə'dʒendə]	Tagesordnung	
to **keep sth to a minimum** [ˌkiːp tu ə 'mɪnɪməm]	etw auf ein Mindestmaß beschränken	
spontaneous [spɒn'teɪniəs]	spontan	
issue ['ɪʃuː]	Frage, Problem	
to **concentrate on sth** ['kɒnsntreɪt ɒn]	sich auf etw konzentrieren	
period of time [ˌpɪəriəd əf 'taɪm]	(gewisse) Zeit	
critical ['krɪtɪkl]	wichtig, unentbehrlich	
the executives pl [ði ɪg'zekjətɪvz]	die Betriebsleitung	
to **be paperless** [bi 'peɪpələs]	kein Papier (mehr) verwenden	
to **favour** ['feɪvə]	favorisieren, bevorzugen	
preference ['prefrəns]	Vorliebe, Wunsch	
to **invest** [ɪn'vest]	investieren	
to **support** [sə'pɔːt]	unterstützen	
concern [kən'sɜːn]	Bedenken, Sorge	
not ... at all [ˌnɒt ət 'ɔːl]	überhaupt nicht	
20 to **chat** [tʃæt]	chatten	

author [ˈɔːθə]	Verfasser/in	
to acknowledge sth [əkˈnɒlɪdʒ]	etw anerkennen	
to pretend [prɪˈtend]	so tun, als ob	
point of view [ˌpɔɪnt əv ˈvjuː]	Sicht	
to set sth aside [set əˈsaɪd]	etw (für etw) vorsehen	
expectation [ˌekspekˈteɪʃn]	Erwartung	
instant(ly) [ˈɪnstənt]	sofortig, sofort	
productivity [ˌprɒdʌkˈtɪvəti]	Produktivität	
starting point [ˈstɑːtɪŋ pɔɪnt]	Ausgangspunkt	
to adjust [əˈdʒʌst]	anpassen, regeln	
as we go along [əz wiː ˌgəʊ əˈlɒŋ]	im Lauf von etw, nach und nach	
lifetime (of a project) [ˈlaɪftaɪm]	Laufzeit (eines Projekts)	
smart [smɑːt]	klug	
21 individual(ly) [ˌɪndɪˈvɪdʒuəl]	einzeln	

T		
invite [ˈɪnvaɪt]	Einladung	
schedule [ˈʃedjuːl]	Zeitplan	
to run behind schedule [rʌn bɪˌhaɪnd ˈʃedjuːl]	im Rückstand sein	
pros and cons pl [ˌprəʊz ənd ˈkɒnz]	Argumente dafür und dagegen, Vor- und Nachteile	
remote working [rɪˌməʊt ˈwɜːkɪŋ]	Arbeit von zu Hause, ortsungebundenes Arbeiten	
to interrupt [ˌɪntəˈrʌpt]	unterbrechen, stören	
to solve [sɒlv]	lösen	
noise [nɔɪz]	Lärm	
separate [ˈseprət]	getrennt, separat, eigen	
meeting room [ˈmiːtɪŋ ruːm]	Sitzungszimmer, Konferenzraum	
drawback [ˈdrɔːbæk]	Nachteil	
distraction [dɪˈstrækʃn]	Ablenkung	
noise level [ˈnɔɪz levl]	Lärmpegel	
downside [ˈdaʊnsaɪd]	Schattenseite, Nachteil	
on the downside [ɒn ðə ˈdaʊnsaɪd]	auf der Negativseite; andererseits	
to turn sth off [ˌtɜːn ˈɒf]	etw ausschalten, etw abstellen	
disaster [dɪˈzɑːstə]	Katastrophe	
upside [ˈʌpsaɪd]	Vorteil, Plus	

to respond to sth [rɪˈspɒnd tə]	auf etw reagieren	
instantaneous(ly) [ɪnstənˈteɪnɪəs]	sofort, augenblicklich	
to progress [prəˈgres]	vorankommen	
to clarify [ˈklærəfaɪ]	klären, abklären	
complex [ˈkɒmpleks]	kompliziert, komplex	
to state [steɪt]	angeben, erklären, nennen, sagen	
22 to leave a message [ˌliːv ə ˈmesɪdʒ]	eine Nachricht hinterlassen	

voicemail [ˈvɔɪsmeɪl]	Mailbox	
to take a message [ˌteɪk ə ˈmesɪdʒ]	etw ausrichten	
to call back [ˌkɔːl ˈbæk]	zurückrufen	
on behalf of sb [ɒn bɪˈhɑːf əv]	für jdn, in jds Namen	
to confirm [kənˈfɜːm]	bestätigen	
update [ˈʌpdeɪt]	Aktualisierung	
database [ˈdeɪtəbeɪs]	Datenbank	
factory manager [ˈfæktəri mænɪdʒə]	Betriebsleiter/in, Werksleiter/in	
technician [tekˈnɪʃn]	Techniker/in	
mobile [ˈməʊbaɪl]	Handy, Mobiltelefon	
to represent [ˌreprɪˈzent]	darstellen, vertreten	
equivalent [ɪˈkwɪvələnt]	Entsprechung, Übersetzung	
engaged [ɪnˈgeɪdʒd]	(Telefon:) besetzt	
to be unavailable [bi ˌʌnəˈveɪləbl]	(Telefon:) nicht zu sprechen sein	
to hold the line [ˌhəʊld ðə ˈlaɪn]	(Telefon:) am Apparat bleiben	
to connect (to/with sth) [kəˈnekt]	(mit etw) verbinden, (an etw) anschließen	
to put sb through [ˌpʊt ˈθruː]	(Telefon:) jdn durchstellen	
23 supplier [səˈplaɪə]	Zulieferer, Lieferant/in	
Speaking. [ˈspiːkɪŋ]	(Telefon:) Am Apparat.	
available [əˈveɪləbl]	lieferbar, verfügbar	
alternative [ɔːlˈtɜːnətɪv]	Alternative	
extension [ɪkˈstenʃn]	Durchwahl	
digit [ˈdɪdʒɪt]	Ziffer	
except for [ɪkˈsept fə]	außer	

P		
to make up sth [ˌmeɪk ˈʌp]	sich etw ausdenken	
contact details pl [ˈkɒntækt diːteɪlz]	Kontaktdaten	
to pass sth on [ˌpɑːs ˈɒn]	etw weiterreichen/-leiten	

KMK Exam practice 1

25 flat [flæt]	flach	
military [ˈmɪlətri]	Militär	
traditional [trəˈdɪʃənl]	traditionell, althergebracht	
corporation [ˌkɔːpəˈreɪʃn]	Unternehmen, Gesellschaft, Konzern	
to rely (heavily) on sth [rɪˌlaɪ ˈhevɪli ɒn]	sich (total) auf etw verlassen, (stark) auf etw angewiesen sein	
hierarchy [ˈhaɪərɑːki]	Hierarchie	
to maintain [meɪnˈteɪn]	aufrecht erhalten	
predictability [prəˌdɪktəˈbɪləti]	Berechenbarkeit	
reliability [rɪˌlaɪəˈbɪləti]	Zuverlässigkeit	
to desire sth [dɪˈzaɪə]	etw wünschen	
predictable [prɪˈdɪktəbl]	berechenbar	
reliable [rɪˈlaɪəbl]	zuverlässig	
to simplify [ˈsɪmplɪfaɪ]	vereinfachen	
planning [ˈplænɪŋ]	Planung	

from the top down [frəm ðə ˌtɒp ˈdaʊn]	von oben nach unten	**fast refresh rate** [ˈfɑːst rɪˈfreʃ reɪt]	hohe Bildwiederholfrequenz
model [ˈmɒdl]	Vorbild, Modell	**unclear** [ˌʌnˈklɪə]	unklar, undeutlich
✗ **entertainment** [ˌentəˈteɪnmənt]	Unterhaltung	to **process** [ˈprəʊses]	verarbeiten
to **waste** [weɪst]	verschwenden, vergeuden	**instruction** [ɪnˈstrʌkʃn]	Befehl, Kommando
to **innovate** [ˈɪnəveɪt]	innovativ sein, kreativ sein	**brain** [breɪn]	Hirn, Gehirn
founder [ˈfaʊndə]	Gründer/in	**input device** [ˈɪnpʊt dɪvaɪs]	Eingabegerät
✗ **opportunity** [ˌɒpəˈtjuːnəti]	Gelegenheit, Möglichkeit	to **interact with sth** [ˌɪntərˈækt wɪð]	auf etw einwirken, Informationen mit etw austauschen
to **take risks** [ˌteɪk ˈrɪsks]	Risiken eingehen	**version** [ˈvɜːʃn]	Ausführung, Modell
✗ to **see sth through** [ˌsiː ˈθruː]	etw zu Ende führen	**button** [ˈbʌtn]	Taste, Knopf, Schalter
barrier [ˈbæriə]	Hindernis, Barriere	to **make a difference** [ˌmeɪk ə ˈdɪfrəns]	sich unterscheiden
✗ to **claim** [kleɪm]	behaupten	**peripheral** [pəˈrɪfərəl]	Peripheriegerät
to **be at the heart of sth** [bi ət ðə ˈhɑːt əv]	zentral für etw sein	**connectivity** [ˌkɒnekˈtɪvəti]	Anschlüsse
✗ to **stop sb from doing sth** [stɒp]	jdn daran hindern, etw zu tun	**freelance** [ˈfriːlɑːns]	freiberuflich, selbstständig
responsibility [rɪˌspɒnsəˈbɪləti]	Verantwortung	**graphic design** [ˌgræfɪk dɪˈzaɪn]	Grafikdesign
talented [ˈtæləntɪd]	begabt, talentiert	to **set up sth** [ˌset ˈʌp]	etw einrichten
✗ to **be capable of doing sth** [bi ˈkeɪpəbl əv]	fähig sein, etw zu tun; etw tun können		

		T **mostly** [ˈməʊstli]	hauptsächlich, meistens
		hands-free [ˌhændz ˈfriː]	Freisprech-, freihändig
		to **pair sth with sth** [peə]	etw an etw koppeln, etw mit etw verbinden
		convenient [kənˈviːniənt]	praktisch, bequem

UNIT 3

26 **work experience** [ˈwɜːk ɪkspɪəriəns]	Praktikum	**speaker** [ˈspiːkə]	Lautsprecher
to **identify** [aɪˈdentɪfaɪ]	identifzieren, bestimmen	**via** [ˈvaɪə]	mit, mittels, über, durch
central processing unit (CPU) [ˌsentrəl ˈprəʊsesɪŋ juːnɪt]	Hauptprozessor	**jack** [dʒæk]	Buchse
		audio quality [ˌɔːdiəʊ ˈkwɒləti]	Tonqualität
graphics card [ˈgræfɪks kɑːd]	Grafikkarte	to **plug** [plʌg]	anschließen, einstecken, verbinden
hard disk [ˈhɑːd dɪsk]	Festplatte	to **charge** [tʃɑːdʒ]	laden, aufladen
keyboard [ˈkiːbɔːd]	Tastatur	to **come with sth** [ˈkʌm wɪð]	(Ware:) über etw verfügen, etw haben
motherboard [ˈmʌðəbɔːd]	Hauptplatine, Motherboard	**in case** [ɪn ˈkeɪs]	für den Fall, dass; falls
mouse, mouses/mice [maʊs, maʊsɪz, maɪs]	Maus, Mäuse	**port** [pɔːt]	Anschluss
random access memory (RAM) [ˌrændəm ˌæksəs ˈmeməri]	Arbeitsspeicher	**at least** [ət ˈliːst]	mindestens
		to **stick** [stɪk]	stecken
to **suppose** [səˈpəʊz]	vermuten, annehmen, glauben	to **unplug** [ˌʌnˈplʌg]	ausstecken, (Kabel) herausziehen
27 to **house** [haʊz]	beherbergen, aufnehmen, unterbringen	to **hook sth to sth** [hʊk]	etw mit etw verbinden
		backup [ˈbækʌp]	Reserve, Ausweich-
to **display** [dɪˈspleɪ]	(auf dem Bildschirm) anzeigen	28 to **expand** [ɪkˈspænd]	expandieren, (in Märkte) vordringen
screen [skriːn]	Bildschirm	**augmented** [ɔːgˈmentɪd]	erweitert
mid-range [ˌmɪd ˈreɪndʒ]	Mittelklasse-, im mittleren Preissegment	**virtual** [ˈvɜːtʃuəl]	virtuell
		to **install** [ɪnˈstɔːl]	installieren
to **upgrade** [ˌʌpˈgreɪd]	hochstufen, upgraden	**instruction manual** [ɪnˈstrʌkʃn mænjuəl]	Bedienungsanleitung
later on [ˌleɪtər ɒn]	später, zu einem späteren Zeitpunkt	**warning** [ˈwɔːnɪŋ]	Hinweis, Warnung
to **turn sth into sth** [ˈtɜːn ɪntə]	etw in etw umwandeln	to **shut down** [ˌʃʌt ˈdaʊn]	herunterfahren, ausschalten
smooth(ly) [ˈsmuːðli]	reibungslos	to **cool** [kuːl]	abkühlen
not necessarily [nɒt ˌnesəˈserəli]	nicht unbedingt	to **disconnect** [ˌdɪskəˈnekt]	trennen
		power adapter [ˈpaʊər ədæptə]	Netzteil

lock [lɒk]	Schloss	
to prevent [prɪ'vent]	verhindern, verhüten	
to turn sth over [ˌtɜːn 'əʊvə]	etw umdrehen, etw auf die andere Seite legen	
screw [skruː]	Schraube	
to secure [sɪ'kjʊə]	befestigen	
case [keɪs]	Gehäuse	
bottom case [ˌbɒtəm 'keɪs]	Gehäuseunterteil	
Phillips screwdriver [ˌfɪlɪps 'skruːdraɪvə]	Kreuzschlitzschraubendreher/-zieher	
to come off [ˌkʌm 'ɒf]	sich ablösen lassen	
fairly ['feəli]	einigermaßen, ziemlich	
lightly ['laɪtli]	etwas, ein wenig	
to force sth [fɔːs]	Kraft (gegen etw) aufwenden	
to hold sth in place [ˌhəʊld ɪn 'pleɪs]	etw fixieren	
to unscrew [ˌʌn'skruː]	(Schraube) herausdrehen	
gently ['dʒentli]	behutsam, vorsichtig	
to lift [lɪft]	heben	
chassis ['ʃæsi]	Montagerahmen	
ribbon (cable) ['rɪbən]	Flachbandkabel	
post [pəʊst]	Säulchen	
to screw [skruː]	schrauben, festschrauben	
to re-attach [ˌriː ə'tætʃ]	wieder einsetzen	
RAM module ['ræm mɒdjuːl]	Speichermodul	
lever ['liːvə]	Hebel	
in an outward direction [ɪn ən ˌaʊtwəd də'rekʃn]	nach außen	
to release sth [rɪ'liːs]	etw lösen	
slot [slɒt]	Steckplatz	
to pop up [ˌpɒp 'ʌp]	hochspringen, herausspringen	
half-circle [ˌhɑːf 'sɜːkl]	halbkreisförmig	
notch [nɒtʃ]	Kerbe, Einkerbung	
to slide out sth [ˌslaɪd 'aʊt]	etw herausschieben	
to align sth with sth [ə'laɪn]	etw auf etw ausrichten	
edge [edʒ]	Kante	
replacement [rɪ'pleɪsmənt]	Austausch, Ersatz	
to tilt [tɪlt]	neigen, kippen	
firm [fɜːm]	fest	
even ['iːvn]	gleichmäßig	
pressure ['preʃə]	Druck	
to insert [ɪn'sɜːt]	einsetzen, hineinstecken	
29	to take it in turns to do sth [ˌteɪk ɪt ɪn 'tɜːnz]	etw abwechselnd tun
application [ˌæplɪ'keɪʃn]	Anwendung, Programm	
degree [dɪ'griː]	Grad	
motion ['məʊʃn]	Bewegung	
to track [træk]	nachvollziehen, verfolgen	
multiple ['mʌltɪpl]	mehrere	
embedded [ɪm'bedɪd]	integriert, eingebettet	
display [dɪ'spleɪ]	Darstellung, Display	
resolution [ˌrezə'luːʃn]	Auflösung	

truly ['truːli]	wirklich, wahrhaftig	
realistic [ˌriːə'lɪstɪk]	realistisch, wirklichkeitsnah	
experience [ɪk'spɪəriəns]	Erlebnis	
to power sth ['paʊə]	etw mit Strom versorgen	
unlimited [ʌn'lɪmɪtɪd]	unbegrenzt	
latency ['leɪtnsi]	Verzögerung, Latenz	
wireless ['waɪələs]	drahtlos, Funk-	
to attach to sth [ə'tætʃ tə]	sich mit etw verbinden lassen	
strap [stræp]	Riemen, Gurt	
to last [lɑːst]	(Zeitraum:) halten	
unit ['juːnɪt]	Einheit, Gerät	
to communicate [kə'mjuːnɪkeɪt]	kommunizieren	
proprietary [prə'praɪətri]	firmeneigen, urheberrechtlich geschützt	
protocol ['prəʊtəkɒl]	Übertragungsprotokoll	
to map [mæp]	erfassen	
battery ['bætəri]	Akku, Batterie	
battery powered ['bætəri paʊəd]	batteriebetrieben, mit Akkus betrieben	
charge [tʃɑːdʒ]	Ladung	
supplied [sə'plaɪd]	mitgeliefert	
30	base station ['beɪs steɪʃn]	Basisstation
physical ['fɪzɪkl]	physisch, räumlich	
to monitor ['mɒnɪtə]	überwachen	
infrared [ˌɪnfrə'red]	Infrarot	
head height ['hed haɪt]	Kopfhöhe	
mounting kit ['maʊntɪŋ kɪt]	Montageset	
to position [pə'zɪʃn]	positionieren	
power source ['paʊə sɔːs]	Stromquelle	
tennis racket ['tenɪs rækɪt]	Tennisschläger	
weapon ['wepən]	Waffe	
to attach sth to sth [ə'tætʃ]	etw mit etw verbinden	
tape [teɪp]	Klebeband	
simultaneous(ly) [ˌsɪml'teɪniəs]	gleichzeitig	
to refer to sth [rɪ'fɜː tə]	auf etw verweisen, sich auf etw beziehen	
function ['fʌŋkʃn]	Funktion	
capability [ˌkeɪpə'bɪləti]	Vermögen, Fähigkeit	
guide [gaɪd]	Leitfaden, Anhaltspunkt	
31	configuration [kənˌfɪgə'reɪʃn]	Konfiguration
store chain ['stɔː tʃeɪn]	Ladenkette	
to operate ['ɒpəreɪt]	geschäftlich tätig sein	
throughout ... [θruː'aʊt]	in ganz ...	
to assess [ə'ses]	beurteilen, einschätzen	
branding ['brændɪŋ]	Markenführung, Markenbildung	
performance [pə'fɔːməns]	Leistung	
to appear [ə'pɪə]	erscheinen	
accurate(ly) ['ækjərət]	exakt, genau	
colour reproduction ['kʌlə riːprə'dʌkʃn]	Farbdarstellung	

	instead of [ɪnˈsted əv]	statt, anstatt
	to **input** [ˈɪnpʊt]	(Daten) eingeben
	customer support [ˌkʌstəmə səˈpɔːt]	Kundenbetreuung, Kundendienst
	warranty [ˈwɒrənti]	Gewährleistung
	return [rɪˈtɜːn]	Retoure, Rücksendung
	sb doesn't mind [dʌznt ˈmaɪnd]	etw ist jdm egal
	to **look sth up** [ˌlʊk ˈʌp]	etw (Informationen) nachschlagen, etw suchen
	high-powered [ˌhaɪˈpaʊəd]	leistungsstark, Hochleistungs-
	account manager [əˈkaʊnt mænɪdʒə]	Kundenbetreuer/in
	lightweight [ˈlaɪtweɪt]	leicht
	to **load** [ləʊd]	laden
	to **compile** [kəmˈpaɪl]	kompilieren
	spreadsheet [ˈspredʃiːt]	Tabellenkalkulation, Tabelle
	to **perform sth** [pəˈfɔːm]	etw ausführen, etw durchführen
	calculation [ˌkælkjuˈleɪʃn]	Berechnung, Rechenvorgang
	in a rush [ɪn ə ˈrʌʃ]	hektisch, in Eile
	feature [ˈfiːtʃə]	Merkmal, Eigenschaft
	processing power [ˈprəʊsesɪŋ paʊə]	Rechenleistung
	load time [ˈləʊd taɪm]	Ladezeit
32	**sales representative** [ˈseɪlz reprɪzentətɪv]	Vertreter/in
T	**based on** [ˈbeɪst ɒn]	anhand von, auf Grundlage von
	to **stick to sth** [ˈstɪk tə]	sich an etw halten
	to **be on the road** [bi ɒn ðə ˈrəʊd]	unterwegs sein
	fit-for-purpose [ˌfɪt fə ˈpɜːpəs]	tauglich, geeignet
	appropriate [əˈprəʊpriət]	passend, geeignet
	projector [prəˈdʒektə]	Beamer
	portability [pɔːtəˈbɪləti]	Transportierbarkeit, Mobilität
	long-lasting [ˌlɒŋ ˈlɑːstɪŋ]	langlebig, (Akku:) leistungsstark
	spot on [ˌspɒt ˈɒn]	genau richtig
	storage space [ˈstɔːrɪdʒ speɪs]	Speicherplatz
	likewise [ˈlaɪkwaɪz]	ebenso
	overly [ˈəʊvəli]	allzu, übermäßig
	processor [ˈprəʊsesə]	Prozessor
	advisable [ədˈvaɪzəbl]	ratsam, empfehlenswert
	due to [ˈdjuː tə]	aufgrund von, wegen
	inappropriate [ˌɪnəˈprəʊpriət]	unpassend, ungeeignet
	to **impress** [ɪmˈpres]	beeindrucken
	all things considered [ˌɔːl θɪŋz kənˈsɪdəd]	insgesamt, alles in allem, unterm Strich
	to **be a good fit for sb** [bi ə ˌɡʊd ˈfɪt fə]	für jdn richtig sein, gut zu jdm passen
	assessment [əˈsesmənt]	Einschätzung, Bewertung
	to **customize** [ˈkʌstəmaɪz]	anpassen, individuell/kundengerecht anfertigen

	to **meet requirements** [miːt rɪˈkwaɪəmənts]	Anforderungen erfüllen
	to **request sth** [rɪˈkwest]	um etw bitten
	to **give reasons for sth** [ˌɡɪv ˈriːznz fə]	etw begründen
33	to **manipulate sth** [məˈnɪpjuleɪt]	mit etw umgehen, etw bearbeiten
	poster [ˈpəʊstə]	Plakat
	ticketing system [ˈtɪkɪtɪŋ sɪstəm]	Ticketsystem
	to **view sth** [vjuː]	etw betrachten, sich etw ansehen
	to **edit** [ˈedɪt]	(Text) bearbeiten
	model [ˈmɒdl]	Modell, Ausführung
	operating system [ˈɒpəreɪtɪŋ sɪstəm]	Betriebssystem
	dual-core processor [ˌdjuːəl kɔː ˈprəʊsesə]	Doppelkernprozessor
	inch [ɪntʃ]	Zoll (= 2,54 cm)
	integrated [ˈɪntɪɡreɪtɪd]	integriert
	headphones pl [ˈhedfəʊnz]	Kopfhörer
	battery life [ˈbætəri laɪf]	Akkulaufzeit
	weight [weɪt]	Gewicht
34	**tool** [tuːl]	Werkzeug
	trade [treɪd]	Gewerbe, Branche
	to **take care of sth** [teɪk ˈkeər əv]	sich um etw kümmern, etw bearbeiten, etw erledigen
	enquiry [ɪnˈkwaɪəri]	Anfrage
	to **appear** [əˈpɪə]	vorkommen, auftauchen
	dot [dɒt]	Punkt
	hyphen [ˈhaɪfn]	Bindestrich, Minus
	underscore [ˈʌndəskɔː]	Unterstrich
	to **dictate** [dɪkˈteɪt]	diktieren
	subject line [ˈsʌbdʒɪkt laɪn]	Betreffzeile
	indication [ˌɪndɪˈkeɪʃn]	Hinweis, Anzeichen
	request (for sth) [rɪˈkwest]	Bitte (um etw)
	assistance [əˈsɪstəns]	Hilfe, Unterstützung
	to **announce** [əˈnaʊns]	ankündigen
	covering letter [ˈkʌvərɪŋ letə]	Anschreiben, Begleitschreiben
	brochure [ˈbrəʊʃə]	Broschüre, Prospekt
	venue [ˈvenjuː]	Veranstaltungsort
	event [ɪˈvent]	Veranstaltung
	flyer [ˈflaɪə]	Faltblatt
	application [ˌæplɪˈkeɪʃn]	Antrag, Bewerbung
	stand [stænd]	(Messe-)Stand
	fair [feə]	Messe
35	**reply** [rɪˈplaɪ]	Antwort
	to **reply** [rɪˈplaɪ]	antworten
	catalogue [ˈkætəlɒg]	Katalog
	slotted screw [ˈslɒtɪd skruː]	Schlitzschraube
	item [ˈaɪtəm]	Artikel
	in stock [ɪn ˈstɒk]	auf Lager, verfügbar
	Yours faithfully [ˌjɔːz ˈfeɪθfəli]	(Brief:) Mit freundlichen Grüßen

Ltd [ˈlɪmɪtɪd]		GmbH
to **dispatch** [dɪˈspætʃ]		versenden
to **do business with sb**		mit jdm Geschäfte machen
[du ˈbɪznəs wɪð]		
complimentary close		(Brief:) Schlussformel
[ˌkɒmplɪˌmentri ˈkləʊz]		
polite(ly) [pəˈlaɪtli]		höflich
salutation [ˌsæljuˈteɪʃn]		(Brief:) Anrede
business partner		Geschäftspartner/in
[ˈbɪznəs pɑːtnə]		
Dear Sir or Madam		(Brief:) Sehr geehrte Damen
[ˌdɪə sɜː ɔː ˈmædəm]		und Herren,
unknown [ˌʌnˈnəʊn]		unbekannt
Best regards/Regards		(Brief:) Viele Grüße,
[rɪˈɡɑːdz]		Mit freundlichen Grüßen
Best wishes [best ˈwɪʃɪz]		(Brief:) Mit freundlichen
		Grüßen
Yours sincerely		(Brief:) Mit freundlichen
[ˌjɔːz sɪnˈsɪəli]		Grüßen

UNIT 4

36	to **navigate sth**	sich bei/in etw zurecht-
	[ˈnævɪɡeɪt]	finden, durch etw steuern
	past [pɑːst]	Vergangenheit
	button [ˈbʌtn]	Schaltfläche, Button
	to **maximize** [ˈmæksɪmaɪz]	maximal vergrößern,
		maximieren
	menu [ˈmenjuː]	Menü
	menu bar [ˈmenjuː bɑː]	Menüleiste
	to **minimize** [ˈmɪnɪmaɪz]	maximal verkleinern,
		minimieren
	wastepaper basket	Papierkorb
	[ˌweɪstˈpeɪpə bɑːskɪt]	
37	to **maintain sth**	etw unterhalten, etw
	[meɪnˈteɪn]	betreiben
	portrait [ˈpɔːtreɪt]	(Bild:) Hochformat
	landscape [ˈlændskeɪp]	(Bild:) Querformat
	mode [məʊd]	Betriebsart, Modus
	destination [ˌdestɪˈneɪʃn]	(Reise-, Fahrt-)Ziel, Zielort
	to **rotate** [rəʊˈteɪt]	drehen
	to **press** [pres]	drücken
	to **mark** [mɑːk]	kennzeichnen, markieren
	pin [pɪn]	Stecknadel, Reißzwecke
	to **drop** [drɒp]	fallen
	to **tap** [tæp]	tippen
	route [ruːt]	Strecke, Weg, Route
	to **zoom in** [ˌzuːm ˈɪn]	vergrößern, einzoomen
	to **spread** [spred]	spreizen
	to **zoom out** [ˌzuːm ˈaʊt]	verkleinern, auszoomen
	to **pinch** [pɪntʃ]	(zwei Finger) zusammen-
		führen
	to **scroll** [skrəʊl]	scrollen, blättern
	to **drag** [dræɡ]	ziehen
	direction [dəˈrekʃn]	Richtung
	to **swipe** [swaɪp]	(Touchscreen:) wischen
	non-native [ˌnɒnˈneɪtɪv]	mit etw nicht vertraut
	gesture [ˈdʒestʃə]	Geste
	to **delete** [dɪˈliːt]	löschen

	flashlight AE [ˈflæʃlaɪt]	Taschenlampe
	widget [ˈwɪdʒɪt]	Steuerelement, Widget
38	**release** [rɪˈliːs]	Freigabe, (Software-)Version
	to **take place** [ˌteɪk ˈpleɪs]	stattfinden
	entire [ɪnˈtaɪə]	gesamte/r/s, ganze/r/s
	progress [ˈprəʊɡres]	Fortgang, aktueller Stand
	to **purchase** [ˈpɜːtʃəs]	kaufen
	licence [ˈlaɪsns]	Lizenz
	extension [ɪkˈstenʃn]	Erweiterung
	package [ˈpækɪdʒ]	Paket
	pre-installation	vor der (eigentlichen)
	[ˌpriː ɪnstəˈleɪʃn]	Installation
	sufficient [səˈfɪʃnt]	ausreichend, genügend
	privilege [ˈprɪvəlɪdʒ]	Berechtigung, (Zugriffs-)
		Recht
	administrative level	Administratorenebene
	[ədˌmɪnɪstrətɪv ˈlevl]	
	to **enter** [ˈentə]	(Daten) eingeben
	confirmation	Bestätigung
	[ˌkɒnfəˈmeɪʃn]	
	valid [ˈvælɪd]	gültig
	tick [tɪk]	Häkchen
	transfer [ˈtrænsfɜː]	Übertragung
	validation [ˌvælɪˈdeɪʃn]	Gültigkeitsprüfung
	to **unpack** [ʌnˈpæk]	entpacken
	temporary [ˈtemprəri]	provisorisch, vorübergehend
	settings pl [ˈsetɪŋz]	Einstellungen
	uncompressed	unkomprimiert
	[ˌʌnkəmˈprest]	
	connected [kəˈnektɪd]	(mit etw) zusammenhängend,
		(mit etw) verbunden
	acceptable [əkˈseptəbl]	zulässig, akzeptabel
	to **transmit** [trænsˈmɪt]	übertragen
	post-installation	nach der Installation
	[ˌpəʊst ɪnstəˈleɪʃn]	
	to **note** [nəʊt]	beachten
	to **verify** [ˈverɪfaɪ]	überprüfen
	visible [ˈvɪzəbl]	sichtbar
	extended [ɪkˈstendɪd]	erweitert
39	**third party** [ˌθɜːd ˈpɑːti]	Dritte/r, von Dritten
	logged out [ˌlɒɡd ˈaʊt]	ausgeloggt
	heading [ˈhedɪŋ]	Rubrik, Überschrift
	to **grant sth** [ɡrɑːnt]	etw gewähren, etw ein-
		räumen
	to **cancel** [ˈkænsl]	(Vorgang) abbrechen
	to **ping** [pɪŋ]	pingen, anpingen
	background [ˈbækɡraʊnd]	Hintergrund
	to **be required to do sth**	etw tun müssen
	[bi rɪˌkwaɪəd tə ˈduː]	
	logged in [ˌlɒɡd ˈɪn]	eingeloggt
	panel [ˈpænl]	Bedienfeld, Panel
	failure [ˈfeɪljə]	Fehler
	error [ˈerə]	Fehler, Irrtum
	error message	Fehlermeldung
	[ˈerə mesɪdʒ]	
	automated [ˈɔːtəmeɪtɪd]	automatisch
	overnight [ˌəʊvəˈnaɪt]	über Nacht
	patch-deployment	Patch-Bereitstellung
	[ˈpætʃ dɪplɔɪmnt]	

to **deploy** [dɪˈplɔɪ]	bereitstellen
to **fail** [feɪl]	fehlschlagen
to **delay sth** [dɪˈleɪ]	etw verschieben
to **log in/on** [ˌlɒg ˈɪn, ˈɒn]	sich einloggen
to **release** [rɪˈliːs]	freigeben, veröffentlichen
insufficient [ˌɪnsəˈfɪʃnt]	unzureichend
security flaw [sɪˈkjʊərəti flɔː]	Sicherheitslücke
dependent (on sb/sth) [dɪˈpendənt]	abhängig (von jdm/etw)
connectivity interruption [ˌkɒnekˈtɪvəti ɪntərʌpʃn]	Unterbrechung der Netzwerkverbindung
40 **percentage** [pəˈsentɪdʒ]	Prozentsatz, Anteil
rate [reɪt]	Quote
cause [kɔːz]	Ursache
to **be in progress** [bi ɪn ˈprəʊgres]	(aktuell) durchgeführt werden
respective [rɪˈspektɪv]	jeweilig
completion [kəmˈpliːʃn]	Ausführung, Abschluss
to **attempt sth** [əˈtempt]	etw versuchen
execution [ˌeksɪˈkjuːʃn]	Ausführung
to **execute sth** [ˈeksɪkjuːt]	etw ausführen
impacted [ɪmˈpæktɪd]	betroffen
41 **enterprise** [ˈentəpraɪz]	Unternehmen
to **advise sb on sth** [ədˈvaɪz]	jdn in einer Sache beraten
to **configure** [kənˈfɪgə]	konfigurieren
to **set** [set]	einstellen
preferences pl [ˈprefrənsɪz]	Einstellungen
maintenance [ˈmeɪntənəns]	Wartung, Instandhaltung
selection [sɪˈlekʃn]	Auswahl
to **make a selection** [ˌmeɪk ə sɪˈlekʃn]	eine Auswahl treffen
default [dɪˈfɔːlt]	Standard(einstellung)
to **force install** [ˌfɔːs ɪnˈstɔːl]	eine/die Installation erzwingen
duration [djuˈreɪʃn]	Dauer, Zeitspanne
to **occur** [əˈkɜː]	geschehen
delay [dɪˈleɪ]	Verschiebung
radio button [ˈreɪdiəʊ bʌtn]	Optionsschaltfläche
check box [ˈtʃek bɒks]	Kontrollkästchen, Auswahlfeld
field [fiːld]	Feld
to **check** [tʃek]	(Kontrollfeld) markieren, (Schaltfläche) anklicken
populated [ˈpɒpjuleɪtɪd]	(Feld:) ausgefüllt
unpopulated [ʌnˈpɒpjuleɪtɪd]	(Feld:) nicht ausgefüllt
42 **administrator** [ədˈmɪnɪstreɪtə]	Administrator/in, Systemverwalter/in
freedom [ˈfriːdəm]	Freiheit
section [ˈsekʃn]	Bereich, Abschnitt
value [ˈvæljuː]	Wert
to **achieve** [əˈtʃiːv]	(Ziel) erreichen
outcome [ˈaʊtkʌm]	Ergebnis, Resultat, Auswirkung(en)

T **on the one hand** [ɒn ðə ˈwʌn hænd]	einerseits
on the other hand [ɒn ði ˈʌðə hænd]	andererseits
to **restrict** [rɪˈstrɪkt]	einschränken, begrenzen
to **force sth** [fɔːs]	etw erzwingen
stability [stəˈbɪləti]	Stabilität
efficient(ly) [ɪˈfɪʃnt]	effizient
flexibility [ˌfleksəˈbɪləti]	Flexibilität
to **consider sth** [kənˈsɪdə]	etw berücksichtigen
impression [ɪmˈpreʃn]	Eindruck
confusion [kənˈfjuːʒn]	Verwirrung
install [ɪnˈstɔːl]	Installation
startup [ˈstɑːtʌp]	Start, Einschalten, Hochfahren
restart [ˌriːˈstɑːt]	Neustart
to **go flat** [ˌgəʊ ˈflæt]	(Akku:) schwach sein
prompt [prɒmpt]	Stichwort
secure [sɪˈkjʊə]	sicher
consequence [ˈkɒnsɪkwəns]	Folge
43 **agreement** [əˈgriːmənt]	Vereinbarung, Übereinkunft
recommendation [ˌrekəmenˈdeɪʃn]	Empfehlung
force [fɔːs]	Zwang, Macht
shutdown [ˈʃʌtdaʊn]	Herunterfahren, Abschalten
inactivity [ˌɪnækˈtɪvəti]	Untätigkeit, Inaktivität
to **restart** [ˌriːˈstɑːt]	neu starten
to **force restart** [ˌfɔːs ˌriːstɑːt]	einen Neustart erzwingen
to **appreciate sth** [əˈpriːʃieɪt]	für etw dankbar sein
reference [ˈrefərəns]	Anspielung, Verweis
44 **signpost** [ˈsaɪnpəʊst]	Hinweise zur Orientierung der Zuhörer in einer Präsentation
conclusion [kənˈkluːʒn]	Schluss
to **invite sth** [ɪnˈvaɪt]	zu etw auffordern, um etw bitten
clarity [ˈklærəti]	Klarheit, Deutlichkeit
correctness [kəˈrektnəs]	Richtigkeit
spelling [ˈspelɪŋ]	Rechtschreibung
prompt card [ˈprɒmt kɑːd]	Moderationskarte
to **come across** [ˌkʌm əˈkrɒs]	wirken
presenter [prɪˈzentə]	Redner/in
either [ˈaɪðə]	eines (von mehreren)
index card [ˈɪndeks kɑːd]	Karteikarte
manufacturing company [ˌmænjʊˈfæktʃərɪŋ kʌmpəni]	Fertigungsbetrieb, Produktionsunternehmen
45 **talk** [tɔːk]	Vortrag
to **be happy to do sth** [bi ˈhæpi tə duː]	etw gern tun
to **divide** [dɪˈvaɪd]	teilen, unterteilen
To begin with, … [tə bɪˈgɪn wɪð]	Zunächst …
To conclude, … [tə kənˈkluːd]	Abschließend …

To sum up, … [tə ˌsʌm ˈʌp]	Zusammenfassend …
to **be one's turn** [bi wʌnz ˈtɜːn]	an der Reihe sein
to **support** [səˈpɔːt]	(Argumentation) unter- mauern
to **deal with sth** [ˈdiːl wɪð]	mit etw umgehen, sich mit etw befassen
manner [ˈmænə]	Art (und Weise)
overall score [ˌəʊvərˌɔːl ˈskɔː]	Gesamtpunktzahl

KMK Exam practice 2

46	to **imagine sth** [ɪˈmædʒɪn]	sich etw vorstellen
T	to **fumble around** [ˌfʌmbl əˈraʊnd]	herumtasten, herumfummeln
	just in time [ˌdʒʌst ɪn ˈtaɪm]	gerade (noch) rechtzeitig
	to **get hold of sb** [get ˈhəʊld əv]	jdn erreichen
	to **go ahead** [ˌgəʊ əˈhed]	loslegen
	glance [glɑːns]	(schneller) Blick
	to **be live** [bi ˈlaɪv]	(Programm:) laufen
	to **launch** [lɔːntʃ]	starten
	to **be familiar with sth** [bi fəˈmɪliə wɪð]	etw kennen
	coloured [ˈkʌləd]	farbig, bunt
	to **track** [træk]	verfolgen, nachverfolgen
	workout [ˈwɜːkaʊt]	Training(seinheit)
	proud (of sth) [praʊd]	stolz (auf etw)
	to **motivate** [ˈməʊtɪveɪt]	motivieren
	exercise [ˈeksəsaɪz]	Bewegung, Sport
	blood pressure [ˈblʌd preʃə]	Blutdruck
	built-in [ˌbɪltˈɪn]	eingebaut
	to **work sth out** [ˌwɜːk ˈaʊt]	etw berechnen
	heart rate [ˈhɑːt reɪt]	Herzfrequenz
	moreover [mɔːrˈəʊvə]	außerdem, darüber hinaus
	motion sensor [ˈməʊʃn sensə]	Bewegungssensor
	to **figure out sth** [ˌfɪgər ˈaʊt]	etw herausfinden, etw berechnen
	to **redesign** [ˌriːdɪˈzaɪn]	neugestalten, umgestalten
	to **put sb within one tap of sth** [pʊt wɪðɪn ˌwʌn ˈtæp əv]	damit man etw mit einem Tipp/Klick tun kann
	altimeter [ˈæltɪmiːtə]	Höhenmesser
	ordinary [ˈɔːdnri]	gewöhnlich, normal
	waterproof [ˈwɔːtəpruːf]	wasserdicht
	to **take a dip** [ˌteɪk ə ˈdɪp]	schwimmen
	scuba-diving [ˈskuːbə daɪvɪŋ]	Gerätetauchen

47	**ink** [ɪŋk]	Tinte, Tätowierung
	hunter [ˈhʌntə]	Jäger/in
	to **ink** [ɪŋk]	tätowieren
	to **repent** [rɪˈpent]	bereuen

to **toy with sth** [ˈtɔɪ wɪð]	mit etw (Gedanke usw.) spielen
to **tattoo** [təˈtuː]	tätowieren
shoulder [ˈʃəʊldə]	Schulter
to **lack sth** [læk]	etw nicht haben
courage [ˈkʌrɪdʒ]	Mut
to **enter sth** [ˈentə]	etw betreten
tattoo [təˈtuː]	Tätowierung
to **try sth on** [ˌtraɪ ˈɒn]	etw anprobieren
marker [ˈmɑːkə]	Markierung
to **project** [prəˈdʒekt]	projizieren
gallery [ˈgæləri]	Galerie
sketch [sketʃ]	Skizze
collection [kəˈlekʃn]	Sammlung
angle [ˈæŋgl]	Winkel
needle [ˈniːdl]	Nadel
to **encourage sb** [ɪnˈkʌrɪdʒ]	jdn ermutigen, jdn ermuntern
artist [ˈɑːtɪst]	Künstler/in, Grafiker/in

UNIT 5

48	**unauthorized** [ˌʌnˈɔːθəraɪzd]	unbefugt
	auditing [ˈɔːdɪtɪŋ]	Wirtschaftsprüfung, Revision
	tax consultancy [ˈtæks kənsʌltənsi]	Steuerberatung
	to **avoid sth** [əˈvɔɪd]	einer Sache aus dem Weg gehen
	cybercrime [ˈsaɪbə kraɪm]	Cyber-Kriminalität
	attack [əˈtæk]	Angriff
T	to **gain** [geɪn]	gewinnen, erlangen
	findings pl [ˈfaɪndɪŋz]	(Untersuchungs-)Ergebnisse
	disappointing [ˌdɪsəˈpɔɪntɪŋ]	enttäuschend
	to **pay attention to sth** [ˌpeɪ əˈtenʃn tə]	etw beachten
	to **pretend** [prɪˈtend]	vorgeben, vortäuschen
	trustworthy [ˈtrʌstwɜːði]	glaubwürdig, verlässlich
	auction [ˈɔːkʃn]	Versteigerung, Auktion
	infected [ɪnˈfektɪd]	infiziert
	malware [ˈmælweə]	Schadprogramm(e)
	frustrating [frʌˈstreɪtɪŋ]	frustrierend
	to **beware of sth** [bɪˈweər əv]	sich vor etw in Acht nehmen
	worm [wɜːm]	Wurm
	to **spread** [spred]	sich ausbreiten
	sensitive [ˈsensətɪv]	(Informationen:) vertraulich
	to **use sth up** [ˌjuːz ˈʌp]	etw verbrauchen, etw auf- brauchen
	bandwidth [ˈbændwɪdθ]	Bandbreite
	usage [ˈjuːsɪdʒ]	Verbrauch, Nutzung
	account records pl [əˈkaʊnt rekɔːdz]	Kontodaten, Kundendaten
	monitoring [ˈmɒnɪtərɪŋ]	Überwachung
	to **keep an eye out for sth** [ˌkiːp ən ˈaɪ aʊt fə]	nach etw Ausschau halten

backdoor ['bækdɔː]	Hintertür	
to **bypass** sth ['baɪpɑːs]	etw umgehen	
authentication [ɔːθentɪ'keɪʃn]	Authentifizierung	
to **hide** [haɪd]	sich verstecken	
inactive [ɪn'æktɪv]	untätig, inaktiv	
state [steɪt]	Zustand	
to **detect** [dɪ'tekt]	aufspüren, entdecken	
continually [kən'tɪnjuəli]	kontinuierlich	
to **watch out for** sth [ˌwɒtʃ 'aʊt fə]	nach etw Ausschau halten	
unidentified [ˌʌnaɪ'dentɪfaɪd]	unbekannt	
not … yet [nɒt 'jet]	noch nicht	
unlikely [ʌn'laɪkli]	unwahrscheinlich	
injection [ɪn'dʒekʃn]	Einschleusung	
to **exploit** sth [ɪk'splɔɪt]	etw ausnutzen	
hidden ['hɪdn]	verborgen, versteckt	
command [kə'mɑːnd]	Befehl	
to **pick up on** sth [ˌpɪk 'ʌp ɒn]	auf etw reagieren, auf etw aufmerksam machen	
weakness ['wiːknəs]	Schwäche	
to **persuade** [pə'sweɪd]	überreden, überzeugen	
to **guard against** sth ['gɑːd əgenst]	sich vor etw schützen	
to **make a point** [ˌmeɪk ə 'pɔɪnt]	ein Argument vortragen	

to **infect** [ɪn'fekt]	infizieren
public ['pʌblɪk]	öffentlich
recipient [rɪ'sɪpiənt]	Empfänger/in
trojan ['trəʊdʒn]	Trojaner
49 **caution** ['kɔːʃn]	Vorsicht
to **exercise** sth ['eksəsaɪz]	etw üben, etw walten lassen
suspicious [sə'spɪʃəs]	verdächtig
immediately [ɪ'miːdiətli]	sofort, unverzüglich
untrustworthy [ʌn'trʌstwɜːði]	nicht vertrauenswürdig
to **appear** [ə'pɪə]	scheinen, den Eindruck erwecken
fake [feɪk]	falsch, gefälscht
to **threaten** ['θretn]	drohen, bedrohen
to **address** sb [ə'dres]	jdn anreden, jdn ansprechen
valuable ['væljuəbl]	wertvoll, geschätzt
colour scheme ['kʌlə skiːm]	Farbgebung, Farbzusammenstellung
criminal ['krɪmɪnl]	Kriminelle/r, Verbrecher/in
to **punish** ['pʌnɪʃ]	bestrafen
to **display** [dɪ'spleɪ]	zeigen, darstellen
credible ['kredəbl]	glaubwürdig
to **refer to** sb [rɪ'fɜː tə]	sich an jdn wenden, jdn (beim Namen) nennen
to **panic** ['pænɪk]	in Panik geraten
50 **acceptable use** [əkˌseptəbl 'juːz]	zulässige Nutzung
access privileges pl ['ækses prɪvəlɪdʒɪz]	Zugriffsrechte

T	**corporate** ['kɔːprət]	Unternehmens-
	corporate auditing [ˌkɔːprət 'ɔːdɪtɪŋ]	interne Revision
	access level ['ækses levl]	Berechtigungsstufe, Zugriffsstufe
	to **be permitted to do** sth [bi pə'mɪtɪd tə duː]	etw tun dürfen; die Erlaubnis haben, etw zu tun
	to **pre-approve** sth [ˌpriː ə'pruːv]	etw im Voraus genehmigen
	to **approve** sth [ə'pruːv]	etw genehmigen, etw zulassen
	to **be considered** sth [bi kən'sɪdəd]	als etw gelten
	confidential [ˌkɒnfɪ'denʃl]	vertraulich
	to **end up in the wrong hands** [end ˌʌp ɪn ðə ˌrɒŋ 'hændz]	in falsche Hände gelangen
	clarification [ˌklærɪfɪ'keɪʃn]	Klarstellung, Klärung

restriction [rɪ'strɪkʃn]	Beschränkung, Einschränkung
security mechanism [sɪ'kjʊərəti mekənɪzəm]	Schutzmechanismus, Sicherheitsmaßnahme
to **put** sth **in place** [ˌpʊt ɪn 'pleɪs]	etw einrichten
to **remind** sb [rɪ'maɪnd]	jdn (an etw) erinnern
51 **policy** ['pɒləsi]	Linie, Vorgehensweise, Politik
to **demonstrate** sth ['demənstreɪt]	etw nachweisen
discrimination [dɪˌskrɪmɪ'neɪʃn]	Diskriminierung
race [reɪs]	Rasse
press release ['pres rɪliːs]	Pressemitteilung
to **support** [sə'pɔːt]	unterstützen, fördern
circumstances pl ['sɜːkəmstənsɪz]	Umstände
harmful (to sb/sth) ['hɑːmfl]	schädlich, nachteilig (für jdn/etw)
to **result in** sth [rɪ'zʌlt ɪn]	zu etw führen, etw ergeben
harm (to sb/sth) [hɑːm]	Schaden, Nachteil (für jdn/etw)
exception [ɪk'sepʃn]	Ausnahme
prohibited [prə'hɪbɪtɪd]	verboten
distribution [ˌdɪstrɪ'bjuːʃn]	Verbreitung
reputation [ˌrepjʊ'teɪʃn]	Ruf, Ansehen
violent ['vaɪələnt]	gewalttätig
controversial [ˌkɒntrə'vɜːʃl]	umstritten
to **impact** sth **negatively** [ɪmˌpækt 'negətɪvli]	sich negativ auf etw auswirken
defamation [ˌdefə'meɪʃn]	Verleumdung
day-to-day functioning [deɪ tə ˌdeɪ 'fʌŋkʃnɪŋ]	täglicher Betriebsablauf
to **slow down** [ˌsləʊ 'daʊn]	verlangsamen, bremsen
excessive [ɪk'sesɪv]	unverhältnismäßig viel
illegal [ɪ'liːgl]	gesetzeswidrig, illegal

strictly [ˈstrɪktli]	streng, strengstens
theft [θeft]	Diebstahl
to **contravene sth**	gegen etw verstoßen
[ˌkɒntrəˈviːn]	
copyright laws pl	Urheberrechtsgesetze
[ˈkɒpiraɪt lɔːz]	
patent laws pl	Patentgesetze
[ˈpætnt lɔːz]	
52 **cellular** [ˈseljʊlə]	Mobilfunk(-), Handy
mobile cellular coverage	Mobilfunkempfang
[ˌməʊbaɪl ˌseljʊlə ˈkʌvərɪdʒ]	
to **forward sth** [ˈfɔːwəd]	etw weiterleiten
token [ˈtəʊkən]	Marke, Token
to **register** [ˈredʒɪstə]	anmelden, registrieren
working [ˈwɜːkɪŋ]	funktionierend
notification	Benachrichtigung
[ˌnəʊtɪfɪˈkeɪʃn]	
weak [wiːk]	schwach
terms pl [tɜːmz]	Bedingungen, Bestimmungen
53 to **maintain** [meɪnˈteɪn]	betreuen
accessible [əkˈsesəbl]	zugänglich
to **secure** [sɪˈkjʊə]	sichern, schützen
highly [ˈhaɪli]	hochgradig, in hohem Maße
security procedures pl	Sicherheitsverfahren,
[sɪˈkjʊərəti prəsiːdʒəz]	Sicherheitsmaßnahmen
flow chart [ˈfləʊ tʃɑːt]	Flussdiagramm
two-factor authentication	Zwei-Faktoren-
[tuː ˌfæktər ɔːθentɪˈkeɪʃn]	Authentifizierung
to **determine** [dɪˈtɜːmɪn]	bestimmen
to **request access**	Zugang anfordern
[rɪˌkwest ˈækses]	
to **authenticate**	authentifizieren
[ɔːˈθentɪkeɪt]	
prompt [prɒmpt]	Eingabeaufforderung
to **disable sth** [dɪsˈeɪbl]	(Zugang) sperren
one-time [ˌwʌn ˈtaɪm]	einmalig
to **fail to do sth** [feɪl]	versäumen, etw zu tun; es nicht schaffen, etw zu tun
to **prompt sb for sth**	(Eingabeaufforderung:) jdn
[prɒmpt]	nach etw fragen
54 to **fail sth** [feɪl]	etw nicht schaffen
to **reset** [ˌriːˈset]	zurücksetzen
passcode [ˈpɑːskəʊd]	Zugangscode, Passwort
fingerprint [ˈfɪŋgəprɪnt]	Fingerabdruck
up to date [ˌʌp tə ˈdeɪt]	auf dem neuesten Stand
to **inform sb of sth**	jdn über etw informieren,
[ɪnˈfɔːm əv]	jdm etw mitteilen
cutting edge [ˌkʌtɪŋ ˈedʒ]	hochmodern, auf dem neuesten Stand der Technik
to **strengthen** [ˈstreŋθn]	stärken, verbessern
character [ˈkærəktə]	Zeichen
out of date [ˌaʊt əv ˈdeɪt]	veraltet, überholt
to **crack sth** [kræk]	etw knacken
best practice	optimale Vorgehensweise
[ˌbest ˈpræktɪs]	
previously [ˈpriːviəsli]	vorher, zuvor
encryption [ɪnˈkrɪpʃn]	Verschlüsselung

state of the art	(auf dem neuesten) Stand
[ˌsteɪt əv ði ˈɑːt]	der Technik
federal government	Bundesregierung
[ˌfedərəl ˈgʌvənmənt]	
obsolete [ˈɒbsəliːt]	veraltet, überholt
disablement	Sperrung
[dɪsˈeɪblmənt]	
attempt [əˈtempt]	Versuch
failed [feɪld]	gescheitert
55 **frequent** [ˈfriːkwənt]	häufig
unregistered	unregistriert
[ʌnˈredʒɪstəd]	
single sign-on	einmaliges Anmelden
[ˌsɪŋgl ˌsaɪn ɒn]	
certificate file	Zertifikatdatei
[səˈtɪfɪkət faɪl]	
capital (letter)	Großbuchstabe
[ˈkæpɪtl letə]	
to **reuse** [ˌriːˈjuːz]	wiederverwenden, nochmals verwenden
identity provider	Identitätsprovider
[aɪˈdentəti prəvaɪdə]	
session [ˈseʃn]	Sitzung, Session
56 **graph** [grɑːf]	Diagramm, Grafik
chart [tʃɑːt]	Diagramm, Tabelle
constant [ˈkɒnstənt]	ständig, fortwährend
T **straight** [streɪt]	sogleich, sofort
to **rise** [raɪz]	ansteigen
steadily [ˈstedɪli]	kontinuierlich, stetig
peak [piːk]	Spitze, Höchstwert
trough [trɒf]	Tiefpunkt, Tiefstand, Talsohle
midway through	mitten in
[ˌmɪdˈweɪ θruː]	
to **decline** [dɪˈklaɪn]	abnehmen, zurückgehen
slightly [ˈslaɪtli]	leicht, etwas
to **tend to do sth**	dazu neigen, etw zu tun
[ˈtend tə]	
to **increase** [ɪnˈkriːs]	zunehmen, ansteigen
sharp(ly) [ˈʃɑːpli]	(Anstieg:) steil, stark
steady [ˈstedi]	gleichbleibend, stabil
to **climb** [klaɪm]	klettern, steigen
significant(ly)	erheblich, bedeutend,
[sɪgˈnɪfɪkəntli]	signifikant
drastic(ally) [ˈdræstɪkli]	drastisch
fluctuation [ˌflʌktʃuˈeɪʃn]	Schwankung
random [ˈrændəm]	zufällig, willkürlich, beliebig
to **be aware of sth**	sich über etw im Klaren sein,
[bi əˈweər əv]	auf etw achten
to **jump** [dʒʌmp]	springen, emporschnellen
to **decrease** [dɪˈkriːs]	abnehmen, sinken
marginal(ly) [ˈmɑːdʒɪnl]	unerheblich, geringfügig
to **grow** [grəʊ]	zunehmen, steigen
gradual(ly) [ˈgrædʒuəli]	allmählich
quarter [ˈkwɔːtə]	Quartal
increase [ˈɪŋkriːs]	Zunahme, Anstieg
steep(ly) [stiːp]	steil
unchanged [ʌnˈtʃeɪndʒd]	unverändert

	to **level off** [ˌlevl ˈɒf]	sich stabilisieren, sich einpendeln (bei)	
	figures pl [ˈfɪgəz]	Zahlen, Ziffern	
P	**line graph** [ˈlaɪn grɑːf]	Liniendiagramm	
	the day before yesterday [ðə deɪ bɪˌfɔː ˈjestədeɪ]	vorgestern	

57	**pie chart** [ˈpaɪ tʃɑːt]	Tortendiagramm
	approximate(ly) [əˈprɒksɪmət]	ungefähr, zirka
	roughly [ˈrʌfli]	ungefähr
	to **account for sth** [əˈkaʊnt fə]	(Anteil:) etw ausmachen
	malicious [məˈlɪʃəs]	schädlich, bösartig
	to **make up sth** [ˌmeɪk ˈʌp]	(Anteil:) etw ausmachen
	costs pl **incurred** [ˌkɒsts ɪnˈkɜːd]	entstandene Kosten
	breakdown [ˈbreɪkdaʊn]	Aufstellung, Aufschlüsselung

UNIT 6

58	to **deal with sb** [ˈdiːl wɪð]	mit jdm zu tun haben, mit jdm umgehen, sich mit jdm auseinandersetzen
	robot [ˈrəʊbɒt]	Roboter
	retailer [ˈriːteɪlə]	Einzelhändler
	wide variety [ˌwaɪd vəˈraɪəti]	große Auswahl, breites Sortiment
	artificial intelligence [ɑːtɪˌfɪʃl ɪnˈtelɪdʒəns]	künstliche Intelligenz
	call centre agent [ˈkɔːl sentər eɪdʒənt]	Callcenteragent/in, Telefonberater/in
T	to **serve sb** [sɜːv]	jdn bedienen
	natural language [ˌnætʃrəl ˈlæŋgwɪdʒ]	natürliche Sprache
	to **interpret** [ɪnˈtɜːprɪt]	übersetzen
	everyday [ˈevrideɪ]	Alltags-, alltäglich
	to **engage in conversation** [ɪnˌgeɪdʒ ɪn kɒnvəˈseɪʃn]	sich unterhalten
	to **pop up** [ˌpɒp ˈʌp]	(auf dem Bildschirm) erscheinen
	greeting [ˈgriːtɪŋ]	Gruß, Begrüßung
	latest [ˈleɪtɪst]	neue/r/s, neuste/r/s, letzte/r/s
	copy [ˈkɒpi]	Exemplar
	right away [raɪt əˈweɪ]	sofort, gleich
	cart [kɑːt]	Einkaufswagen, Warenkorb
	credit [ˈkredɪt]	Guthaben
	to **be of assistance** [bi əv əˈsɪstəns]	helfen
	gift [gɪft]	Geschenk
	kit [kɪt]	Set
	starter kit [ˌstɑːtə kɪt]	Einsteigerset
	time of day [taɪm əv ˈdeɪ]	Tageszeit
	to **assist sb with sth** [əˈsɪst]	jdm bei etw helfen

	to **personalize** [ˈpɜːsnəlaɪz]	individuell anpassen, persönlich gestalten
	interaction [ˌɪntərˈækʃn]	Austausch, Kommunikation
	review [rɪˈvjuː]	Rezension, Kritik
	purchase decision [ˈpɜːtʃəs dɪsɪʒn]	Kaufentscheidung
	to **predict** [prɪˈdɪkt]	vorhersagen
	purchase [ˈpɜːtʃəs]	Kauf

	existing customer [ɪgˌzɪstɪŋ ˈkʌstəmə]	Bestandskunde/-kundin
59	**delivery time** [dɪˈlɪvəri taɪm]	Lieferzeit
	behaviour [bɪˈheɪvjə]	Verhalten
	to **be unable to do sth** [bi ʌnˈeɪbl tə]	etw nicht können; nicht in der Lage sein, etw zu tun
	satisfaction [ˌsætɪsˈfækʃn]	Zufriedenheit
	to **sb's satisfaction** [tə ˌsʌmbədiz sætɪsˈfækʃn]	zu jds Zufriedenheit
	to **transfer** [trænsˈfɜː]	weiterleiten, vermitteln
	light bulb [ˈlaɪt bʌlb]	Glühbirne
	to **dim** [dɪm]	dimmen
	to **have sth in mind** [həv ɪn ˈmaɪnd]	etw vorhaben, etw im Sinn haben, an etw denken
	lighting [ˈlaɪtɪŋ]	Beleuchtung
	brand [brænd]	Marke
	customer service representative [ˌkʌstəmə ˌsɜːvɪs ˌreprɪˈzentətɪv]	Kundenbetreuer/in
60	**set-up** [ˈsetʌp]	Einrichtung
	customization [kʌstəmaɪˈzeɪʃn]	(individuelle) Anpassung
	reference material [ˈrefərəns mətɪəriəl]	Material zum Nachschlagen
	to **upload** [ˌʌpˈləʊd]	hochladen
	to **import** [ɪmˈpɔːt]	laden, importieren
	wizard [ˈwɪzəd]	Assistent
	criterion, criteria [kraɪˈtɪəriən, kraɪˈtɪəriə]	Kriterium, Kriterien
	row [rəʊ]	Reihe, Zeile
	to **survey sb** [ˈsɜːveɪ]	jdn befragen
	mandatory [ˈmændətəri]	obligatorisch, zwingend notwendig
	column [ˈkɒləm]	(Text:) Spalte
	file extension [ˈfaɪl ɪkstenʃn]	Dateiendung, Dateierweiterung
	special character [ˌspeʃl ˈkærəktə]	Sonderzeichen
	punctuation [ˌpʌŋktʃuˈeɪʃn]	Satzzeichen
	sheet of data [ˌʃiːt əv ˈdeɪtə]	Datenblatt
	to **unprotect** [ʌnprəˈtekt]	den Schutz aufheben
	to **start from scratch** [stɑːt frəm ˈskrætʃ]	(ganz) von vorne anfangen
	template [ˈtempleɪt]	Vorlage, Dokumentvorlage
	to **proceed** [prəˈsiːd]	fortfahren, weitermachen
	error code [ˈerə kəʊd]	Fehlercode

in the event that	falls	
[ɪn ði ɪ'vent ðət]		
at any stage	jederzeit	
[ət ˌeni 'steɪdʒ]		
to **reverse** sth [rɪ'vɜːs]	etw umkehren	
by **mistake** [baɪ mɪ'steɪk]	versehentlich, irrtümlich	

61 **password protection** — Kennwortschutz
[ˌpɑːswɜːd prə'tekʃn]
participation — Beteiligung, Teilnahme
[pɑːˌtɪsɪ'peɪʃn]
to **submit** sth [səb'mɪt] — etw einreichen
data range ['deɪtə reɪndʒ] — Datenbereich
vertical ['vɜːtɪkl] — senkrecht, vertikal
bar [bɑː] — Balken
shaded ['ʃeɪdɪd] — schattiert
to **indicate** ['ɪndɪkeɪt] — anzeigen
rated question — bewertete Frage
[ˌreɪtɪd 'kwestʃən]
horizontal [ˌhɒrɪ'zɒntl] — waagrecht, horizontal
to **demonstrate** — darstellen, anzeigen
['demənstreɪt]
engagement — Engagement
[ɪn'geɪdʒmənt]
yet [jet] — doch, aber
powerful ['paʊəfl] — aussagekräftig
cell [sel] — Zelle
score [skɔː] — Punktzahl, Punkte
confidence (in sb/sth) — Zutrauen, Vertrauen (in jdn/
['kɒnfɪdəns] — etw)
alignment [ə'laɪnmənt] — Ausrichtung
involvement — Beteiligung, Engagement
[ɪn'vɒlvmənt]
collaboration — Zusammenarbeit
[kəˌlæbə'reɪʃn]
impact ['ɪmpækt] — Relevanz, Wirkung
favourable score — positive Bewertung
[ˌfeɪvərəbl 'skɔː]
leadership ['liːdəʃɪp] — Mitarbeiterführung,
Führungsqualitäten
career opportunities pl — Aufstiegsmöglichkeiten,
[kəˌrɪər ɒpə'tjuːnətiz] — berufliche Perspektiven

62 to **feel comfortable** — sich wohlfühlen
[ˌfiːl 'kʌmftəbl]
T **at some point** — irgendwann
[ət ˌsʌm 'pɔɪnt]
to **tailor** sth ['teɪlə] — etw individuell anpassen
to **toggle** [tɒgl] — hin- und herschalten,
umschalten
ascending [ə'sendɪŋ] — aufsteigend
descending [dɪ'sendɪŋ] — absteigend
to **refine** [rɪ'faɪn] — verfeinern
to **focus on** sth — sich auf etw konzentrieren
['fəʊkəs ɒn]
custom report — benutzerdefinierter Bericht
[ˌkʌstəm rɪ'pɔːt]

baseline ['beɪslaɪn] — Basis
to **export** [ɪk'spɔːt] — exportieren
to **filter** ['fɪltə] — filtern

category ['kætəgəri] — Kategorie, Klasse
enablement [ɪ'neɪblmnt] — Umsetzung, Förderung
data line ['deɪtə laɪn] — Datenzeile
sub-criteria pl — Unterkriterien
[ˌsʌb kraɪ'tɪəriə]

63 to **extract** (sth from sth) — entnehmen, extrahieren,
[ɪk'strækt] — (etw aus etw) ziehen

T **raw data** pl [ˌrɔː 'deɪtə] — Rohdaten
to **enable** sth [ɪ'neɪbl] — etw einschalten,
etw aktivieren
design feature — Konstruktionsmerkmal
[dɪ'zaɪn fiːtʃə]
data extraction — Datenextraktion
['deɪtə ɪkstrækʃn]
to **disable** sth [dɪs'eɪbl] — etw ausschalten,
etw deaktivieren
by default [baɪ dɪ'fɔːlt] — standardmäßig
commitment [kə'mɪtmənt] — Verpflichtung, Bindung
anonymous [ə'nɒnɪməs] — anonym
to **make sense** — nachvollziehbar sein,
[meɪk 'sens] — einleuchten
to **trust** [trʌst] — vertrauen
to **walk** sb **through** sth — jdm etw schrittweise erklären
[wɔːk 'θruː]
administration — Verwaltung
[ədˌmɪnɪ'streɪʃn]
dummy ['dʌmi] — Attrappe, Schein-, Blind-
Not quite. [ˌnɒt 'kwaɪt] — Nicht ganz.
to **uncheck** [ʌn'tʃek] — Auswahl/Markierung
aufheben
to **acknowledge** — bestätigen
[ək'nɒlɪdʒ]
record ['rekɔːd] — Aufzeichnung, Eintrag

survey taker ['sɜːveɪ teɪkə] — Umfrageteilnehmer/in
64 to **integrate** ['ɪntɪgreɪt] — integrieren
to **authorize** ['ɔːθəraɪz] — genehmigen, zulassen,
autorisieren
authorization — Genehmigung, Autorisierung
[ˌɔːθəraɪ'zeɪʃn]
65 **synchronization** — Synchronisierung
[ˌsɪŋkrənaɪ'zeɪʃn]
to **role-play** ['rəʊl pleɪ] — mit verteilten Rollen spielen
66 **arrangement** — (Termin-)Vereinbarung,
[ə'reɪndʒmənt] — Vorbereitung
to **set up a meeting** — ein Treffen vereinbaren
[set ˌʌp ə 'miːtɪŋ]
to **get in touch with** sb — sich bei jdm melden, sich mit
[get ɪn 'tʌtʃ wɪð] — jdm in Verbindung setzen
to **let** sb **know** [ˌlet 'nəʊ] — jdm Bescheid geben
67 **appointment** — Termin
[ə'pɔɪntmənt]
to **reserve** [rɪ'zɜːv] — reservieren
with a room attached — mit einem Nebenraum
[wɪð ə ˌruːm ə'tætʃt]
working breakfast — Arbeitsfrühstück
[ˌwɜːkɪŋ 'brekfəst]
to **postpone** [pə'spəʊn] — (nach hinten) verschieben
itinerary [aɪ'tɪnərəri] — Reiseplan

68 to **steal** [stiːl] stehlen
T **exam papers** pl Prüfungsunterlagen
  [ɪgˈzæm peɪpəz]
headmaster [ˌhedˈmɑːstə] (Schul-)Direktor
bond (to sb/sth) [bɒnd] Bindung (zu jdm/etw)
principle [ˈprɪnsəpl] Grundsatz, Prinzip
to **litter sth** [ˈlɪtə] etw zumüllen,
    etw verunreinigen
car manufacturer Autohersteller
  [ˌkɑː ˌmænjuˈfæktʃərə]
flaw [flɔː] Mangel
That reminds me … Da fällt mir ein …
  [ðæt rɪˈmaɪndz miː]
the other day neulich
  [ði ˌʌðə ˈdeɪ]
How come? [ˌhaʊ ˈkʌm] Wieso?
to **think twice** sich etw gut überlegen
  [ˌθɪŋk ˈtwaɪs]
charging card Ladekarte
  [ˈtʃɑːdʒɪŋ kɑːd]
insecure [ˌɪnsɪˈkjʊə] unsicher
provider [prəˈvaɪdə] Anbieter
as sb sees fit nach jds Ermessen
  [əz ˌsʌmbədi ˌsiːz ˈfɪt]
to **clone** [kləʊn] klonen
attacker [əˈtækə] Angreifer/in
to **link sth to sth** [ˈlɪŋk tə] eine Verbindung von etw zu
    etw herstellen
to **have a hard time doing** etw nur schwer tun können
  sth [həv ə ˌhɑːd ˈtaɪm]
to **prove sth** [pruːv] etw nachweisen, etw
    beweisen
unbelievable unglaublich
  [ˌʌnbɪˈliːvəbl]
to **take action** Maßnahmen ergreifen
  [ˌteɪk ˈækʃn]
not until [nɒt ənˈtɪl] erst wenn
scandal [ˈskændl] Skandal

69 **methodology** Methodik
  [ˌmeθəˈdɒlədʒi]
agile [ˈædʒaɪl] agil, beweglich
iterative [ˈɪtrətɪv] iterativ, sich wiederholend
approach [əˈprəʊtʃ] Ansatz, Vorgehen
adaptable [əˈdæptəbl] anpassungsfähig
sequential [sɪˈkwenʃl] sequenziell, fortlaufend
waterfall [ˈwɔːtəfɔːl] Wasserfall
uncertainty [ʌnˈsɜːtnti] Unsicherheit
scope [skəʊp] Umfang, Geltungs-/
    Anwendungsbereich
deadline [ˈdedlaɪn] Frist, Fertigstellungstermin
methodical [məˈθɒdɪkl] systematisch, planvoll
to **encourage sth** etw fördern,
  [ɪnˈkʌrɪdʒ] etw begünstigen
in turn [ɪn ˈtɜːn] wiederum, seiner-/ihrerseits
quick course correction schnelle Korrektur
  [kwɪk ˌkɔːs kəˈrekʃn]

experimentation Experimentieren
  [ɪksperɪmenˈteɪʃn]
creativity [ˌkriːeɪˈtɪvəti] Kreativität
breakthrough [ˈbreɪkθruː] Durchbruch, bahnbrechend
to **overcomplicate sth** etw verkomplizieren
  [ˌəʊvəˈkɒmplɪkeɪt]
repeatable [rɪˈpiːtəbl] reproduzierbar

UNIT 7

70 to **collaborate** zusammenarbeiten
  [kəˈlæbəreɪt]
publishing company Verlag
  [ˈpʌblɪʃɪŋ kʌmpəni]
maturity [məˈtʃʊərəti] Reifung, Reife
individually einzeln, separat, privat
  [ˌɪndɪˈvɪdʒuəli]
to **publish** [ˈpʌblɪʃ] veröffentlichen
multiple [ˈmʌltɪpl] mehrere, mehrfach
transparent erkennbar, transparent
  [trænsˈpærənt]
to **lose track of sth** etw aus den Augen verlieren,
  [ˌluːz ˈtræk əv] die Übersicht über etw
    verlieren
version control Versionsverwaltung,
  [ˈvɜːʃn kəntrəʊl] -kontrolle
71 **set-up** [ˈsetʌp] Aufbau, Einrichtung
front page [ˌfrʌnt ˈpeɪdʒ] Titelseite
overview [ˈəʊvəvjuː] Übersicht
project health Projektzustand
  [ˈprɒdʒekt helθ]
amber [ˈæmbə] (Ampelfarbe:) gelb
stakeholder [ˈsteɪkhəʊldə] Projektbeteiligte/r
backlog [ˈbæklɒg] Arbeitsrückstand, Arbeits-
    überhang
sub-page [ˈsʌb peɪdʒ] Unterseite
adjacent [əˈdʒeɪsnt] angrenzend, benachbart
prioritized [praɪˈɒrətaɪzd] nach Priorität geordnet
to **be impacted by sth** von etw betroffen sein, von
  [bi ɪmˈpæktɪd baɪ] etw beeinflusst werden
associated with sth mit etw verbunden
  [əˈsəʊʃieɪtɪd wɪð]
T to **run sth** [rʌn] etw ausführen,
    etw betreiben
layout [ˈleɪaʊt] Anordnung, Aufbau, Layout
to **limit** [ˈlɪmɪt] begrenzen, beschränken
editing rights pl Bearbeitungsrechte
  [ˈedɪtɪŋ raɪts]
consistent [kənˈsɪstənt] einheitlich
to **perform** [pəˈfɔːm] sich entwickeln
to **generate** [ˈdʒenəreɪt] erzeugen
upcoming [ˈʌpkʌmɪŋ] bevorstehend, künftig
typically [ˈtɪpɪkli] normalerweise, üblicherweise
to **revise sth** [rɪˈvaɪz] etw überarbeiten, etw
    ändern
access rights pl Zugriffsrechte
  [ˈækses raɪts]

	to **notify sb** ['nəʊtɪfaɪ]	jdn benachrichtigen	
	to **inform** [ɪn'fɔːm]	informieren, mitteilen	
	consistency [kən'sɪstənsi]	Einheitlichkeit	
	transparency	Transparenz	
	[træns'pærənsi]		
72	to **expand** [ɪk'spænd]	sich vergrößern	
	network design	Netzwerkkonzeption,	
	['netwɜːk dɪzaɪn]	-auslegung, -design	
	consideration	Überlegung	
	[kənˌsɪdə'reɪʃn]		

T	**off the shelf** [ɒf ðə 'ʃelf]	handelsüblich
	to **plug in sth** [ˌplʌg 'ɪn]	etw anschließen
	after all [ˌɑːftər 'ɔːl]	schließlich, immerhin
	business-grade	professionell, Industrie-
	['bɪznəs greɪd]	
	to **operate** ['ɒpəreɪt]	funktionieren, arbeiten, laufen
	for starters [fə 'stɑːtəz]	zunächst (einmal)
	gear [gɪə]	Gerät(e), Ausrüstung, Ausstattung
	to **be designed for sth**	für etw ausgelegt sein
	[bi dɪ'zaɪnd fə]	
	load [ləʊd]	Last
	to **take sth into account**	etw berücksichtigen
	[ˌteɪk ɪntu ə'kaʊnt]	
	That's a good point.	Da hast du / haben Sie
	[ˌðæts ə ˌgʊd 'pɔɪnt]	recht. Da ist was dran.
	rock-solid [ˌrɒk 'sɒlɪd]	(absolut) stabil
	to **bear sth in mind**	etw berücksichtigen, an etw
	[ˌbeər ɪn 'maɪnd]	denken
	frequency ['friːkwənsi]	Frequenz
	frequency band	Frequenzband
	['friːkwənsi bænd]	
	range [reɪndʒ]	Reichweite
	square metre	Quadratmeter
	['skweə miːtə]	
	access point	Zugangspunkt, Access Point
	['ækses pɔɪnt]	
	to **cover sth** ['kʌvə]	etw abdecken
	spare [speə]	Ersatz, Reserve
	to **keep in mind**	daran denken
	[ˌkiːp ɪn 'maɪnd]	
	to **interfere with sth**	etw stören
	[ˌɪntə'fɪə wɪð]	
	to **decrease sth** [dɪ'kriːs]	etw senken
	I didn't realize that.	Das war mir nicht klar.
	[aɪ ˌdɪdnt 'rɪəlaɪz ðæt]	
	interference [ˌɪntə'fɪərəns]	Störung, Interferenz
	noise [nɔɪz]	Rauschen
	placement ['pleɪsmənt]	Platzierung, Anordnung
	painless ['peɪnləs]	schmerzfrei
	to **determine** [dɪ'tɜːmɪn]	festlegen
	to **place sth** [pleɪs]	etw platzieren
	usable ['juːzəbl]	nutzbar

	to **take sth into consideration**	etw in Betracht ziehen, etw berücksichtigen
	[ˌteɪk ɪntə kənˌsɪdə'reɪʃn]	

73	**estimate** ['estɪmət]	Schätzung, Kosten- voranschlag
	to **justify** ['dʒʌstɪfaɪ]	rechtfertigen, begründen
	draft [drɑːft]	Entwurf
	approval [ə'pruːvl]	Genehmigung, Freigabe
	need [niːd]	Bedarf
	to **point out sth**	auf etw hinweisen
	[ˌpɔɪnt 'aʊt]	
	investment [ɪn'vestmənt]	Investition
	justification	Rechtfertigung, Begründung
	[dʒʌstɪfɪ'keɪʃn]	
	midday [ˌmɪd'deɪ]	Mittag
	crucial ['kruːʃl]	entscheidend, unerlässlich
	failure (to do sth) ['feɪljə]	Unterlassen, Unterlassung
	to **suffer** ['sʌfə]	leiden
	vital ['vaɪtl]	unverzichtbar
	wise(ly) [waɪz]	klug
	bulk discount	Mengenrabatt
	[bʌlk 'dɪskaʊnt]	
	testing equipment	Prüfgeräte
	['testɪŋ ɪkwɪpmənt]	
	strength [streŋθ]	Stärke
	measurement unit	Messgerät
	['meʒəmənt juːnɪt]	
	coverage ['kʌvərɪdʒ]	Abdeckung
	to **approve** [ə'pruːv]	genehmigen, freigeben
	unless [ən'les]	wenn nicht, sofern nicht
74	to **fail** [feɪl]	ausfallen
	compatibility	Kompatibilität
	[kəmˌpætə'bɪləti]	
	shielded ['ʃiːldɪd]	abgeschirmt
	corrupted data pl	beschädigte/fehlerhafte
	[kəˌrʌptɪd 'deɪtə]	Daten
	funding ['fʌndɪŋ]	Finanzierung, Geldmittel
	volume ['vɒljuːm]	Volumen
75	**processing** ['prəʊsesɪŋ]	(Daten-)Verarbeitung
	to **render** ['rendə]	berechnen, erzeugen, rendern
	GPU (graphics processing unit) [ˌdʒiː piː 'juː]	Grafikprozessor
	process flow	Prozessablauf
	['prəʊses fləʊ]	
	to **convert** [kən'vɜːt]	umwandeln
	to **facilitate sth**	etw erleichtern,
	[fə'sɪlɪteɪt]	etw begünstigen
76	to **argue the case for sth**	für etw plädieren, für etw
	[ˌɑːgjuː ðə 'keɪs fə]	eintreten
	particular [pə'tɪkjələ]	bestimmt, speziell
	in theory [ɪn 'θɪəri]	theoretisch, in der Theorie
	computing power	Rechenleistung
	[kəm'pjuːtɪŋ paʊə]	
	that said, … [ˌðæt 'sed]	vor diesem Hintergrund
	to **benefit** ['benɪfɪt]	(davon) profitieren
	workforce ['wɜːkfɔːs]	Arbeitskräfte, Belegschaft
	to **hand sth to sb** [hænd]	jdm etw übergeben
	shift [ʃɪft]	Schicht
	incredible [ɪn'kredəbl]	unglaublich
	reluctance [rɪ'lʌktəns]	Abneigung, Widerwille, Widerstand

	gain [geɪn]	Gewinn
	to **win sb over** [ˌwɪn ˈəʊvə]	jdn überzeugen
	intellectual property [ɪntəˌlektʃʊəl ˈprɒpəti]	geistiges Eigentum
	to **host** [həʊst]	(Daten) hosten
	excessive [ɪkˈsesɪv]	übermäßig, zu hoch/groß
	latency [ˈleɪtnsi]	Latenzzeiten
	uptake [ˈʌpteɪk]	(Daten-)Aufnahme
	savings pl [ˈseɪvɪŋz]	Einsparung(en)
	switch (to sth) [swɪtʃ]	Umstellung (auf etw)
	counterargument [ˌkaʊntəˈɑːgjumnt]	Gegenargument
77	to **acknowledge sth** [əkˈnɒlɪdʒ]	etw würdigen, etw zur Kenntnis nehmen
	to **state one's case** [ˌsteɪt wʌnz ˈkeɪs]	sein Anliegen vorbringen, seine Sache vertreten

T	**heavy computation** [ˌhevi kɒmpjuˈteɪʃn]	hohes Rechenaufkommen
	resource [rɪˈsɔːs]	Quelle, Resource
	to **transfer** [trænsˈfɜː]	übertragen
	on the road [ɒn ðə ˈrəʊd]	unterwegs
	to **contribute to sth** [kənˈtrɪbjuːt tə]	zu etw beitragen
	entirely [ɪnˈtaɪəli]	völlig, voll und ganz
	obviously [ˈɒbviəsli]	natürlich, offensichtlich
	to **pick up sth** [ˌpɪk ˈʌp]	mit etw weitermachen
	amazing [əˈmeɪzɪŋ]	irre, fantastisch
	in terms of [ɪn ˈtɜːmz əv]	was … anbelangt
	employee satisfaction [ɪmˈplɔɪiː sætɪsfækʃn]	Mitarbeiterzufriedenheit
	to a point [tʊ ə ˈpɔɪnt]	bis zu einem gewissen Punkt
	a valid concern [ə ˌvælɪd kənˈsɜːn]	eine berechtigte Sorge
	night-owl [ˈnaɪt aʊl]	Nachteule
	thin [θɪn]	dünn, schlank
	potentially [pəˈtenʃəli]	eventuell, potenziell
	I'm with you on that. [aɪm ˌwɪð juː ɒn ˈðæt]	Da bin ich ganz deiner/Ihrer Meinung.
	partially [ˈpɑːʃəli]	teilweise, zum Teil

	agreement [əˈgriːmənt]	Zustimmung
	doubt [daʊt]	Zweifel
P	to **mess sth up** [ˌmes ˈʌp]	etw durcheinanderbringen
78	to **adopt sth** [əˈdɒpt]	etw einführen, etw anwenden
	in good shape [ɪn ˌgʊd ˈʃeɪp]	in gutem Zustand
	formatting [ˈfɔːmətɪŋ]	Formatierung
	inconsistent [ˌɪnkənˈsɪstənt]	uneinheitlich
	to **figure out sth** [ˌfɪgər ˈaʊt]	sich etw erklären
	in bold [ɪn ˈbəʊld]	(Schrift:) fett
	in italics [ɪn ɪˈtælɪks]	(Schrift:) kursiv

	reference time [ˈrefərəns taɪm]	Referenzzeit, Bezugszeit
	sign-in [ˈsaɪn ɪn]	Login
	to **get sth right** [ˌget ˈraɪt]	etw richtig verstehen
	spelling mistake [ˈspelɪŋ mɪsteɪk]	Rechtschreibfehler
	to **slip through** [ˌslɪp ˈθruː]	durchrutschen
	font [fɒnt]	Zeichensatz, Schrift
	Feel free to call me. [fiːl friː tə ˈkɔːl miː]	Du kannst / Sie können mich gerne anrufen.
79	to **rush sth** [rʌʃ]	etw hastig erledigen

T	to **sign sth in** [ˌsaɪn ˈɪn]	etw anmelden, etw eintragen
	to **appreciate sth** [əˈpriːʃieɪt]	für etw Verständnis haben
	rush [rʌʃ]	Hast, Eile

UNIT 8

80	**a wide range of** [ə ˈreɪndʒ əv]	eine große Auswahl von/an
	standardized [ˈstændədaɪzd]	genormt
	to **regulate** [ˈregjuleɪt]	(durch Vorschriften) regeln, reglementieren
	charging [ˈtʃɑːdʒɪŋ]	Laden, Aufladen

T	**range** [reɪndʒ]	Produktreihe
	Agreed. [əˈgriːd]	Stimmt.
	to **optimize** [ˈɒptɪmaɪz]	optimieren
	pairing [ˈpeərɪŋ]	Kopplung, Pairing
	annoying [əˈnɔɪɪŋ]	nervig
	selling point [ˈselɪŋ pɔɪnt]	Verkaufsargument
	to **enhance** [ɪnˈhɑːns]	verbessern
	optimization [ˌɒptɪmaɪˈzeɪʃn]	Optimierung
	power usage [ˈpaʊə juːsɪdʒ]	Stromverbrauch

	initially [ɪˈnɪʃəli]	ursprünglich, anfangs
	casual [ˈkæʒuəl]	Gelegenheits-
81	**trade fair** [ˈtreɪd feə]	Fachmesse, Branchenmesse
	vacuum robot [ˈvækjuəm rəʊbɒt]	Staubsaugerroboter
	purpose [ˈpɜːpəs]	Zweck
	to **vacuum** [ˈvækjuəm]	staubsaugen
	charge [tʃɑːdʒ]	Ladevorgang, Aufladen
	to **do exercise** [duː ˈeksəsaɪz]	Sport treiben
	to **care about sth** [ˈkeə əbaʊt]	es liegt einem etw an etw
	appearance [əˈpɪərəns]	Erscheinungsbild, Auftreten
	to **be short of time** [bi ˌʃɔːt əf ˈtaɪm]	wenig Zeit haben
82	**educational** [ˌedʒuˈkeɪʃənl]	Bildungs-, Lern-
	professional [prəˈfeʃənl]	Fachkraft, Profi

T	**booth** [ˌdʒæki ˈbuːð]	(Messe-)Stand	
	show [ʃəʊ]	Messe, Ausstellung	
	to **be impressed with sth** [bi ɪmˈprest wɪð]	von etw beeindruckt sein	
	to **be precise** [tə bi prɪˈsaɪs]	genau gesagt, um genau zu sein	
	to **be headquartered in** [bi ˈhedkwɔːtəd ɪn]	seinen Sitz in … haben	
	passion [ˈpæʃn]	Leidenschaft	
	sth in particular [ɪn pəˈtɪkjələ]	etw Spezielles	
	medical procedure [ˌmedɪk lprəˈsiːdʒə]	medizinischer Eingriff	
	to **educate sb** [ˈedʒukeɪt]	jdn schulen, jdn ausbilden	
	to **demonstrate sth** [ˈdemənstreɪt]	etw vorführen	
	holographic [ˌhɒləˈgræfɪk]	holographisch	
	anatomy [əˈnætəmi]	Anatomie	

to **engage sb** [ɪnˈgeɪdʒ]	mit jdm ins Gespräch kommen, auf jdn (gesprächsweise) zugehen
to **establish rapport** [ɪˌstæblɪʃ ræˈpɔː]	eine persönliche Beziehung aufbauen
83 to **augment** [ɔːgˈment]	erweitern
to **establish a reputation** [ɪˌstæblɪʃ ə repjuˈteɪʃn]	sich einen Ruf erwerben
trusted brand [ˌtrʌstɪd ˈbrænd]	vertrauenswürdige Marke
flagship product [ˌflægʃɪp ˈprɒdʌkt]	Top-Produkt, Vorzeigeprodukt
expertise [ˌekspəˈtiːz]	Fachwissen, Know-how
to **transform** [trænsˈfɔːm]	verwandeln
capable [ˈkeɪpəbl]	kompetent
to **be confident of being able to handle sth** [bi ˌkɒnfɪdənt əv bɪɪŋ ˌeɪbl tə ˈhændl]	sicher im Umgang mit etw sein
respected [rɪˈspektɪd]	angesehen
sophisticated [səˈfɪstɪkeɪtɪd]	anspruchsvoll, hochentwickelt
adoption [əˈdɒpʃn]	Annahme, (Produkt-)Verwendung, Akzeptanz
countless [ˈkaʊntləs]	unzählig, zahllos
to **accompany sb** [əˈkʌmpəni]	jdn begleiten
testimonial [ˌtestɪˈməʊniəl]	Erfahrungsbericht
to **exceed sth** [ɪkˈsiːd]	etw übertreffen
to **be dedicated to sth** [bi ˈdedɪkeɪtɪd tə]	sich einer Sache verschreiben, sich für etw einsetzen
healthcare [ˈhelθkeə]	Gesundheitswesen, Medizin
to **benefit sb** [ˈbenɪfɪt]	jdm nützen
to **compare to sth** [kəmˈpeə tə]	im Vergleich mit etw dastehen, sich mit etw vergleichen lassen
84 to **follow up** [ˌfɒləʊ ˈʌp]	nachfassen, nachbereiten
to **have sth in common** [həv ɪn ˈkɒmən]	etw gemeinsam haben

demonstration [ˌdemənˈstreɪʃn]	Vorführung
capabilities pl [ˌkeɪpəˈbɪlətiz]	Kompetenzen
impressive [ɪmˈpresɪv]	beeindruckend
lastly [ˈlɑːstli]	zuletzt, zu guter Letzt
to **relive sth** [ˌriːˈlɪv]	etw noch einmal erleben
to **hesitate** [ˈhezɪteɪt]	zögern
85 to **run a project** [ˌrʌn ə ˈprɒdʒekt]	ein Projekt leiten/durchführen
to **estimate a project** [ˌestɪmeɪt ə ˈprɒdʒekt]	ein Projekt kalkulieren
overall cost [əʊvərˌɔːl ˈkɒst]	Gesamtkosten
bar chart [ˈbɑː tʃɑːt]	Säulendiagramm
to **name sth after sb** [neɪm]	etw nach jdm benennen
mechanical engineer [mɪˌkænɪkl ˌendʒɪˈnɪə]	Maschinenbauer/in
management consultant [ˌmænɪdʒmənt kənˈsʌltənt]	Unternehmensberater/in
to **illustrate sth** [ˈɪləstreɪt]	etw veranschaulichen
project schedule [ˈprɒdʒekt ʃedjuːl]	Projektplan
to **schedule** [ˈʃedjuːl]	planen, (Termin) ansetzen
kick-off [ˈkɪk ɒf]	Projektstart
launch [lɔːntʃ]	(Produkt-)Vorstellung, Start, Markteinführung
slack [slæk]	Pufferzeit
due date [ˌdjuː ˈdeɪt]	Fälligkeitstermin
milestone [ˈmaɪlstəʊn]	Projektabschnitt, Meilenstein
86 **counterpart** [ˈkaʊntəpɑːt]	Gegenüber, Ansprechpartner/in
to **be due to do sth** [bi ˈdjuː tə]	etw (zu einem bestimmten Zeitpunkt) tun sollen
to **write sth up** [ˌraɪt ˈʌp]	etw ausarbeiten, etw formulieren
ahead of schedule [əˌhed əv ˈʃedjuːl]	vorzeitig
to **hit a snag** [ˌhɪt ə ˈsnæg]	ein (unerwartetes) Problem haben
to **come across sth** [ˌkʌm əˈkrɒs]	auf etw stoßen
specifications pl [ˌspesɪfɪˈkeɪʃnz]	Technische Daten, Spezifikationen
import [ˈɪmpɔːt]	Einlesen, Importieren
optical character recognition (OCR) [ˌɒptɪkl ˈkærəktə rekəgnɪʃn]	optische Zeichenerkennung
on a (more) positive note [ɒn ə ˌpɒzətɪv ˈnəʊt]	positiv zu vermerken ist, dass …
to **track** [træk]	laufen
to **make up ground** [meɪk ˌʌp ˈgraʊnd]	Boden gutmachen
bug [bʌg]	Fehler, Bug
slightly [ˈslaɪtli]	geringfügig

	co-ordination [kəʊˌɔːdɪˈneɪʃn]	Abstimmung, Koordination
87	to **review sth** [rɪˈvjuː]	etw besprechen, etw Revue passieren lassen
	a lesson learned [ə ˌlesn ˈlɜːnd]	eine Lehre (aus etw)
T	**involved (in sth)** [ɪnˈvɒlvd]	(an etw) beteiligt
	in hindsight [ɪn ˈhaɪndsaɪt]	rückblickend
	to **standardize** [ˈstændədaɪz]	normieren, standardisieren
	if I recall correctly [ɪf aɪ rɪˌkɔːl kəˈrektli]	wenn ich mich richtig erinnere
	to **rush** [rʌʃ]	eilen, hetzen
	to **reflect sth** [rɪˈflekt]	über etw nachdenken
	upset [ˌʌpˈset]	verärgert
	to **be proactive** [bi ˌprəʊˈæktɪv]	die Initiative ergreifen, von selbst aktiv werden
	to **gather** [ˈgæðə]	zusammentragen, sammeln
	to **cancel** [ˈkænsl]	(Termin) absagen
	sign-off [ˈsaɪn ɒf]	Abnahme, Abschluss
	wireframe [ˈwaɪəfreɪm]	Entwurf einer Webseite/ Software
	user acceptance [ˌjuːzər əkˈseptəns]	Nutzerakzeptanz
	Easter [ˈiːstə]	Ostern
	to **allow time for sth** [əˌlaʊ ˈtaɪm fə]	Zeit für etw vorsehen
88	**award** [əˈwɔːd]	Auszeichnung, Preis
	prize-giving ceremony [ˌpraɪz gɪvɪŋ ˈserəməni]	Preisverleihung
	receptionist [rɪˈsepʃənɪst]	Empfangsmitarbeiter/in
	to **check in** [ˌtʃek ˈɪn]	sich anmelden, einchecken
T	**reservation** [ˌrezəˈveɪʃn]	Reservierung
	to **serve** [sɜːv]	servieren
	buffet breakfast [ˈbʌfeɪ brekfəst]	Frühstücksbüfett
	dining room [ˈdaɪnɪŋ ruːm]	(Hotel:) Speisesaal
	wheelchair [ˈwiːltʃeə]	Rollstuhl
	access [ˈækses]	Zugang
	facilities pl [fəˈsɪlətiz]	Einrichtungen
	secure [sɪˈkjʊə]	sicher, bewacht
	gate [geɪt]	Tor, Einfahrt
	to **check out** [ˌtʃek ˈaʊt]	sich abmelden, auschecken
89	**Pleased to meet you.** [ˌpliːzd tə ˈmiːt ju]	Schön, Sie kennen zu lernen.
	to **get ready** [get ˈredi]	sich bereit machen, sich fertig machen
	Is this seat taken? [ɪz ðɪs ˌsiːt ˈteɪkən]	Ist hier besetzt?
	cultural awareness [ˌkʌltʃərəl əˈweənəs]	Kulturbewusstsein, kulturelle Sensibilität
	to **bow** [baʊ]	sich verbeugen
	to **shake hands with sb** [ˌʃeɪk ˈhændz wɪð]	jdm die Hand geben
	to **respect** [rɪˈspekt]	respektieren, achten
	aggressive [əˈgresɪv]	aggressiv

	dominant [ˈdɒmɪnənt]	dominant
	powerful [ˈpaʊəfl]	mächtig
	to **pray** [preɪ]	beten
	to **pin sth to sth** [pɪn]	etw an etw befestigen

KMK Exam practice 4

91 T	**wallet** [ˈwɒlɪt]	Brieftasche, (Herren-) Portemonnaie
	presently [ˈprezntli]	im Moment, gegenwärtig
	variety [vəˈraɪəti]	Vielzahl
	ranging from … to … [ˈreɪndʒɪŋ frəm tə]	von … bis …
	cryptocurrency [ˈkrɪptəʊˌkʌrnsi]	Kryptowährung
	depending on … [dɪˈpendɪŋ ɒn]	je nachdem, je nach
	fee [fiː]	Gebühr
	transfer [ˈtrænsfɜː]	Überweisung
	limitation [ˌlɪmɪˈteɪʃn]	Begrenzung
	savings pl [ˈseɪvɪŋz]	Ersparnisse
	lost property [lɒst prɒpəti]	verlorene Gegenstände
	pickpocket [ˈpɪkpɒkɪt]	Taschendieb/in
	burglar [ˈbɜːglə]	Einbrecher/in
	to **break sth** [breɪk]	etw kaputtmachen
	contents [ˈkɒntents]	Inhalt
	on a regular basis [ɒn ə ˌregjələ ˈbeɪsɪs]	regelmäßig
	to **encrypt** [ɪnˈkrɪpt]	verschlüsseln
	funds pl [fʌndz]	Geldmittel, Geld
	to **patent** [ˈpeɪtnt, ˈpætnt]	patentieren
	on the occasion of sth [ɒn ði əˈkeɪʒn əv]	aus Anlass von etw
	anniversary [ˌænɪˈvɜːsəri]	Jubiläum
	to **outline** [ˈaʊtlaɪn]	skizzieren, darstellen
	invention [ɪnˈvenʃn]	Erfindung
	mess [mes]	Chaos, Durcheinander
	tremendous [trɪˈmendəs]	enorm
	misuse [mɪsˈjuːs]	Missbrauch
	to **federate** [ˈfedəreɪt]	zu einem Bund zusammen-schließen
	federation [ˌfedəˈreɪʃn]	Bund
	to **be welcome to do sth** [bi ˈwelkəm tə duː]	etw gern tun können
	to **revise** [rɪˈvaɪz]	(Text) überarbeiten, redigieren
	ownership [ˈəʊnəʃɪp]	Besitz, Eigentum
	abuse [əˈbjuːs]	Missbrauch

UNIT 9

92	to **re-play sth** [ˌriːˈpleɪ]	etw (erneut) abspielen
	trial [ˈtraɪəl]	Test, Probe, Ausprobieren
	recording [rɪˈkɔːdɪŋ]	Aufzeichnung, Aufnahme
T	**Never mind.** [ˌnevə ˈmaɪnd]	Egal.
	to **supply** [səˈplaɪ]	liefern, zur Verfügung stellen
	expert [ˈekspɜːt]	Fachmann/-frau

93	operator	[ˈɒpəreɪtə]	Telefonist/in
	to feature	[ˈfiːtʃə]	(Merkmal) haben, aufweisen
94	to enable sb to do sth		jdn in die Lage versetzen,
		[ɪˈneɪbl tə duː]	etw zu tun
T	participant	[pɑːˈtɪsɪpənt]	Teilnehmer/in
	to collate	[kəˈleɪt]	(Dokumente) zusammen-
			tragen, abgleichen
	time-consuming		zeitraubend
		[ˈtaɪmkənsjuːmɪŋ]	
	horrible	[ˈhɒrəbl]	grässlich, scheußlich
	to elaborate	[ɪˈlæbəreɪt]	ins Detail geben,
			etw genauer ausführen
	to recreate sth	[ˌriːkriˈeɪt]	etw wiederherstellen
	obvious	[ˈɒbviəs]	klar, offensichtlich
	easily accessible		leicht zugänglich
		[ˌiːzəli əkˈsesəbl]	
95	collation	[kəˈleɪʃn]	Abgleich, Zusammenstellung
			(von Dokumenten)
	high usage	[ˌhaɪ ˈjuːsɪdʒ]	intensive Nutzung
	two-step verification		Überprüfung in zwei
		[tuː ˌstep verɪfɪˈkeɪʃn]	Schritten
	reversion	[rɪˈvɜːʃn]	Rückkehr
	unique selling proposition (USP)		Alleinstellungsmerkmal
		[juˌniːk ˈselɪŋ prɒpəzɪʃn]	
	immediate	[ɪˈmiːdiət]	sofortig, unverzüglich
P	shareable	[ˈʃeərəbl]	gemeinsam nutzbar
	generous	[ˈdʒenərəs]	großzügig
	to deny sb sth	[dɪˈnaɪ]	jdm etw verweigern
	usage rate	[ˈjuːsɪdʒ reɪt]	Nutzungsquote, Auslastung
96	contract	[ˈkɒntrækt]	Vertrag
	to negotiate	[nɪˈgəʊʃieɪt]	verhandeln
	negotiation	[nɪˌgəʊʃiˈeɪʃn]	Verhandlung
	legally binding		rechtsverbindlich
		[ˌliːgəli ˈbaɪndɪŋ]	
	to reach an agreement		sich einigen
		[riːtʃ ən əˈgriːmənt]	
	to review sth	[rɪˈvjuː]	etw überprüfen
	proposal	[prəˈpəʊzl]	Vorschlag
	to sign	[saɪn]	unterschreiben, unter-
			zeichnen
	terms and conditions pl		Allgemeine Geschäfts-
		[ˌtɜːmz ənd kənˈdɪʃnz]	bedingungen
	with a view to doing sth		mit dem Ziel, etw zu tun
		[wɪð ə ˈvjuː tə]	
	term	[tɜːm]	Laufzeit
	rather than	[ˈrɑːðə ðən]	anstatt
	storage capacity		Speicherkapazität
		[ˈstɔːrɪdʒ kəpæsəti]	
	assuming …	[əˈsjuːmɪŋ]	angenommen, …
	briefing	[ˈbriːfɪŋ]	Einweisung
	Please note that …		Wir weisen Sie darauf hin,
		[ˌpliːz ˈnəʊt ðət]	dass …
	to constitute sth		etw darstellen, etw sein
		[ˈkɒnstɪtjuːt]	
	obligation	[ˌɒblɪˈgeɪʃn]	Verpflichtung

	Kind regards		(Brief:) Mit freundlichen
		[kaɪnd rɪˈgɑːdz]	Grüßen
	procurement		Beschaffung
		[prəˈkjʊəmənt]	
97	to get down to business		zur Sache kommen
T		[get ˌdaʊn tə ˈbɪznəs]	
	to quote	[kwəʊt]	(Preis) nennen, anbieten
	discount	[ˈdɪskaʊnt]	Rabatt
	growth	[grəʊθ]	Wachstum
	annual licence		Jahreslizenz
		[ˌænjuəl ˈlaɪsns]	
	subscription	[səbˈskrɪpʃn]	Abonnement
	to accommodate changes		Änderungswünschen
		[əˌkɒmədeɪt ˈtʃeɪndʒɪz]	entgegenkommen
	to refuse	[rɪˈfjuːz]	ablehnen, verweigern
P	inclusion	[ɪnˈkluːʒn]	inbegriffene Leistung
	to raise a question		eine Frage vorbringen
		[ˌreɪz ə ˈkwestʃən]	
98	body	[ˈbɒdi]	(Brief:) Haupttext
	enclosure	[ɪnˈkləʊʒə]	(Brief:) Anlage
	inside address		Innenadresse
		[ˌɪnsaɪd əˈdres]	
	reference initials pl		(Brief:) Zeichen
		[ˈrefərəns ɪnɪʃlz]	
	signature	[ˈsɪgnətʃə]	Unterschrift
	to enclose	[ɪnˈkləʊz]	(Brief:) beifügen
	to pack	[pæk]	verpacken
	operating theatre		Operationssaal
		[ˈɒpəreɪtɪŋ θɪətə]	
	terms pl of delivery		Lieferbedingungen
		[ˌtɜːmz əv dɪˈlɪvəri]	
	to place an order		einen Auftrag erteilen, eine
		[ˌpleɪs ən ˈɔːdə]	Bestellung aufgeben
	wooden	[ˈwʊdn]	hölzern, aus Holz
	packing crate		Packkiste
		[ˈpækɪŋ kreɪt]	
99	trade magazine		Fachzeitschrift
		[ˈtreɪd mægəziːn]	
	outpatient clinic		Ambulanz
		[ˈaʊtpeɪʃnt klɪnɪk]	
	high-definition		hochauflösend
		[ˌhaɪ ˌdefɪˈnɪʃn]	
	trial order	[ˌtraɪəl ˈɔːdə]	Probebestellung
	housing	[ˈhaʊzɪŋ]	Gehäuse
	sealed	[siːld]	dicht, abgedichtet
	dustproof	[ˈdʌstpruːf]	staubdicht
	terms pl of payment		Zahlungsbedingungen
		[ˌtɜːmz əf ˈpeɪmənt]	
	packaging	[ˈpækɪdʒɪŋ]	Verpackung

UNIT 10

100	disabled	[dɪsˈeɪbld]	behindert
	the disabled	[ðə dɪsˈeɪbld]	Menschen mit
			Behinderung
	prosthetics pl		Prothesen
		[prɒsˈθetɪks]	

property [ˈprɒpəti]	Eigenschaft	
digitization [dɪdʒɪtaɪˈzeɪʃn]	Digitalisierung	
to enable sth [ɪˈneɪbl]	etw ermöglichen	
affordable [əˈfɔːdəbl]	erschwinglich	
reprint [ˌriːˈprɪnt]	Neudruck	
wearer [ˈweərə]	Träger/in	
to handle sth [ˈhændl]	etw aushalten	
force [fɔːs]	Kraft	
impact [ˈɪmpækt]	Aufprall, Wucht	
to twist [twɪst]	(sich) verdrehen	
to turn [tɜːn]	(sich) drehen	
durable [ˈdjʊərəbl]	strapazierfähig, dauerhaft, stark	
support [səˈpɔːt]	Halt	
silicone [ˈsɪlɪkəʊn]	Silikon	
aesthetics [esˈθetɪks]	Ästhetik	
confidence [ˈkɒnfɪdəns]	Selbstvertrauen, Selbstbewusstsein	
layer [ˈleɪə]	Schicht	
to cover sth [ˈkʌvə]	etw bedecken, etw überziehen	
skin [skɪn]	Haut	
complexion [kəmˈplekʃn]	Teint, Hautfarbe	
surface [ˈsɜːfɪs]	Oberfläche, Fläche	
to sign up to sth [ˌsaɪn ˈʌp tə]	sich bei etw anmelden	
agreed [əˈgriːd]	vereinbart	

101 prospective customer [prəˌspektɪv ˈkʌstəmə] — potenzielle/r Kunde/Kundin

P **in bulk** [ɪn ˈbʌlk] — en gros, in großen Mengen

protective [prəˈtektɪv]	Schutz-	
insured [ɪnˈʃʊəd]	versichert	
by registered post [baɪ ˌredʒɪstəd ˈpəʊst]	per Einschreiben	
receipt [rɪˈsiːt]	Beleg, Quittung	

102 smart [smɑːt] — intelligent

wristband [ˈrɪstbænd]	Armband	
induction course [ɪnˈdʌkʃn kɔːs]	Einarbeitung, Einführungskurs	
to direct [dəˈrekt]	leiten, lenken, führen	
to incorporate [ɪnˈkɔːpəreɪt]	integrieren	
state-of-the-art [ˌsteɪt əv ðɪ ˈɑːt]	modernste/r/s	
triangulation [traɪæŋjʊˈleɪʃn]	Dreiecksbildung, Triangulation	
to receive a signal [rɪˌsiːv ə ˈsɪgnəl]	ein Signal empfangen	
algorithm [ˈælgərɪðm]	Algorithmus	
to calculate sth [ˈkælkjuleɪt]	etw berechnen	
distance [ˈdɪstəns]	Entfernung, Strecke	
pace [peɪs]	Tempo	
optical [ˈɒptɪkl]	optisch	
to measure [ˈmeʒə]	messen	

light-sensitive [ˌlaɪt ˈsensɪtɪv]	lichtempfindlich	
to detect sth [dɪˈtekt]	etw ermitteln, etw feststellen	
to flow [fləʊ]	fließen	
wrist [rɪst]	Handgelenk	
to absorb [əbˈsɔːb]	schlucken, absorbieren	
heartbeat [ˈhɑːtbiːt]	Herzschlag	
accelerometer [əkˌseləˈrɒmɪtə]	Beschleunigungsmesser	
piezoelectric [paɪˌiːzəʊˈlektrɪk]	piezoelektrisch	
crystal [ˈkrɪstl]	Kristall	
to become stressed [bɪˌkʌm ˈstrest]	unter Druck geraten, belastet werden	
accelerative forces pl [əkˌselərətɪv ˈfɔːsɪz]	Beschleunigungskräfte	
stress [stres]	Druck, Belastung	
to interpret sth [ɪnˈtɜːprɪt]	etw deuten	
velocity [vɪˈlɒsɪti]	Geschwindigkeit	
orientation [ˌɔːriənˈteɪʃn]	Orientierung, Ausrichtung	
unlike sth [ˌʌnˈlaɪk]	im Gegensatz zu etw	
operator [ˈɒpəreɪtə]	Betreiber/in	
to embed [ɪmˈbed]	einbetten	

103 lens [lenz] — Linse

sapphire crystal [ˌsæfaɪə ˈkrɪstl]	Saphirglas	
strengthened glass [ˌstreŋθnd ˈglɑːs]	gehärtetes Glas	
stainless steel [ˌsteɪnləs ˈstiːl]	Edelstahl	
titanium [tɪˈteɪniəm]	Titan	
strap [stræp]	Armband	
splashproof [ˈsplæʃpruːf]	spritzwassergeschützt	
battery life [ˈbætəri laɪf]	Batterielaufzeit	
rating [ˈreɪtɪŋ]	Bewertung, Einstufung	
subjective [səbˈdʒektɪv]	subjektiv	
scratch resistance [ˈskrætʃ rɪzɪstəns]	Kratzfestigkeit	
fashionable [ˈfæʃnəbl]	in Mode, modisch	
practicality [ˌpræktɪˈkæləti]	Zweckmäßigkeit	
comprehensiveness [ˌkɒmprɪˈhensɪvnəs]	Ausstattungsumfang	
ease of reading information [ˌiːz əv ˌriːdɪŋ ɪnfəˈmeɪʃn]	leichte Ablesbarkeit der Werte	

104 to overhear sth [ˌəʊvəˈhɪə] — etw (zufällig) mithören

T | | | |
|---|---|---|
| occasional(ly) [əˈkeɪʒənəli] | gelegentlich | |
| notification [ˌnəʊtɪfɪˈkeɪʃn] | Benachrichtigung, Meldung | |
| altitude [ˈæltɪtjuːd] | Höhe (über NN) | |
| coast [kəʊst] | Küste | |
| handy [ˈhændi] | praktisch | |
| water resistance [ˈwɔːtə rɪzɪstəns] | Wasserdichtigkeit | |
| to intend to do sth [ɪnˈtend tə duː] | beabsichtigen, etw zu tun | |

casually ['kæʒuəli]	gelegentlich, nach Lust und Laune	
fashion-conscious ['fæʃn kɒnʃəs]	modebewusst	
writer ['raɪtə]	Autor/in, Schriftsteller/in	
to break [breɪk]	kaputtgehen	
to be on call [bi ɒn 'kɔːl]	erreichbar sein	
105 recurring [rɪ'kɜːrɪŋ]	wiederkehrend	
up front [ʌp 'frʌnt]	im Voraus	
household ['haʊshəʊld]	Haushalt	
initial [ɪ'nɪʃl]	erste/r/s, Anfangs-	
cancellation policy [ˌkænsə'leɪʃn pɒləsi]	(Vertrag:) Kündigungs- bedingungen	
to cancel ['kænsl]	kündigen	
to expire [ɪk'spaɪə]	(Vertrag) auslaufen	
106 order form ['ɔːdə fɔːm]	Bestellformular	
bundle ['bʌndl]	Paket	
107 commitment [kə'mɪtmənt]	Vertragsbindung	
108 reference ['refərəns]	Referenz	
calibration equipment [kalɪ'breɪʃn ɪkwɪpmənt]	Kalibriergerät	
quality control ['kwɒləti kəntrəʊl]	Qualitätskontrolle	
industrial estate [ɪnˌdʌstriəl ɪ'steɪt]	Gewerbegebiet	
to extend [ɪk'stend]	erweitern	
109 VAT (value added tax) [ˌvæljuː 'ædɪd tæks]	MwSt (Mehrwertsteuer)	
scheme [skiːm]	Schema	
working day ['wɜːkɪŋ deɪ]	Werktag	

KMK Exam practice 5

110 host [həʊst]	Moderator/in	
T science ['saɪəns]	(Natur-)Wissenschaft	
carpet ['kɑːpɪt]	Teppich	
astonishing [ə'stɒnɪʃɪŋ]	erstaunlich	
magic carpet [ˌmædʒɪk 'kɑːpɪt]	fliegender Teppich	
joking apart [ˌdʒəʊkɪŋ ə'pɑːt]	Scherz beiseite	
sex [seks]	Geschlecht	
to be willing to do sth [bi 'wɪlɪŋ tə]	bereit sein, etw zu tun	
to go on air [ˌgəʊ ɒn 'eə]	auf Sendung gehen	
to distinguish [dɪ'stɪŋgwɪʃ]	unterscheiden	
stride [straɪd]	Schritt	
to reveal sth [rɪ'viːl]	etw verraten, etw enthüllen	
centre of gravity [ˌsentər əv 'grævəti]	Schwerpunkt	
optical fibre [ˌɒptɪkl 'faɪbə]	Glasfaser	
to bend [bend]	sich biegen	
according to [ə'kɔːdɪŋ tə]	je nach, entsprechend	
footfall ['fʊtfɔːl]	Schritt(e)	
semiconductor [ˌsemikən'dʌktə]	Halbleiter	
to guide [gaɪd]	leiten, führen	

radio-frequency identification (RFID) [ˌreɪdiəʊ ˌfriːkwənsi aɪdentɪfɪ'keɪʃn]	Funkerkennung	
motionless ['məʊʃnləs]	regungslos	
footprint ['fʊtprɪnt]	Fußabdruck, Fußstapfen	
emergency service [ɪ'mɜːdʒənsi sɜːvɪs]	Notdienst	
scatter-brained ['skætə breɪnd]	zerstreut, schusselig	
gender ['dʒendə]	Geschlecht	

111 to explore [ɪk'splɔː]	erkunden, erforschen	
cadaver [kə'dɑːvə]	Leiche	
dead body [ded 'bɒdi]	Leichnam	
lungs pl [lʌnz]	Lunge	
texture ['tekstʃə]	(Gewebe-)Konsistenz	
allergy ['ælədʒi]	Allergie	
laboratory [lə'bɒrətri]	Labor	
mask [mɑːsk]	Maske	
scalpel ['skælpəl]	Skalpell	
storage ['stɔːrɪdʒ]	Lagerung	
imaging ['ɪmɪdʒɪŋ]	Bildgebung, Abbildung(en)	
to go beyond sth [ˌgəʊ bɪ'jɒnd]	über etw hinausgehen	
professional [prə'feʃnl]	professionell, Berufs-	
actor ['æktə]	Schauspieler/in	
diagnosis [ˌdaɪəg'nəʊsɪs]	Diagnose	
tap [tæp]	Tipp, Klick	
to strip sth [strɪp]	etw abstreifen	
to navigate ['nævɪgeɪt]	navigieren	
muscle ['mʌsl]	Muskel	
vein [veɪn]	Vene	
artery ['ɑːtəri]	Arterie	
skeleton ['skelɪtn]	Skelett	
to pump [pʌmp]	pumpen	
slice [slaɪs]	Schnitt	
air tap command ['eə tæp kəmɑːnd]	Befehl per Tipp in der Luft	
to interact [ˌɪntər'ækt]	kommunizieren, interagieren	
surgeon ['sɜːdʒən]	Chirurg/in	
surgical ['sɜːdʒɪkl]	chirurgisch	
technique [tek'niːk]	Methode, Technik	

UNIT 11

112 sustainability [səˌsteɪnə'bɪləti]	Nachhaltigkeit	
influence ['ɪnfluəns]	Auswirkung(en)	
non-harmful [ˌnɒn 'hɑːmfl]	unschädlich	
consumption [kən'sʌmpʃn]	Verbrauch	
non-renewable [ˌnɒn rɪ'njuːəbl]	nicht erneuerbar	
renewable [rɪ'njuːəbl]	erneuerbar	
to renew [rɪ'njuː]	sich erneuern	
waste [weɪst]	Müll, Abfall	
pollution [pə'luːʃn]	Verschmutzung	

disposal [dɪˈspəʊzl]	Entsorgung	
to dispose of sth [dɪˈspəʊz əv]	etw entsorgen	
to feed sb [fiːd]	jdn ernähren	
understanding [ˌʌndəˈstændɪŋ]	Verständnis	
hazard [ˈhæzəd]	Gefahr	
toxic [ˈtɒksɪk]	giftig	
to be addicted to sth [bi əˈdɪktɪd tə]	nach etw süchtig sein	
addiction [əˈdɪkʃn]	Sucht	
obesity [əʊˈbiːsəti]	Fettleibigkeit	
paperless [ˈpeɪpələs]	papierlos	
to disrupt [dɪsˈrʌpt]	stören, aus dem Gleichgewicht bringen	
habitat [ˈhæbɪtæt]	Lebensraum	
to destroy [dɪˈstrɔɪ]	zerstören	
to contaminate [kənˈtæmɪneɪt]	verunreinigen, kontaminieren	
climate change [ˈklaɪmət tʃeɪndʒ]	Klimawandel	
intelligence [ɪnˈtelɪdʒəns]	Intelligenz	
impact (on sth) [ˈɪmpækt]	Einfluss (auf etw)	

113 impact [ˈɪmpækt] — Auswirkung, Folge
to influence [ˈɪnfluəns] — beeinflussen
to multiply [ˈmʌltɪplaɪ] — (sich) vervielfachen, vervielfältigen
to push sth up [ˌpʊʃ ˈʌp] — etw in die Höhe treiben
emission [ɪˈmɪʃn] — Ausstoß, Emission
carbon footprint [ˌkɑːbən ˈfʊtprɪnt] — CO_2-Fußabdruck
CRT (cathode ray tube) [ˌsiː ɑː ˈtiː] — Kathodenstrahlröhre

T to look into sth [ˌlʊk ˈɪntə] — etw untersuchen, etw prüfen
greenhouse gas [ˌɡriːnhaʊs ˈɡæs] — Treibhausgas
commonly [ˈkɒmənli] — normalerweise, gewöhnlich
carbon dioxide [ˌkɑːbən daɪˈɒksaɪd] — Kohlendioxid
surprising [səˈpraɪzɪŋ] — erstaunlich
to emit sth [ɪˈmɪt] — etw ausstoßen
to file [faɪl] — (Dokument) ablegen
unique [juˈniːk] — einzigartig
to reflect sth [rɪˈflekt] — etw widerspiegeln
study [ˈstʌdi] — Untersuchung, Studie
shift [ʃɪft] — Verlagerung, Umschwung
to rent sth [rent] — etw leihen
to consume [kənˈsjuːm] — konsumieren
to specify sth [ˈspesɪfaɪ] — etw (genau) angeben
to ship sth [ʃɪp] — etw verschicken, etw versenden
to commit to sth [kəˈmɪt tə] — sich zu etw verpflichten

record [ˈrekɔːd] — Bilanz
to expand on sth [ɪkˈspænd ɒn] — ausführlich über etw sprechen

to cut down on sth [ˌkʌt ˈdaʊn ɒn] — Kosten für etw reduzieren
surroundings pl [səˈraʊndɪŋz] — Umgebung
to damage sth [ˈdæmɪdʒ] — etw schädigen, einer Sache schaden

114 in-house [ˌɪn ˈhaʊs] — betriebsintern
This is a fail. [ˌðɪs ɪz ə ˈfeɪl] — Das ist eine glatte Sechs.
conveniently [kənˈviːniəntli] — praktischerweise
sure enough [ˌʃʊər ɪˈnʌf] — selbstverständlich
entry [ˈentri] — Eintragung
to demand sth [dɪˈmɑːnd] — etw verlangen
refund [ˈriːfʌnd] — Erstattung
tone [təʊn] — Tonfall, Ton
to refund [rɪˈfʌnd] — (Kosten) erstatten
in full [ɪn ˈfʊl] — vollständig
to fail [feɪl] — versagen
asap (as soon as possible) [ˌeɪ es eɪ ˈpiː] — schnellstmöglich
to request sth [rɪˈkwest] — etw verlangen, etw wünschen
to appreciate sth [əˈpriːʃieɪt] — etw schätzen, etw zu schätzen wissen

115 impolite [ˌɪmpəˈlaɪt] — unhöflich
in the meantime [ɪn ðə ˈmiːntaɪm] — in der Zwischenzeit
upset [ˌʌpˈset] — Ärger, Aufregung
request [rɪˈkwest] — Bitte, Anfrage
to take sth seriously [teɪk ˈsɪəriəsli] — etw ernst nehmen
fraud investigation [ˈfrɔːd ɪnvestɪgeɪʃn] — Betrugsermittlung, Betrugsbekämpfung
to investigate sth [ɪnˈvestɪgeɪt] — etw untersuchen, in einer Sache ermitteln
to compromise sth [ˈkɒmprəmaɪz] — etw gefährden, etw (Daten) unberechtigt nutzen
to request [rɪˈkwest] — darum bitten
action [ˈækʃn] — Maßnahme
to resolve [rɪˈzɒlv] — (Problem) klären, lösen
to apologize [əˈpɒlədʒaɪz] — sich entschuldigen
patience [ˈpeɪʃns] — Geduld
to assure sb that … [əˈʃʊə] — jdm etw versichern/ zusichern
to regret sth [rɪˈgret] — etw bedauern
Please bear with us. [ˌpliːz ˈbeə wɪð ʌs] — Bitte geben Sie uns etwas Zeit. / Bitte haben Sie etwas Geduld.
to handle sth [ˈhændl] — mit etw umgehen

116 confusing [kənˈfjuːzɪŋ] — verwirrend
to expire [ɪkˈspaɪə] — (Gültigkeit) ablaufen
to advise sb of sth [ədˈvaɪz] — jdn über etw informieren
to disrupt [dɪsˈrʌpt] — stören, unterbrechen
default [dɪˈfɔːlt] — Standard-
billing details pl [ˈbɪlɪŋ diːteɪlz] — Rechnungsdaten

	to **cut sth off** [ˌkʌt ˈɒf]	etw abschalten, etw sperren	
	over the counter [ˌəʊvə ðə ˈkaʊntə]	am Schalter	
	frustrated [frʌˈstreɪtɪd]	frustriert	
117	**dispute** [dɪˈspjuːt]	Auseinandersetzung, Streit	
	invoice [ˈɪnvɔɪs]	Rechnung	
	consulting fee [kənˈsʌltɪŋ fiː]	Beratungshonorar	
	cabling [ˈkeɪblɪŋ]	Verkabelung	
	mount [maʊnt]	Halterung	
	charge [tʃɑːdʒ]	Gebühr, Kosten	
	subtotal [ˈsʌbtəʊtl]	Zwischensumme	
	deposit [dɪˈpɒzɪt]	Anzahlung	
	in advance [ɪn ədˈvɑːns]	im Voraus	
	prompt [prɒmpt]	umgehend, prompt	

118 T	**misunderstanding** [ˌmɪsʌndəˈstændɪŋ]	Missverständnis
	to **rectify** [ˈrektɪfaɪ]	korrigieren, *(Fehler)* beheben
	to **apply sth** [əˈplaɪ tə]	etw anwenden
	sincere(ly) [sɪnˈsɪə]	aufrichtig
	recollection [ˌrekəˈlekʃn]	Erinnerung
	to **discount sth** [dɪsˈkaʊnt]	etw vergünstigen, einen Rabatt auf etw geben
	to **break even** [breɪk ˈiːvn]	die Kosten wieder hereinholen, die Gewinnzone erreichen
	courier company [ˈkʊriə kʌmpəni]	Kurierdienstunternehmen
	to **waive sth** [weɪv]	auf etw verzichten
	typing error [ˈtaɪpɪŋ erə]	Tippfehler
	to **cut sth** [kʌt]	etw reduzieren
	to **settle sth** [ˈsetl]	etw regeln, etw erledigen
	to **revise sth** [rɪˈvaɪz]	etw überarbeiten, etw korrigieren

119	**disputed** [dɪˈspjuːtɪd]	umstritten
	boardroom [ˈbɔːdruːm]	Vorstandszimmer, Besprechungsraum
	desk-mounted [ˌdesk ˈmaʊntɪd]	zur Tischmontage, Tisch-
120	**X-ray machine** [ˈeks reɪ məʃiːn]	Röntgengerät

T	**dental clinic** [ˌdentl ˈklɪnɪk]	Zahnklinik
	scratched [skrætʃt]	verkratzt
	dented [ˈdentɪd]	verbeult
	casing [ˈkeɪsɪŋ]	Gehäuse
	to **get sth sorted** [ˌget ˈsɔːtɪd]	etw klären, sich um etw kümmern
	business [ˈbɪznəs]	Angelegenheit, Sache
	superior [suːˈpɪəriə]	Vorgesetzte/r

	spelling [ˈspelɪŋ]	Schreibweise
	consignment [kənˈsaɪnmənt]	Warensendung
	to **fulfil an order** [fʊlˌfɪl ən ˈɔːdə]	einen Auftrag abwickeln, eine Bestellung ausführen

121	**transcript** [ˈtrænskrɪpt]	Mitschrift
	record [ˈrekɔːd]	Datensatz
	I realize that. [aɪ ˈrɪəlaɪz ðæt]	Das ist mir bewusst.

UNIT 12

122	**(job) application** [ˌæplɪˈkeɪʃn]	Bewerbung
	to **apply for a job** [əˌplaɪ fər ə ˈdʒɒb]	sich um eine Stelle bewerben
	to **qualify** [ˈkwɒlɪfaɪ]	einen/den Abschluss machen
	job agency [ˈdʒɒb eɪdʒənsi]	Arbeitsagentur, Arbeitsvermittlung

T	to **gain** [geɪn]	erwerben
	wholesale [ˈhəʊlseɪl]	Großhandel
	varied [ˈveərɪd]	vielfältig
	to **capture** [ˈkæptʃə]	*(Daten)* erfassen
	to **back up** [ˌbæk ˈʌp]	*(Daten)* sichern
	to **corrupt** [kəˈrʌpt]	*(Daten)* beschädigen
	to **keep up with sth** [ˌkiːp ˈʌp wɪð]	mit etw Schritt halten
	hands on [ˌhændz ˈɒn]	praktisch, konkret
	individual [ˌɪndɪˈvɪdʒuəl]	(Einzel-)Person
	insurance [ɪnˈʃʊərəns]	Versicherung
	mixture [ˈmɪkstʃə]	Mischung
	vocational school [vəʊˌkeɪʃənl ˈskuːl]	Berufsschule
	to **diagnose** [ˈdaɪəgnəʊz]	diagnostizieren

123	**job opportunities** *pl* [dʒɒb ˌɒpəˈtjuːnətiz]	Arbeitsmöglichkeiten
	career prospects *pl* [kəˈrɪə prɒspekts]	berufliche Perspektiven
	job offer [ˈdʒɒb ɒfə]	Stellenangebot
	CV (curriculum vitae) [ˌsiː ˈviː, kəˌrɪkjələm ˈviːtaɪ]	Lebenslauf
	agent [ˈeɪdʒənt]	*hier:* zuständige/r Mitarbeiter/in
	potential [pəˈtenʃl]	möglich, potenziell
	self-assessment [ˌself əˈsesmənt]	Selbsteinstufung
	mobility [məʊˈbɪləti]	Freizügigkeit, Mobilität
	to **acquire** [əˈkwaɪə]	erlangen, erwerben
	supplement [ˈsʌplɪmənt]	Zusatz, Ergänzung
	holder [ˈhəʊldə]	Inhaber/in
124	**job advert(isement)** [ˈdʒɒb ædvɜːt, ədvɜːtɪsmənt]	Stellenanzeige
	to **be shortlisted** [bi ˈʃɔːtlɪstɪd]	in die engere Auswahl kommen
	recruiter [rɪˈkruːtə]	Anwerber/in, Personalbeschaffer/in
	recruitment agency [rɪˈkruːtmənt eɪdʒənsi]	Personalvermittlung
	salary [ˈsæləri]	Gehalt
	negotiable [nɪˈgəʊʃiəbl]	verhandelbar
	renewable [rɪˈnjuːəbl]	verlängerbar

	to **face** sth [feɪs]	mit etw konfrontiert sein	
	chronic ['krɒnɪk]	dauerhaft	
	shortage ['ʃɔːtɪdʒ]	Mangel	
	in high demand	sehr gefragt	
	[ɪn ˌhaɪ dɪ'mɑːnd]		
	commitment [kə'mɪtmənt]	Engagement	
	willingness ['wɪlɪŋnəs]	Bereitschaft	
	ability [ə'bɪləti]	Fähigkeit	
	drive [draɪv]	Tatendrang, Motivation	
	starting salary	Einstiegsgehalt	
	['stɑːtɪŋ sæləri]		
	to **conduct** sth [kən'dʌkt]	etw durchführen	
125	**vacancy** ['veɪkənsi]	offene Stelle	
	data capture	Datenerfassung	
	[ˌdeɪtə 'kæptʃə]		
	to **validate** ['vælɪdeɪt]	(Daten) überprüfen, validieren	
	permanent ['pɜːmənənt]	unbefristet	
	full-time [ˌfʊl 'taɪm]	Vollzeit-	
	paid holiday	bezahlter Urlaub	
	[ˌpeɪd 'hɒlədeɪ]		
	public holiday	gesetzlicher Feiertag	
	[ˌpʌblɪk 'hɒlədeɪ]		
	equivalent [ɪ'kwɪvələnt]	gleichwertig	

P
	duty ['djuːti]	Pflicht, Aufgabe	
	data entry [ˌdeɪtə entri]	Dateneingabe	
	user creation	Anlegen von neuen Benutzern	
	['juːzə krieɪʃn]		
	candidate ['kændɪdət]	Bewerber/in	
	attention to detail	Liebe zum Detail	
	[ə'tenʃn tə 'diːteɪl]		
	preliminary [prɪ'lɪmɪnəri]	vorläufig, Vor-	
	specialist ['speʃəlɪst]	Fach-, Spezial-	
	troubleshooting	Fehlersuche	
	['trʌblʃuːtɪŋ]		
	unsupervised	unbeaufsichtigt	
	[ʌn'suːpəvaɪzd]		
	problem solver	Problemlöser/in	
	['prɒbləm sɒlvə]		
	to **assume** [ə'sjuːm]	davon ausgehen	
	occasion [ə'keɪʒn]	Gelegenheit	
	to **arise** [ə'raɪz]	sich ergeben	

126	**(job) interview** ['ɪntəvjuː]	Vorstellungsgespräch	
	interviewer ['ɪntəvjuːə]	Person, die ein Vorstellungs-gespräch führt	
	to **irritate** ['ɪrɪteɪt]	stören, irritieren	
	to **flick through**	durchblättern	
	['flɪk θruː]		
	to **disconnect** [ˌdɪskə'nekt]	abschalten	
	landline ['lændlaɪn]	Festnetz(telefon)	
	to **get disconnected**	(Telefonverbindung:) unter-brochen werden	
	[get ˌdɪskə'nektɪd]		
	to **dress** [dres]	sich kleiden	
	strange [streɪndʒ]	seltsam, merkwürdig	
	bored [bɔːd]	gelangweilt	
	uninterested	uninteressiert	
	[ʌn'ɪntrəstɪd]		
	to **focus** ['fəʊkəs]	sich konzentrieren	

	to **hang on** [ˌhæŋ 'ɒn]	(Telefon:) warten	
	to **swallow** ['swɒləʊ]	schlucken	
	to **look the part**	entsprechend (rollengerecht) aussehen	
	[ˌlʊk ðə 'pɑːt]		

127 P
	to **indicate** ['ɪndɪkeɪt]	andeuten, darauf hinweisen	
	to **stress** [stres]	betonen	
	selection process	Auswahlverfahren	
	[sɪ'lekʃn prəʊses]		
	expression [ɪk'spreʃn]	Ausdruck	

T
	My pleasure. [maɪ 'pleʒə]	Ganz meinerseits. Gern geschehen.	
	in good time	rechtzeitig	
	[ɪn ˌgʊd 'taɪm]		
	to **calm down**	sich beruhigen	
	[ˌkɑːm 'daʊn]		
	Not particularly.	Eigentlich nicht	
	[ˌnɒt pə'tɪkjələli]		
	smart [smɑːt]	(Kleidung:) schick	
	confident(ly) ['kɒnfɪdənt]	selbstbewusst	
	shy [ʃaɪ]	schüchtern	
	habit ['hæbɪt]	Gewohnheit	
	to **get into the habit of doing** sth	sich daran gewöhnen, etw zu tun	
	[ˌget ɪntə ðə 'hæbɪt əv]		
	to **relate** sth **to** sth	etw auf etw beziehen	
	[rɪ'leɪt]		
	panel ['pænl]	Gremium	
	to **occur to** sb [ə'kɜː tə]	jdm einfallen	
	concerning sth	etw betreffend	
	[kən'sɜːnɪŋ]		

128	**mixed up** [ˌmɪkst 'ʌp]	durcheinander	
	set [set]	vorgegeben, starr, fest	
	to **grab** sb's **attention**	jds Aufmerksamkeit fesseln	
	[ˌgræb ə'tenʃn]		
	achievement [ə'tʃiːvmənt]	Leistung	
	brief [briːf]	kurz, knapp	
	academic [ˌækə'demɪk]	universitär	
	reverse order	umgekehrte Reihenfolge	
	[rɪˌvɜːs 'ɔːdə]		
	socializing ['səʊʃəlaɪzɪŋ]	Ausgehen	
	data protection	Datenschutz	
	['deɪtə prətekʃn]		
	referee [ˌrefə'riː]	Referenz(geber)	
129	to **widen** ['waɪdn]	erweitern	
	interpersonal	zwischenmenschlich	
	[ˌɪntə'pɜːsənl]		
	economy [ɪ'kɒnəmi]	Wirtschaft	
	equal to ['iːkwəl tə]	gleichwertig mit	
	GNVQ (General National Vocational Qualifica-tion) [ˌdʒiː en viː 'kjuː]	brit. Berufsschulabschluss	
	on request [ɒn rɪ'kwest]	auf Anfrage	
130	**electrical engineering**	Elektrotechnik	
	[ɪˌlektrɪkl ˌendʒɪ'nɪərɪŋ]		
131	**Attn.** [ə'tenʃn]	(Brief:) z. Hdn.	
	post [pəʊst]	Stelle	
	particularly [pə'tɪkjələli]	insbesondere	

to **be keen to do sth** [bi ˈkiːn]	jdm liegt sehr daran, etw zu tun
on a daily basis [ɒn ə ˌdeɪli ˈbeɪsɪs]	jeden Tag, täglich
fluent [ˈfluːənt]	*(Sprache:)* fließend
at short notice [ət ˌʃɔːt ˈnəʊtɪs]	kurzfristig

KMK Exam practice 6

132	**vacuum cleaner** [ˈvækjuəm kliːnə]	Staubsauger
	clever [ˈklevə]	klug, intelligent, schlau
	to **weigh** [weɪ]	wiegen
	recharge [ˌriːˈtʃɑːdʒ]	Wiederaufladen
	to **carry on doing sth** [ˌkæri ˈɒn]	mit etw weitermachen
	to **glide** [glaɪd]	gleiten
	edge [edʒ]	Rand, Kante
	stomach [ˈstʌmək]	Bauch
	remote control [rɪˌməʊt kənˈtrəʊl]	Fernbedienung
	to **adapt to sth** [əˈdæpt tə]	sich an etw anpassen
	artificial [ˌɑːtɪˈfɪʃl]	künstlich
	to **recognize** [ˈrekəgnaɪz]	erkennen
	accordingly [əˈkɔːdɪŋli]	entsprechend (rollengerecht) aussehen
	to **mop** [mɒp]	feudeln, wischen
	tile [taɪl]	Fliese
	dust free [ˈdʌst friː]	staubfrei
	to **disinfect** [ˌdɪsɪnˈfekt]	desinfizieren
	bacteria *pl* [bækˈtɪəriə]	Bakterien
	ultrasound [ˈʌltrəsaʊnd]	Ultraschall
	to **manoeuvre** [məˈnuːvə]	manövrieren
	to **equip sth with sth** [ɪˈkwɪp]	etw mit etw ausstatten
	bumper [ˈbʌmpə]	Stoßfänger, Puffer
	antique [ænˈtiːk]	antik
	chest of drawers [ˌtʃest əv ˈdrɔːz]	Kommode
	to **screen sth off** [ˌskriːn ˈɒf]	etw abteilen
	featuring sth [ˈfiːtʃərɪŋ]	mit etw
	homemaker [ˈhəʊmmeɪkə]	Hausfrau/-mann

133	**racing boat** [ˈreɪsɪŋ bəʊt]	Rennboot
T	**skipper** [ˈskɪpə]	Kapitän/in
	competitor [kəmˈpetɪtə]	Teilnehmer/in (an einem Wettbewerb)
	speedboat [ˈspiːdbəʊt]	Schnellboot

The thing is, … [ðə ˈθɪŋ ɪz]	Es geht darum, dass …
by the way [baɪ ðə ˈweɪ]	übrigens
spearhead [ˈspɪəhed]	Speerspitze
lightning [ˈlaɪtnɪŋ]	Blitz
radio control [ˌreɪdiəʊ kənˈtrəʊl]	Funksteuerung
To cut a long story short, … [tə kʌt ə lɒŋ ˌstɔːri ˈʃɔːt]	Lange Rede, kurzer Sinn: …
radio link [ˈreɪdiəʊ lɪŋk]	Funkverbindung
transmitter [trænsˈmɪtə]	Sender
receiver [rɪˈsiːvə]	Empfänger
shark [ʃɑːk]	Hai
antenna [ænˈtenə]	Antenne
flash [flæʃ]	Blitz
competitive racing [kəmˌpetətɪv ˈreɪsɪŋ]	Wettrennen
acceleration [əkˌseləˈreɪʃn]	Beschleunigung
to **come up with sth** [ˌkʌm ˈʌp wɪð]	sich etw einfallen lassen, sich etw ausdenken
It's a deal. [ˌɪts ə ˈdiːl]	Abgemacht!

cyclist [ˈsaɪklɪst]	Radfahrer/in
athlete [ˈæθliːt]	Sportler/in
tiny [ˈtaɪni]	klein, winzig
remote area [rɪˌməʊt ˈeɪriə]	entlegene Gegend
billion [ˈbɪliən]	Milliarde
trillion [ˈtrɪljən]	Billion
to **cover** [ˈkʌvə]	*(Entfernung)* zurücklegen
Department of Defense *AE* [dɪˌpɑːtmənt əv dɪˈfens]	Verteidigungsministerium
soldier [ˈsəʊldʒə]	Soldat/in
to **distribute** [dɪˈstrɪbjuːt]	verteilen
military personnel [ˌmɪlətri pɜːsəˈnel]	Soldaten, Militärangehörige
to **browse** [braʊz]	durchblättern, stöbern
to **inhabit** [ɪnˈhæbɪt]	bewohnen
civilian [səˈvɪliən]	Zivilist/in
to **trace** [treɪs]	nachzeichnen, verfolgen
forces *pl* [ˈfɔːsɪz]	Streitkräfte
to **go out on patrol** [ɡəʊ ˌaʊt ɒn pəˈtrəʊl]	auf Patrouille gehen
to **patrol** [pəˈtrəʊl]	patrouillieren
alike [əˈlaɪk]	gleichermaßen

Dieses Wörterverzeichnis enthält alle neuen Wörter aus *IT Matters – 3rd Edition* in alphabetischer Reihenfolge. Nicht angeführt sind Wörter, die zum Grundwortschatz (*Basic word list,* in den Handreichungen für den Unterricht) gehören. Die Zahl nach dem Stichwort bezieht sich auf die Seite, auf der das Wort zum ersten Mal erscheint. Wörter aus den Hörverständnisübungen sind zusätzlich mit einem **T** (Transkript) und Wörter aus den *Partner files* mit einem **P** gekennzeichnet.

A

ability *124* Fähigkeit

abroad, from ~ *6* aus dem Ausland

to **absorb** *102* schlucken, absorbieren

abuse *91* Missbrauch

academic *128* universitär

acceleration *133T* Beschleunigung

accelerative forces *pl 102* Beschleunigungskräfte

accelerometer *102* Beschleunigungsmesser

acceptable *38* zulässig, akzeptabel; **~ use** *50* zulässige Nutzung

acceptance, user ~ *87* Nutzerakzeptanz

to **access sth** *15T* auf etw zugreifen

access *88T* Zugang; **~ (to sth)** *15T* Zugriff (auf etw); to **request ~** *53* Zugang anfordern; **~ level** *50T* Berechtigungsstufe, Zugriffsstufe; **~ point** *72T* Anschlusspunkt, Zugang; **~ privileges** *pl 50* Zugriffsrechte; **~ rights** *pl 71T* Zugriffsrechte

accessible *53* zugänglich; **easily ~** *94T* leicht zugänglich

to **accommodate changes** *97* Änderungswünschen entgegenkommen

to **accompany sb** *83* jdn begleiten

according to *7* gemäß, entsprechend, zufolge; *110T* je nach

accordingly *132* entsprechend (rollengerecht) aussehen

to **account for sth** *57* (*Anteil:*) etw ausmachen

account: to **take sth into ~** *72T* etw berücksichtigen; **~ manager** *31* Kundenbetreuer/in; **~ records** *pl 48T* Kontodaten, Kundendaten

accurate(ly) *31* genau

to **achieve** *42* (*Ziel*) erreichen

achievement *128* Leistung

to **acknowledge sth** *20* etw anerkennen; *63T* etw bestätigen; *77* etw würdigen, etw zur Kenntnis nehmen

to **acquire** *123* erlangen, erwerben

action *115* Maßnahme; to **take ~** *68T* Maßnahmen ergreifen

actor *111* Schauspieler/in

to **adapt to sth** *132* sich an etw anpassen

adaptable *69* anpassungsfähig

adapter, power ~ *28* Netzteil

addicted, to **be ~ to sth** *112* nach etw süchtig sein

addiction *112* Sucht

addition, in ~ *16T* außerdem

address, inside ~ *98* Innenadresse

to **address sb** *49* jdn anreden, jdn ansprechen

adjacent *71* angrenzend, benachbart

to **adjust** *20* anpassen, regeln

administration *63T* Verwaltung

administrative level *38* Administratorenebene

administrator *42* Administrator/in, Systemverwalter/in; **IT ~** *6* IT-Kaufmann/-frau

to **adopt sth** *78* etw einführen, etw anwenden

adoption *83* Annahme, (Produkt-)Verwendung, Akzeptanz

advance, in ~ *117* im Voraus

advert(isement), job ~ *124* Stellenanzeige

advisable *32T* ratsam, empfehlenswert

to **advise: ~ sb of sth** *116* jdn über etw informieren; **~ sb on sth** *41* jdn in einer Sache beraten

aesthetics *100* Ästhetik

to **affect sb/sth** *17* sich auf jdn/etw auswirken

affordable *100* erschwinglich

after all *72T* schließlich, immerhin

agency, job ~ *122* Arbeitsagentur, Arbeitsvermittlung; **recruitment ~** *124* Personalvermittlung

agenda *19* Tagesordnung

agent *123* *hier:* zuständige/r Mitarbeiter/in; **call centre ~** *58* Callcenteragent/in, Telefonberater/in

aggressive *89* aggressiv

agile *69* agil, beweglich

agreed *100* vereinbart; **A~.** *80T* Stimmt.

agreement *43* Vereinbarung, Übereinkunft; *77* Zustimmung; to **reach an ~** *96* sich einigen

air, to **go on ~** *110T* auf Sendung gehen; **~ tap command** *111* Befehl per Tipp in der Luft

algorithm *102* Algorithmus

to **align sth with sth** *28* etw auf etw ausrichten

alignment *61* Ausrichtung

alike *133* gleichermaßen

allergy *111* Allergie

to **allow time for sth** *87* Zeit für etw vorsehen

along, as we go ~ *20* im Lauf von etw, nach und nach

altimeter *46T* Höhenmesser

altitude *104T* Höhe (*über NN*)

amazing *77T* irre, fantastisch

amber *71* (*Ampelfarbe:*) gelb

to **analyse** *11* analysieren

analysis, system ~ *10T* Systemanalyse

anatomy *82T* Anatomie

and so on *15T* und so weiter

angle *47* Winkel

anniversary *91* Jubiläum

to **announce** *34* ankündigen

annoying *80T* nervig

annual: ~ leave *16T* Jahresurlaub; **~ licence** *97T* Jahreslizenz

anonymous *63T* anonym

antenna *133T* Antenne

antique *132* antik

to **apologize** *115* sich entschuldigen

to **appear** *31* erscheinen; *34* vorkommen, auftauchen; *49* scheinen, den Eindruck erwecken

appearance *81* Erscheinungsbild, Auftreten

applicant *17* Bewerber/in

application *29* Anwendung, Programm; *34* Antrag, Bewerbung

to **apply: ~ sth** *118T* etw anwenden; **~ for a job** *122* sich um eine Stelle bewerben

appointment *67* Termin

to **appreciate sth** *43* für etw dankbar sein; *79T* für etw Verständnis haben; *114* etw schätzen, etw zu schätzen wissen

apprentice *6* Auszubildende/r, Lehrling

apprenticeship *6* Lehre, Ausbildung

approach *69* Ansatz, Vorgehen

appropriate *32T* passend, geeignet

approval *73* Genehmigung, Freigabe

to **approve sth** *50T* etw genehmigen, etw zulassen, etw freigeben

approximate(ly) *57* ungefähr, zirka

architecture, system ~ *10T* Systemarchitektur

to **argue the case for sth** *76* für etw plädieren, für etw eintreten to **arise** *125P* sich ergeben

arrangement *66* (Termin-)Vereinbarung, Vorbereitung

artery *111* Arterie

artificial *132* künstlich; **~ intelligence** *58* künstliche Intelligenz

artist *47* Künstler/in, Grafiker/in

asap (as soon as possible) *114* schnellstmöglich

ascending *62T* aufsteigend

aspect *16* Gesichtspunkt, Aspekt

to **assess** *31* beurteilen, einschätzen

assessment *32* Einschätzung, Bewertung; **self-~** *123* Selbsteinstufung

to **assist sb with sth** *58T* jdm bei etw helfen

assistance *34* Hilfe, Unterstützung; **to be of ~** *58T* helfen

associated with sth *71* mit etw verbunden

to **assume** *125P* davon ausgehen

assuming ... *96* angenommen, ...

assurance, quality ~ *8* Qualitätssicherung

to **assure sb that ...** *115* jdm etw versichern/zusichern

astonishing *110T* erstaunlich

at all, not ... ~ *19* überhaupt nicht

athlete *133* Sportler/in

to **attach** *15T* (E-Mail:) anhängen; **~ to sth** *29* sich mit etw verbinden lassen; **~ sth to sth** *30* etw mit etw verbinden

attached, with a room ~ *67* mit einem Nebenraum

attachment *15* (E-Mail:) Anhang

attack *48* Angriff

attacker *68T* Angreifer/in

attempt *54* Versuch

to **attempt sth** *40* etw versuchen

attention, to grab sb's ~ *128* jds Aufmerksamkeit fesseln; **to pay ~ to sth** *48T* etw beachten; **~ to detail** *125P* Liebe zum Detail

Attn. *131* (Brief:) z. Hdn.

auction *48T* Versteigerung, Auktion

audience *7* Publikum

audio quality *27T* Tonqualität

auditing *48* Wirtschaftsprüfung, Revision; **corporate ~** *50T* interne Revision

to **augment** *83* erweitern

augmented *28* erweitert

to **authenticate** *53* authentifizieren

authentication *48T* Authentifizierung; **two-factor ~** *53* Zwei-Faktoren-Authentifizierung

author *20* Verfasser/in

authorization *64* Genehmigung, Autorisierung

to **authorize** *64* genehmigen, zulassen, autorisieren

automated *39* automatisch

automation *6* Automatisierung, Automation

automotive *7T* Automobil-

available *23* lieferbar, verfügbar

to **avoid sth** *13* etw vermeiden; *48* einer Sache aus dem Weg gehen

award *88* Auszeichnung, Preis

aware, to be ~ of sth *56T* sich über etw im Klaren sein, auf etw achten

awareness, cultural ~ *89* Kulturbewusstsein, kulturelle Sensibilität

B

backdoor *48T* Hintertür

background *39* Hintergrund

backlog *71* Arbeitsrückstand, Arbeitsüberhang

to **back up** *122T* (Daten) sichern

backup *27T* Reserve, Ausweich-

bacteria *pl 132* Bakterien

balance *16T* Gleichgewicht

bandwidth *48T* Bandbreite

bar *61* Balken; **menu ~** *36* Menüleiste; **~ chart** *85* Säulendiagramm

barrier *25* Hindernis, Barriere

base station *30* Basisstation

based, to be ~ in ... *13* seinen Sitz in ... haben, in ... sein; **~ on** *32T* anhand von, auf Grundlage von

baseline *62* Basis

basis, on a daily ~ *131* jeden Tag, täglich; **on a regular ~** *91T* regelmäßig

battery *29* Akku, Batterie; **~ life** *33* Akkulaufzeit; *103* Batterielaufzeit; **~ powered** *29* batteriebetrieben, mit Akkus betrieben

to **bear: ~ sth in mind** *72T* etw berücksichtigen, an etw denken; **Please ~ with us.** *115* Bitte geben Sie uns etwas Zeit. / Bitte haben Sie etwas Geduld.

begin, to ~ with *45* zunächst

behalf, on ~ of sb *22* für jdn, in jds Namen

behaviour *59* Verhalten

believer, to be big ~s in sth *16T* fest von etw überzeugt sein

to **bend** *110T* sich biegen

to **benefit** *76* (davon) profitieren; **~ sb** *83* jdm nützen

benefit *10T* Nutzen, Vorteil(e); **~s** *pl 9* Zusatzleistungen, Sozialleistungen

Best regards *35* (Brief:) Viele Grüße, Mit freundlichen Grüßen

to **beware of sth** *48T* sich vor etw in Acht nehmen

billing *11* Abrechnung, Rechnungsstellung; **~ details** *pl 116* Rechnungsdaten

billion *133* Milliarde

binding, legally ~ *96* rechtsverbindlich

birth, place of ~ *12* Geburtsort

blood pressure *46T* Blutdruck

board *6* Aufsichtsrat; **~room** *119* Vorstandszimmer, Besprechungsraum

body *98* (Brief:) Hauptext; **dead ~** *111* Leichnam

bold, in ~ *78* (Schrift:) fett

bond (to sb/sth) *68T* Bindung (zu jdm/etw)

booth *82T* (Messe-)Stand

bored *126* gelangweilt

bottom case *28* Gehäuseunterteil

to **bow** *89* sich verbeugen

brain *27* Hirn, Gehirn

to **brainstorm** *15* Ideen sammeln

brand *59* Marke; **trusted ~** *83* vertrauenswürdige Marke

branding *31* Markenführung, Markenbildung

to **break** *104* kaputtgehen; **~ sth** *91T* etw kaputtmachen; **~ even** *118T* die Kosten wieder hereinholen, die Gewinnzone erreichen

breakdown *57* Aufstellung, Aufschlüsselung

breakthrough *69* Durchbruch, bahnbrechend

brief *128* kurz, knapp

briefing *96* Einweisung

to **bring up sth** *15T* etw zur Sprache bringen

brochure *34* Broschüre, Prospekt

to **browse** *133* durchblättern, stöbern

buffet breakfast *88T* Frühstücksbüfett

bug *86* Fehler, Bug

building *7* Bauwesen

built-in *46T* eingebaut

bulb, light ~ *59* Glühbirne

bulk, in ~ *101P* en gros, in großen Mengen; **~ discount** *73* Mengenrabatt

bumper *132* Stoßfänger, Puffer

bundle *106* Paket

burglar *91T* Einbrecher/in

business *120T* Angelegenheit, Sache; **to do ~ with sb** *35* mit jdm Geschäfte machen; **to get down to ~** *97T* zur Sache kommen; **~ partner** *35* Geschäftspartner/in

business-grade *72T* professionell, Industrie-

button *27* Taste, Knopf, Schalter; *36* Schaltfläche, Button; **radio ~** *41* Optionsschaltfläche

to **bypass sth** *48T* etw umgehen

comprehensiveness *103* Ausstattungs-umfang

to **compromise sth** *115* etw gefährden, etw *(Daten)* unberechtigt nutzen

computation, heavy ~ *77T* hohes Rechenaufkommen

computerized *12* Computer-

computing power *76* Rechenleistung

to **concentrate on sth** *19* sich auf etw konzentrieren

concern *19* Bedenken, Sorge; **a valid ~** *77T* eine berechtigte Sorge

concerning sth *127T* etw betreffend

conclude, to ~ *45* abschließend

conclusion *44* Schluss

condition *16* Bedingung; **terms and ~s pl** *96* Allgemeine Geschäfts-bedingungen

to **conduct sth** *124* etw durchführen

confidence *100* Selbstvertrauen, Selbstbewusstsein; **~ (in sb/sth)** *61* Zutrauen, Vertrauen (in jdn/etw)

confident *127T* selbstbewusst; **to be ~ of being able to handle sth** *83* sicher im Umgang mit etw sein

confidential *50T* vertraulich

configuration *31* Konfiguration

to **configure** *41* konfigurieren

to **confirm** *22* bestätigen

confirmation *38* Bestätigung

confusing *116* verwirrend

confusion *42T* Verwirrung

to **connect (to/with sth)** *22* (mit etw) verbinden, (an etw) anschließen

connected *38* (mit etw) zusammen-hängend, (mit etw) verbunden

connection *6* Verbindung, Anschluss

connectivity *27* Anschlüsse; **~ interruption** *39* Unterbrechung der Netzwerkverbindung

connector *6* Verbinder, Stecker

conscious, fashion-~ *104* modebewusst

consequence *42* Folge

to **consider sth** *15T* etw in Betracht ziehen, über etw nachdenken; *42T* etw berücksichtigen

consideration *72* Überlegung; **to take sth into ~** *72* etw in Betracht ziehen, etw berücksichtigen

considered, all things ~ *32T* insgesamt, alles in allem, unterm Strich; **to be ~ sth** *50T* als etw gelten

consignment *120* Warensendung

consistency *71* Einheitlichkeit

consistent *71T* einheitlich

constant *56* ständig, fortwährend

to **constitute sth** *96* etw darstellen, etw sein

construction *7* Bau

consultancy, tax ~ *48* Steuerberatung

consultant, management ~ *85* Unter-nehmensberater/in

consulting fee *117* Beratungshonorar

to **consume** *113T* konsumieren

consumption *112* Verbrauch

contact details pl *23P* Kontaktdaten

to **contaminate** *112* verunreinigen, kontaminieren

contents *91T* Inhalt

continually *48T* kontinuierlich

to **continue** *9T* weitermachen, fortfahren

contract *96* Vertrag

to **contravene sth** *51* gegen etw verstoßen

to **contribute to sth** *77T* zu etw beitragen

control, quality ~ *108* Qualitäts-kontrolle; **radio ~** *133T* Funk-steuerung; **remote ~** *132* Fern-bedienung; **version ~** *70* Versionsverwaltung, -kontrolle

controversial *51* umstritten

convenient *27T* praktisch, bequem

conveniently *114* praktischerweise

conversation *19* Gespräch; **to engage in ~** *58T* sich unterhalten

to **convert** *75* umwandeln

to **cool** *28* abkühlen

copy *58T* Exemplar

to **copy in sb** *15T* jdn auf CC in den Verteiler setzen

copyright laws pl *51* Urheberrechts-gesetze

corporate *50T* Unternehmens-; **~ auditing** *50T* interne Revision

corporation *25* Unternehmen, Gesell-schaft, Konzern

correction, quick course ~ *69* schnelle Korrektur

correctness *44* Richtigkeit

corridor *9T* Flur, Gang

to **corrupt** *122T* *(Daten)* beschädigen

corrupted data pl *74* beschädigte/fehlerhafte Daten

cost, overall ~ *85* Gesamtkosten; **~s pl incurred** *57* entstandene Kosten

counter, over the ~ *116* am Schalter

counterargument *76* Gegenargument

counterpart *86* Gegenüber, Ansprech-partner/in

countless *83* unzählig, zahllos

courage *47* Mut

courier company *118T* Kurierdienst-unternehmen

to **cover** *7* *(Thema)* behandeln; *133* *(Entfernung)* zurücklegen; **~ sth** *72T* etw abdecken; *100* etw bedecken, etw überziehen

coverage *73* Abdeckung; **mobile cellular ~** *52* Mobilfunkempfang

covering letter *34* Anschreiben, Begleit-schreiben

to **crack sth** *54* etw knacken

crate, packing ~ *98* Packkiste

to **create** *9* *(Software)* erstellen, *(Produkt)* gestalten

creation, user ~ *125P* Anlegen von neuen Benutzern

creative *17* kreativ

creativity *69* Kreativität

credible *49* glaubwürdig

credit *58T* Guthaben

crime, cyber~ *48* Cyber-Kriminalität

criminal *49* Kriminelle/r, Verbrecher/in

criterion, criteria *60* Kriterium, Kriterien; **sub-criteria pl** *62* Unter-kriterien

critical *19* wichtig, unentbehrlich, wesentlich, kritisch

CRT (cathode ray tube) *113* Kathoden-strahlröhre

crucial *73* entscheidend, unerlässlich

cryptocurrency *91T* Kryptowährung

crystal *102* Kristall; **sapphire ~** *103* Saphirglas

cultural awareness *89* Kulturbewusst-sein, kulturelle Sensibilität

custom report *62T* benutzerdefinierter Bericht

customer, existing ~ *58* Bestandskunde/-kundin; **prospective ~** *101* potenzielle/r Kunde/Kundin; **~ service** *8* Kundendienst; **~ representative** *59* Kundenbetreuer/in; **~ support** *31* Kundenbetreuung, Kundendienst

customization *60* (individuelle) Anpas-sung

to **customize** *32* anpassen, individuell/kundengerecht anfertigen

to **cut: ~ sth** *118T* etw reduzieren; **~ down on sth** *113* Kosten für etw reduzieren; **~ sth off** *116* etw abschal-ten, etw sperren; **To ~ a long story short, …** *133T* Lange Rede, kurzer Sinn: …

cutting edge *54* hochmodern, auf dem neuesten Stand der Technik

CV (curriculum vitae) *123* Lebenslauf

cybercrime *48* Cyber-Kriminalität

cyclist *133* Radfahrer/in

D

daily *10T* täglich, Alltags-; **on a ~ basis** *131* jeden Tag, täglich

to **damage sth** *113* etw schädigen, einer Sache schaden

data pl: corrupted ~ *74* beschädigte/fehlerhafte Daten; **test ~** *17* Prüf-daten; **raw ~ pl** *63* Rohdaten; **sheet**

of ~ *60* Datenblatt; **capture** *125* Datenerfassung; ~ **entry** *125P* Dateneingabe; ~ **extraction** *63T* Datenextraktion; ~ **line** *62* Datenzeile; ~ **processing** *6* Datenverarbeitung; ~ **protection** *128* Datenschutz; ~ **range** *61* Datenbereich

database *22* Datenbank

date, due ~ *85* Fälligkeitstermin; **out of ~** *54* veraltet, überholt; **up to ~** *54* auf dem neuesten Stand

day, the other ~ *68T* neulich; **time of ~** *58T* Tageszeit; **working ~** *109* Werktag

day-to-day functioning *51* täglicher Betriebsablauf

dead body *111* Leichnam

deadline *69* Frist, Fertigstellungstermin

to deal: ~ with sth *10T* sich um etw kümmern; *45* mit etw umgehen, sich mit etw befassen; **~ with sb** *58* mit jdm zu tun haben, mit jdm umgehen, sich mit jdm auseinandersetzen

deal, It's a ~. *133T* Abgemacht!

dealer *7T* Händler/in

to debug *9* Fehler beseitigen, debuggen

decision, purchase ~ *58T* Kaufentscheidung

to decline *56T* abnehmen, zurückgehen

to decrease *56T* abnehmen, sinken; **~ sth** *72T* etw senken

dedicated, to be ~ to sth *83* sich einer Sache verschreiben, sich für etw einsetzen

defamation *51* Verleumdung

default *41* Standard(einstellung); *116* Standard-; **by ~** *63T* standardmäßig

defect *17* Mangel, Fehler

defense *AE*, **Department of D~** *133* Verteidigungsministerium

definition, high-~ *99* hochauflösend

degree *29* Grad

delay *41* Verschiebung

to delay sth *39* etw verschieben

to delete *37* löschen

delivery, terms *pl* **of ~** *98* Lieferbedingungen; **~ time** *59* Lieferzeit

demand, in high ~ *124* sehr gefragt

to demand sth *114* etw verlangen

to demonstrate *61* darstellen, anzeigen; **~ sth** *51* etw nachweisen; *82T* etw vorführen

demonstration *84* Vorführung

dental clinic *120T* Zahnklinik

dented *120T* verbeult

to deny sb sth *95P* jdm etw verweigern

department, legal ~ *8* Rechtsabteilung; **D~ of Defense** *AE* *133* Verteidigungsministerium

dependent (on sb/sth) *39* abhängig (von jdm/etw)

depending on … *91T* je nachdem, je nach

to deploy *39* bereitstellen

deployment, patch-~ *39* Patch-Bereitstellung

deposit *117* Anzahlung

descending *62T* absteigend

description, job ~ *12* Stellenbeschreibung

design, network ~ *72* Netzwerkkonzeption, -auslegung, -design; **~ feature** *63T* Konstruktionsmerkmal

designed, to be ~ for sth *72T* für etw ausgelegt sein

to desire sth *25* etw wünschen

desk-mounted *119* zur Tischmontage, Tisch-

destination *37* (Reise-, Fahrt-)Ziel, Zielort

to destroy *112* zerstören

detail, attention to ~ *125P* Liebe zum Detail

detailed *17* ausführlich, genau

to detect *48T* aufspüren, entdecken; **~ sth** *102* etw ermitteln, etw feststellen

to determine *53* bestimmen; *72T* festlegen

to develop *6* entwickeln

developer *11* Entwickler/in

development *8* Entwicklung

device *6* Gerät, Apparat; **input ~** *27* Eingabegerät

to diagnose *122T* diagnostizieren

diagnosis *111* Diagnose

to dictate *34* diktieren

difference, to make a ~ *27* sich unterscheiden

digit *23* Ziffer

digitization *100* Digitalisierung

to dim *59* dimmen

dining room *88T* *(Hotel:)* Speisesaal

dip, to take a ~ *46T* schwimmen

to direct *102* leiten, lenken, führen

direction *37* Richtung; **in an outward ~** *28* nach außen; **~s** *pl* *9* Wegbeschreibung; **to give ~s** *9* den Weg beschreiben

disabled *100* behindert; **the ~** *100* Menschen mit Behinderung

to disable sth *53* etw *(Zugang)* sperren; *63T* etw ausschalten, etw deaktivieren

disablement *54* Sperrung

disappointing *48T* enttäuschend

disaster *21T* Katastrophe

to disconnect *28* trennen; *126* abschalten

disconnected, to get ~ *126* *(Telefonverbindung:)* unterbrochen werden

discount *97T* Rabatt; **bulk ~** *73* Mengenrabatt

to discount sth *118T* etw vergünstigen, einen Rabatt auf etw geben

discrimination *51* Diskriminierung

to disinfect *132* desinfizieren

to dispatch *35* versenden

display *29* Darstellung, Display

to display *27* *(auf dem Bildschirm)* anzeigen; *49* zeigen, darstellen

disposal *112* Entsorgung

to dispose of sth *112* etw entsorgen

dispute *117* Auseinandersetzung, Streit

disputed *119* umstritten

to disrupt *112* stören, aus dem Gleichgewicht bringen; *116* unterbrechen

distance *102* Entfernung, Strecke

to distinguish *110T* unterscheiden

distraction *21T* Ablenkung

to distribute *133* verteilen

distribution *51* Verbreitung

to disturb *9T* stören

to divide *45* teilen, unterteilen

to document *9* dokumentieren

dominant *89* dominant

dot *34* Punkt

doubt *77* Zweifel

downside *21T* Schattenseite, Nachteil; **on the ~** *21T* auf der Negativseite; andererseits

draft *73* Entwurf

to drag *37* ziehen

drastic(ally) *56T* drastisch

drawback *21T* Nachteil

drawer, chest of ~s *132* Kommode

to dress *126* sich kleiden

drive *124* Tatendrang, Motivation

to drop *37* fallen

dual-core processor *33* Doppelkernprozessor

due: ~ to *32T* aufgrund von, wegen; **to be ~ to do sth** *86* etw *(zu einem bestimmten Zeitpunkt)* tun sollen; **~ date** *85* Fälligkeitstermin

dummy *63T* Attrappe, Schein-, Blind-

durable *100* strapazierfähig, dauerhaft, stark

duration *41* Dauer, Zeitspanne

dust free *132* staubfrei

dustproof *99* staubdicht

duty *125P* Pflicht, Aufgabe

E

ease of reading information *103* leichte Ablesbarkeit der Werte

easily: ~ accessible *94T* leicht zugänglich; **~ understandable** *17* leicht verständlich

Easter *87* Ostern

economy *129* Wirtschaft

edge *28* Kante; *132* Rand; **cutting ~** *54* hochmodern, auf dem neuesten Stand der Technik
to **edit** *33* *(Text)* bearbeiten, redigieren
editing rights *pl 71T* Bearbeitungsrechte
to **educate sb** *82T* jdn schulen, jdn ausbilden
educational *82* Bildungs-, Lern-
efficient(ly) *42T* effizient
either *44* eines (von mehreren)
to **elaborate** *94T* ins Detail geben, etw genauer ausführen
electrical engineering *130* Elektrotechnik
elevator *AE 8* Aufzug, Lift
to **embed** *102* einbetten
embedded *29* integriert, eingebettet
emergency service *110T* Notdienst
emission *113* Ausstoß, Emission
to **emit sth** *113T* etw ausstoßen
to **employ sb** *6* jdn beschäftigen
employee *7* Angestellte/r, Beschäftigte/r; **~ satisfaction** *77T* Mitarbeiterzufriedenheit
to **enable: ~ sth** *63T* etw einschalten, etw aktivieren; *100* etw ermöglichen; **~ sb to do sth** *94* jdn in die Lage versetzen, etw zu tun
enablement *62* Umsetzung, Förderung
to **enclose** *98* *(Brief:)* beifügen
enclosure *98* *(Brief:)* Anlage
to **encourage: ~ sb** *47* jdn ermutigen, jdn ermuntern; **~ sth** *69* etw fördern, etw begünstigen
to **encrypt** *91T* verschlüsseln
encryption *54* Verschlüsselung
to **end up in the wrong hands** *50T* in falsche Hände gelangen
to **engage: ~ sb** *82* mit jdm ins Gespräch kommen, auf jdn (gesprächsweise) zugehen; **~ in conversation** *58T* sich unterhalten
engaged *22* *(Telefon:)* besetzt
engagement *61* Engagement
engineer, mechanical ~ *85* Maschinenbauer/in
engineering *12* Technik, Ingenieurwissenschaft, Maschinenbau; **electrical ~** *130* Elektrotechnik; **mechanical ~** *6* Maschinenbau; **software ~** *10T* Softwareentwicklung
to **enhance** *80T* verbessern
enquiry *34* Anfrage
to **ensure** *18* dafür sorgen, sicherstellen
to **enter** *38* *(Daten)* eingeben; **~ sth** *47* etw betreten
enterprise *41* Unternehmen
entertainment *25* Unterhaltung
entire *38* gesamte/r/s, ganze/r/s

entirely *77T* völlig, voll und ganz
entry *114* Eintragung; **data ~** *125P* Dateneingabe
equal to *129* gleichwertig mit
to **equip sth with sth** *132* etw mit etw ausstatten
equipment *7T* Geräte, Ausstattung
equivalent *22* Entsprechung, Übersetzung; *125* gleichwertig
error *39* Fehler, Irrtum; **typing ~** *118T* Tippfehler; **~ code** *60* Fehlercode; **~ message** *39* Fehlermeldung
to **establish: ~ rapport** *82* eine persönliche Beziehung aufbauen; **~ a reputation** *83* sich einen Ruf erwerben
estate, industrial ~ *108* Gewerbegebiet
estimate *73* Schätzung, Kostenvoranschlag
to **estimate a project** *85* ein Projekt kalkulieren
even *28* gleichmäßig; **~ though** *19* obwohl
event *34* Veranstaltung; **in the ~ that** *60* falls
everyday *58T* Alltags-, alltäglich
exam papers *pl 68T* Prüfungsunterlagen
to **exceed sth** *83* etw übertreffen
except for *23* außer
exception *51* Ausnahme
excessive *51* unverhältnismäßig viel; *76* übermäßig, zu hoch/groß
to **excuse: E~ me.** *13* Verzeihung./ Entschuldigung.
to **execute sth** *40* etw ausführen
execution *40* Ausführung
the executives *pl 19* die Betriebsleitung
exercise *46T* Bewegung, Sport; to **do ~** *81* Sport treiben
to **exercise sth** *49* etw üben, etw walten lassen
existing *9* bestehend, existierend; **~ customer** *58* Bestandskunde/-kundin
to **expand** *28* expandieren, (in Märkte) vordringen; *72* sich vergrößern; **~ on sth** *113* ausführlich über etw sprechen
expectation *20* Erwartung
experience *29* Erlebnis
experimentation *69* Experimentieren
expert *92T* Fachmann/-frau
expertise *83* Fachwissen, Know-how
to **expire** *105* *(Vertrag)* auslaufen; *116* *(Gültigkeit)* ablaufen
to **explain** *8* erklären, erläutern
to **exploit sth** *48T* etw ausnutzen
to **explore** *111* erkunden, erforschen
to **export** *62* exportieren
expression *127* Ausdruck
to **extend** *9T* sich erstrecken, sich ausdehnen; *108* erweitern
extended *38* erweitert

extension *23* Durchwahl; *38* Erweiterung; **file ~** *60* Dateiendung, Dateierweiterung
external *9* extern
to **extract (sth from sth)** *63* entnehmen, extrahieren, (etw aus etw) ziehen
extraction, data ~ *63T* Datenextraktion
eye, to keep an ~ out for sth *48T* nach etw Ausschau halten

F
to **face sth** *124* mit etw konfrontiert sein
face-to-face *15T* persönlich
to **facilitate sth** *75* etw erleichtern, etw begünstigen
facilities *pl 88T* Einrichtungen
fact, in ~ *13* tatsächlich, eigentlich
factory *6* Fabrik, Werk; **~ manager** *22* Betriebsleiter/in, Werksleiter/in
to **fail** *39* fehlschlagen; *74* ausfallen; *114* versagen; **~ sth** *54* etw nicht schaffen; **~ to do sth** *53* versäumen, etw zu tun; es nicht schaffen, etw zu tun
fail, This is a ~. *114* Das ist eine glatte Sechs.
failed *54* gescheitert
failure *39* Fehler; **~ (to do sth)** *73* Unterlassen, Unterlassung
fair *34* Messe; **trade ~** *81* Fachmesse, Branchenmesse
fairly *28* einigermaßen, ziemlich
faithfully, Yours ~ *35* *(Brief:)* Mit freundlichen Grüßen
fake *49* falsch, gefälscht
familiar, to be ~ with sth *46T* etw kennen
family business *6* Familienunternehmen
fantastic *13* phantastisch, toll
fashion-conscious *104* modebewusst
fashionable *103* in Mode, modisch
to **favour** *19* favorisieren, bevorzugen
favourable score *61* positive Bewertung
feature *31* Merkmal, Eigenschaft; **design ~** *63T* Konstruktionsmerkmal
to **feature** *93* *(Merkmal)* haben, aufweisen
featuring sth *132* mit etw
federal government *54* Bundesregierung
to **federate** *91* zu einem Bund zusammenschließen
federation *91* Bund
fee *91T* Gebühr; **consulting ~** *117* Beratungshonorar
to **feed sb** *112* jdn ernähren
feedback *19* Rückmeldung(en)
fibre, optical ~ *110T* Glasfaser
field *41* Feld

to **figure out sth** *46T* etw herausfinden, etw berechnen; *78* sich etw erklären

figures *pl 56* Zahlen, Ziffern

to **file** *113T* (Dokument) ablegen

file, certificate ~ *55* Zertifikatdatei; **personnel ~** *12* Personalakte; **~ extension** *60* Dateiendung, Dateierweiterung

to **filter** *62* filtern

finance *6* Finanz, Finanzen

findings *pl 48T* (Untersuchungs-) Ergebnisse

fingerprint *54* Fingerabdruck

finish *17* Ende

firm *28* fest

fit, as sb sees ~ *68T* nach jds Ermessen; to **be a good ~ for sb** *32T* für jdn richtig sein, gut zu jdm passen; **~-for-purpose** *32T* tauglich, geeignet

to **fix** *18* (etw) in Ordnung bringen, reparieren

flagship product *83* Top-Produkt, Vorzeigeprodukt

flash *133T* Blitz

flashlight *AE 37* Taschenlampe

flat *25* flach; to **go ~** *42T* (Akku:) schwach sein

flaw *68T* Mangel; **security ~** *39* Sicherheitslücke

flexibility *42T* Flexibilität

flexible *16T* variabel, flexibel

to **flick through** *126* durchblättern

floor, ground ~ *9T* Erdgeschoss; **~ plan** *9* Grundriss, Lageplan

to **flow** *102* fließen

flow, process ~ *75* Prozessablauf; **~ chart** *53* Flussdiagramm

fluctuation *56T* Schwankung

fluent *131* (Sprache:) fließend

flyer *34* Faltblatt

to **focus** *126* sich konzentrieren; **~ on sth** *62T* sich auf etw konzentrieren

to **follow up** *84* nachfassen, nachbereiten

font *78* Zeichensatz, Schrift

footfall *110T* Schritt(e)

footprint *110T* Fußabdruck, Fußstapfen; **carbon ~** *113* CO_2-Fußabdruck

for starters *72T* zunächst (einmal)

to **force** *17* zwingen

to **force: ~ sth** *28* Kraft (gegen etw) aufwenden; *42T* etw erzwingen; **~ install** *41* eine/die Installation erzwingen; **~ restart** *43* einen Neustart erzwingen

force *43* Zwang, Macht; *100* Kraft

forces *pl 133* Streitkräfte; **accelerative ~** *102* Beschleunigungskräfte

form, order ~ *106* Bestellformular

formal *13* formell, förmlich

formatting *78* Formatierung

to **forward sth** *52* etw weiterleiten

to **found** *6* gründen

foundation *6* Grundlage

founder *25* Gründer/in

fraud investigation *115* Betrugsermittlung, Betrugsbekämpfung

free, Feel ~ to call me. *78* Du kannst / Sie können mich gerne anrufen.

freedom *42* Freiheit

freelance *27* freiberuflich, selbstständig

frequency *72T* Frequenz; **~ band** *72T* Frequenzband

frequent *55* häufig

front, up ~ *105* im Voraus; **~ page** *71* Titelseite

frustrated *116* frustriert

frustrating *48T* frustrierend

to **fulfil an order** *120* einen Auftrag abwickeln, eine Bestellung ausführen

full, in ~ *114* vollständig

full-time *125* Vollzeit-

to **fumble around** *46T* herumtasten, herumfummeln

function *30* Funktion

functionality *17* Funktionen

functioning, day-to-day ~ *51* täglicher Betriebsablauf

funding *74* Finanzierung, Geldmittel

funds *pl 91T* Geldmittel, Geld

G

gain *76* Gewinn

to **gain** *48T* gewinnen, erlangen; *122T* erwerben

gallery *47* Galerie; **~ walk** *18* Galerierundgang

gate *88T* Tor, Einfahrt

to **gather** *87* zusammentragen, sammeln

gear *72T* Gerät(e), Ausrüstung, Ausstattung

gender *110T* Geschlecht

general partner *6* Gesellschafter/in, Teilhaber/in

to **generate** *71T* erzeugen

generous *95P* großzügig

gently *28* behutsam, vorsichtig

gesture *37* Geste

to **get: ~ at sth** *15T* auf etw hinauswollen; **~ a message across** *14* eine Botschaft vermitteln; **~ hold of sb** *46T* jdn erreichen; **~ sth right** *78* etw richtig verstehen; **~ ready** *89* sich bereit machen, sich fertig machen; **~ down to business** *97T* zur Sache kommen

gift *58T* Geschenk

glance *46T* (schneller) Blick

glass, strengthened ~ *103* gehärtetes Glas

to **glide** *132* gleiten

GNVQ (General National Vocational Qualification) *129* brit. Berufsschulabschluss

to **go: ~ ahead** *46T* loslegen; **~ beyond sth** *111* über etw hinausgehen

goal *10T* Ziel

government, federal ~ *54* Bundesregierung

GPU (graphics processing unit) *75* Grafikprozessor

to **grab sb's attention** *128* jds Aufmerksamkeit fesseln

gradual(ly) *56T* allmählich

graduate *17* mit Abschluss

to **grant sth** *39* etw gewähren, etw einräumen

graph *56* Diagramm, Grafik; **line ~** *56P* Liniendiagramm

graphic: ~ design *27* Grafikdesign; **~ image** *15T* Grafik

graphics card *26* Grafikkarte

gravity, centre of ~ *110T* Schwerpunkt

greenhouse gas *113T* Treibhausgas

greeting *58T* Gruß, Begrüßung

grid *7* Raster

ground, to make up ~ *86* Boden gutmachen; **~ floor** *8* Erdgeschoss

to **grow** *56T* zunehmen, steigen

growth *97T* Wachstum

to **guard against sth** *48T* sich vor etw schützen

guide *30* Leitfaden, Anhaltspunkt

to **guide** *110T* leiten, führen

guided tour *9* Führung

guideline *19* Richtlinie, Leitfaden

H

habit *127T* Gewohnheit; to **get into the ~ of doing sth** *127T* sich daran gewöhnen, etw zu tun

habitat *112* Lebensraum

half-circle *28* halbkreisförmig

to **hand sth to sb** *76* jdm etw übergeben

hand, on the one ~ *42T* einerseits; **on the other ~** *42T* andererseits; to **end up in the wrong ~s** *50T* in falsche Hände gelangen; to **shake ~s with sb** *89* jdm die Hand geben; **~s on** *122T* praktisch, konkret; **~s-free** *27T* Freisprech-, freihändig

hand-out *15T* Arbeitsblatt, Informationsblatt, Merkblatt

to **handle: ~ sth** *100* etw aushalten; *115* mit etw umgehen; to **be confident of being able to ~ sth** *83* sicher im Umgang mit etw sein

handy *104T* praktisch

to **hang on** *126* (Telefon:) warten

happy, to be ~ to do sth *45* etw gern tun

hard disk *26* Festplatte
hard time, to have a ~ doing sth *68T* etw nur schwer tun können
harm (to sb/sth) *51* Schaden, Nachteil (für jdn/etw)
harmful (to sb/sth) *51* schädlich, nachteilig (für jdn/etw); **non-~** *112* unschädlich
hazard *112* Gefahr
head: ~ height *30* Kopfhöhe; **~ office** *6* Zentrale, Hauptsitz
heading *39* Rubrik, Überschrift
headline *6* Überschrift
headmaster *68T* (Schul-)Direktor
headphones *pl* *33* Kopfhörer
headquartered, to be ~ in *82T* seinen Sitz in … haben
headquarters *pl* *16* Zentrale, Hauptsitz
health, project ~ *71* Projektzustand
healthcare *83* Gesundheitswesen, Medizin
heart, to be at the ~ of sth *25* zentral für etw sein
heartbeat *102* Herzschlag
heart rate *46T* Herzfrequenz
heavy computation *77T* hohes Rechenaufkommen
height, head ~ *30* Kopfhöhe
to hesitate *84* zögern
hidden *48T* verborgen, versteckt
to hide *48T* sich verstecken
hierarchy *25* Hierarchie
high-definition *99* hochauflösend
high-powered *31* leistungsstark, Hochleistungs-
high usage *95* intensive Nutzung
to highlight *11* hervorheben
highly *53* hochgradig, in hohem Maße
hindsight, in ~ *87T* rückblickend
to hit a snag *86* ein (unerwartetes) Problem haben
to hold: ~ up sb *13* jdn aufhalten; **~ sth in place** *28* etw fixieren; **~ the line** *22* (Telefon:) am Apparat bleiben
hold, to get ~ of sb *46T* jdn erreichen
holder *123* Inhaber/in
holiday, paid ~ *125* bezahlter Urlaub; **public ~** *125* gesetzlicher Feiertag
holographic *82T* holographisch
homemaker *132* Hausfrau/-mann
to hook sth to sth *27T* etw mit etw verbinden
horizontal *61* waagrecht, horizontal
horrible *94T* grässlich, scheußlich
to host *76* (Daten) hosten
host *110T* Moderator/in
to house *27* beherbergen, aufnehmen, unterbringen
household *105* Haushalt

housing *99* Gehäuse
How come? *68T* Wieso?
Human Resources (HR) *8* Personalabteilung
hunter *47* Jäger/in
hyphen *34* Bindestrich, Minus

I

identification, radio-frequency ~ (RFID) *110T* Funkerkennung
to identify *26* identifzieren, bestimmen
identity provider *55* Identitätsprovider
illegal *51* gesetzeswidrig, illegal
illness *13* Krankheit
to illustrate sth *85* etw veranschaulichen
to imagine sth *46T* sich etw vorstellen
imaging *111* Bildgebung, Abbildung(en)
immediate(ly) *49* sofortig, sofort, unverzüglich
impact *61* Relevanz, Wirkung; *100* Aufprall, Wucht; *112* Einfluss; *113* Auswirkung, Folge
to impact sth negatively *51* sich negativ auf etw auswirken
impacted *40* betroffen; **to be ~ by sth** *71* von etw betroffen sein, von etw beeinflusst werden
impolite *115* unhöflich
import *86* Einlesen, Importieren
to import *60* laden, importieren
to impress *32T* beeindrucken
impressed, to be ~ with sth *82T* von etw beeindruckt sein
impression *42T* Eindruck
impressive *84* beeindruckend
improvement *14* Verbesserung
inactive *48T* untätig, inaktiv
inactivity *43* Untätigkeit, Inaktivität
inappropriate *32T* unpassend, ungeeignet
inch *33* Zoll (= 2,54 cm)
to include *11* einbeziehen, aufnehmen
including *6* einschließlich
inclusion *97P* inbegriffene Leistung
inconsistent *78* uneinheitlich
to incorporate *102* integrieren
increase *56T* Zunahme, Anstieg
to increase *56T* zunehmen, ansteigen; **~ sth** *9* etw steigern, etw erhöhen
incredible *76* unglaublich
to incur: costs *pl* **~rred** *57* entstandene Kosten
index card *44* Karteikarte
to indicate *61* anzeigen; *127P* andeuten, darauf hinweisen
indication *34* Hinweis, Anzeichen
individual *122T* (Einzel-)Person
individual(ly) *21* einzeln, separat, privat

induction *8* Einführung, Einarbeitung; **~ course** *102* Einarbeitung, Einführungskurs
industrial: ~ electronics *6* Industrieelektronik; **~ estate** *108* Gewerbegebiet
to infect *48* infizieren
infected *48T* infiziert
influence *112* Auswirkung(en)
to influence *113* beeinflussen
to inform *71* informieren, mitteilen; **~ sb of sth** *54* jdn über etw informieren, jdm etw mitteilen
infrared *30* Infrarot
to inhabit *133* bewohnen
in-house *114* betriebsintern
initial *105* erste/r/s, Anfangs-
initials *pl*, **reference ~** *98* (Brief:) Zeichen
initially *80* ursprünglich, anfangs
injection *48T* Einschleusung
ink *47* Tinte, Tätowierung
to ink *47* tätowieren
to innovate *25* innovativ sein, kreativ sein
innovative *9* innovativ
to input *31* (Daten) eingeben
input *11* Idee(n), Anregung(en); **~ device** *27* Eingabegerät
insecure *68T* unsicher
to insert *28* einsetzen, hineinstecken
inside address *98* Innenadresse
install *42T* Installation
to install *28* installieren; **to force ~** *41* eine/die Installation erzwingen
installation, post-~ *38* nach der Installation; **pre-~** *38* vor der (eigentlichen) Installation
instant(ly) *20* sofortig, sofort
instantaneous(ly) *21T* sofort, augenblicklich
instead of *31* statt, anstatt
instruction *15* Anweisung; *27* Befehl, Kommando; **~ manual** *28* Bedienungsanleitung
insufficient *39* unzureichend
insurance *122T* Versicherung
insured *101* versichert
to integrate *64* integrieren; **~ with one another** *11* ineinandergreifen
integrated *33* integriert
intellectual property *76* geistiges Eigentum
intelligence *112* Intelligenz; **artificial ~** *58* künstliche Intelligenz
to intend to do sth *104T* beabsichtigen, etw zu tun
to interact *111* kommunizieren, interagieren; **~ with sth** *27* auf etw

Ltd *35* GmbH
lungs *pl 111* Lunge

M

madam, Dear Sir or M~ *35* (*Brief:*) Sehr geehrte Damen und Herren,
magazine, trade ~ *99* Fachzeitschrift
magic carpet *110T* fliegender Teppich
to **maintain** *9* warten, instand halten; *25* aufrecht erhalten; *53* betreuen; **~ sth** *37* etw unterhalten, etw betreiben
maintenance *41* Wartung, Instand-haltung
to **make up: ~ sth** *23P* sich etw ausden-ken; *57* (*Anteil:*) etw ausmachen; **~ ground** *86* Boden gutmachen
malicious *57* schädlich, bösartig
malware *48T* Schadprogramm(e)
manager, account ~ *31* Kunden-betreuer/in; **factory ~** *22* Betriebs-leiter/in, Werksleiter/in
management consultant *85* Unterneh-mensberater/in
mandatory *60* obligatorisch, zwingend notwendig
to **manipulate sth** *33* mit etw umgehen, etw bearbeiten
manner *45* Art (und Weise)
to **manoeuvre** *132* manövrieren
manual, instruction ~ *28* Bedienungs-anleitung
to **manufacture** *6* fertigen, herstellen
manufacturer, car ~ *68T* Autohersteller
manufacturing company *44* Ferti-gungsbetrieb, Produktionsunternehmen
to **map** *29* erfassen
marginal(ly) *56T* unerheblich, gering-fügig
to **mark** *37* kennzeichnen, markieren
marker *47* Markierung
mask *111* Maske
material, reference ~ *60* Material zum Nachschlagen
maturity *70* Reifung, Reife
to **maximize** *10T* maximieren; *36* maximal vergrößern
means of communication *14* Kommunikationsmittel
meantime, in the ~ *115* in der Zwischenzeit
measure *14* Maßnahme
to **measure** *102* messen
measurement unit *73* Messgerät
mechanical: ~ engineer *85* Maschinenbauer/in; **~ engineering** *6* Maschinenbau
mechanism, security ~ *50* Schutz-mechanismus, Sicherheitsmaßnahme

medical *7T* medizinisch, Medizin-; **~ procedure** *82T* medizinischer Eingriff
medium-sized *7* mittelgroß, mittel-ständisch
to **meet: ~ requirements** *32* Anforderungen erfüllen; **~ standards** *9* Normen erfüllen
meeting room *21T* Sitzungszimmer, Konferenzraum
member *11* Mitglied
memory, random access ~ (RAM) *26* Arbeitsspeicher
to **mention (sth to sb)** *15T* (etw jdm gegenüber) erwähnen
menu *36* Menü; **~ bar** *36* Menüleiste
mess *91* Chaos, Durcheinander
to **mess sth up** *77P* etw durcheinander-bringen
message, to get a ~ across *14* eine Botschaft vermitteln; to **leave a ~** *22* eine Nachricht hinterlassen; to **take a ~** *22* etw ausrichten; **error ~** *39* Fehler-meldung; **text ~** *15T* SMS
method *9* Art, Weise, Methode
methodical *69* systematisch, planvoll
methodology *69* Methodik
mid-range *27* Mittelklasse-, im mittleren Preissegment
midday *73* Mittag
midway through *56T* mitten in
milestone *85* Projektabschnitt, Meilenstein
military *25* Militär; **~ personnel** *133* Soldaten, Militärangehörige
mind, to bear sth in ~ *72T* etw berück-sichtigen, an etw denken; to **have sth in ~** *59* etw vorhaben, etw im Sinn haben, an etw denken; to **keep in ~** *72T* daran denken
to **mind: sb doesn't ~** *31* etw ist jdm egal; **Never ~.** *92T* Egal.
to **minimize** *36* maximal verkleinern, minimieren
minimum, to keep sth to a ~ *19* etw auf ein Mindestmaß beschränken
mistake, by ~ *60* versehentlich, irrtümlich
misunderstanding *118T* Missverständ-nis
misuse *91* Missbrauch
mixed up *128* durcheinander
mixture *122T* Mischung
mobile *22* Handy, Mobiltelefon; **~ cellular coverage** *52* Mobilfunk-empfang
mobility *123* Freizügigkeit, Mobilität
mode *37* Betriebsart, Modus
model *25* Vorbild, Modell; *33* Ausführung

to **monitor** *30* überwachen
monitoring *48T* Überwachung
to **mop** *132* feudeln, wischen
moreover *46T* außerdem, darüber hinaus
most, to make the ~ of sth *10T* etw (bestmöglich) nutzen
mostly *27T* hauptsächlich, meistens
motherboard *26* Hauptplatine, Mother-board
motion *29* Bewegung; **~ sensor** *46T* Bewegungssensor
motionless *110T* regungslos
to **motivate** *46T* motivieren
mount *117* Halterung
mounting kit *30* Montageset
mouse, mouses/mice *26* Maus, Mäuse
multinational (company) *7* inter-/ multinationaler Konzern
multiple *29* mehrere; *70* mehrfach
to **multiply** *113* (sich) vervielfachen, vervielfältigen
muscle *111* Muskel

N

to **name sth after sb** *85* etw nach jdm benennen
native, non-~ *37* mit etw nicht vertraut
natural language *58T* natürliche Sprache
to **navigate** *111* navigieren; **~ sth** *36* sich bei/in etw zurechtfinden, durch etw steuern
neat *16T* sauber, ordentlich
necessarily, not ~ *27* nicht unbedingt
need *73* Bedarf
needle *47* Nadel
negatively, to impact sth ~ *51* sich negativ auf etw auswirken
negotiable *124* verhandelbar
to **negotiate** *96* verhandeln
negotiation *96* Verhandlung
network *6* Netzwerk; **~ design** *72* Netzwerkkonzeption, -auslegung, -design
night-owl *77T* Nachteule
noise *21T* Lärm; *72T* Rauschen; **~ level** *21T* Lärmpegel
non-harmful *112* unschädlich
non-native *37* mit etw nicht vertraut
non-renewable *112* nicht erneuerbar
notch *28* Kerbe, Einkerbung
to **note** *38* beachten; **Please ~ that …** *96* Wir weisen Sie darauf hin, dass …
notice, at short ~ *131* kurzfristig
note, on a (more) positive ~ *86* positiv zu vermerken ist, dass …
notification *52* Benachrichtigung; *104T* Meldung
to **notify sb** *71* jdn benachrichtigen

O

obesity *112* Fettleibigkeit
obligation *96* Verpflichtung
obsolete *54* veraltet, überholt
obstacle *18* Hindernis
obvious *94T* klar, offensichtlich
obviously *77T* natürlich, offensichtlich
occasion *125P* Gelegenheit; **on the ~ of sth** *91* aus Anlass von etw
occasional(ly) *104T* gelegentlich
to **occur** *41* geschehen; **~ to sb** *127T* jdm einfallen
offer, job ~ *123* Stellenangebot
office, head ~ *6* Zentrale, Hauptsitz; **open-plan ~** *9T* Großraumbüro
one-time *53* einmalig
to **operate** *31* geschäftlich tätig sein; *72T* funktionieren, arbeiten, laufen
operating: ~ system *33* Betriebssystem; **~ theatre** *98* Operationssaal
operator *93* Telefonist/in; *102* Betreiber/in
opportunity *25* Gelegenheit, Möglichkeit; **career ~ies** *pl 61* Aufstiegsmöglichkeiten, berufliche Perspektiven; **job ~ies** *pl 123* Arbeitsmöglichkeiten
optical *102* optisch; **~ character recognition (OCR)** *86* optische Zeichenerkennung; **~ fibre** *110T* Glasfaser
optimization *80T* Optimierung
to **optimize** *80T* optimieren
order, to fulfil an ~ *120* einen Auftrag abwickeln, eine Bestellung ausführen; to **place an ~** *98* einen Auftrag erteilen, eine Bestellung aufgeben; **trial ~** *99* Probebestellung; **~ form** *106* Bestellformular
ordinary *46T* gewöhnlich, normal
organization chart *11* Organigramm
orientation *102* Orientierung, Ausrichtung
out of date *54* veraltet, überholt
outcome *42* Ergebnis, Resultat, Auswirkung(en)
to **outline** *91* skizzieren, darstellen
outpatient clinic *99* Ambulanz
output *19* Arbeitsergebnis(se)
outward, in an ~ direction *28* nach außen
overall *10T* Gesamt-, allgemein; **~ cost** *85* Gesamtkosten; **~ score** *45* Gesamtpunktzahl
to **overcomplicate sth** *69* etw verkomplizieren
to **overhear sth** *104* etw (zufällig) mithören
overly *32T* allzu, übermäßig
overnight *39* über Nacht
overview *71* Übersicht

owl, night-~ *77T* Nachteule
own, on one's ~ *7* alleine
ownership *91* Besitz, Eigentum

P

pace *102* Tempo
to **pack** *98* verpacken
package *38* Paket
packaging *99* Verpackung
packing crate *98* Packkiste
paid holiday *125* bezahlter Urlaub
painless *72T* schmerzfrei
to **pair sth with sth** *27T* etw an etw koppeln, etw mit etw verbinden
pairing *80T* Kopplung, Pairing
panel *39* Bedienfeld, Panel; *127T* Gremium
to **panic** *49* in Panik geraten
paperless *112* papierlos; to **be ~** *19* kein Papier (mehr) verwenden
part, to look the ~ *126* entsprechend (rollengerecht) aussehen
partially *77T* teilweise, zum Teil
participant *94T* Teilnehmer/in
participation *61* Beteiligung, Teilnahme
particular *76* bestimmt, speziell; **sth in ~** *82T* etw Spezielles
particularly *131* insbesondere; **Not ~.** *127T* Eigentlich nicht
partner *6* Gesellschafter/in, Teilhaber/in
party, third ~ *39* Dritte/r, von Dritten
pass, security ~ *9T* Firmenausweis, Zugangskarte
to **pass sth on** *23P* etw weiterreichen/-leiten
passcode *54* Zugangscode, Passwort
passion *82T* Leidenschaft
password protection *61* Kennwortschutz
past *36* Vergangenheit
patch-deployment *39* Patch-Bereitstellung
to **patent** *91* patentieren
patent laws *pl 51* Patentgesetze
patience *115* Geduld
to **patrol** *133* patrouillieren
patrol, to go out on ~ *133* auf Patrouille gehen
pay *13* Bezahlung, Gehalt
payment, terms *pl* **of ~** *99* Zahlungsbedingungen
peak *56T* Spitze, Höchstwert
percentage *40* Prozentsatz, Anteil
to **perform** *10T* (Tätigkeit) ausführen; *71T* sich entwickeln; **~ sth** *31* etw ausführen, etw durchführen
performance *31* Leistung
period of time *19* (gewisse) Zeit
peripheral *27* Peripheriegerät
permanent *125* unbefristet

permission *16T* Genehmigung, Erlaubnis
permitted, to be ~ to do sth *50T* etw tun dürfen; die Erlaubnis haben, etw zu tun
to **personalize** *58T* individuell anpassen, persönlich gestalten
personnel *12* Personal; **military ~** *133* Soldaten, Militärangehörige; **~ file** *12* Personalakte
to **persuade** *48T* überreden, überzeugen
phase *19* Stadium, Phase
Phillips screwdriver *28* Kreuzschlitzschraubendreher/-zieher
physical *30* physisch, räumlich
to **pick up: ~ sth** *77T* mit etw weitermachen; **~ on sth** *48T* auf etw reagieren, auf etw aufmerksam machen
pickpocket *91T* Taschendieb/in
pie chart *57* Tortendiagramm
piezoelectric *102* piezoelektrisch
pin *37* Stecknadel, Reißzwecke
to **pin** *18* (mit einer Nadel) befestigen, anheften; **~ sth to sth** *89* etw an etw befestigen
to **pinch** *37* (zwei Finger) zusammenführen
to **ping** *39* pingen, anpingen
to **place: ~ sth** *72T* etw platzieren; **~ an order** *98* einen Auftrag erteilen, eine Bestellung aufgeben
place, all over the ~ *15T* überall (in der Weltgeschichte); to **hold sth in ~** *28* etw fixieren; to **put sth in ~** *50* etw einrichten; to **take ~** *38* stattfinden; **~ of birth** *12* Geburtsort
placement *72T* Platzierung, Anordnung
planning *25* Planung
platform *10T* Plattform
pleased, P~ to meet you. *89* Schön, Sie kennen zu lernen.
pleasure, My ~. *127T* Ganz meinerseits. Gern geschehen.
to **plug** *27T* anschließen, einstecken, verbinden; **~ in sth** *72T* etw anschließen
point, at some ~ *62T* irgendwann; **That's a good ~.** *72T* Da hast du / haben Sie recht. Da ist was dran.; **to a ~** *77T* bis zu einem gewissen Punkt; to **make a ~** *48T* ein Argument vortragen; **access ~** *72T* Zugangspunkt, Access Point; **selling ~** *80T* Verkaufsargument; **starting ~** *20* Ausgangspunkt; **~ of view** *20* Sicht
to **point out sth** *73* auf etw hinweisen
policy *51* Linie, Vorgehensweise, Politik; **cancellation ~** *105* (Vertrag:) Kündigungsbedingungen
polite(ly) *35* höflich
politics *13* Politik

pollution *112* Verschmutzung

to **pop up** *28* hochspringen, herausspringen; *58T* (auf dem Bildschirm) erscheinen

populated *41* (Feld:) ausgefüllt

port *27T* Anschluss

portability *32P* Transportierbarkeit, Mobilität

portrait *37* (Bild:) Hochformat

to **position** *30* positionieren

positive, on a (more) ~ note *86* positiv zu vermerken ist, dass …

post *28* Säulchen; *131* Stelle

post-installation *38* nach der Installation

poster *33* Plakat

to **postpone** *67* (nach hinten) verschieben

potential *123* möglich, potenziell

potentially *77T* eventuell, potenziell

power, computing ~ *76* Rechenleistung; **processing ~** *31* Rechenleistung; **~ adapter** *28* Netzteil; **~ source** *30* Stromquelle; **~ usage** *80T* Stromverbrauch

to **power sth** *29* etw mit Strom versorgen

powerful *61* aussagekräftig; *89* mächtig

practicality *103* Zweckmäßigkeit

practice, best ~ *54* optimale Vorgehensweise

to **pray** *89* beten

to **pre-approve sth** *50T* etw im Voraus genehmigen

precise, to be ~ *82T* genau gesagt, um genau zu sein

to **predict** *58T* vorhersagen

predictability *25* Berechenbarkeit

predictable *25* berechenbar

preference *19* Vorliebe, Wunsch; **~es** *pl* *41* Einstellungen

pre-installation *38* vor der (eigentlichen) Installation

preliminary *125P* vorläufig, Vor-

premises *pl* *8* (Betriebs-)Gelände, Räumlichkeiten

prepared *7* bereit, vorbereitet

presenter *44* Redner/in

presently *91T* im Moment, gegenwärtig

to **press** *37* drücken

press release *51* Pressemitteilung

pressure *28* Druck; **blood ~** *46T* Blutdruck

to **pretend** *20* so tun, als ob; *48T* vorgeben, vortäuschen

to **prevent** *28* verhindern, verhüten

previously *54* vorher, zuvor

principle *68T* Grundsatz, Prinzip

prioritized *71* nach Priorität geordnet

privilege *38* Berechtigung, (Zugriffs-) Recht; **access ~es** *pl* *50* Zugriffsrechte

prize-giving ceremony *88* Preisverleihung

proactive, to be ~ *87* die Initiative ergreifen, von selbst aktiv werden

problem solver *125P* Problemlöser/in

procedure, medical ~ *82T* medizinischer Eingriff; **security ~s** *pl* *53* Sicherheitsverfahren, Sicherheitsmaßnahmen

to **proceed** *60* fortfahren, weitermachen

to **process** *27* verarbeiten

process, selection ~ *127P* Auswahlverfahren; **~ flow** *75* Prozessablauf

processing *75* (Daten-)Verarbeitung; **data ~** *6* Datenverarbeitung; **~ power** *31* Rechenleistung

processor *32T* Prozessor; **dual-core ~** *33* Doppelkernprozessor

procurement *96* Beschaffung

producer *6* Hersteller, Produzent

production *7* Produktion, Fertigung, Herstellung

productive *17* produktiv

productivity *20* Produktivität

professional *82* Fachkraft, Profi; *111* professionell, Berufs-

profile *6* Porträt, Beschreibung, Profil

progress *38* Fortgang, aktueller Stand; **to be in ~** *40* (aktuell) durchgeführt werden

to **progress** *21* vorankommen

prohibited *51* verboten

project: to run a ~ *85* ein Projekt leiten/durchführen; **~ health** *71* Projektzustand; **~ schedule** *85* Projektplan

to **project** *47* projizieren

projector *32T* Beamer

to **promote sth** *9* für etw Werbung machen

prompt *42* Stichwort; *53* Eingabeaufforderung; *117* umgehend, prompt; **~ card** *44* Moderationskarte

to **prompt sb for sth** *53* (Eingabeaufforderung:) jdn nach etw fragen

property *100* Eigenschaft; **intellectual ~** *76* geistiges Eigentum; **lost ~** *91T* verlorene Gegenstände

proposal *96* Vorschlag

to **propose** *19* vorschlagen

proposition, unique selling ~ (USP) *95* Alleinstellungsmerkmal

proprietary *29* firmeneigen, urheberrechtlich geschützt

pros and cons *pl* *21T* Argumente dafür und dagegen, Vor- und Nachteile

prospective customer *101* potenzielle/r Kunde/Kundin

prospects *pl*, **career ~** *123* berufliche Perspektiven

prosthetics *pl* *100* Prothesen

protection, data ~ *128* Datenschutz; **password ~** *61* Kennwortschutz

protective *101* Schutz-

protocol *29* Übertragungsprotokoll

proud (of sth) *46T* stolz (auf etw)

to **prove sth** *68T* etw nachweisen, etw beweisen

provider *68T* Anbieter; **identity ~** *55* Identitätsprovider

public *48* öffentlich; **~ holiday** *125* gesetzlicher Feiertag

to **publish** *70* veröffentlichen

publishing company *70* Verlag

to **pump** *111* pumpen

punctuation *60* Satzzeichen

to **punish** *49* bestrafen

to **purchase** *38* kaufen

purchase *58T* Kauf; **~ decision** *58T* Kaufentscheidung

purchasing *6* Einkauf

purpose *81* Zweck; **fit-for-~** *32T* tauglich, geeignet

to **push sth up** *113* etw in die Höhe treiben

to **put: ~ sb through** *22* (Telefon:) jdn durchstellen; **~ sth in place** *50* etw einrichten

Q

to **qualify** *122* einen/den Abschluss machen

quality: ~ assurance *8* Qualitätssicherung; **~ control** *108* Qualitätskontrolle

quantity *15* Menge, Anzahl

quarter *56T* Quartal

question, to raise a ~ *97P* eine Frage vorbringen

question, rated ~ *61* bewertete Frage

quick course correction *69* schnelle Korrektur

quiet, to keep ~ *9T* sich ruhig verhalten

quite, Not ~. *63T* Nicht ganz.

to **quote** *97T* (Preis) nennen, anbieten

R

R&D (Research & Development) *8* Forschung und Entwicklung

race *51* Rasse

racing, competitive ~ *133T* Wettrennen; **~ boat** *133T* Rennboot

racket, tennis ~ *30* Tennisschläger

radio: ~ button *41* Optionsschaltfläche; **~ control** *133T* Funksteuerung; **~ link** *133T* Funkverbindung; **~-frequency identification (RFID)** *110T* Funkerkennung

to **raise: ~ sth** *17* etw ansprechen, auf etw aufmerksam machen; **~ a question** *97P* eine Frage vorbringen

to **result in sth** *51* zu etw führen, etw ergeben

retailer *58* Einzelhändler

return *31* Retoure, Rücksendung

to **reuse** *55* wiederverwenden, nochmals verwenden

to **reveal sth** *110T* etw verraten, etw enthüllen

reverse order *128* umgekehrte Reihenfolge

to **reverse sth** *60* etw umkehren

reversion *95* Rückkehr

review *58T* Rezension, Kritik

to **review sth** *87* etw besprechen, etw Revue passieren lassen; *96* etw überprüfen

to **revise** *91* *(Text)* überarbeiten, redigieren; ~ **sth** *71T* etw ändern; *118T* etw korrigieren

ribbon (cable) *28* Flachbandkabel

right, to get sth ~ *78* etw richtig verstehen; ~ **away** *58T* sofort, gleich

rights *pl*, **editing ~** *71T* Bearbeitungsrechte; **access ~** *71T* Zugriffsrechte

to **rise** *56T* ansteigen

risk, to take ~s *25* Risiken eingehen

road, on the ~ *77T* unterwegs; to **be on the ~** *32T* unterwegs sein

roadblock *17* Hindernis

robot *58* Roboter; **vacuum ~** *81* Staubsaugerroboter

rock-solid *72T* (absolut) stabil

role *6* Rolle, Funktion

to **role-play** *65* mit verteilten Rollen spielen

to **rotate** *37* drehen

roughly *57* ungefähr

route *37* Strecke, Weg, Route

row *60* Reihe, Zeile

to **run** *6* *(Unternehmen usw.)* führen; ~ **sth** *71T* etw ausführen, etw betreiben; ~ **behind schedule** *21T* im Rückstand sein; ~ **a project** *85* ein Projekt leiten

rush *79T* Hast, Eile; **in a ~** *31* hektisch, in Eile

to **rush** *87T* eilen, hetzen; ~ **sth** *79T* etw hastig erledigen

S

salary *124* Gehalt; **starting ~** *124* Einstiegsgehalt

sales *6* Verkauf, Vertrieb; ~ **representative** *32* Vertreter/in

salutation *35* *(Brief:)* Anrede

sapphire crystal *103* Saphirglas

satisfaction *59* Zufriedenheit; **to sb's ~** *59* zu jds Zufriedenheit; **employee ~** *77T* Mitarbeiterzufriedenheit

savings *pl* *76* Einsparung(en); *91T* Ersparnisse

to **say: that said, ...** *76* vor diesem Hintergrund

scalpel *111* Skalpell

scandal *68T* Skandal

scatter-brained *110T* zerstreut, schusselig

schedule *21T* Zeitplan; **ahead of ~** *86* vorzeitig; to **run behind ~** *21T* im Rückstand sein; **project ~** *85* Projektplan

to **schedule** *85* planen, *(Termin)* ansetzen

scheme *109* Schema; **colour ~** *49* Farbgebung, Farbzusammenstellung

science *110T* (Natur-)Wissenschaft

scope *69* Umfang, Geltungs-/Anwendungsbereich

score *61* Punktzahl, Punkte; **favourable ~** *61* positive Bewertung; **overall ~** *45* Gesamtpunktzahl

scratch, to start from ~ *60* (ganz) von vorne anfangen; ~ **resistance** *103* Kratzfestigkeit

scratched *120T* verkratzt

screen *27* Bildschirm

to **screen sth off** *132* etw abteilen

to **screw** *28* schrauben, festschrauben

screw *28* Schraube; **slotted ~** *35* Schlitzschraube

screwdriver, Phillips ~ *28* Kreuzschlitzschraubendreher/-zieher

to **scroll** *37* scrollen, blättern

scuba-diving *46T* Gerätetauchen

sealed *99* dicht, abgedichtet

seat, Is this ~ taken? *89* Ist hier besetzt?

section *42* Bereich, Abschnitt

sector *7* Bereich, Branche, Sektor

secure *42* sicher; *88T* bewacht

to **secure** *28* befestigen; *53* sichern, schützen

security: ~ doors *pl* *9T* Sicherheitsschleuse, Sicherheitstüren; ~ **flaw** *39* Sicherheitslücke; ~ **mechanism** *50* Schutzmechanismus, Sicherheitsmaßnahme; ~ **pass** *9T* Firmenausweis, Zugangskarte; ~ **procedures** *pl* *53* Sicherheitsverfahren, Sicherheitsmaßnahmen

to **see sth through** *25* etw zu Ende führen

to **select** *15T* auswählen

selection *41* Auswahl; to **make a ~** *41* eine Auswahl treffen; ~ **process** *127P* Auswahlverfahren

self-assessment *123* Selbsteinstufung

selling point *80T* Verkaufsargument

semiconductor *110T* Halbleiter

senior *11* leitend

sense, to make ~ *63T* nachvollziehbar sein, einleuchten

sensitive *48T* *(Informationen:)* vertraulich

to **separate** *17* trennen

separate *21T* getrennt, separat, eigen

sequential *69* sequenziell, fortlaufend

seriously, to take sth ~ *115* etw ernst nehmen

to **serve** *88T* servieren; ~ **sb** *58T* jdn bedienen

service *7* Dienst, Dienstleistung

session *55* Sitzung, Session

to **set** *41* einstellen; ~ **sth aside** *20* etw (für etw) vorsehen; ~ **up sth** *27* etw einrichten; ~ **up a meeting** *66* ein Treffen vereinbaren

set *128* vorgegeben, starr, fest

set-up *60* Einrichtung; *71* Aufbau

settings *pl* *38* Einstellungen

to **settle sth** *118T* etw regeln, etw erledigen

sex *110T* Geschlecht

shaded *61* schattiert

to **shake hands with sb** *89* jdm die Hand geben

shape, in good ~ *78* in gutem Zustand

shareable *95P* gemeinsam nutzbar

shark *133T* Hai

sharp(ly) *56T* *(Anstieg:)* steil, stark

sheet of data *60* Datenblatt

shelf, off the ~ *72T* handelsüblich

shielded *74* abgeschirmt

shift *76* Schicht; *113T* Verlagerung, Umschwung

to **ship sth** *113T* etw verschicken, etw versenden

short, to be ~ of time *81* wenig Zeit haben

shortage *124* Mangel

shortlisted, to be ~ *124* in die engere Auswahl kommen

shoulder *47* Schulter

show *82T* Messe, Ausstellung

to **show sb around** *9* jdn herumführen

to **shut down** *28* herunterfahren, ausschalten

shutdown *43* Herunterfahren, Abschalten

shy *127T* schüchtern

to **sign** *96* unterschreiben, unterzeichnen; ~ **sth in** *79T* etw anmelden, etw eintragen; ~ **up to sth** *100* sich bei etw anmelden

signal, to receive a ~ *102* ein Signal empfangen

signature *98* Unterschrift

significant(ly) *56T* erheblich, bedeutend, signifikant

sign-in *78* Login

sign-off *87* Abnahme, Abschluss

sign-on, single ~ *55* einmaliges Anmelden

signpost *44* *Hinweise zur Orientierung der Zuhörer in einer Präsentation*

silicone *100* Silikon

to **simplify** *25* vereinfachen

simultaneous(ly) *30* gleichzeitig

sincerely *118T* aufrichtig; **Yours ~** *35* *(Brief:)* Mit freundlichen Grüßen

single sign-on *55* einmaliges Anmelden

sir, Dear S~ or Madam *35* *(Brief:)* Sehr geehrte Damen und Herren,

size *7* Größe

skeleton *111* Skelett

sketch *47* Skizze

skin *100* Haut

skipper *133T* Kapitän/in

slack *85* Pufferzeit

slice *111* Schnitt

slide *15T* *(Präsentation:)* Folie

to **slide out sth** *28* etw herausschieben

slight(ly) *56T* leicht, etwas; *86* geringfügig

to **slip through** *78* durchrutschen

slot *28* Steckplatz

slotted screw *35* Schlitzschraube

to **slow: ~ down** *51* verlangsamen, bremsen; **~ sb down** *17* jdn aufhalten, jdn bremsen

smart *20* klug; *102* intelligent; *127T* *(Kleidung:)* schick

smooth(ly) *27* reibungslos

snag, to hit a ~ *86* ein (unerwartetes) Problem haben

socializing *128* Ausgehen

software engineering *10T* Softwareentwicklung

soldier *133* Soldat/in

solution *7* Lösung

to **solve** *21T* lösen

sophisticated *83* anspruchsvoll, hochentwickelt

to **sort sth out** *15T* etw klären, etw in Ordnung bringen

sorted, to get sth ~ *120T* etw klären, sich um etw kümmern

source, power ~ *30* Stromquelle

space, storage ~ *32T* Speicherplatz

spare *72T* Ersatz, Reserve

speaker *27T* Lautsprecher

Speaking. *23* *(Telefon:)* Am Apparat.

spearhead *133T* Speerspitze

special character *60* Sonderzeichen

specialist *125P* Fach-, Spezial-

specification *18* technische Anforderung(en); **~s** *pl 86* Technische Daten, Spezifikationen

to **specify sth** *113T* etw (genau) angeben

speedboat *133T* Schnellboot

spelling *44* Rechtschreibung; *120* Schreibweise; **~ mistake** *78* Rechtschreibfehler

splashproof *103* spritzwassergeschützt

spontaneous *19* spontan

spot on *32T* genau richtig

to **spread** *37* spreizen; *48T* sich ausbreiten

spreadsheet *31* Tabellenkalkulation, Tabelle

square metre *72T* Quadratmeter

stability *42T* Stabilität

stage, at any ~ *60* jederzeit

stainless steel *103* Edelstahl

stairs *pl 9T* Treppe

stakeholder *71* Projektbeteiligte/r

stand *34* (Messe-)Stand

stand-up *19* im Stehen

standard *18* üblich, normal; to **meet ~s** *9* Normen erfüllen

to **standardize** *87T* normieren, standardisieren

standardized *80* genormt

to **start from scratch** *60* (ganz) von vorne anfangen

starter, for ~s *72T* zunächst (einmal); **~ kit** *58T* Einsteigerset

starting: ~ point *20* Ausgangspunkt; **~ salary** *124* Einstiegsgehalt

startup *42T* Start, Einschalten, Hochfahren

to **state** *21* angeben, erklären, nennen, sagen; **~ one's case** *77* sein Anliegen vorbringen, seine Sache vertreten

state *48T* Zustand; **~ of the art** *54* (auf dem neuesten) Stand der Technik; *102* modernste/r/s

steadily *56T* kontinuierlich, stetig

steady *56T* gleichbleibend, stabil

to **steal** *68T* stehlen

steel, stainless ~ *103* Edelstahl

steep(ly) *56* steil

to **stick** *27T* stecken; **~ to sth** *32T* sich an etw halten

stock, in ~ *35* auf Lager, verfügbar

stomach *132* Bauch

to **stop sb from doing sth** *25* jdn daran hindern, etw zu tun

storage *15T* (Daten-)Speicherung; *111* Lagerung; **~ capacity** *96* Speicherkapazität; **~ space** *32T* Speicherplatz

store chain *31* Ladenkette

story, To cut a long ~ short, ... *133T* Lange Rede, kurzer Sinn: ...

straight *56T* sogleich, sofort; **~ ahead** *9T* geradeaus

strange *126* seltsam, merkwürdig

strap *29* Riemen, Gurt; *103* Armband

strategy *10T* Strategie

strength *73* Stärke

to **strengthen** *54* stärken, verbessern

strengthened glass *103* gehärtetes Glas

stress *102* Druck, Belastung

to **stress** *127P* betonen

stressed, to become ~ *102* unter Druck geraten, belastet werden

strictly *51* streng, strengstens

stride *110T* Schritt

to **strip sth** *111* etw abstreifen

structure *6* Aufbau, Struktur

to **structure** *7* aufbauen, strukturieren

structured *15T* strukturiert

study *113T* Untersuchung, Studie

sub-criteria *pl 62* Unterkriterien

sub-page *71* Unterseite

subject line *34* Betreffzeile

subjective *103* subjektiv

to **submit sth** *61* etw einreichen

subscription *97* Abonnement

subsidiary *8* Niederlassung

subtotal *117* Zwischensumme

to **suffer** *73* leiden

sufficient *38* ausreichend, genügend

to **suit sb/sth** *16T* (zu) jdm/etw passen

suitable *13* geeignet, passend

sum up, to ~ *45* zusammenfassend

superior *120T* Vorgesetzte/r

to **supervise** *10T* führen, leiten, vorgesetzt sein

supervisor *12* Ausbildungsleiter/in, Abteilungsleiter/in, Vorgesetzte/r

supplement *123* Zusatz, Ergänzung

supplied *29* mitgeliefert

supplier *23* Zulieferer, Lieferant/in

to **supply** *92T* liefern, zur Verfügung stellen

support *8* Hilfe, Unterstützung, Betreuung, Kundendienst, Support; *100* Halt; **customer ~** *31* Kundenbetreuung, Kundendienst

to **support** *19* unterstützen; *45* (Argumentation) untermauern; *51* fördern

to **suppose** *26* vermuten, annehmen, glauben

sure, to make ~ *9* sicherstellen, gewährleisten; **~ enough** *114* selbstverständlich

surface *100* Oberfläche, Fläche

surgeon *111* Chirurg/in

surgical *111* chirurgisch

surprising *113T* erstaunlich

surroundings *pl 113* Umgebung

to **survey sb** *60* jdn befragen

survey *14* Umfrage; **~ taker** *63* Umfrageteilnehmer/in

suspicious *49* verdächtig

sustainability *112* Nachhaltigkeit

to **swallow** *126* schlucken

to **swap** *9* tauschen
to **swipe** *37* (*Touchscreen:*) wischen
switch (to sth) *76* Umstellung (auf etw)
synchronization *65* Synchronisierung
to **synchronize** *15T* abgleichen, synchronisieren
system: ~ **analysis** *10T* Systemanalyse; ~ **architecture** *10T* Systemarchitektur

T

to **tailor sth** *62T* etw individuell anpassen
to **take:** ~ **up sth** *9T* etw ausmachen, etw in Anspruch nehmen; ~ **up time** *15T* Zeit beanspruchen; ~ **sth seriously** *115* etw ernst nehmen; ~ **place** *38* stattfinden
talented *25* begabt, talentiert
talk *45* Vortrag
to **tap** *37* tippen
tap *111* Tipp, Klick; to **put sb within one** ~ **of sth** *46T* damit man etw mit einem Tipp/Klick tun kann; **air** ~ **command** *111* Befehl per Tipp in der Luft
tape *30* Klebeband
target group *7* Zielgruppe
to **tattoo** *47* tätowieren
tattoo *47* Tätowierung
tax consultancy *48* Steuerberatung
technician *22* Techniker/in
technique *111* Methode, Technik
telecommunication(s) *6* Fernmelde-technik, Telekommunikation
template *60* Vorlage, Dokumentvorlage
temporary *38* provisorisch, vorüber-gehend
to **tend to do sth** *56T* dazu neigen, etw zu tun
tennis racket *30* Tennisschläger
term *96* Laufzeit
terms *pl 52* Bedingungen, Bestimmungen; ~ **and conditions** *pl 96* Allgemeine Geschäftsbedingungen; ~ **of delivery** *98* Lieferbedingungen; ~ **of payment** *99* Zahlungsbedingungen; **in** ~ **of** *77T* was … anbelangt
to **test** *17* prüfen, testen
test: ~ **data** *pl 17* Prüfdaten; ~ **plan** *18* Prüfplan
testimonial *83* Erfahrungsbericht
testing *10T* Prüfung, Erprobung; ~ **equipment** *73* Prüfgeräte
text (message) *15T* SMS
texture *111* (Gewebe-)Konsistenz
theatre, operating ~ *98* Operationssaal
theft *51* Diebstahl
theory, in ~ *76* theoretisch, in der Theorie
thin *77T* dünn, schlank
thing, The ~ **is,** … *133T* Es geht darum, dass …

to **think twice** *68T* sich etw gut überlegen
third party *39* Dritte/r, von Dritten
to **threaten** *49* drohen, bedrohen
throughout … *31* in ganz …
tick *38* Häkchen
ticketing system *33* Ticketsystem
tile *132* Fliese
to **tilt** *28* neigen, kippen
time, full-~ *125* Vollzeit-; **in good** ~ *127T* rechtzeitig; **just in** ~ *46T* gerade (noch) rechtzeitig; **on** ~ *10T* rechtzei-tig, pünktlich; **one-~** *53* einmalig; **period of** ~ *19* (gewisse) Zeit; **reference** ~ *78* Referenzzeit, Bezugs-zeit; **waste of** ~ *15T* Zeitverschwen-dung; to **allow** ~ **for sth** *87* Zeit für etw vorsehen; to **be short of** ~ *81* wenig Zeit haben; to **have a hard** ~ **doing sth** *68T* etw nur schwer tun können; to **take up** ~ *15T* Zeit beanspruchen; ~ **of day** *58T* Tageszeit; **~-consuming** *94T* zeitraubend; **load** ~ *31* Ladezeit
timeline *18* Zeitschiene
tiny *133* klein, winzig
titanium *103* Titan
title, job ~ *11* Stellenbezeichnung
to **toggle** *62T* hin- und herschalten, umschalten
token *52* Marke, Token
tone *114* Tonfall, Ton
tool *34* Werkzeug
top, from the ~ **down** *25* von oben nach unten
touch, to get in ~ **with sb** *66* sich bei jdm melden, sich mit jdm in Verbindung setzen
tour *9* Rundgang; **guided** ~ *9* Führung
toxic *112* giftig
to **toy with sth** *47* mit etw (*Gedanke usw.*) spielen
to **trace** *133* nachzeichnen, verfolgen
to **track** *29* nachvollziehen, verfolgen; *46T* nachverfolgen; *86* laufen
track, to lose ~ **of sth** *70* etw aus den Augen verlieren, die Übersicht über etw verlieren
trade *34* Gewerbe, Branche; ~ **fair** *81* Fachmesse, Branchenmesse; ~ **magazine** *99* Fachzeitschrift
traditional *25* traditionell, altherge-bracht
trainee *6* Auszubildende/r, Praktikant/in
training *7T* Ausbildung; ~ **company** *8* Ausbildungsbetrieb
transcript *121* Mitschrift
transfer *38* Übertragung; *91T* Überweisung

to **transfer** *59* weiterleiten, vermitteln; *77T* übertragen
to **transform** *83* verwandeln
to **transmit** *38* übertragen
transmitter *133T* Sender
transparency *71* Transparenz
transparent *70* erkennbar, transparent
tremendous *91* enorm
trial *92* Test, Probe, Ausprobieren; ~ **order** *99* Probebestellung
triangulation *102* Dreiecksbildung, Triangulation
trillion *133* Billion
trojan *48* Trojaner
troubleshooting *125P* Fehlersuche
trough *56T* Tiefpunkt, Tiefststand, Talsohle
truly *29* wirklich, wahrhaft
to **trust** *63T* vertrauen
trusted brand *83* vertrauenswürdige Marke
trustworthy *48T* glaubwürdig, verlässlich
to **try sth on** *47* etw anprobieren
to **turn** *100* (sich) drehen; ~ **sth into sth** *27* etw in etw umwandeln; ~ **sth off** *21T* etw ausschalten, etw abstellen; ~ **sth over** *28* etw umdrehen, etw auf die andere Seite legen
turn, in ~ *69* wiederum, seiner-/ihrer-seits; to **be one's** ~ *45* an der Reihe sein; to **take it in** ~**s to do sth** *29* etw abwechselnd tun
twice, to think ~ *68T* sich etw gut überlegen
to **twist** *100* (sich) verdrehen
two-factor authentication *53* Zwei-Faktoren-Authentifizierung
two-step verification *95* Überprüfung in zwei Schritten
typically *71T* normalerweise, üblicher-weise
typing error *118T* Tippfehler

U

ultrasound *132* Ultraschall
unable, to be ~ **to do sth** *59* etw nicht können; nicht in der Lage sein, etw zu tun
unauthorized *48* unbefugt
unavailable, to be ~ *22* (*Telefon:*) nicht zu sprechen sein
unbelievable *68T* unglaublich
uncertainty *69* Unsicherheit
unchanged *56* unverändert
to **uncheck** *63T* Auswahl/Markierung aufheben
unclear *27* unklar, undeutlich
uncompressed *38* unkomprimiert
underscore *34* Unterstrich

understandable, easily ~ *17* leicht verständlich

understanding *112* Verständnis

unidentified *48T* unbekannt

uninterested *126* uninteressiert

unique *113T* einzigartig; **~ selling proposition (USP)** *95* Alleinstellungsmerkmal

unit *29* Einheit, Gerät; **measurement ~** *73* Messgerät

unknown *35* unbekannt

unless *73* wenn nicht, sofern nicht

unlike sth *102* im Gegensatz zu etw

unlikely *48T* unwahrscheinlich

unlimited *29* unbegrenzt

to **unpack** *38* entpacken

unpaid leave *16T* unbezahlter Urlaub

to **unplug** *27T* ausstecken, *(Kabel)* herausziehen

unpopulated *41* *(Feld:)* nicht ausgefüllt

to **unprotect** *60* den Schutz aufheben

unregistered *55* unregistriert

to **unscrew** *28* *(Schraube)* herausdrehen

unsupervised *125P* unbeaufsichtigt

until, not ~ *68T* erst wenn

untrustworthy *49* nicht vertrauenswürdig

up front *105* im Voraus

up to date *54* auf dem neuesten Stand

upcoming *71T* bevorstehend, künftig

to **update** *18* auf den neuesten Stand bringen

update *22* Aktualisierung; **~ (on sth)** *17* aktuelle Informationen (zu etw)

to **upgrade** *27* hochstufen, upgraden

to **upload** *60* hochladen

upset *115* Ärger, Aufregung; *87T* verärgert

upside *21T* Vorteil, Plus

uptake *76* (Daten-)Aufnahme

usable *72T* nutzbar

usage *48T* Verbrauch, Nutzung; **high ~** *95* intensive Nutzung; **power ~** *80T* Stromverbrauch; **~ rate** *95P* Nutzungsquote, Auslastung

use, acceptable ~ *50* zulässige Nutzung

to **use sth up** *48T* etw verbrauchen, etw aufbrauchen

user *17* Benutzer/in, Anwender/in, User/in; **~ acceptance** *87* Nutzerakzeptanz; **~ creation** *125P* Anlegen von neuen Benutzern

V

vacancy *125* offene Stelle

to **vacuum** *81* staubsaugen

vacuum: ~ cleaner *132* Staubsauger; **~ robot** *81* Staubsaugerroboter

valid *38* gültig; **a ~ concern** *77T* eine berechtigte Sorge

to **validate** *125* *(Daten)* überprüfen, validieren

validation *38* Gültigkeitsprüfung

valuable *49* wertvoll, geschätzt

value *42* Wert

varied *122T* vielfältig

variety *91T* Vielzahl; **wide ~** *58* große Auswahl, breites Sortiment

VAT (value added tax) *109* MwSt (Mehrwertsteuer)

vein *111* Vene

velocity *102* Geschwindigkeit

venue *34* Veranstaltungsort

verification, two-step ~ *95* Überprüfung in zwei Schritten

to **verify** *38* überprüfen

version *27* Ausführung, Modell; **~ control** *70* Versionsverwaltung, -kontrolle

vertical *61* senkrecht, vertikal

via *27T* mit, mittels, über, durch

view *13* Aussicht, Blick; **point of ~** *20* Sicht; **with a ~ to doing sth** *96* mit dem Ziel, etw zu tun

to **view sth** *33* etw betrachten, sich etw ansehen

violent *51* gewalttätig

virtual *28* virtuell

visible *38* sichtbar

vital *73* unverzichtbar

vocational: ~ school *122T* Berufsschule; **~ training** *6* Berufsausbildung

voicemail *22* Mailbox

volume *74* Volumen

W

to **waive sth** *118T* auf etw verzichten

to **walk sb through sth** *63T* jdm etw schrittweise erklären

walkway *9T* Gang, Weg

wallet *91T* Brieftasche, (Herren-) Portemonnaie

warning *28* Hinweis, Warnung

warranty *31* Gewährleistung

to **waste** *25* verschwenden, vergeuden

waste *112* Müll, Abfall; **~ of time** *15T* Zeitverschwendung

wastepaper basket *36* Papierkorb

to **watch out for sth** *48T* nach etw Ausschau halten

water resistance *104T* Wasserdichtigkeit

waterfall *69* Wasserfall

waterproof *46T* wasserdicht

way, by the ~ *133T* übrigens

weak *52* schwach

weakness *48T* Schwäche

weapon *30* Waffe

wearer *100* Träger/in

to **weigh** *132* wiegen

weight *33* Gewicht

welcome, to be ~ to do sth *91* etw gern tun können

well-known *7* bekannt

wheelchair *88T* Rollstuhl

wholesale *122T* Großhandel

wide variety *58* große Auswahl, breites Sortiment

to **widen** *129* erweitern

widget *37* Steuerelement, Widget

willing, to be ~ to do sth *110T* bereit sein, etw zu tun

willingness *124* Bereitschaft

to **win sb over** *76* jdn überzeugen

wireframe *87* Entwurf einer Webseite/ Software

wireless *29* drahtlos, Funk-

wise(ly) *73* klug

wish, Best ~es *35* *(Brief:)* Mit freundlichen Grüßen

with, I'm ~ you on that. *77T* Da bin ich ganz deiner/Ihrer Meinung.

wizard *60* Assistent

wooden *98* hölzern, aus Holz

to **work: ~ sth out** *46T* etw berechnen; **~ closely with sb** *17* eng mit jdm zusammenarbeiten; **~ remotely** *16T* von zu Hause aus arbeiten, ortsungebunden arbeiten

work experience *26* Praktikum

workforce *76* Arbeitskräfte, Belegschaft

working *52* funktionierend; **~ breakfast** *67* Arbeitsfrühstück; **~ day** *109* Werktag

workout *46T* Training(seinheit)

workplace *14* Arbeitsplatz

worm *48T* Wurm

wrist *102* Handgelenk

wristband *102* Armband

to **write sth up** *86* etw ausarbeiten, etw formulieren

writer *104* Autor/in, Schriftsteller/in

writing, in ~ *15T* schriftlich

XYZ

X-ray machine *120* Röntgengerät

yesterday, the day before ~ *56P* vorgestern

yet *61* doch, aber; **not ... ~** *48T* noch nicht

to **zoom in** *37* vergrößern, einzoomen

to **zoom out** *37* verkleinern, auszoomen

Talking about numbers

Cardinal numbers

0	oh/nought/null (*AE*) zero
1	one
2	two
3	three
4	four
5	five
6	six
7	seven
8	eight
9	nine
10	ten
11	eleven
12	twelve
13	thirteen
14	fourteen
15	fifteen
16	sixteen
17	seventeen
18	eighteen
19	nineteen
20	twenty
21	twenty-one
22	twenty-two
23	twenty-three
24	twenty-four
30	thirty
40	forty
50	fifty
60	sixty
70	seventy
80	eighty
90	ninety
100	one hundred

Ordinal numbers

1st	first
2nd	second
3rd	third
4th	fourth
5th	fifth
6th	sixth
7th	seventh
8th	eighth
9th	ninth
10th	tenth
11th	eleventh
12th	twelfth
13th	thirteenth
14th	fourteenth
15th	fifteenth
16th	sixteenth
17th	seventeenth
18th	eighteenth
19th	nineteenth
20th	twentieth
21st	twenty-first
22nd	twenty-second
23rd	twenty-third
24th	twenty-fourth
30th	thirtieth
40th	fortieth
50th	fiftieth
60th	sixtieth
70th	seventieth
80th	eightieth
90th	ninetieth
100th	one hundredth

In English you say:

101	one hundred **and** one
235	two hundred **and** thirty-five
1,563,765	one million, five hundred **and** sixty-three thousand, seven
1 563 765	hundred **and** sixty-five

You use commas or spaces (and not a point) after the thousands (or millions) in large numbers.

Decimals

In English, you write decimals with a point, not a comma.

0.25	oh/nought point two five (*BE*) zero point two five (*AE*)
3.76	three point seven six
55.37	fifty-five point three seven
1.585	one point five eight five

Fractions

$\frac{1}{4}$	a/one quarter
$\frac{1}{3}$	a/one third
$\frac{1}{2}$	a/one half
$\frac{2}{3}$	two-thirds
$\frac{3}{4}$	three-quarters
$\frac{5}{16}$	five sixteenths
$1\frac{1}{2}$	one and a half

$1\,m^2$	one **square** metre
$1\,m^3$	one **cubic** metre
5^2	five **squared**
10^4	ten **to the power** of four

Symbols

+	plus/and
−	minus
±	plus or minus
×	multiplied by/times by (6 mm × 2 mm)
÷	divided by
=	is equal to/equals
≠	isn't equal to/doesn't equal
≈	is approximately equal to
<	is less than
>	is greater/more than
μ	micro- (one millionth)
%	per cent (*auch:* percent)
°	degree

Temperature

Fahrenheit (F) to Celsius: subtract 32, then multiply by 5, then divide by 9
Celsius to Fahrenheit: multiply by 9, then divide by 5, then add 32

Conversion tables

Distance

English to metric	1 inch (in)	= 2.54 centimetres
	1 foot (ft)	= 30.48 centimetres
	1 yard (yd)	= 0.9144 metres
	1 mile (mi)	= 1.609 kilometres
Metric to English	1 centimetre	= 0.3937 inches (⅜ inch)
	1 metre	= 39.37 inches (3 feet, 3 ⅜ inches)
	1 kilometre	= 0.62137 miles
English to English	1 foot	= 12 inches
	1 yard	= 3 feet / 36 inches
	1 mile	= 5,280 feet / 1,760 yards

Area

English to metric	1 square inch (in²)	= 6.452 square centimetres
	1 square foot (ft²)	= 0.0929 square metres
	1 square mile (m²)	= 2.59 square kilometres
Metric to English	1 square centimetre	= 0.155 square inches
	1 square metre	= 10.764 square feet
	1 square kilometre	= 0.3861 square miles
English to English	1 square foot	= 144 square inches
	1 square mile	= 640 acres

Mass / Weight

English to metric	1 ounce (oz)	= 28.35 grams
	1 pound (lb)	= 0.453 kilograms
	1 UK ton ('long ton')	= 1,016 kilograms
	1 US ton ('short ton')	= 907 kilograms
Metric to English	1 gram	= 0.035 ounces
	1 kilogram	= 2 pounds, 3.3 ounces
English to English	1 pound	= 16 ounces
	1 UK ton ('long ton')	= 2,240 pounds
	1 US ton ('short ton')	= 2,000 pounds
Metric to metric	1 metric tonne (t)	= 1,000 kilograms

Volume

English to metric	1 fluid UK ounce (fl oz)	= 28.41 millilitres
	1 UK pint (pt)	= 0.568 litres
	1 UK quart (qt)	= 1.137 litres
	1 UK gallon (gal)	= 4.546 litres
	1 fluid US ounce	= 29.57 millilitres
	1 US pint	= 0.473 litres
	1 US quart	= 0.946 litres
	1 US gallon	= 3.785 litres
	1 cubic inch (in³)	= 16 cubic centimetres
	1 cubic foot (ft³)	= 0.03 cubic metres
Metric to English	1 litre	= 0.568 UK pints
	1 litre	= 0.473 US pints

Irregular verbs

be – was/were – been	sein	let – let – let	lassen
become – became – become	werden	lose – lost – lost	verlieren
begin – began – begun	anfangen, beginnen	make – made – made	machen
break – broke – broken	brechen	mean – meant – meant	meinen, bedeuten
bring – brought – brought	bringen	meet – met – met	treffen
build – built – built	bauen	pay – paid – paid	bezahlen
burn – burnt/burned – burnt/burned	(ver)brennen	put – put – put	setzen, stellen, legen
buy – bought – bought	kaufen	read – read – read	lesen
catch – caught – caught	fangen	ride – rode – ridden	reiten, fahren
choose – chose – chosen	wählen	ring – rang – rung	klingeln, anrufen
come – came – come	kommen	rise – rose – risen	(an)steigen
cost – cost – cost	kosten	run – ran – run	laufen, rennen
cut – cut – cut	schneiden	say – said – said	sagen
do – did – done	tun, machen, erledigen	see – saw – seen	sehen
draw – drew – drawn	zeichnen	sell – sold – sold	verkaufen
dream – dreamt – dreamt	träumen	send – sent – sent	senden, schicken
drink – drank – drunk	trinken	shake – shook – shaken	schütteln
drive – drove – driven	fahren	set – set – set	setzen, stellen
eat – ate – eaten	essen	show – showed – shown	zeigen
fall – fell – fallen	fallen	shut – shut – shut	schließen
feed – fed – fed	füttern, ernähren	sing – sang – sung	singen
feel – felt – felt	(sich) fühlen, empfinden	sit – sat – sat	sitzen
fight – fought – fought	kämpfen	sleep – slept – slept	schlafen
find – found – found	finden	smell – smelt/smelled – smelt/smelled	riechen
fit – fit/fitted – fit/fitted	passen	speak – spoke – spoken	sprechen
fly – flew – flown	fliegen	spell – spelt/spelled – spelt/spelled	buchstabieren
forget – forgot – for- gotten	vergessen	spend – spent – spent	ausgeben, verbringen
get – got – got (*AE* gotten)	bekommen, erhalten	stand – stood – stood	stehen
give – gave – given	geben	steal – stole – stolen	stehlen
go – went – gone	gehen, fahren	swim – swam – swum	schwimmen
grow – grew – grown	wachsen	take – took – taken	nehmen
hang – hung – hung	hängen	teach – taught – taught	unterrichten, beibringen
have – had – had	haben	tear – tore – torn	(zer)reißen
hear – heard – heard	hören	tell – told – told	sagen, erzählen
hide – hid – hidden	(sich) verstecken	think – thought – thought	denken
hit – hit – hit	schlagen, aufprallen auf	throw – threw – thrown	werfen
hold – held – held	halten, festhalten	understand – understood – understood	verstehen
keep – kept – kept	behalten	wake – woke – woken	wecken
know – knew – known	kennen, wissen	wear – wore – worn	tragen (Kleidung)
lay – laid – laid	legen	win – won – won	gewinnen
lead – led – led	führen, leiten	write – wrote – written	schreiben
learn – learnt/learned – learnt/learned	lernen		
leave – left – left	abfahren, verlassen, weggehen		

Acknowledgements

Cover: Fotolia/.shock; **S. 7:** Shutterstock/OPOLJA; **S. 8.1:** Fotolia/itsallgood; **S. 8.2:** ODI; **S. 10:** Shutterstock/leungchopan; **S. 12.1:** Shutterstock/Djomas; **S. 12.2:** Shutterstock/Monkey Business Images; **S. 12.3:** Shutterstock/Kazandzhan; **S. 12.4:** Fotolia/Photozi; **S. 12.5:** Shutterstock/Firma V; **S. 12.6:** Fotolia/ajr_images; **S. 14.1–6:** ODI; **S. 14.7:** Shutterstock/ESB Professional; **S. 14.8:** Shutterstock/mimagephotography; **S. 14.9:** Shutterstock/stockfour; **S. 16:** Shutterstock/Zurijeta; **S. 17.1:** Shutterstock/blvdone; **S. 17.2:** Shutterstock/iko; **S. 17.3:** Shutterstock/Daxiao Productions; **S. 18:** Fotolia/Kzenon; **S. 25:** Shutterstock/nd3000; **S. 26.1:** Shutterstock/Garsya; **S. 26.2:** Shutterstock/Dmitr1ch; **S. 26.3:** Shutterstock/robert_s; **S. 26.4:** Shutterstock/Volodymyr Krasyuk; **S. 26.5:** Shutterstock/HelloRF Zcool; **S. 26.6:** Shutterstock/Tupungato; **S. 26.7:** Shutterstock/Karynav; **S. 26.8:** Shutterstock/AG-PHOTOS; **S. 28:** Shutterstock/zack2701; **S. 29:** ODI; **S. 30.1–8:** ODI; **S. 31.1:** Shutterstock/Olena Zaskochenko; **S. 31.2:** Shutterstock/aastock; **S. 31.3:** Shutterstock/fizkes; **S. 31.4:** Shutterstock/Natan86; **S. 31.5:** Shutterstock/9nong; **S. 31.6:** Shutterstock/ESB Basic; **S. 32:** Shutterstock/Kzenon; **S. 33.1:** Shutterstock/Pieter Beens; **S. 33.2+3:** Shutterstock/Umberto Shtanzman; **S. 36:** Brad Courtney; **S. 37.1:** Fotolia/Vividz Foto; **S. 37.A1–11:** ODI; **S. 38:** Shutterstock/NakoPhotography; **S. 40:** Brad Courtney; **S. 41:** Brad Courtney; **S. 42:** Shutterstock/Dean Drobot; **S. 44:** Shutterstock/ESB Professional; **S. 46:** HUBER IMAGES/Maurizio Rellini; **S. 47:** Shutterstock/guruXOX; **S. 50:** Shutterstock/Andrey_Popov; **S. 52.1–4:** ODI; **S. 61+62:** ODI; **S. 62:** Culture Amp Pty Ltd, Melbourne; **S. 63:** Fotolia/Halfpoint; **S. 66:** Shutterstock/Rawpixel.com; **S. 69:** Brad Courtney; **S. 72:** Shutterstock/PsyComa; **S. 74:** Fotolia/skiminok; **S. 75:** ODI; **S. 77:** Shutterstock/George Rudy; **S. 80.1:** Shutterstock/(©) 1987-1996 Adobe Systems Incorporated All Rights Reserved; **S. 80.2:** Shutterstock/(©)2000-2006 Adobe Systems, Inc. All Rights Reserved; **S. 80.3:** Shutterstock/Radu Bercan; **S. 80.4:** Shutterstock/Piti Tan; **S. 80.5:** © by Logitech/FAKTOR3 AG; **S. 80.6:** The Wireless Power Consortium/GOLIN, USA; **S. 81.1:** Fotolia/Konstantin Kulikov; **S. 81.2:** Shutterstock/Mile Atanasov; **S. 81.3:** Shutterstock/s.chanakanon; **S. 82:** Shutterstock/Tinxi; **S. 83.1:** Shutterstock/Anatomy Insider; **S. 83.2:** Shutterstock/Romaset; **S. 88.1:** Shutterstock/leungchopan; **S. 88.2:** Shutterstock/Lisa F. Young; **S. 88.3:** Shutterstock/Rehan Qureshi; **S. 88.4:** Shutterstock/SnowWhiteimages; **S. 94:** Fotolia/Antonioguillem; **S. 95:** Fotolia/nnudoo; **S. 97:** Fotolia/Antonioguillem; **S. 100:** Shutterstock/belekekin; **S. 103.1:** Fotolia/chesky; **S. 103.2:** Shutterstock/artjazz; **S. 103.3:** Shutterstock/(©)2000-2006 Adobe Systems, Inc. All Rights Reserved; **S. 104:** Fotolia/Maridav; **S. 111:** Shutterstock/Anatomy Insider; **S. 112:** Shutterstock/akiyoko; **S. 114:** Shutterstock/Dean Drobot; **S. 118:** Shutterstock/WAYHOME studio; **S. 120:** Shutterstock/Daniel M Ernst; **S. 122.1:** Fotolia/Spectral-Design; **S. 122.2:** Fotolia/Andrey Popov; **S. 122.3:** Fotolia/nullplus; **S. 127:** Shutterstock/Michal Kowalski; **S. 135:** Brad Courtney; **S. 149.1:** Shutterstock/browndogstudios; **S. 149.2:** Shutterstock/Ben Davis

Wir danken der Firma Culture Amp Pty Ltd, Melbourne für ihre freundliche Unterstützung.